Milk Street is changing how we cook by searching
the world for bold, simple recipes. Adapted
and tested for home cooks everywhere, this is what
we call the *new* home cooking.

CHRISTOPHER KIMBALL

THE
MILK STREET
COOKBOOK

The Definitive Guide to the New Home Cooking
With Every Recipe from Every Episode of the TV Show
2017 to 2020

Christopher Kimball

WITH WRITING AND EDITING BY
J. M. Hirsch and Michelle Locke

RECIPES BY
Matthew Card, Diane Unger and the Cooks at Milk Street

ART DIRECTION BY
Jennifer Baldino Cox and Brianna Coleman

VORACIOUS
LITTLE, BROWN AND COMPANY
NEW YORK   BOSTON   LONDON

Little, Brown and Company
Hachette Book Group
1290 Avenue of the Americas, New York, NY 10104
littlebrown.com

Revised and Expanded Edition: October 2019

Voracious is an imprint of Little, Brown and Company, a division of Hachette Book Group, Inc.
The Voracious name and logo are trademarks of Hachette Book Group, Inc.

The publisher is not responsible for websites (or their content) that are not owned by the publisher.

The Hachette Speakers Bureau provides a wide range of authors for speaking events. To find out more, go to hachettespeakersbureau.com or call (866) 376-6591.

Photography Credits: Connie Miller of CB Creatives except as noted by page: Brian Samuels, pages 72, 86, 214, 217, 227, 261, 273, 447, 462, 468, 489, 493; Channing Johnson, pages V, VI, 545; Shannon Frandsen, page XI; Sylvian Cherkaoui, pages XII-XIII; Marco Simola, pages XIV-XV; Kristin Teig, pages 22, 24-25, 172, 297; Heidi Murphy of White Loft Studios, page 83; Michael Piazza, pages 415, 436.

Food Styling Credits: Christine Tobin except as noted by page: Catherine Smart, pages 111, 128, 143, 148, 158, 183, 204, 212, 250, 253, 324-325, 334, 475; Catrine Kelty, pages 22, 24-26, 54, 75-77, 83, 93, 107, 116, 121, 152, 172, 209, 297, 302, 307, 413, 415, 427-428, 434, 436, 438, 440, 497, 499; Sally Staub, page 398; and Monica Mariano, pages 340, 346, 444; and Molly Shuster, pages 29, 88, 94, 179, 190, 323, 465, 513.

ISBN 978-0-316-45615-9
LCCN 2019938007

10 9 8 7 6 5 4 3 2 1

IM

Print book interior design by Gary Tooth / Empire Design Studio
Printed in China

This book is dedicated to the
notion that cooking is the universal language
of the human spirit.

Contents

The New Home Cooking / IX

1 Pantry / 1

2 Eggs / 20

3 Soups / 38

4 Vegetables / 74

5 Grains / 136

6 Noodles / 160

7 Suppers / 200

8 Dinners / 290

9 Breads / 372

10 Small Sweets / 400

11 Desserts / 424

12 Staples, Sauces and Seasonings / 490

Index / 545

Acknowledgments / 558

THE NEW HOME COOKING

The Marché Tilène, or Tilene Market, in Dakar, Senegal, is a vast airplane hangar of a place, with light filtering down through the open roof. I walked past long stretches of wooden benches covered with fish, from sardines and the popular thiof (similar to sea bass) to grouper, prawns and large barracuda, one specimen reaching 7 feet. We found a good spot to introduce our episode on the cooking of Senegal, then I did two takes (cameras are not welcome in Dakar, so we did not linger). Then we bought mangoes, oranges, a couple of cheap blue plastic grocery sacks and an assortment of Maggi seasoning cubes on the way out.

The previous afternoon, we cooked the local seafood gumbo and then, after our market visit, we spent the day with Pierre Thiam, a Dakar-born New York chef who prepared a sweet potato/black eyed pea stew, a mango-avocado salad and rice pudding with coconut milk. We also stopped by a cavernous "dibi" restaurant, where thin slices of beef, liver and chicken are cooked over table braziers, the guests seated around, paying for whatever they eat. The meat is served on used green-lined computer paper along with mustard, hot sauce, grilled onions and powdered spices. Hold the skewer at one end, dip the cooked meat in the condiments, slide the seasoned meat into your mouth.

This book is about that trip and others like it, including Cape Town, Taipei, Armenia, Peru, Columbia, Thailand, Italy, Mexico and dozens of other destinations. We travel the world to spend time with cooks who help us appreciate new ways of thinking about cooking, flavor and the art of eating. Our journeys leave us feeling both humble (how did we live so long without harissa?) and thrilled to discover that the development of flavor in cooking does not have to be a function of time and expertise. It's actually rather simple—start with big flavors and the cooking takes care of itself. With liberal use of spices, herbs, chilies and fermented sauces, anyone can become a good cook virtually overnight.

In this volume, you will find all of the recipes from the first three seasons of Milk Street Television. These are not authentic reproductions of the recipes we enjoyed elsewhere; these are adaptations of those recipes for the American kitchen. We don't call for ingredients you won't find in the supermarket (no smoked catfish in the gumbo, for example) or techniques that make no sense in our homes (no pounding of okra in a 3-foot-high wooden mortar and pestle). We have limited time in the kitchen, as do you, and our batterie-de-cuisine is a bit different than Dakar or Chiang Mai.

But the kitchens we visited in Dakar are not all that different than what you might find in Europe or America. The world is growing smaller and it is time to reach out across the oceans and continents to find better ways to put food on the table. Nothing fancy. No feasts; only suppers. But the world has a lot to teach us about flavor, about combinations of ingredients, even about how to cook an egg.

I hope that you enjoy the television show, as well as this book. Milk Street was founded to change the way we cook. It has already changed mine.

Christopher Kimball
Founder, Christopher Kimball's Milk Street

Pantry

1

PANTRY

FATS

Butter

Breaking with convention, we use salted butter for everything. Our reason? It simply tastes better. Not to mention it's simpler to keep just one variety of butter on hand for all uses, whether for toast or cooking. Our recipes are written with the extra salt of salted butter in mind (roughly ¼ teaspoon per 4-ounce stick). To use salted butter in other recipes that assume unsalted, scale back slightly on other salt added during cooking. If using unsalted butter in Milk Street recipes, add a pinch more salt than specified. Butter readily absorbs surrounding flavors, so store it tightly wrapped in the refrigerator. For longer storage, it can be frozen.

Coconut Oil

Coconut oil is a fat we use sparingly, generally with other coconut ingredients. Its flavor is particularly good in Indian and Southeast Asian dishes. Be mindful of its low smoke point.

Cooking Spray

We use nonstick cooking spray judiciously. It's convenient and works well (the lecithin in it ensures that even the stickiest foods release). Baking spray, which contains flour, is ideal for coating baking pans, especially a Bundt pan's deep grooves.

Grapeseed Oil

We like the neutral flavor, light mouthfeel and high smoke point of grapeseed oil. It's our go-to choice for a neutral cooking oil.

Lard

Though it's a four-letter word for many, we think lard has a place in modern cooking. It tastes awfully good stirred into a pot of beans or used to add flakiness to savory baked goods. Most supermarkets sell Armour brand lard, which is hydrogenated (in some stores, it will be easier to find Armour labeled in Spanish as "manteca"). Lately, high-quality lard has become more widely available; look for it in jars. If you can find it, "leaf" lard has the lightest flavor. Lard keeps indefinitely in the refrigerator or freezer but will absorb other flavors; wrap it well.

Olive Oil

We probably use olive oil more than any other oil. In most cases, we favor full-flavored extra-virgin olive oil. Buying extra-virgin olive oil is a gamble; expense doesn't always guarantee quality, and there are few safeguards against adulterated oils. While there are wonderful imported oils, we think California oils are generally fresher and a better bet. California Olive Ranch extra-virgin olive oil, for example, is a terrific product that can be found in most any supermarket. Regular olive oil—not extra-virgin—is made from subsequent pressings and thus lacks the more robust flavor of extra-virgin. Its mild flavor and higher smoke point make it better for sautéing.

Peanut Oil

The light, nutty flavor and high smoke point of peanut oil make it particularly good for deep-frying. Toasted peanut oil has a more pronounced nutty flavor.

Sesame Oil

Sesame oil is pressed from either raw or toasted seeds; we prefer the richer flavor of the latter, which we drizzle over many Asian dishes. As with most seed and nut oils, sesame oil is volatile and can go rancid. We recommend buying small bottles that can be used within a couple of months. Sesame oil has a low smoke point and is not suitable for sautéing.

Tahini

Tahini is a paste made from ground sesame seeds. Good tahini is pleasantly bitter. As with sesame oil, it can be made from raw or toasted sesame seeds. We often prefer the stronger flavor of the latter and, when possible, stone-ground varieties (the label should indicate). Tahini is fine for a month or less at room temperature, though we recommend refrigeration beyond that to maintain freshness. Try stirring it into yogurt with a little jam, smearing it on toast with honey or drizzling it over roasted chicken or vegetables.

ACIDS

Cider Vinegar

The mildly acidic, lightly fruity flavor of cider vinegar is neutral enough to work in numerous dishes, making it a vinegar we turn to often. The flavor varies by brand; we prefer Bragg Organic Raw Unfiltered Apple Cider Vinegar.

Citrus

The zest and juice of lemons, limes and oranges show up repeatedly in our cooking. They are excellent for balancing the flavors of other ingredients, especially anything heavy or fatty. A spritz of lemon or lime juice before serving can brighten most any finished dish. When shopping for lemons and limes, look for round, plump fruit that feel heavy for their size. They should also give when squeezed; hard fruit won't produce much juice. Citrus should be stored in the crisper drawer of your refrigerator to maintain freshness. Use a wand-style grater for zesting citrus. It produces light, feathery shreds that blend easily into dishes. Make sure to avoid the white pith beneath the zest, which can be bitter. If you need the zest but not the juice of citrus, be sure to wrap the fruit in plastic or a bag, otherwise it will dry out quickly. There are countless ways to juice citrus fruits (juicer, reamer, fork, tong tips), though we do recommend squeezing it over a small mesh strainer to catch seeds. For recipes calling for both zest and juice, it's easier to zest before juicing.

Pomegranate Molasses

Intensely sweet and sour, pomegranate molasses is used throughout the Middle East in both sweet and savory dishes. It's essentially boiled-down pomegranate juice that is rounded out with a bit of sugar and acid. We like it drizzled over grilled or roasted meats or vegetables just before serving, mixed with Greek-style yogurt for a simple dip, or added to vinaigrettes. It pairs particularly well with Aleppo pepper. Refrigerated, an open bottle will last indefinitely, though it may need to be warmed in hot water or the microwave before it will flow freely.

Sherry Vinegar

Used liberally in Spanish and French cooking, sherry vinegar has a complex, slightly nutty flavor. The best sherry vinegars have a little age on them, which softens the harsh edges. Look for labels indicating the vinegar is at least 3 years old. It will cost a little more than unaged vinegar, but the difference in flavor is worth it.

Unseasoned Rice Vinegar

Rice vinegar is a staple of Japanese cooking and packs a mild, neutral acidity well suited to vegetables, seafood and poultry. It can also add kick to citrus juice. Be sure to purchase unseasoned rice vinegar; seasoned rice vinegar is used for making sushi rice and already contains salt and sugar, which can make it difficult to balance in dressings.

Verjus

Verjus is the cooking wine substitute you've been searching for. While fruit juices or vinegar can work, verjus—made from the juice of unripe wine grapes—adds a gentle mineral tang and a wine-like body. Verjus can be tricky to find and may require purchasing online. Refrigerate after opening to prevent spoilage. It will last for two to three months.

White Balsamic Vinegar

White balsamic has little to do with the dark, sweet, long-aged stuff most people are familiar with. But its light, neutral flavor and mild sweetness make it an acid we use often. White balsamic is perfect for when we want a clean flavor that highlights, but doesn't compete with, other flavors.

FRESH HERBS

We use fresh herbs with reckless abandon to add bold, bright flavor to many of our recipes. Instead of scant tablespoons, think in terms of handfuls. It's important to wash and dry herbs well. Any moisture clinging to them can turn them mushy during chopping and dilute the flavors of the dishes to which they are added. Salad spinners work best. Herbs can also be dried by rolling them in a towel and gently squeezing. With a little care, most fresh herbs can be

refrigerated in the crisper drawer for a week or more. Wrap loosely in paper towels, then place in a plastic bag. Some fresh herbs, such as cilantro, mint and parsley have edible stems. We like to use them to flavor stocks, soups and stews. As for dried herbs, we rarely use them. They lack much of the nuance of fresh and generally require long, steady cooking to coax out their flavors. Exceptions to that rule include oregano (both Mexican and Turkish varieties, which offer different flavors) and mint, which packs a deeper, earthier flavor than fresh.

SPICES

Despite their seeming durability, spices contain volatile oils and are perishable. For best flavor, we recommend buying whole spices in small quantities. It's easy to grind them as needed in a spice mill (a cheap blade-style coffee grinder works well) or a mortar and pestle. If purchasing ground spices, choose amounts you can consume within six months. Older, flat-tasting spices can be perked up with a quick toast in a hot skillet.

Aleppo Pepper
Fruity and only moderately spicy, coarsely ground Aleppo pepper is used throughout Middle Eastern cooking. We use it frequently and consider it a valuable flavoring for dishes that benefit from a little spark of heat. For a quick substitute mix 1 part cayenne to 4 parts sweet paprika. Aleppo pepper can be found at most Middle Eastern shops and spice dealers. It's typically processed with a little salt and safflower oil.

Allspice
With a flavor tasting subtly of cinnamon, clove, nutmeg and black pepper, allspice works in both sweet and savory dishes. We typically buy whole allspice berries and grind them fresh for the best flavor. We also use whole allspice berries when pickling, though the berries should be removed before serving.

Bay Leaves
We think of bay leaves as we do of vanilla—it's a flavor noticed mostly by omission. Bay leaves lend a certain aroma and savory note to soups, stews and pickles. They're also great tossed with roasted vegetables (just be sure to remove them before serving). We even use them in syrups and sweets. Turkish bay leaves, which come from laurel trees, contribute the best flavor; California bay leaves are from a different tree and have a harsher flavor. Buy in bulk for economy's sake and store in the freezer to maintain flavor and aroma.

Black Pepper
Black pepper adds depth and nominal heat to dishes. We use it to give a mild kick—and not always hand-in-hand with salt. For best flavor, buy whole peppercorns and grind as needed (find a good-quality adjustable pepper mill). Pre-ground pepper lacks the aroma and much of the flavor of freshly ground. Consider tasting different varieties of black pepper to see which you prefer, as some are more aggressive than others.

Cardamom
We use cardamom widely in both sweet and savory recipes. It is sold whole in pods (white, black and green—each with a slightly different flavor), corticated (removed from the papery husk) and ground. More often than not, we use ground, as it can be difficult to grind finely. We also like to make Arabic coffee by grinding the whole pods into our coffee beans, then brewing as normal. Use 1 tablespoon of cardamom pods per 1 cup of whole coffee beans.

Coriander
Coriander is the seed of the cilantro plant. It has a bright, citrusy flavor with a hint of mint. The seeds are tender enough to use whole, though it is typically used ground. We prefer to buy it whole and grind as needed.

Cumin
One of our more liberally used spices, cumin packs an earthy flavor and pungency that lends backbone to all manner of Latin, Middle Eastern and even Indian dishes. Buy whole and grind fresh, if possible.

Dried Chilies

Dried chilies are used in many cuisines to add complexity and heat. Latin varieties tend to be the easiest to find. New Mexico chilies are perhaps the most common and most adaptable in flavor. Look for glossy, pliant-looking chilies in the Latin section of your grocer. We recommend pulling the stems off and shaking them out before using; the seeds can be bitter and overly spicy. Depending on the recipe, the chilies should be toasted or fried to deepen the flavor. Ancho chilies—which have a deep, almost prune-like flavor and mild spiciness—are interchangeable with pasilla chilies. Tangy, very fruity guajillo chilies taste hot and bright; they pair well with tomatoes and can be substituted for New Mexico chilies. Chipotle chilies are smoked red jalapeños; chipotle chilies en adobo, sold in cans, are the chilies packed in a tomato-vinegar sauce. The latter are often used in our recipes to add both smoke and spice. Pointy little árbol chilies can be quite hot; simmer them whole in a dish and pull them out before serving.

Fennel Seeds

We use both whole and ground fennel seeds to add a licorice-like flavor to meats, vegetables and sauces. Fennel pairs well with coriander and chili flakes.

Mustard Seeds

We pickle them or stir them into curries and the occasional bean dish for a pop of flavor. We prefer brown, though yellow mustard seeds are fine, too. Mustard seeds can be found in the spice section of most markets, either packaged or in bulk bins.

Nutmeg

The warm, sharp flavor of ground nutmeg works in sweet and savory dishes, both on its own and blended with other warm spices. It's especially important in cream sauces and often paired with lemon. The flavor is particularly volatile, so it is best to buy whole nutmeg and grate fresh as needed. A wand-style grater works well for this.

Paprika

Paprika adds deep, sweet and earthy flavor to countless dishes. It also has a bit of a thickening property when used in soups, stews and sauces. All paprika is made from dried red peppers. Whether it's hot or sweet depends on the variety of pepper used and if the seeds were removed. Though paprika originated in Latin America, it is often associated with Hungary or Spain. Hungarian paprika tends to be the most flavorful; it's usually identified as sweet or hot on the package. Smoked paprika is made from peppers that are slow-dried over a fire; we prefer pimentón de La Vera, which is produced only in the La Vera region of Spain. We use all types of paprika, depending on the flavor profile that we are aiming for in the recipe.

Red Pepper Flakes

The sharp bite of red pepper flakes serves to punctuate many dishes. We don't aim for spicy food per se, just balanced dishes with a compelling range of flavors to keep things interesting start to finish. Red pepper flakes are produced from various dried peppers, and intensity can vary from brand to brand. Age affects heat level as well; the older the flakes, the less intense they will be.

Salt

We use kosher salt in our cooking and baking because the larger granules are easier to measure and sprinkle with your fingers. The two most common brands are Diamond Crystal Kosher Salt and Morton Coarse Kosher Salt; we use the former. Grains of Diamond Crystal are slightly larger and fluffier than those of Morton, which are dense and compact, so the same volume of Diamond is less salty than Morton. If you use Morton in our recipes, reduce the amount called for to just over half. Flaky finishing salts, such as Maldon Sea Salt Flakes, add a delicious crunch and salty pop but should be used only at the table, not during cooking.

Shichimi Togarashi

One of our favorite seasoning blends is shichimi togarashi, a seven-ingredient mix that includes chili peppers, sesame seeds, citrus peel, seaweed and sometimes black peppercorns, poppy seeds and hemp seeds. We use the mix to enliven Japanese noodle dishes. It's also great as a seasoning for scrambled or fried eggs, broiled fish or chicken, or even roasted vegetables. Look for shichimi togarashi, sold in small glass bottles, in the international foods section of your grocer or an Asian specialty market.

Sichuan Peppercorns

Not technically pepper, Sichuan peppercorns have a sharp flavor and unique ability to "numb" the mouth. They are used broadly in Sichuan cooking in tandem with whole chilies in a combination known as "ma la." Make sure to sort well and remove the black seeds, which can contribute a gritty texture.

Sumac

Deep red and bursting with zesty flavor, sumac has been an essential flavoring of Middle Eastern cooking—and, closer to home, Native American cooking—for centuries. It's made from the berries of the sumac bush and is usually sold ground. You can find it online, at Middle Eastern markets and at some larger grocers. (Though they're related, this is not the poison sumac you've been warned to stay away from in the wild.) Sumac has a sour, lemony flavor and is a good way to add a bright pop of color and a tart note of citrus without the liquid of lemon juice. It works well as a condiment and can be dusted over just about anything—hummus and baba ghanoush are traditional, but it also makes a good popcorn topper. And it's good in dry rubs for chicken and fish.

White Pepper

While we use white pepper less than black, its unique flavor and pungent aroma make it an important pantry staple for some Scandinavian and Asian dishes. It comes from the same berry (pepper nigrum) as black, but is processed differently. Like black pepper, white is best when freshly ground. For a complex flavor, use a blend of black and white peppercorns in your pepper mill.

SEASONINGS

Anchovies

Few ingredients are as polarizing as anchovies. We love them and use them often. The best come jarred, though canned will suffice. Skip those rolled around a caper. And forget about anchovy paste—it may be convenient, but the poor-quality, salty flavor isn't worth it. Buy a jar of anchovies and keep it in the back of the refrigerator to add to sauces, soups and vegetables. Once they're heated and dissolved into a dish, they add tremendous savory flavor, but you'll never detect anything "fishy."

Chili Sauces

We use a variety of hot sauces in our cooking; you should taste different varieties to figure out which suits your heat threshold. We like Dynasty Thai Chili Garlic Paste. For a general Southeast Asian-style sauce, there are many Sriracha sauces ranging in potency; Shark brand Thai Sriracha Chili Sauce is milder, sweeter and tangier than most.

Dried Mushrooms

Umami-rich dried mushrooms pack a flavor punch well above their weight. For the most part, we use dried shiitake mushrooms, which add deep, savory flavor. To use them, dust them off, then soak them in hot water to soften before slicing and adding to dishes. Sometimes we add them whole to stocks and soups. They can also be ground to a powder and used in stews and sautés to add umami flavor without mushroom texture.

Fish Sauce

Fish sauce is just that: the fermented broth of salted, aged fish. The heady, amber-colored liquid is used throughout Southeast Asia as a seasoning, as well as for the base of countless sauces. We use it beyond Asian cuisines to add deep flavor to sauces. Brands vary widely in flavor. After tasting our way through a host of options, we found Red Boat Fish Sauce to be the best. It costs more than other brands, but the clean, rich flavor makes it well worth it. And a little goes a long way.

Kimchi

Kimchi—a spicy, pungent mix of fermented cabbage and other vegetables—has been an essential part of Korean cooking for more than 2,000 years. It began as a way to preserve food without refrigeration. The red and relatively fiery version has become more common in the U.S. as interest in Korean food has risen. You'll often find jars of it in the grocer's refrigerated section. But kimchi can also be quite mild and even white; there are more than 100 varieties. It usually contains a seafood element, such as fish sauce for flavoring. Served as a small plate at just about every Korean meal, kimchi can be offered as a vegetable side dish or pickle-like accompaniment to a main dish, or it can be used as a cooking ingredient. It stores well in the refrigerator, but its flavor becomes sharper and tangier over time.

Miso

Miso is fermented soybean paste, and there are many varieties, from white and smooth to dark and chunky. Two versions commonly found in the U.S. are shiro (white), which has a mild, sweet-and-salty flavor, and shinshu (yellow), which is fermented a little longer than shiro but still has a delicate flavor and light golden color. Red miso, fermented longer than shiro or shinshu, is saltier and works best where a heartier flavor is desired. The classic use of miso is in soup, though it can add a shot of umami to many dishes. Try white or yellow miso in sauces and dressings. One of our favorite ways to use miso is blended with an equal amount of softened butter and, if you like, grated fresh ginger. This mixture is terrific tossed with pasta for a carbonara-like dish or used to dress roasted or grilled vegetables.

Peppadew Peppers

A little sweet, a little tart, a little spicy, Peppadews are bright red, pleasantly spicy peppers that are about the size of a cherry tomato. They are a trademarked brand that originated in South Africa. The peppers are now widely available at grocers, usually jarred, but sometimes sold loose at the olive bar. Use the peppers to add mild piquancy to a salad, as part of an antipasto spread, as a pizza topping or as a companion to cheese. Peppadews are sold in mild, hot and golden varieties; we most often use mild.

Soy Sauce

Called soy sauce in China and shoyu in Japan, the inky-dark sauce is made from fermented, salted soybeans and typically a bit of wheat. It has a deep, umami-rich flavor; we use it frequently in both Asian and Western cooking. Soy sauce comes in a variety of styles. For the most part, we use regular soy sauce. "Light" soy sauce is a lighter color from the first pressing. It's light only in color; the flavor is salty and strong. Tamari is a Japanese variety that is often wheat-free (check the label). If sodium is an issue, choose a reduced-sodium version. "White" soy sauce is a high-end variety that should be used only as a dipping sauce. Sweet soy sauce, sometimes known as kecap manis, is soy sauce sweetened with molasses or palm sugar. It's not an appropriate substitute.

Tamarind

Tamarind is an intensely tart fruit used to add sour flavors in the cooking of Latin America, the Indian subcontinent and Southeast Asia. While some supermarkets sell whole tamarind pods—which look like long brown, leathery seed-pods—it's most often found as a jarred concentrate or a semi-dried block of pulp. We prefer the latter for its clearer, stronger flavor. To use, cut off a chunk of the sticky, dark pulp and soak in hot water to soften, about 10 minutes. Stir to loosen and discard the large seeds, then force the pulp through a fine-mesh strainer. We use the tangy, slightly molasses-y juice in dipping sauces, but it also adds a pleasant tartness to a variety of sauces, dressings and even cocktails. Try adding a splash to a gin and tonic, or do as Portland, Oregon's Pok Pok restaurant does and use it in a whiskey sour.

Za'atar

Za'atar can refer to two things—a dried herb and an herb blend that contains it. Both are used widely in Middle Eastern cooking. The plant is reminiscent of wild thyme and oregano. The herb blend comes in many varieties, differing by region and cook. Most contain the za'atar herb, as well as sesame seeds and other spices, such as sumac. The blend is often used as a substitute for lemon or vinegar where a liquid won't work. Za'atar can be found in Middle Eastern markets, better-stocked grocers or online. It can be mixed into olive oil and spread onto flatbread as one would butter, or swirled into labneh (yogurt cheese) with vinegar and oil. It can also be baked into bread, sprinkled on salads, pizza or hummus, or rubbed into meat and vegetables.

SWEETENERS

Whenever possible, we try to use sweeteners that contribute depth and flavor beyond sweetness.

Agave
A honey-like syrup made from the agave plant, agave has a clean, simple flavor and blends easily into other liquids, making it ideal for vinaigrettes and sauces. It can be purchased in a variety of shades, from light to dark. The lighter varieties are a good substitute for simple syrup in cocktails.

Brown Sugar
We like brown sugar because it adds earthy, caramel flavors that contribute so much more than basic sweetness. It may look like "raw" sugar, but it is really just white sugar blended with molasses. Light brown sugar has less molasses; dark brown has more (and consequently is more acidic).

Honey
We use honey in both sweet and savory dishes. In addition to its flavor, we like to take advantage of its hygroscopic (moisture-retaining) properties. This helps keep baked goods tender, but it also can prevent vegetables and other foods from drying out. As a general rule, we favor mild-flavored honeys, such as clover, which combine well with other flavors. Honey with assertive flavors, such as buckwheat and orange blossom, can compete with the other ingredients.

Palm Sugar
Produced from the sap of coconut palm trees, palm sugar has a creamy mouthfeel and earthy taste slightly reminiscent of maple sugar. It's used as a sweetener throughout Asia and is easily found at Asian markets. Light brown sugar is a good substitute.

STARCHES

All-Purpose Flour
For cooking and general baking, we prefer all-purpose flour with a lower protein level to ensure tender cookies and crisp pie dough. Brands we like include Gold Medal and Bob's Red Mill.

Bread Flour
High-protein bread flour is the best choice for chewy flatbreads and hearty loaves and boules. Don't substitute it for all-purpose, as it will make your pancakes and muffins dense and tough.

Graham Flour
Graham flour is coarse-ground whole-wheat flour. We like using it in cookies and breads because it can contribute a strong, wheaty flavor without the gumminess of finer whole-wheat flour. Look for it in natural foods stores or in bulk bins at a co-op. It is perishable and should be stored in the refrigerator or freezer. To intensify the flavor of graham flour, toast it in a dry skillet until it darkens.

Potato Starch
Potato starch is essential for the crisp texture of Korean pancakes and worth keeping around to use as a dusting for a variety of fried foods, such as chicken and fish. Look for potato starch in the baking aisle or Jewish foods section of the grocery store or at Asian markets. Note: Potato flour is different and should not be substituted.

Rye Flour
Rye flour has a slightly spicy, earthy flavor that we use to add complexity and a pleasant bitterness to baked goods. Try substituting it for a small amount of the all-purpose flour in pizza dough and pancakes for more complex flavor (no more than a 20 percent swap; otherwise the texture will be affected). Rye flour is more perishable than wheat flour and should be stored in the refrigerator or freezer.

Semolina Flour

Semolina is a coarse protein-rich flour produced from hard durum wheat. It's most commonly used to make dried pasta, and we also use it for dusting a peel for transferring pizza dough. In Italy and the Middle East, it turns up in recipes for cookies and sweets that benefit from a bit of added texture.

GRAINS & PASTA

Asian Noodles

There are dozens of varieties of Asian noodles made from an array of starches. Most Asian wheat noodles are made from a lower-protein wheat than is used for Italian pasta, so they tend to be softer and chewier. In our experience, udon noodles are the most widely available of this style. Japanese soba noodles are made with buckwheat and are brownish-gray in color, with nutty, mineral notes. If you can't find any Asian wheat noodles, substitute dried Italian linguine or fettuccine.

Bulgur

Chewy and firm with a nutty flavor, bulgur is an ancient ingredient. Though often confused with plain cracked wheat, which is uncooked, bulgur is a cooked and dried cracked wheat. It is made by boiling wheat berries, usually durum (a hard protein-rich wheat), until they are about to crack open, then allowing them to dry. The outer bran layers are rubbed off, and the grains are ground in grades ranging from fine to coarse. Preparation can be as simple as a cold soak (for fine) to a gentle simmer (for coarse). As with many grains, bulgur can be toasted to intensify its flavor. If you can't find fine-grain bulgur, process coarse bulgur in a spice grinder in short pulses until fine, light and fluffy, six to 10 pulses.

Italian Pasta

We always keep on hand a package of long, thin noodles—such as spaghetti or linguine—to use with creamy or thin sauces, as well as a pack of short or round stocky noodles—such as penne, gemelli or orecchiette—for chunkier sauces. Most of our pasta recipes are designed to use 12 ounces (3 ounces per serving—Italian-style), 4 ounces less than the average box of pasta. Either cook the extra pasta and save for the next day (terrific fried crisp in olive oil and topped with grated Parmesan and a fried egg), or save the surplus for a future batch. We like using tongs for stirring pasta; it makes it easy to separate any stuck pieces.

Rice

For pilafs and day-to-day eating, we like long-grain white rice. For Southeast Asian dishes, long-grain jasmine rice is ideal (note that U.S.-grown jasmine lacks the aroma and flavor of Asian-grown rice). For Indian dishes, long, thin grains of basmati are best. Rice is easy to make, though it does take a bit of time. For convenience, we often make a batch or two ahead and freeze it in zip-close bags. It thaws in just minutes in the microwave.

WINE & SPIRITS

Dry Sherry

Dry sherry is frequently used in Chinese cooking as a good substitute for hard-to-find Shaoxing cooking wine. It adds a sweet-sharp flavor that rounds out the herbs and ginger in the broth and works wonders on the flavor of the chicken. It's not necessary to spend much on a bottle. Palo cortado is a good varietal (a good bit cheaper than manzanilla or fino), and the Lustau brand is a reliable choice.

Mirin

Mirin is Japanese sweet rice wine. Aji-mirin varieties are sweetened with added sugar and sometimes seasoned with salt; hon-mirin varieties have no added sugar (and are more expensive). As with many things, the more you spend, the better the quality. Lower-quality varieties are made largely from corn syrup and flavorings. We prefer hon-mirin when available.

Rye Whiskey

The spicy flavors of rye are particularly well suited to flavoring spiced baked goods. Among good brands for cooking, Rittenhouse Rye packs a lot of spice and doesn't cost a fortune (and it makes a great Manhattan).

Rum

We use the spicy, earthy flavor of dark rum in some baking because it does a terrific job of accenting spices, vanilla and brown sugar. Myers's Rum Original Dark and Gosling's Black Seal Bermuda Black Rum are excellent choices for cooking.

Vermouth

Vermouth is wine fortified with additional alcohol and flavored with a variety of botanicals. The herbal notes of vermouth make it particularly well suited for pairing with vegetables, poultry and seafood. An opened bottle of vermouth stores well for up to a month in the refrigerator. For cooking, be sure to use dry vermouth; sweet vermouth is best in a Manhattan or negroni.

Wine

The basic rule for selecting a cooking wine: Don't spend a fortune, but do make sure it's drinkable. When choosing wines to cook with, look for neutral, dry varietals and blends. For whites, we stick with sauvignon blanc, pinot gris, Côtes du Rhône and Spanish Rueda wines. Avoid anything oaky, such as chardonnay, or overly aromatic, like riesling and gewürztraminer. For reds, we like Côtes du Rhône again, as well as grenache and syrah. If you have leftover drinking wine that won't be consumed within a few days, consider simmering it down until it reduces by half, then freeze it in an ice cube tray. It's a quick way to add big flavor to soups, stews, stocks and sauces.

Eggs

Fluffy Olive Oil Scrambled Eggs / 23

Sunny-Side Up Fried Eggs / 23

Baked Persian Herb Omelet
(*Kuku Sabzi*) / 27

Curry Braised Eggs / 28

Spanish-Style Eggs with Garlicky
Crumbs and Chorizo (*Migas*) / 31

Chinese Stir-Fried Eggs
with Tomatoes / 33

Korean Scallion Pancakes (*Pajeon*) / 35

Turkish Scrambled Eggs with Spicy
Tomato and Capers (*Menemen*) / 37

2

GET A BETTER SCRAMBLE WITH OLIVE OIL, NOT BUTTER

Making scrambled eggs in a hot skillet with extra-virgin olive oil instead of butter allows the proteins to link up more easily, trapping steam and scrambling faster to create creamier, fluffier, more tender eggs.

Fluffy Olive Oil **Scrambled Eggs**

Start to finish: **10 minutes** / Servings: 4

We'd never questioned the French rule that butter is best for cooking eggs. But then we noticed that chefs at hotel breakfast stations use oil to make omelets in carbon-steel pans. Likewise, the Chinese cook their well-seasoned, well-browned omelets in oil, as do the Japanese. But scrambled eggs? As a test, we heated olive oil until just smoking and poured in whisked eggs. Whoosh! In a quick puff of steam, we had light, fluffy eggs. The oil needed a full 3 minutes at medium heat to get hot enough. Higher temperatures cooked the eggs too fast, toughening them. Two tablespoons of oil was enough to coat the bottom of the skillet and flavor the eggs without making them greasy. We like our scrambled eggs particularly wet and not entirely cooked through, which takes just 30 seconds. Leave them a little longer for drier eggs. Either way, take them off the heat before they are fully cooked and let them rest on a warm plate for 30 seconds. They finish cooking off the heat. Mixing the salt into the eggs before cooking was the best way to season them.

Don't warm your plates too much. It sounds minor, but hot plates will continue to cook the eggs, making them tough and dry. Cold plates will cool the eggs too fast. The plates should be warm to the touch, but not so hot that you can't comfortably hold them.

2 tablespoons extra-virgin olive oil

8 large eggs

Kosher salt and ground black pepper

1. In a 12-inch nonstick or seasoned carbon-steel skillet over medium, heat the oil until just starting to smoke, about 3 minutes. While the oil heats, in a bowl, use a fork to whisk the eggs and ¾ teaspoon salt until blended and foamy. Pour the eggs into the center of the pan.

2. Using a rubber spatula, continuously stir the eggs, pushing them toward the middle as they set at the edges and folding the cooked egg over on itself. Cook until just set, 60 to 90 seconds. The curds should be shiny, wet and soft, but not translucent or runny. Immediately transfer to warmed plates. Season with salt and pepper.

SUNNY-SIDE UP FRIED EGGS

Start to finish: **8 minutes**
Makes 4 eggs

Hot oil gave us the best scrambled eggs, but fried eggs turned out to be a different game. Here, butter truly was better; oil produced tough, greasy fried eggs. Every stovetop has a different low setting, and skillets vary in thickness and heat conductivity. It may take a few attempts to determine the best timing for your equipment. For us, 3 minutes was perfect for completely set whites and thick but runny yolks. If you like very loose yolks, shave off a minute; for lightly browned whites and firm yolks, add a minute. To make 2 eggs, use an 8-inch skillet and 2 teaspoons of butter.

Don't break the yolks when cracking the eggs into the bowl. If you're not confident in your egg-cracking skills, break the eggs one at a time into a small bowl before combining them.

4 large eggs

1 tablespoon salted butter

Kosher salt and ground black pepper

1. Heat a 10-inch nonstick skillet over low for 3 minutes. Crack the eggs into a bowl. Add the butter to the hot pan and swirl until melted. When the butter stops foaming, slowly pour the eggs into the skillet. If necessary, gently nudge the yolks with a wooden spoon to space them evenly in the pan.

2. Working quickly, season the eggs with salt and pepper, then cover the skillet and cook until the whites are completely set and the yolks are bright yellow, about 3 minutes. Slide out of the pan and onto plates.

WELL-SEASONED STEEL

Here at Milk Street, we think equipment can be every bit as important in changing the way you cook as the recipes we develop and the ingredients we source. Case in point: the wok. The pan's thin metal composition, gently curved sides and broad surface area allow for rapid heating and quick searing; foods won't stew in their own juices.

When shopping for a wok, look for a flat-bottomed model, which will sit flat on a conventional burner and heat evenly (round-bottomed woks, designed for a different kind of burner, require a stabilizing ring to use on Western stoves and will never heat quite as well).

We prefer the quick heating and light weight of carbon-steel pans. A roughly 14-inch diameter is ideal because it's large enough to stir-fry up to four servings at once, but won't require a ton of storage space. Look for a wok with a heat-safe handle and a helper handle on the opposite side; a full wok can be unwieldy without it.

While you're shopping for a wok, make sure to pick up a wok spatula (or wok shovel), which is designed to fit the wok's curvature. If you don't have one, try a flexible fish spatula and tongs.

We also like carbon-steel skillets. Like woks, they're inexpensive and rugged and can develop a natural nonstick coating without the worrying chemicals of typical nonstick surfaces.

To get that surface, carbon-steel skillets and woks must be seasoned before use. We do this just after buying them. We also use a technique cooks at Chinese restaurants use. When it's time to cook, we ladle oil into the hot pan to coat it, then dump it before adding fresh oil for cooking. This fills divots in the coating caused by daily wear.

INITIAL SEASONING: Scrub the wok or skillet with hot soapy water to remove any protective layer of oil or wax coating the surface, then dry and set over medium heat. Use a paper towel held with tongs to spread 1 tablespoon vegetable oil evenly over the pan. Leave on the heat until it smokes, then hold it at that stage for 1 minute. Use a paper towel held with tongs to wipe the pan clean. Repeat the process until the pan develops a golden-brown patina, three to five repetitions. The pan may look blotchy, but will even out with use.

DAILY USE: Set the pan over medium heat and add 1 teaspoon of vegetable oil. Use a paper towel held with tongs to wipe the oil evenly over the pan. When the oil smokes, hold it at that stage for 1 minute, then wipe clean with another paper towel held with tongs. Allow the pan to cool for 3 to 5 minutes, then add the oil or butter for cooking. Don't skip the cooling step or the pan will be too hot and burn the cooking fat.

DAILY CARE: Treat your seasoned pan well. Never plunge a hot carbon-steel pan into cold water; the thermal shock can crack the pan. And avoid soap; it will dissolve the seasoning. After cooking, clean the pan with a wet sponge (and a little coarse salt mixed with oil if needed to scrub away stubborn bits), dry it well and wipe lightly with oil before storing.

Baked Persian Herb Omelet
(*Kuku Sabzi*)

Start to finish: **1 hour (20 minutes active)** / Servings: 6

5 tablespoons extra-virgin olive oil, divided

2 cups lightly packed fresh flat-leaf parsley leaves

2 cups lightly packed fresh cilantro leaves and tender stems

1 cup coarsely chopped fresh dill

6 scallions, trimmed and coarsely chopped

1½ teaspoons baking powder

1 teaspoon kosher salt

¾ teaspoon ground cardamom

¾ teaspoon ground cinnamon

½ teaspoon ground cumin

¼ teaspoon ground black pepper

6 large eggs

½ cup walnuts, toasted and chopped (optional)

⅓ cup dried cranberries, coarsely chopped (optional)

Whole-milk Greek-style yogurt, to serve (optional)

As France claims the omelet, Italy the frittata and Spain the tortilla, Iran has kuku, a baked egg dish. The kuku sabzi variation gets its flavor—and a deep green color—from tons of fresh herbs. We love this approach to fresh herbs. Using heaps of them delivers big flavor effortlessly, and keeps heavy dishes feeling light and fresh. Kuku sabzi—which is served at Persian New Year's feasts—remains light despite six eggs and a handful of walnuts (for texture and richness) thanks to five cups of parsley, cilantro and dill. Also helping is baking powder, which forms tiny air bubbles that catch the steam released as the eggs cook, causing the dish to rise. While some recipes for kuku sabzi opt for stovetop cooking (with copious oil), we preferred the ease of baking. Pulsing the herbs and scallions in the food processor was easier and faster than hand chopping, and the texture was better. Dried cranberries were a good stand-in for traditional Persian barberries—lending a sweet-and-savory balance—but the recipe works without them.

Don't use less than 2 tablespoons of oil to grease the pan; the oil should pool at the bottom and generously coat the sides. This crisps the edges and boosts the omelet's flavor.

1. Heat the oven to 375°F with a rack in the upper-middle position. Coat the bottom and sides of an 8-inch square or 9-inch round cake pan with 2 tablespoons of the oil. Line the bottom of the pan with a square of kitchen parchment, then turn the parchment to coat both sides with oil.

2. In a food processor, combine the parsley, cilantro, dill, scallions and the remaining 3 tablespoons oil. Process until finely ground. In a large bowl, whisk together the baking powder, salt, cardamom, cinnamon, cumin and pepper. Add 2 of the eggs and whisk until blended. Add the remaining 4 eggs and whisk until just combined. Fold in the herb-scallion mixture and the walnuts and cranberries, if using. Pour into the prepared pan and smooth the top. Bake until the center is firm, 20 to 25 minutes.

3. Let the kuku cool in the pan on a rack for 10 minutes. Run a knife around the edges, then invert onto a plate and remove the parchment. Reinvert onto a cutting board or serving platter. Cut into wedges and serve warm, cold or room temperature with a dollop of yogurt, if desired. The kuku can be refrigerated for up to 3 days, tightly wrapped.

CHANGE THE WAY YOU COOK:
FOR LIGHTER EGGS, BORROW A BAKING INGREDIENT

Baking powder can help lighten baked frittatas such as this kuku, a Persian herb omelet. Just as it does in more traditional baking, the baking powder reacts with the heat of the oven to form carbon dioxide gas—or bubbles—that adds air to the frittata's structure.

Curry Braised Eggs

Start to finish: 1 hour 15 minutes (50 minutes active)
Servings: 4

3 tablespoons grapeseed or other neutral oil

1 large yellow onion, halved and thinly sliced lengthwise

Kosher salt

2 tablespoons finely grated fresh ginger

4 teaspoons garam masala

1 teaspoon ground turmeric

¼ teaspoon cayenne pepper

Three 14½-ounce cans diced tomatoes, drained

14-ounce can coconut milk

1 tablespoon packed brown sugar

Ground black pepper

1 tablespoon lime juice, plus lime wedges to serve

8 large eggs

⅓ cup chopped fresh cilantro

Steamed basmati rice, naan or boiled potatoes, to serve (optional)

Eggs are bit players in Western dinners. We eat them for breakfast and brunch, but come evening they rarely appear except as accessories for the put-an-egg-on-it crowd. The rest of the world knows better. Portugal, for example, has ervilhas com ovos, braised eggs with spicy or sweet Portuguese chourico sausage and/or bacon and peas. In India, there is muttai kuzhambu, a type of egg curry. Both dishes are built on layers of seasoning that balance the richness of the eggs. We liked the way garam masala—a warmly flavored Indian seasoning blend—added complex flavor. For our vegetables, we started with onions and found that sliced worked better than diced, adding texture and helping the sauce hold its shape. We let the sauce cool a bit in the dish before adding the eggs to ensure even cooking. While we like runny yolks, feel free to leave the dish in the oven a bit longer for firm yolks.

Don't forget that every oven is different, not to mention every egg. Cooking times will depend on oven temperature, as well as the size and temperature of the eggs.

1. Heat the oven to 375°F with a rack in the lower-middle position. In a 6- to 8-quart Dutch oven over medium, heat the oil. Add the onion and ½ teaspoon salt. Cook, stirring, until browned, 7 to 9 minutes. Add the ginger, garam masala, turmeric and cayenne. Cook for 30 seconds, stirring constantly. Add the tomatoes, coconut milk, sugar, ¾ teaspoon salt and ½ teaspoon pepper. Bring to a boil, scraping up any browned bits. Reduce heat to medium and simmer, stirring and scraping the pan, until thickened, 20 to 25 minutes.

2. Remove the pan from the heat and let sit for 10 minutes, stirring occasionally. Stir in the lime juice, then taste and season with salt and pepper. Use the back of a spoon to make 8 evenly spaced wells in the sauce. Crack 1 egg into each well, then season the eggs with salt and pepper.

3. Bake until the sauce is bubbling and the egg whites are opaque but still jiggle slightly, 13 to 18 minutes, rotating the pot halfway through. Remove from the oven and let sit for 5 minutes. Sprinkle with cilantro and serve with lime wedges and rice, naan or potatoes, if desired.

Spanish-Style Eggs with Garlicky Crumbs and Chorizo (*Migas*)

Start to finish: **30 minutes** / Servings: 4

8 large eggs

Kosher salt

3 ounces Spanish chorizo, halved lengthwise and thinly sliced crosswise

3 tablespoons extra-virgin olive oil, divided

2½ cups ½-inch chewy bread cubes

1 medium red onion, diced (about 1 cup)

2 garlic cloves, thinly sliced

¼ teaspoon sweet paprika

¼ teaspoon cayenne pepper (optional)

4 cups lightly packed coarsely chopped lacinato kale (about 3 ounces)

Ground black pepper

Migas evolved as a Spanish-Portuguese dish intended to use up stale bread. In fact, the word is Spanish for crumbs. Traditionally, the bread is torn into cubes, sprinkled with water and left overnight. Since most Americans don't have stale bread sitting around, we used ½-inch cubes of rustic bread. The best way to flavor them was to toss them in garlicky oil before toasting them in a skillet. We used Spanish-style chorizo, which is cured, and added a diced red onion along with chopped fresh kale. Lacinato (dinosaur) kale gave the dish heft, color and flavor. Be sure to stem the kale before measuring or weighing it, or substitute baby kale, which requires no stemming. For a variation, reduce or omit the kale and add 1 cup of chopped roasted red peppers or frozen peas (thawed). We found the bread cubes worked best when stirred in at the end of cooking, which gave them a chance to reheat and just begin to soften at the edges without losing their crunch. Their salty, garlicky flavor came through beautifully.

Don't walk away while browning the chorizo. Chorizo brands vary widely in fat content—not to mention flavor—and can go from golden brown to burnt in seconds.

1. In a medium bowl, whisk the eggs and ½ teaspoon salt. In a 12-inch non-stick skillet over medium, cook the chorizo, stirring frequently, until browned and crisp, 2 to 5 minutes. Use a slotted spoon to transfer the chorizo to a medium bowl, leaving any fat in the pan.

2. Add 2 tablespoons of the olive oil to the skillet and return to medium-high. Add the bread and a pinch of salt, then cook, stirring and tossing frequently, until browned and crisp, 3 to 5 minutes. Transfer to the bowl with the chorizo.

3. Return the skillet to medium heat and add the remaining 1 tablespoon oil, the onion, garlic, paprika, cayenne, if using, and ¼ teaspoon salt. Cook,

stirring frequently, until the onion and garlic are softened and lightly browned, 3 to 5 minutes. If the garlic darkens too fast, reduce the heat. Add the kale and cook until wilted but still bright green, 1 to 2 minutes.

4. Whisk the eggs to recombine, then pour into the skillet and immediately reduce the heat to low. Cook, stirring and scraping the edges of the pan constantly, until barely set, about 1 minute. Stir in the bread and chorizo. Cook to desired consistency, 30 to 90 seconds. Transfer to a platter and season with salt and pepper.

Chinese Stir-Fried Eggs with Tomatoes

Start to finish: 15 minutes / Servings: 4

3 plum tomatoes (about 12 ounces), halved, cored and seeded

4 tablespoons unseasoned rice vinegar, divided

Ground white pepper

1 tablespoon ketchup

2 teaspoons finely grated fresh ginger

1 garlic clove, finely grated

½ teaspoon red pepper flakes

1 teaspoon toasted sesame oil

3 teaspoons soy sauce, divided

8 large eggs

3 tablespoons vegetable oil, divided

Kosher salt

Stir-fried eggs with tomatoes is quick Chinese comfort food, and there are endless variations. Our version has more flavor than most since we season the ingredients from the start, rather than relying on condiments. We began by giving our tomatoes a toss in vinegar and white pepper. We didn't add sugar (a classic ingredient), but did add a dollop of sweet tomato flavor via a tablespoon of ketchup. We found the best method was to cook the eggs and tomatoes separately, starting with the eggs. We then added tomatoes to the empty skillet, cooked them until just beginning to blister, then arranged them on the eggs. Finally, our sauce went into the skillet to heat and thicken. This recipe comes together quickly, so have all ingredients assembled and prepared before you begin cooking. We liked the eggs with thinly sliced scallions, toasted sesame seeds and a drizzle of chili oil. Serve it over rice and you have a quick dinner.

Don't forget to seed the tomatoes. *The pulp made the dish watery.*

1. Cut each tomato half into thirds. In a medium bowl, toss the tomatoes with 1 tablespoon of the vinegar and ½ teaspoon white pepper. In a small bowl, combine the remaining 3 tablespoons vinegar, ¼ cup water, ketchup, ginger, garlic, pepper flakes, sesame oil, 2 teaspoons of the soy sauce and ½ teaspoon white pepper. Set aside. In a second medium bowl, whisk the eggs, the remaining 1 teaspoon soy sauce and ½ teaspoon white pepper.

2. Drain the tomatoes and set aside. In a 12-inch nonstick skillet over medium-high, heat 2 tablespoons of the vegetable oil until barely smoking. Pour the eggs into the center of the pan, letting the eggs puff up along the edges. Use a spatula to stir the eggs, pushing them toward the middle as they begin to set at the edges and folding the cooked egg onto itself. Cook until just set, 45 to 60 seconds. Transfer to a plate.

3. In the empty skillet, heat the remaining 1 tablespoon of oil over medium-high until beginning to smoke. Add the drained tomatoes and cook undisturbed until just beginning to blister, 30 to 60 seconds. Arrange the tomatoes on top of the eggs.

4. Return the skillet to high heat and pour the sauce mixture into the skillet. Cook, stirring constantly, until thickened, about 30 seconds. Taste and season with salt and white pepper. Pour over the tomatoes.

Korean Scallion Pancakes (*Pajeon*)

Start to finish: **30 minutes** / Servings: 4

65 grams (½ cup) all-purpose flour

½ cup potato starch

1 teaspoon red pepper flakes

1 teaspoon kosher salt

1 cup ice water

1 large egg, beaten

6 scallions, trimmed and
cut into 1-inch pieces

¼ cup shredded carrot
(about ½ medium carrot)

¼ cup soy sauce

3 tablespoons unseasoned
rice vinegar

½ teaspoon toasted sesame oil

¼ teaspoon ground black pepper

2 tablespoons grapeseed or
other neutral oil, divided

Quick to make and with a crisp exterior but chewy center, pajeon take pancakes from breakfast to dinner. We tried several flour combinations in our search for just the right texture. We found that a combination of all-purpose flour and potato starch gave these pancakes their signature crisp-chewy texture. Using ice water in our batter encouraged the pancakes to puff while cooking, producing slightly crisped edges. Some recipes use as few as two scallions but we preferred more, settling on six. We started our pancake at a medium-high heat, but needed to reduce it after flipping to prevent the scallions from burning. If you can find gochugaru, or Korean chili powder, use it in place of the red pepper flakes for a sweeter, smokier flavor. Looking to switch up the flavors? We've included kimchi and seafood variations.

Don't use potato flour, which has a strong potato flavor and reacts differently with water. Bob's Red Mill makes potato starch, which is usually available in the baking aisle or natural foods section of your grocer.

1. In a medium bowl, whisk together the flour, potato starch, pepper flakes and salt. Add the water and egg and whisk until smooth. Fold in the scallions and carrots. Set aside. In a small bowl, combine the soy sauce, vinegar, sesame oil and pepper; set aside.

2. In a 12-inch nonstick skillet, heat 1 tablespoon of the grapeseed oil over medium-high until barely smoking. Stir the batter to recombine, then add half (1 scant cup) to the skillet, spreading it and the vegetables evenly to the edges of the pan. Cook until the top is set and the pancakes get lightly brown around the edges, 3 to 4 minutes.

3. Reduce heat to medium-low, then use a spatula to flip the pancake. Cook until golden brown on the second side, being careful not to burn the scallions, 1 to 2 minutes. Flip again and cook until

the pancake is charred in spots and crisp around the edges, 2 to 4 minutes. Transfer to a plate. Increase the heat to medium-high and repeat with the remaining 1 tablespoon grapeseed oil and the remaining batter. Cut the pancakes into wedges and serve with the sauce.

VARIATIONS:

For kimchi pancakes: Substitute ⅔ cup sliced napa cabbage kimchi for the scallions and carrots. Squeeze the kimchi gently before adding to remove excess liquid.

For seafood pancakes: Eliminate the carrot and add ½ cup chopped raw shrimp (peeled and deveined) to the batter with the scallions.

Turkish Scrambled Eggs with Spicy Tomato and Capers (*Menemen*)

Start to finish: **20 minutes** / Servings: 4

4 tablespoons extra-virgin olive oil, divided, plus more to serve

2 poblano chilies, stemmed, seeded and finely chopped

1 bunch scallions, thinly sliced

3 medium garlic cloves, minced

1 tablespoon Aleppo pepper or substitute, see p. 7

Kosher salt and ground white pepper

1 plum tomato, cored and finely chopped

2 tablespoons drained capers

8 large eggs

⅓ cup crumbled feta cheese

3 tablespoons chopped fresh dill

Poblano chilies are Mexican in heritage, but their earthy flavor and mild heat make them ideal for this version of Turkish-style scrambled eggs. Using Aleppo pepper nudges the dish closer to the traditional flavor profile, but if you don't have any, see p. 7 for a substitute. Serve on warmed plates to prevent the eggs from cooling too quickly. Round out the meal with crisp slices of toast.

Don't wait until the eggs are firm and fully set before removing the pan from the heat; the eggs continue to cook in the time it takes to portion and serve.

1. In a 12-inch nonstick skillet over medium, heat 2 tablespoons of oil until shimmering. Add the poblanos, scallions, garlic, Aleppo pepper and ½ teaspoon each salt and white pepper. Cover and cook, stirring, until the chilies are softened but not browned, 6 to 8 minutes. Transfer to a medium bowl and stir in the tomato and capers; set aside. Wipe out the skillet.

2. In a medium bowl, whisk the eggs and ¾ teaspoon salt. Return the skillet to medium and heat the remaining 2 tablespoons oil until shimmering. Pour the eggs into the center of the pan.

3. Using a silicone spatula, continuously stir the eggs, pushing them toward the middle as they set at the edges and folding the cooked egg over on itself. Cook until just set, about 1½ minutes. The curds should be shiny, wet and soft. Taste and season with salt and pepper, then divide among warmed serving plates.

4. Top each serving with a portion of the poblano mixture. Sprinkle with feta and dill, then drizzle with oil.

Soups

Miso-Shiitake Soup with
Napa Cabbage / 41

Turkish Red Lentil Soup / 43

Chickpea and Harissa Soup (*Lablabi*) / 45

Korean Pork and Kimchi Stew
(*Kimchi Jjigae*) / 46

Singapore Shrimp and Chicken Noodle
Soup (*Laksa*) / 49

Pork and Vegetable Miso Soup
(*Ton-Jiru*) / 50

Taiwanese Beef Noodle Soup / 52

Georgian Chicken Soup (*Chikhirtma*) / 55

Greek White Bean Soup (Fasolada) / 57

Spicy Red Lentil Stew
with Coconut Milk and Spinach / 59

Mexican Chicken Soup
with Tomatillos and Hominy / 60

Vietnamese Meatball and
Watercress Soup (*Canh*) / 63

Black-Eyed Pea and
Sweet Potato Stew (*Ndambe*) / 65

Spanish Garlic Soup / 67

Thai Rice Soup (*Khao Tom*) / 68

Somali Chicken Soup / 70

Gonzalo Guzmán's Pozole Rojo / 73

3

Miso-Shiitake Soup with Napa Cabbage

Start to finish: **30 minutes** / Servings: **6**

½ pound carrots (2 to 3 medium), peeled, halved lengthwise and cut crosswise into ½-inch pieces

2 tablespoons dried wakame seaweed

8 ounces soft tofu, drained and cut into ½-inch cubes

5 ounces fresh shiitake mushrooms, stems discarded, caps thinly sliced

4 cups chopped napa cabbage (½ small head)

6 tablespoons (3½ ounces) white miso paste

1-inch chunk fresh ginger, grated

1 tablespoon soy sauce, plus more to serve

2 teaspoons toasted sesame oil, plus more to serve

4 ounces (about 4 cups) baby spinach

6 scallions, trimmed and cut into 1-inch lengths

Hot chili oil, to serve (optional)

In Japan, where soup has evolved into high art, nabe (NAH-beh) is shorthand for nabemono, a broad category of soups that may be more recognizable by its Westernized name—hot pot. One such soup, yosenabe, loosely translates to "anything goes hot pot" and relies on layering flavors, adding them to the pot one at a time. Dense or long-cooking items go in first; more delicate ingredients follow. For our simplified yosenabe, we leaned heavily on vegetables. Most Japanese soups begin with dashi, a broth made from kombu seaweed and bonito, or shaved shreds of smoked tuna. We used more common but equally flavorful fresh shiitake mushrooms and dried wakame seaweed. (Wakame tastes slightly sweet and oceanic; look for it in the Asian foods aisle.) Timing was simple: Each ingredient cooked through in the time it took for the pot to return to a simmer. Yosenabe is typically flavored with a blend of soy sauce, sesame oil or scallions. We added all of them.

Don't use firm or extra-firm tofu in this recipe. Soft tofu had the best texture. Silken and medium tofu were decent substitutes.

1. In a medium Dutch oven over medium, combine 7 cups water, the carrots and wakame. Bring to a simmer and cook for 5 minutes. Add the tofu and mushrooms, then return to a simmer. Add the cabbage, then return to a simmer.

2. Place the miso in a 2-cup liquid measuring cup. Ladle out a bit of the cooking water and add to the miso, stirring until smooth. Pour the miso mixture back into the soup, then stir well.

3. As the soup returns to a simmer, stir in the ginger, soy sauce and sesame oil. Once the soup reaches a simmer, remove it from the heat and stir in the spinach and scallions. When the spinach is wilted, ladle the soup into serving bowls. Serve with soy sauce, sesame oil and chili oil, if using.

Turkish Red Lentil Soup

Start to finish: 45 minutes / Servings: 4

3 tablespoons salted butter

1 medium yellow onion, chopped

1 medium garlic clove, finely grated

1 tablespoon tomato paste

1 tablespoon sweet paprika

½ teaspoon ground cumin

1 cup red lentils

2 tablespoons long-grain white rice

Kosher salt

3 tablespoons extra-virgin olive oil

2 teaspoons Aleppo pepper (see note)

Chopped fresh mint, to serve (optional)

Lemon wedges, to serve

This simple yet substantial Turkish soup is made with red lentils, which soften and break down during cooking, adding texture. The Aleppo pepper brings gentle heat to the dish. If you can't find it locally, order online or see substitute, p. 7. The soup can be made vegan by substituting olive oil for the butter.

Don't omit the rice. The grains help thicken the soup.

1. In a large saucepan over medium, melt the butter. Add the onion and cook, stirring occasionally, until softened and translucent, about 5 minutes. Stir in the garlic and cook until fragrant, about 30 seconds. Stir in the tomato paste, paprika and cumin, then cook for about 1 minute.

2. Add the lentils, rice, 5 cups water and 2 teaspoons salt. Stir to combine and bring to a boil over medium-high. Reduce the heat to maintain a steady simmer, cover and cook, stirring occasionally, until the lentils and rice are tender and broken down, about 30 minutes. Season to taste.

3. Meanwhile, in a small skillet over medium, heat the olive oil, swirling to coat the pan. Add the Aleppo pepper and cook until a few bubbles appear and the oil is bright red, 1 to 2 minutes. Remove from the heat and set aside.

4. Serve the soup with Aleppo pepper oil drizzled over each serving and sprinkled with mint, if using, and lemon wedges on the side.

Chickpea and Harissa Soup (*Lablabi*)

Start to finish: 1 hour, plus soaking the chickpeas
Servings: 8

For the soup:

2 cups dried chickpeas

Kosher salt and ground black pepper

5 tablespoons extra-virgin
olive oil, divided

1 large yellow onion, chopped

6 medium garlic cloves, minced

2 tablespoons tomato paste

2 tablespoons ground cumin, toasted

6 tablespoons harissa

3 quarts low-sodium chicken broth
or water

8 ounces crusty white bread,
sliced ½-inch-thick and torn into
bite-size pieces

2 tablespoons lemon juice

For serving:

8 soft-cooked eggs, peeled
and halved

½ cup drained capers

½ cup chopped pitted green olives

½ cup chopped fresh flat-leaf parsley

½ cup chopped fresh cilantro

Extra-virgin olive oil

Harissa

2 tablespoons ground cumin,
toasted

Lemon wedges

This brothy-bready Tunisian chickpea soup gets punches of flavor from garlic, tomato paste and cumin. For the harissa, use our recipe (p. 496) or buy it ready-made; we like the DEA brand. And instead of using stale bread—as is common in Tunisia—we got better texture by toasting chunks of crusty bread in olive oil to make croutons. Toasted ground cumin is used in the soup as well as on it as a garnish; to be efficient, toast it all at once. In a small, dry skillet over medium, toast 5 tablespoons ground cumin, stirring constantly, until fragrant, about 1 minute, then transfer to a small bowl. To make soft-cooked eggs for serving, bring 2 cups water to a simmer in a large saucepan fitted with a steamer basket. Add the desired number of eggs, cover and steam over medium for 7 minutes. Immediately transfer to ice water to stop the cooking.

Don't forget to soak the dried chickpeas. They need to soak for at least 12 hours before cooking.

1. First, soak the chickpeas. In a large bowl, combine 2 quarts water, the chickpeas and 2 tablespoons salt. Let soak at room temperature for at least 12 hours or up to 24 hours. Drain the chickpeas and set aside.

2. To make the soup, in a large Dutch oven, heat 2 tablespoons of oil until shimmering. Add the onion and cook, stirring occasionally, until lightly golden, about 5 minutes. Stir in the garlic and cook until fragrant, about 30 seconds. Add the tomato paste and cook, stirring, until it browns, about 2 minutes. Stir in the cumin and harissa, then cook until fragrant, about 1 minute. Add the chickpeas and broth, then bring to a boil over high. Reduce to medium and simmer, uncovered, stirring occasionally, until the chickpeas are tender, about 1 hour.

3. Meanwhile, in a 12-inch nonstick skillet over medium, combine the bread, the remaining 3 tablespoons oil and 1 teaspoon salt. Cook, stirring occasionally, until crisp and light golden brown, 4 to 6 minutes. Remove from the heat and let the croutons cool in the pan. Transfer to a bowl.

4. When the chickpeas are tender, remove the pot from the heat and stir in the lemon juice. Taste and season with salt and pepper.

5. To serve, place 2 to 3 tablespoons of croutons in each serving bowl. Ladle chickpeas and broth around them, then top each portion with soft-cooked egg halves and 1 tablespoon each capers, olives, parsley and cilantro, or as desired. Drizzle with oil and garnish to taste with harissa and cumin. Serve with lemon wedges.

Korean Pork and Kimchi Stew (*Kimchi Jjigae*)

Start to finish: 1 hour 15 minutes (25 minutes active)
Servings: 6

1 cup boiling water,
plus 5 cups cold water

½ ounce dried shiitake mushrooms,
brushed clean

6 scallions, white parts finely
chopped, green parts thinly sliced
on diagonal, reserved separately

3 garlic cloves, smashed and peeled

1 tablespoon toasted sesame oil

1 tablespoon soy sauce

16-ounce container napa cabbage
kimchi, drained (¼ cup liquid
reserved) and coarsely chopped

4 teaspoons gochujang

1 pound baby back ribs, separated
into individual ribs

12 ounces medium-firm or firm tofu,
drained and cut into ¾-inch cubes

2 teaspoons white sugar

Looking for a stew with big flavor and easy prep, we were delighted to encounter Korean pork and kimchi stew. The assertively seasoned dish uses purchased kimchi—the pungent fermented cabbage that is a staple of Korean cooking—to easily add both vegetables and flavor. We built on our kimchi base with bone-in, baby back ribs for meaty flavor, cutting them into individual ribs so they tenderized quickly in the simmering broth. The bones and connective tissue of the ribs also add body to the broth. We layered the heat by combining another Korean favorite, gochujang chili paste, as well as the juice from the drained kimchi. For another time-saver, look for pre-sliced dried shiitake mushrooms. Serve with bowls of steamed white rice for a complete meal.

Don't use extra-firm or soft tofu. Soft or silken tofu was too fragile, and extra-firm added too much chew. Textures vary by brand, but we preferred medium-firm and firm.

1. In a small bowl, combine the boiling water and mushrooms. Let sit for 30 minutes.

2. Drain the mushrooms, reserving the soaking liquid. Discard the stems and thinly slice the caps. In a large Dutch oven over medium-high, combine the scallion whites, garlic, sesame oil and soy sauce. Cook, stirring occasionally, until the scallions have softened, 3 to 4 minutes. Stir in half of the kimchi, the sliced mushrooms and the gochujang. Add the cold water, the mushrooms' soaking liquid, the ribs and ¼ cup kimchi liquid and bring to a boil. Cover, leaving the lid slightly ajar, reduce the heat to medium-low and cook until rib meat is easily pierced with a knife, about 50 minutes, adjusting the heat to maintain a lively simmer.

3. Remove the pot from the heat. Using tongs, transfer the ribs to a plate and let rest until cool enough to handle, about 15 minutes.

4. Shred the meat into bite-size pieces, discarding the bones and cartilage. Add the meat to the stew along with the tofu, scallion greens, sugar and remaining kimchi. Bring to a simmer over medium and cook for 5 minutes.

Singapore Shrimp and Chicken Noodle Soup (*Laksa*)

Start to finish: **1 hour 20 minutes** / Servings: 6

6 medium shallots, peeled and halved

6 medium garlic cloves, peeled

3 tablespoons Thai red curry paste

2 lemon grass stalks, trimmed to the bottom 6 inches, dry outer layers discarded, chopped

2-inch piece fresh ginger, peeled and sliced into coins

2 teaspoons ground turmeric

1 bunch fresh cilantro, tender stems and leaves chopped, reserved separately, plus cilantro leaves, to serve

2 tablespoons grapeseed or other neutral oil

1 pound jumbo shrimp, peeled (shells reserved) and deveined

1 pound boneless, skinless chicken thighs, trimmed

14-ounce container firm tofu, drained, patted dry and cut into ½-inch cubes

6 tablespoons fish sauce, divided

3 tablespoons chili-garlic sauce, divided, plus more to serve

6 ounces wide (¼ inch) rice stick noodles

14-ounce can coconut milk

Kosher salt and ground white pepper

3 tablespoons lime juice, plus lime wedges, to serve

CHANGE THE WAY YOU COOK:
SAVE YOUR SHRIMP SHELLS

Don't toss the shells after peeling shrimp for soups or stews. Simmering shells in water or broth is a simple way to add flavor and they're easily strained out before other ingredients are added.

Laksa is a vibrant seafood and chicken noodle soup eaten from breakfast through dinner in Singapore. We use the shrimp shells to give maximum flavor to a broth that is seasoned with shallots, lemon grass and Thai red curry paste. You can boost the spiciness of the soup with extra chili-garlic sauce. If you like, garnish with chopped cucumber, halved hard-cooked eggs and chopped roasted peanuts.

Don't purchase shrimp that have been treated with sodium tripolyphosphate, an additive that improves the shrimps' appearance but also gives them an undesirable saltiness and unappealing texture. Check the label on the package or ask at the seafood counter. Don't discard the shrimp shells; you'll need them to make the broth. If you purchased already peeled shrimp, use just the tails for the broth.

1. In a food processor, combine the shallots, garlic, curry paste, lemon grass, ginger, turmeric and cilantro stems. Process until finely chopped, about 20 seconds.

2. In a large Dutch oven over medium-high, heat the oil until barely smoking. Add the shrimp shells and cook, stirring frequently, until they begin to char, 2 to 3 minutes. Stir in the shallot mixture and cook, stirring constantly, until fragrant and the paste begins to stick to the pot, about 2 minutes. Add 2 quarts water and bring to a boil over high, then reduce to medium-low, cover and simmer for 30 minutes.

3. Strain the broth through a fine mesh strainer set over a large heat-safe bowl, pressing on the solids to extract as much liquid as possible. Discard the solids. Return the broth to the pot and bring to a simmer over medium-high. Stir in the chicken, tofu, 1 tablespoon of fish sauce and 1 tablespoon of chili-garlic sauce. Return to a simmer, cover and reduce to low. Cook until a skewer inserted into the chicken meets no resistance, about 30 minutes.

4. Meanwhile, in a small bowl, toss the shrimp with 1 tablespoon of the remaining fish sauce and 1 tablespoon of the remaining chili-garlic sauce. Cover and refrigerate until needed.

5. Bring a large pot of water to a boil, then remove from the heat. Stir in the noodles and let soak until softened but still chewy, about 10 minutes. Drain in a colander, rinse under cold water and drain again. Divide the noodles evenly among 6 serving bowls.

6. When the chicken is cooked, transfer to a bowl, then use 2 forks to shred it into bite-size pieces. Return the chicken to the pot and stir in the coconut milk. Bring to a simmer over medium, then reduce to low. Add the shrimp and cook, stirring occasionally, until the shrimp are cooked through and opaque, 1 to 2 minutes.

7. Off heat, stir in the cilantro leaves, the remaining 4 tablespoons fish sauce, the remaining 1 tablespoon chili-garlic sauce and the lime juice. Taste and season with salt and white pepper. Ladle the soup over the noodles. Sprinkle with cilantro leaves and serve with lime wedges and chili-garlic sauce.

Pork and Vegetable Miso Soup (*Ton-Jiru*)

Start to finish: **40 minutes** / Servings: **4**

6 to 8 ounces pork tenderloin, trimmed of silver skin, halved lengthwise, cut into ¼-inch slices

¼ cup soy sauce

14-ounce container firm tofu, drained

One 4-by-6-inch piece kombu seaweed

4 medium dried shiitake mushrooms

3 small carrots, peeled and cut into ½-inch pieces

2-inch chunk daikon (about 5 ounces), peeled, cut into ½-inch pieces

3 scallions, thinly sliced on diagonal, white and green parts reserved separately

3 tablespoons sake

5 tablespoons white miso

Miso gives this simple soup—inspired by a recipe from Japanese cooking expert Elizabeth Andoh—great depth of flavor and a unique savoriness. Of the various types of miso, we liked the mild, subtle sweetness of white (shiro) miso best in this dish, but use any variety you like. For more complexity, you can even blend several different ones.

Don't allow the kombu-shiitake broth to reach a full boil. High heat damages the kombu's delicate flavors and will result in a pungent, overpowering broth.

1. In a small bowl, stir together the pork and soy sauce. Cover and refrigerate for at least 20 minutes or up to 1 hour. Meanwhile, line a baking dish with a triple layer of paper towels. Set the tofu in it and cover with additional paper towels. Place a second baking dish or plate on top, then weigh it down with several cans. Let stand for 10 minutes, then discard any accumulated liquid. Pat the tofu dry, cut it into ½-inch cubes and set aside.

2. Meanwhile, in a large saucepan over medium-high, bring 5 cups water, the kombu and mushrooms to a simmer; do not boil. Reduce to medium-low and cook, adjusting the heat to maintain a gentle simmer, for about 15 minutes, skimming off any small particles or foam on the surface.

3. Remove and discard the kombu and mushrooms. Add the tofu, carrots, daikon, scallion whites and sake. Bring to a gentle simmer over medium and cook until the vegetables are tender, 5 to 9 minutes.

4. Pour off and discard the excess pork marinade, then stir the pork into the soup. Cook until the pork is no longer pink, about 2 minutes. In a small bowl, whisk the miso and ¼ cup of the hot broth until dissolved, then stir into the soup. Ladle into bowls and sprinkle with scallion greens.

Taiwanese Beef **Noodle Soup**

Start to finish: 2 hours 45 minutes (45 minutes active)
Servings: 6

---

1 tablespoon grapeseed
or other neutral oil

6 medium garlic cloves, smashed
and peeled

4-inch piece fresh ginger, peeled,
cut into 6 to 8 pieces and smashed

6 scallions, white parts roughly
chopped, green parts thinly sliced,
reserved separately

3 star anise pods

1 tablespoon Sichuan peppercorns

3 tablespoons chili bean sauce (toban
djan, see note)

2 tablespoons tomato paste

2 tablespoons packed dark
brown sugar

⅓ cup soy sauce

⅓ cup sake

2 to 2½ pounds beef shanks
(about 1 inch thick), trimmed

Kosher salt

1 pound baby bok choy, trimmed
and cut crosswise into 1-inch pieces

8 ounces dried wheat noodles

Fragrant star anise and Sichuan peppercorns flavor this meaty broth, along with toban djan, a spicy, fermented chili-bean paste. It's sold in most Asian markets, but if you can't find it, substitute with 2 tablespoons white miso mixed with 4 teaspoons chili-garlic sauce and 2 teaspoons soy sauce. The soup is lightly spicy; you can add more toban djan and/or some ground Sichuan pepper at the table for more heat and spice. Chinese wheat noodles of any thickness worked well, as did Japanese udon and long, thin Italian pastas, such as spaghetti.

Don't forget to skim the fat off the strained cooking liquid. This prevents the soup from tasting greasy. And don't rinse the drained noodles under cold water. Lukewarm water will keep them from cooling down completely.

1. In a large Dutch oven over medium, combine the oil, garlic, ginger and scallion whites. Cook, stirring, until sizzling, about 3 minutes. Stir in the star anise and peppercorns, then cook until fragrant, about 30 seconds. Stir in the chili-bean sauce, tomato paste, brown sugar, soy sauce, sake and 2½ cups water. Bring to a boil over high.

2. Add the beef shanks and return to a simmer. Cover, reduce to low and cook, adjusting as needed to maintain a gentle simmer, until the beef is tender and beginning to fall apart, about 2 hours.

3. Use a slotted spoon to transfer the beef shanks to a bowl and set aside. Pour the cooking liquid through a fine mesh strainer set over a large bowl; discard the solids. Reserve the pot. Skim off and discard the fat from the surface

of the liquid, then return to the pot. When cool enough to handle, shred the meat into bite-size pieces, discarding the bones, fat and gristle. Add the meat to the pot and bring to a simmer over medium-high, then reduce to low and cover to keep warm.

4. In a large pot, bring 4 quarts water to a boil. Add 2 tablespoons salt and the bok choy. Cook until the stems are crisp-tender, about 3 minutes. Use a slotted spoon to transfer the bok choy to a large plate and set aside. Add the noodles to the water and cook until tender. Drain, rinse under lukewarm water, then drain again.

5. Divide the noodles and bok choy among serving bowls, then ladle in the soup and sprinkle with scallion greens.

Georgian Chicken Soup (*Chikhirtma*)

Start to finish: 1 hour 45 minutes (45 minutes active)
Servings: 6

For the broth and chicken:

1 bunch fresh cilantro

1 bunch fresh dill

1 garlic head

2½ to 3 pounds bone-in
skin-on chicken legs

10 cups water

1 large yellow onion, quartered

2 teaspoons kosher salt

1 teaspoon black peppercorns

½ teaspoon coriander seeds

½ teaspoon red pepper flakes
(optional)

3-inch cinnamon stick

2 bay leaves

For the soup:

1 pound carrots (about 5 medium),
peeled, halved lengthwise and cut
crosswise into ½-inch pieces

1 large yellow onion, coarsely
chopped

3 tablespoons salted butter

½ teaspoon kosher salt

½ cup dry vermouth

1 tablespoon all-purpose flour

6 large egg yolks

¼ cup lemon juice

Ground black pepper

It's easy to overcomplicate chicken soup. Too often, the broths are watery and flavorless, so we compensate by piling on the ingredients. But that only leads to a muddle of flavors and textures. We wanted a chicken soup that tastes fresh and light, yet also robust and satisfying. We wanted just the right vegetables—and in the right volumes—balanced by a gentle acidity and spice. We found our answer in chikhirtma, a traditional soup from Georgia, the Eurasian country that bridges Turkey and Russia. Georgian cuisine often marries Western techniques with Eastern flavors. We used a recipe from Darra Goldstein, author of "The Georgian Feast," as our starting point. Her chikhirtma calls for a whole chicken, but that much meat made the soup feel heavy, so we used just chicken legs. We built flavor with bunches of dill and cilantro stems and a head of garlic, as well as coriander, cinnamon and bay leaves.

Don't simmer the soup after adding the eggs. Heat it gently just until warm, otherwise the eggs will curdle.

1. To make the broth, tie the stems of the cilantro and dill into bundles, then trim off the leaves, reserving ¼ cup of each for garnish. Cut off and discard the top third of the garlic head, leaving the head intact. In a large pot, combine both sets of stems, the garlic, the chicken and the remaining broth ingredients. Bring to a boil, then reduce heat to medium-low. Simmer until chicken is tender, about 45 minutes. Remove and set aside the garlic head. Transfer the chicken to a plate and cool until easily handled. Shred the chicken into bite-size pieces, discarding the skin, bones and cartilage. Set aside.

2. To make the soup, strain the broth into another pot or bowl, discarding the solids. Using tongs, squeeze the garlic head into the broth; the tender cloves should easily pop out of their skins. Whisk into the broth. Wipe out the empty pot, then add the carrots, onion, butter and salt. Set over medium-high and cook, stirring occasionally, until the onion is browned, 10 to 12 minutes. Add the vermouth, scraping up any browned bits, and cook until evaporated, 1 to 2 minutes. Add the flour and cook, stirring constantly, for 1 minute. Add 2 cups of the broth and stir until smooth, then add the remaining broth and bring to a simmer.

3. In a medium bowl, whisk the yolks. Continue whisking while slowly adding 1 cup of hot broth from the pot. Whisk in the lemon juice, then return the mixture to the pot and whisk to combine. Add the chicken and any accumulated juices and cook until just heated through (do not simmer). Taste and season with salt and pepper. Serve with the reserved chopped cilantro and dill leaves.

Greek White Bean Soup (*Fasolada*)

Start to finish: 1½ hours, plus soaking time for beans
Servings: 6

---

6 tablespoons extra-virgin olive oil, divided, plus more to serve

1 large red onion, chopped

3 medium celery stalks, chopped

3 medium carrots, peeled and chopped, divided

Kosher salt and ground black pepper

4 medium garlic cloves, minced

½ teaspoon red pepper flakes

3 tablespoons tomato paste

1 pound dried cannellini beans, soaked and drained (see note)

2½ quarts low-sodium chicken broth

4 teaspoons red wine vinegar

½ cup finely chopped fresh flat-leaf parsley

½ cup pitted Kalamata olives, chopped

2 ounces feta cheese, crumbled (½ cup)

CHANGE THE WAY YOU COOK:
WHISK, DON'T DRIZZLE, OIL FOR BODY AND FLAVOR

Vigorously whisking extra-virgin olive oil into soup toward the end of cooking adds body as well as peppery richness.

This soup is built on fresh ingredients and contrasting flavors. Carrots lend a sweetness that's balanced by briny olives and salty feta cheese. Half are added at the start and the rest at the end to preserve their taste and texture. Acid, in the form of red wine vinegar added at the end, lightens the soup while ample parsley brings freshness. Dried cannellini beans that are soaked before cooking yield a full-flavored soup and creamy, silky-textured beans. To soak the beans, in a large bowl, stir together 2 quarts water and 1 tablespoon kosher salt. Add the beans, soak at room temperature for at least 12 hours or up to 24 hours, then drain well. Canned beans work in a pinch; see instructions below. We do as we were taught in Greece and use extra-virgin olive oil to give the soup a little body and fruity, peppery richness throughout. Vigorously whisking in a few tablespoons just before serving—rather than just drizzling it on—does the trick. Refrigerate leftovers in an airtight container for up to two days; reheat in a saucepan over low, adding water as needed to thin the consistency.

Don't skip the step of mashing 1 cup of the cooked beans to stir back into the soup. The mashed beans give the soup a creamy, slightly thickened consistency.

1. In a large pot over medium, heat 3 tablespoons of oil until shimmering. Add the onion, celery, half the carrots and ½ teaspoon salt, then cook, stirring occasionally, until the vegetables begin to brown, about 5 minutes. Add the garlic and red pepper flakes, then cook, stirring, until fragrant, about 30 seconds. Add the tomato paste and cook, stirring, until the paste begins to brown, about 2 minutes. Stir in the beans and the broth, then bring to a simmer over medium-high. Cover partially, reduce to low and simmer, stirring occasionally, until the beans are tender, about 1 hour.

2. Using a slotted spoon, transfer 1 cup of the beans to a medium bowl. Using a potato masher or fork, mash the beans to a paste, then whisk the mixture back into the soup. Add the remaining carrots, bring to a simmer over medium and cook, stirring occasionally, until the carrots are just tender, about 10 minutes.

3. Off heat, stir in the vinegar, then vigorously whisk in the remaining 3 tablespoons oil. Taste and season with salt and pepper. Ladle into bowls and top with the parsley, olives and cheese.

GREEK WHITE BEAN SOUP (*FASOLADA*) WITH CANNED BEANS:

Rinse and drain four 15½-ounce cans cannellini beans; measure 1 cup of the beans into a medium bowl, then use a potato masher or fork to mash to a paste. Follow the recipe as written, making the following changes: Add all of the carrots with the onion and celery; reduce the broth to 1½ quarts; and add both the whole and mashed beans at once. After bringing to a simmer over medium-high, reduce to medium-low, cover and cook, stirring occasionally and maintaining a gentle simmer, until the carrots are just tender,

Spicy Red Lentil Stew with Coconut Milk and Spinach

Start to finish: **1 hour (10 minutes active)** / Servings: **4 to 6**

1 medium yellow onion, chopped

2 tablespoons coconut
or peanut oil

4 garlic cloves, smashed and peeled

Kosher salt

3 teaspoons finely grated
fresh ginger, divided

2 teaspoons mustard seeds

2 teaspoons ground turmeric

1 teaspoon ground coriander

1 teaspoon ground fennel seeds

¾ teaspoon red pepper flakes

14-ounce can coconut milk

1 cup red lentils, rinsed
and drained

6 ounces (about 6 cups)
baby spinach, roughly chopped

2 tablespoons lime juice

Unsweetened coconut flakes
and chopped tomato, to garnish
(optional)

Located on the southwestern coast of India, Goa is known for its use of chilies, spices, coconut and bright acid (an influence from Portuguese colonization). Our spicy red lentil soup is a simplified take on a Goan staple that delivers a complete vegetarian meal in about an hour. Split red lentils, the foundation of the dish, cook in minutes. Blending turmeric, coriander and fennel created complex flavor. Fresh ginger brought welcome brightness, and adding a portion of it at the end kept the flavor vibrant. Both virgin and refined coconut oil worked, but virgin had a slightly stronger flavor. Mustard seeds added a peppery pop to the dish.

Don't substitute brown or green lentils for the split red lentils. Red lentils break down as they cook, thickening the cooking liquid and providing the ideal texture for the soup. Other lentil varieties remain intact even when fully cooked.

1. In a large saucepan over medium-high, combine the onion, oil, garlic and 1½ teaspoons of salt. Cook, stirring occasionally, until the onions have softened and are just beginning to color, 7 to 9 minutes. Stir in 2 teaspoons of ginger, the mustard seeds, turmeric, coriander, fennel and pepper flakes. Cook, stirring frequently, until fragrant, about 1 minute. Add 3½ cups water, coconut milk and lentils, then bring to a boil. Reduce heat to low, cover and cook until the lentils have broken down, 30 to 40 minutes.

2. Stir in the spinach and return to a simmer. Off the heat, add the remaining 1 teaspoon of ginger and the lime juice. Season with salt. Serve, garnished with coconut flakes and tomato, if using.

Mexican Chicken Soup
with Tomatillos and Hominy

Start to finish: **2 hours (1 hour active)** / Servings: **6**

2 large white onions,
1 quartered and 1 chopped

1 bunch fresh cilantro, stems
and leaves separated

2 whole dried ancho or pasilla
chilies, stemmed, seeded and
torn into rough pieces

2 tablespoons coriander seeds,
toasted, plus 1 tablespoon ground
coriander

2 tablespoons cumin seeds,
toasted, plus 1 tablespoon
ground cumin

Kosher salt

1 head of garlic

2½ to 3 pounds bone-in
skin-on chicken legs

2 fresh poblano chilies

2 fresh jalapeño chilies

1 pound fresh tomatillos,
husked and quartered

2 tablespoons grapeseed
or other neutral oil

2 teaspoons dried oregano,
preferably Mexican

15-ounce can hominy, drained

Toasted pepitas, lime wedges and
sour cream or Mexican crema
(optional), to serve

For a fresh take on chicken soup we looked to Mexico for inspiration and came up with one that builds layer upon layer of flavor—spice, chilies and herbs. We used charred fresh jalapeño and poblano peppers, a flavor-boosting technique common to Mexican and Latin American cooking. For our dried spices we added depth with relatively little effort by using toasted whole as well as ground coriander and cumin. Bone-in, skin-on chicken legs gave us broth-thickening collagen. For more spice, use serranos instead of jalapeños, or include the chilies' seeds. If you can't find fresh tomatillos, substitute canned tomatillos, drained. The broth and chicken can be made a day ahead and refrigerated separately before proceeding. However, shred the chicken while it's still warm. We liked garnishing the soup with chopped avocado, sliced jalapeños, crumbled queso fresco and fried tortilla strips.

Don't leave out the tomatillos. They give the soup acidity and texture.

1. In a large pot, combine 10 cups water, the quartered onion, cilantro stems, dried chilies, coriander seeds, cumin seeds and 1 teaspoon salt. Cut off and discard the top third of the garlic head, leaving the head intact, and add to the pot. Cover and bring to a boil, then simmer for 10 minutes. Add the chicken and return to a boil. Reduce heat to medium-low and cook partially covered for 30 minutes, maintaining a gentle simmer.

2. Meanwhile, heat the broiler to high with an oven rack 6 inches from the element. Arrange the poblanos and jalapeños on a rimmed baking sheet and broil, turning frequently, until evenly blackened and blistered, 10 to 12 minutes. Transfer to a bowl, cover tightly and set aside. Chop the cilantro leaves and set aside.

3. Peel, stem and seed the charred chilies, then roughly chop and add to a food processor along with the tomatillos. Pulse until coarsely chopped, 6 to 8 pulses.

4. Transfer the chicken and garlic head to a plate and let cool. Strain the broth, discarding the solids. Wipe out the pot. Add the oil, chopped onion and ½ teaspoon salt. Cook over medium-high, stirring occasionally, until softened and beginning to brown, 7 to 9 minutes. Add the ground coriander, ground cumin and oregano and cook, stirring constantly, for 1 minute. Add the tomatillo-chili mixture and cook, stirring frequently and scraping up any browned bits, until most of the moisture has evaporated, about 5 minutes. Add the broth and bring to a boil.

5. Shred the chicken into bite-size pieces, discarding the skin, bones and cartilage. Using tongs, squeeze the garlic head into the soup. The tender cloves should easily pop out of their skins. Add the chicken and hominy. Return to a simmer and cook until heated through, about 5 minutes. Stir in ½ cup of the chopped cilantro, then taste and season with salt. Top the soup with toasted pepitas, lime juice, more chopped cilantro and sour cream, if desired.

Vietnamese Meatball and Watercress Soup (*Canh*)

Start to finish: **40 minutes** / Servings: 4

---

1 pound ground pork

6 scallions, white parts finely chopped, green parts thinly sliced, reserved separately

1 large egg white, lightly beaten

3 tablespoons fish sauce, divided

4 teaspoons finely grated fresh ginger, divided

Kosher salt and ground white pepper

2 tablespoons grapeseed or other neutral oil

1 medium yellow onion, chopped

4 medium garlic cloves, thinly sliced

2 quarts low-sodium chicken broth or water

1 bunch watercress, cut into 1½-inch lengths (4 cups lightly packed)

2 tablespoons lime juice

This refreshing supper is a take on canh, a type of quick, brothy Vietnamese soup. The soups (pronounced KUN) can be sour, rich with vegetables, or loaded with seafood. But whatever variety, the unifying factor is simplicity. Our version stays true to the simplicity, but scales up the ingredients so it can serve as a satisfying meal on its own. Watercress adds a peppery note; look for "live" watercress, which is packaged with its roots attached. It stays fresher longer and is easier to clean. To prep it, trim off and discard the roots, rinse and drain the greens, then cut them into 1½-inch lengths, discarding any stems that are thick or tough. If you prefer, substitute an equal amount of baby spinach for the watercress, but roughly chop the leaves before using. We also liked this soup made with chicken bouillon paste instead of chicken broth; use 2 tablespoons of paste dissolved in 2 quarts of water.

Don't leave the meatballs at room temperature after shaping them. Chilling firms them so they hold together in the simmering broth.

1. Line a rimmed baking sheet with kitchen parchment and mist with cooking spray. In a medium bowl, combine the pork, scallion whites, egg white, 1 tablespoon of fish sauce, 2 teaspoons of ginger, 1¼ teaspoons salt and 1 teaspoon white pepper. Mix with your hands. Lightly moisten your hands with water and form into 20 balls, each about a generous tablespoon. Set on the prepared baking sheet, cover and refrigerate.

2. In a large Dutch oven over medium, heat the oil until shimmering. Add the onion and cook, stirring, until beginning to soften, about 5 minutes. Stir in the remaining 2 teaspoons ginger and the garlic, then cook until fragrant, about

30 seconds. Add the broth and bring to a boil over high. Reduce to medium-low and simmer, uncovered, until the onion is fully softened, about 10 minutes.

3. Add the meatballs, then bring to a simmer over medium-high. Reduce the heat to maintain a gentle simmer and cook without stirring until the meatballs are cooked through, 8 to 10 minutes; they should reach 160°F at the center.

4. Off heat, stir in the watercress and the remaining 2 tablespoons fish sauce. Let stand until the greens are wilted and tender, about 1 minute. Stir in the lime juice. Taste and season with salt and pepper, then stir in the scallion greens.

CHANGE THE WAY YOU COOK:
CHILL YOUR MEATBALLS

Chilling meatballs before cooking them firms them up so they hold their shape better and won't fall apart when cooked in liquid, such as soups and sauces.

Black-Eyed Pea and Sweet Potato Stew (*Ndambe*)

Start to finish: **40 minutes** / Servings: **6**

2 tablespoons unrefined coconut oil

1 large yellow onion, finely chopped

Kosher salt and ground black pepper

8 medium garlic cloves, minced

2 Fresno chilies, stemmed and sliced into thin rings

Three 14½-ounce cans black-eyed peas, rinsed and drained

2 bay leaves

1 pound sweet potatoes, peeled and cut into ½-inch cubes

1 pound plum tomatoes, cored and chopped

1 cup finely chopped fresh flat-leaf parsley

2 tablespoons lemon juice, plus lemon wedges, to serve

Both sweet potatoes and black-eyed peas are staples of West African cooking. In this recipe for Senegalese ndambe (pronounced NAM-bay), they're simmered together to make a hearty vegetarian stew. Canned black-eyed peas keep this dish fast and simple.

Don't use neutral-flavored oil in place of the coconut oil. Coconut oil—particularly unrefined—infuses the stew with a sweet flavor while adding richness.

1. In a large Dutch oven over medium, heat the coconut oil until shimmering. Add the onion, 2 teaspoons salt and ½ teaspoon pepper, then cook, stirring, until the onion is light golden brown and softened, 7 to 10 minutes.

2. Stir in the garlic and chilies, then cook until fragrant, about 30 seconds. Add the black-eyed peas, bay leaves and 5 cups water. Bring to a simmer over medium-high, then reduce to medium and cook, uncovered, stirring occasionally, for about 15 minutes.

3. Stir in the sweet potatoes and 2 teaspoons salt. Cover, reduce to medium-low and cook until the potatoes are tender, 10 to 15 minutes. Off heat, stir in the tomatoes, parsley and lemon juice. Taste and season with salt and pepper. Serve with lemon wedges.

Spanish Garlic Soup

Start to finish: 45 minutes / Servings: 4

6 scallions, trimmed and thinly sliced, whites and greens divided

6 medium garlic cloves, thinly sliced

6 tablespoons extra-virgin olive oil, divided, plus extra

4 teaspoons sweet paprika

1½ teaspoons smoked paprika

6 ounces sourdough or other rustic bread, cut into ½-inch cubes (about 4 cups), divided

2 tablespoons chicken bouillon

Kosher salt and ground black pepper

4 large egg yolks

Sherry vinegar, to taste

José Andrés taught us this "end of month" recipe—the sort of meal to make quickly with whatever is on hand and when money is tight. His approach: garlic cooked in copious amounts of olive oil with handfuls of thinly sliced stale bread and several tablespoons of smoked paprika. Add some water and simmer, then off heat stir in four or five whisked eggs. Supper is served. For our version, we realized the leftover bread, garlic and smoked paprika we had in our cupboards weren't up to Andrés' standards. So we needed to tweak. We boosted flavor by using chicken bouillon (an easy pantry flavor enhancer) instead of plain water, and we sautéed both sweet and smoked paprika with garlic and scallions. We actually didn't have stale bread, so we turned a loaf of rustic sourdough (a baguette or any crusty loaf will do) into delicious croutons, and added a bit of bread directly to the broth to thicken it. To serve, the soup and croutons are married in the serving bowls, allowing each person to adjust the ratio of soup to bread, as well as how long they soak.

Don't skip tempering the egg yolks with some of the hot broth before adding to the soup. This prevents them from curdling in the hot broth.

1. In a medium saucepan over medium-low, combine the scallion whites, garlic and 3 tablespoons of the oil. Cook, stirring occasionally, until beginning to color, 8 to 10 minutes. Add both paprikas and cook, stirring, until fragrant and darkened, 30 seconds.

2. Add 1 cup of the bread cubes and stir well. Whisk in 6 cups water and bouillon, increase heat to medium-high and bring to a simmer. Reduce heat to medium-low and simmer, whisking occasionally, for 15 minutes. Whisk vigorously to ensure bread is thoroughly broken up.

3. Meanwhile, in a 12-inch skillet over medium, combine the remaining 3 tablespoons of oil, the remaining 3 cups of bread, the scallion greens and ½ teaspoon each salt and pepper. Cook, stirring occasionally, until browned and crisp, 8 to 10 minutes.

4. In a medium bowl, whisk the egg yolks. Slowly whisk in 1 cup of the hot broth. Remove the soup from the heat. Off heat, vigorously whisk the egg yolks into the soup, then whisk in the vinegar. Taste and season with salt and pepper. To serve, fill individual bowls with the crouton mixture, then ladle the soup over them. Drizzle with additional oil, if desired.

Thai Rice Soup (*Khao Tom*)

Start to finish: 35 minutes / Servings: 4

8 ounces ground pork

3 tablespoons fish sauce, divided, plus extra to serve

2 tablespoons chili-garlic sauce, divided, plus extra to serve

Ground white pepper

3 tablespoons lard or refined coconut oil

5 large shallots, peeled, halved lengthwise and thinly sliced (2 cups)

Kosher salt

8 medium garlic cloves, thinly sliced

3 lemon grass stalks, trimmed to bottom 6 inches, dry outer leaves removed, smashed

2 tablespoons finely grated fresh ginger

2½ quarts low-sodium chicken broth

4 cups cooked and chilled jasmine rice (see note)

1 cup chopped fresh cilantro

3 tablespoons lime juice, plus lime wedges, to serve

Fried shallots, to serve (see recipe p. 69)

Soft- or hard-cooked eggs, peeled and halved, to serve

Savory pork meatballs and jasmine rice give this Thai soup heft, but its aromatic broth—made with plenty of shallots, garlic, lemon grass and ginger—has excellent flavor on its own. The soup is a sort of blank canvas for garnishes; the recipe calls for our favorites, but feel free to offer only those that appeal to you.

Don't use freshly cooked rice, as the grains will turn mushy. Rice that was cooked at least a day in advance, then chilled, held its shape better than rice that was cooked the same day. To chill just-cooked rice, mist a parchment-lined baking sheet with cooking spray and spread the hot rice on it evenly. Let cool to room temperature, cover and refrigerate for at least four hours or up to three days.

1. In a medium bowl, combine the pork, 1 tablespoon of fish sauce, 1 tablespoon of chili-garlic sauce and ¾ teaspoon white pepper. Mix with your hands. Form the mixture into 20 meatballs (about 2 teaspoons each), rolling each between the palms of your hands. Place on a large plate.

2. In a large Dutch oven over medium-high, heat the lard until shimmering. Add the shallots and ½ teaspoon salt and cook, stirring occasionally, until browned, about 5 minutes. Stir in the garlic and cook until fragrant, about 30 seconds. Stir in the lemon grass and ginger and cook until fragrant, about 30 seconds. Add the broth and bring to a boil, scraping up any browned bits, then reduce to medium and simmer uncovered for about 15 minutes.

3. Remove and discard the lemon grass. Add the meatballs, stir gently to combine and simmer over medium until the meatballs are just cooked through, 3 to 4 minutes. Stir in the rice and cook until heated through, about 1 minute. Off heat, stir in the remaining 2 tablespoons fish sauce, the remaining 1 tablespoon chili-garlic sauce, 1 teaspoon white pepper, the cilantro and lime juice. Ladle into bowls and serve with fried shallots, egg halves, chili-garlic sauce and lime wedges.

FRIED SHALLOTS

A mandoline works well for slicing the shallots, but a sharp knife does the job, too. Fried shallots are a great garnish on soups, salads, fried rice and noodle dishes. The oil left over from frying the shallots is infused with flavor; use it for stir-frying, sautéing and in salad dressings.

Don't be tempted to turn the heat up once the shallots are added to the oil. Moderate heat and frequent stirring ensure the shallots brown evenly and without scorching.

Start to finish: **20 minutes**
Makes about **1½ cups**

1 cup grapeseed or other neutral oil

12 ounces shallots, thinly sliced

1. Line a large plate with a triple layer of paper towels. Place a mesh strainer over a heat-safe medium bowl and set near the stove.

2. In a large saucepan over medium-high, heat the oil to about 275°F; a slice of shallot dropped in the oil should sizzle immediately. Add the shallots and reduce to medium. Cook, stirring, until golden brown, 8 to 10 minutes. Drain immediately in the strainer and shake the strainer to remove excess oil.

3. Using tongs, transfer the shallots to the prepared plate, spreading them in an even layer. Let cool completely. Store the shallots and oil separately in airtight containers. The shallots will keep for up to 1 week at room temperature; the oil will keep for up to 1 month in the refrigerator.

Somali Chicken Soup

Start to finish: 50 minutes / Servings: 6

1 tablespoon grapeseed or other neutral oil

2 large yellow onions, chopped

Kosher salt and ground white pepper

2 serrano chilies, stemmed and sliced into thin rounds

4 medium garlic cloves, smashed and peeled

4 teaspoons ground coriander

2 teaspoons ground cardamom

1 bunch fresh cilantro, stems chopped, leaves finely chopped, reserved separately

4 plum tomatoes, cored, seeded and chopped, divided

1½ quarts low-sodium chicken broth or water

Four 12-ounce bone-in, skin-on chicken breasts

1½ cups jasmine or basmati rice, rinsed and drained

2 tablespoons lime juice, plus lime wedges, to serve

Thinly sliced radishes and/or chopped red cabbage, to serve (optional)

Green chili sauce, berbere sauce or other hot sauce, to serve (see recipes p. 71)

Serve this soup family style: Bring the pot to the table along with the radishes, cabbage and lime wedges, then have diners fill and garnish their bowls as they like. Offer a simple homemade or store-bought hot sauce alongside. Hot steamed rice, added to bowls before the soup is ladled in, is a satisfying addition.

Don't use boneless, skinless chicken breasts. Both the bones and skin contribute flavor to the broth.

1. In a large Dutch oven over medium, heat the oil until shimmering. Add the onions and ½ teaspoon salt and cook, stirring, until beginning to brown, about 5 minutes. Add the chilies, garlic, coriander, cardamom, cilantro stems and half of the tomatoes. Cook, stirring constantly, until fragrant, about 30 seconds.

2. Add the broth and bring to a simmer over high. Submerge the chicken breasts in the broth, cover and cook over low until a skewer inserted in the thickest part of the chicken meets no resistance or the chicken reaches 160°F, about 30 minutes.

3. Meanwhile, in a medium saucepan, combine the rice, 2 cups water and 1 teaspoon salt. Bring to a simmer over medium-high, then reduce to low and cook, covered, until the liquid is absorbed and the rice is tender, 15 to 20 minutes. Off heat, remove the lid, lay a clean dish towel over the pot, replace the cover and let stand for about 10 minutes or until ready to serve.

4. Using tongs, transfer the chicken to a large plate and set aside to cool. Pour the broth through a fine mesh strainer set over a large heatproof bowl; discard the solids. Return the broth to the pot. When the chicken is cool enough to handle, shred the meat into bite-size pieces, discarding the skin and bones.

5. Add the chicken to the broth and bring to a simmer over medium-high. Remove from the heat and stir in the remaining tomatoes, the cilantro leaves and lime juice. Taste and season with salt and pepper.

6. To serve, fluff the rice with a fork, then mound a portion into each serving bowl. Ladle the soup over the rice, then top each portion with radishes and/or cabbage (if using) and the hot sauces. Serve with lime wedges.

GREEN CHILI SAUCE

This sauce is spicy and sharp on its own, but a spoonful stirred into a serving of soup provides the perfect flavor accent. Refrigerate leftovers in an airtight container for up to a week.

Start to finish: **5 minutes**
Makes about **1 cup**

1 plum tomato, cored and quartered

5 serrano chilies, stemmed

3 tablespoons lime juice

2 medium garlic cloves, smashed and peeled

1½ teaspoons kosher salt

In a blender, combine all ingredients and process until smooth, 1 to 2 minutes, scraping the sides as needed.

BERBERE SAUCE

For this bold, paste-like sauce, macerating the onion in lime juice tempers its harsh bite. For a brighter flavor, substitute sweet paprika instead of smoked. This sauce is best used the day it is made.

Start to finish: **15 minutes**
Makes about: **¼ cup**

3 tablespoons lime juice

1 tablespoon minced red onion

½ teaspoon kosher salt

1 tablespoon smoked paprika

1 teaspoon ground coriander

1 teaspoon ground ginger

½ teaspoon cayenne pepper

¼ teaspoon ground cardamom

1. In a small bowl, stir together the lime juice, onion and salt. Let stand for 10 minutes.

2. Meanwhile, in a small skillet over medium-low, toast the paprika, coriander, ginger, cayenne and cardamom, stirring constantly, until fragrant, 1 to 2 minutes. Remove from the heat and let cool for 10 minutes. Stir the spices into the lime juice-onion mixture.

Gonzalo Guzmán's Pozole Rojo

Start to finish: 2¼ hours (50 minutes active)
Servings: 6

4 large ancho chilies,
stemmed and seeded

Boiling water

2 medium garlic cloves, divided

½ large white onion, roughly chopped

¾ teaspoon dried Mexican oregano

½ teaspoon cumin seeds

Kosher salt

¼ medium yellow onion

4 cilantro stems

1 bay leaf

2 pounds boneless pork shoulder,
trimmed and cut into 1-inch cubes

4 cups rinsed and drained
canned hominy (from two 29-ounce
cans)

For serving:

Shredded green cabbage

Thinly sliced radishes

Thinly sliced red onion

Chili powder

Chopped fresh oregano
or dried oregano

Cilantro leaves

Tortilla chips

Lime halves

Chef Gonzalo Guzmán's pozole rojo (pork, red chili and hominy stew), from his book "Nopalito," is boldly flavored with ancho chilies, herbs, cumin and aromatics. He blends some of the hominy (dried corn kernels treated with alkali then cooked until tender) with some of the braising liquid, then adds the puree back into the soup to give the broth body. Guzmán says garnishes are a key component of pozole and encourages piling them high onto individual servings. A long list is included here, but you can offer as many or as few as you like. The pozole can be made a few days in advance, then reheated for serving.

Don't discard the chili soaking water after removing the chilies. You will need some of it to thin the chili mixture in the blender so it breaks down into a smooth puree.

1. Place the chilies in a medium heat-proof bowl and add boiling water to cover. Let stand until the chilies are softened, about 20 minutes. Remove the chilies from the water and transfer to a blender; reserve the water. Add 1 garlic clove, the white onion, oregano, cumin and a generous pinch of salt to the blender, then puree until smooth, about 2 minutes, scraping down the jar as needed and adding just enough of the soaking water to form a thick, smooth paste.

2. In a piece of cheesecloth, wrap the remaining garlic clove, yellow onion, cilantro stems and bay; secure with kitchen twine to form a small bundle. Set aside.

3. Season the pork with salt. In a large pot, combine the pork, chili puree and cheesecloth bundle, then stir in 3 quarts water. Season generously with salt and

bring to a boil. Reduce to a simmer and cook, uncovered, until a skewer inserted into the pork meets no resistance, about 1 hour. Remove from the heat.

4. In the blender, puree ½ cup of hominy with about ½ cup of the braising liquid from the pork until smooth, about 20 seconds. Stir the puree and the remaining 3½ cups hominy into the pot and bring to a simmer over medium-high. Remove from the heat and let stand for 5 minutes. Using a wide, shallow spoon, skim off and discard the fat on the surface.

5. Bring the pozole back to a simmer over medium-high. Taste and adjust the seasoning with salt. Ladle into bowls and serve with cabbage, radishes, red onion, oregano, chili powder, cilantro, tortilla chips and limes.

Vegetables

Avocado Salad with Pickled Mustard Seeds and Marjoram Vinaigrette / 76

Lebanese-Style Tabbouleh / 79

Apple, Celery Root and Fennel Salad with Hazelnuts / 81

Thai-Style Napa Coleslaw with Mint and Cilantro / 82

Kale Salad with Smoked Almonds and Picada Crumbs / 85

Eventide Green Salad with Nori Vinaigrette / 87

Smashed Cucumber Salad / 89

Greens with Walnuts, Parmesan and Pancetta Vinaigrette / 90

French Carrot Salad / 92

Japanese Potato Salad / 95

Fattoush / 97

Shaved Zucchini and Herb Salad with Parmesan / 99

Bulgur-Tomato Salad with Herbs and Pomegranate Molasses (*Eetch*) / 101

Austrian Potato Salad / 103

Senegalese Avocado and Mango Salad with Rof / 104

Skillet-Charred Brussels Sprouts with Garlic, Anchovy and Chili / 106

Roasted Cauliflower with Miso Glaze / 109

Cumin-Coriander Potatoes with Cilantro (*Patates Mekhalel*) / 111

Hot Oil–Flashed Chard with Ginger, Scallions and Chili / 112

Cracked Potatoes with Vermouth, Coriander and Fennel / 117

Thai Stir-Fried Spinach / 119

Sweet Potato Gratin with Vanilla Bean and Bay Leaves / 120

Spicy Egyptian Eggplant with Fresh Herbs / 123

Celery Root Puree / 125

Sweet-and-Spicy Ginger Green Beans / 126

Mashed Potatoes with Caraway-Mustard Butter / 129

Cauliflower with Tahini and Egyptian
Nut-and-Seed Seasoning (*Dukkah*) / 130

Harissa Roasted Potatoes / 133

Stir-Fried Broccoli with
Sichuan Peppercorns / 135

4

Avocado Salad with Pickled Mustard Seeds and Marjoram Vinaigrette

Start to finish: **1 hour** / Servings: **6**

For the pickled mustard seeds:

¼ cup yellow mustard seeds

½ cup cider vinegar

¼ cup white sugar

¼ cup water

1½ teaspoons black peppercorns

½ teaspoon coriander seeds

3 allspice berries

1 bay leaf

⅛ teaspoon red pepper flakes

For the dressing:

2 tablespoons pickled mustard seeds and brine

1 tablespoon minced shallot

2 teaspoons whole-grain mustard

1 teaspoon honey

¼ teaspoon kosher salt

¼ teaspoon ground black pepper

¼ cup chopped fresh marjoram

3 tablespoons canola oil

3 tablespoons extra-virgin olive oil

For the salad:

3 firm but ripe avocados

Kosher salt

6 teaspoons lemon juice

Thinly sliced ricotta salata cheese

Fresh marjoram leaves

It was the simplicity that we loved. Half an avocado, sliced and fanned across a plate. Over it, marjoram vinaigrette studded with tender spheres of pickled mustard seeds. One thing was quite clear: A handful of simple ingredients can take a stunning turn when the right flavors tie them together. In this case, that is the role of the whole mustard seeds, an ingredient Americans rarely encounter outside pickle brine. We discovered this at Stephen Oxaal's Branch Line restaurant in Watertown, Massachusetts, where the seeds take an avocado salad from simple to stunning. The pickling process takes just a few minutes and the result adds a tang and crunch that balance the lushness of the other ingredients. Conventional vinaigrettes–blends of fat and acid–tended to slide off the avocados. Instead, we eliminated the lemon juice from the dressing and drizzled it directly over the avocado slices, where it mingled with the dressing. We liked ricotta salata best, but Parmesan was a fine substitute.

1. To make the pickled mustard seeds, in a small saucepan over high, combine the mustard seeds and enough water to cover by 2 inches. Bring to a boil, then reduce heat to medium-low and simmer until the seeds are tender, about 8 minutes. Strain the seeds through a mesh strainer and transfer to a bowl. Wipe out and reserve the pan.

2. To the pan, add the remaining pickling ingredients. Place over high heat. Bring to a boil, then reduce to medium-low and simmer until fragrant and the sugar has dissolved, 3 to 5 minutes. Strain over the mustard seeds, discarding the solids. Let the mixture cool to room temperature. Use immediately or cover and refrigerate for up to 4 weeks.

3. To make the dressing, in a small bowl, mix together 2 tablespoons of the pickled mustard seeds and brine, the shallot, mustard, honey, salt and pepper. Let sit for 10 minutes. Add the marjoram and both oils and whisk until emulsified.

4. To assemble and serve, halve the avocados lengthwise, remove the pits and peel away the skins. Cut each half into slices (see sidebar), leaving the halves intact, and fan onto serving plates, cut sides down. Sprinkle a pinch of salt and 1 teaspoon of lemon juice over each half. Spoon the dressing over the avocados and garnish with ricotta salata and marjoram.

HOW TO FAN AN AVOCADO

1. Halve each avocado lengthwise and remove the pit. Peel the skin from each half.

2. Place the avocado halves cut side down. Starting at the larger end of each half, cut each into 6 lengthwise slices, leaving the top 1 inch intact.

3. Set each half on a plate, cut side down. Gently press the large end to fan the slices.

Lebanese-Style **Tabbouleh**

Start to finish: **15 minutes** / Servings: **4**

½ cup boiling water

⅓ cup fine-grain bulgur

1 teaspoon ground sumac (optional)

½ teaspoon ground allspice

Kosher salt and ground black pepper

3 tablespoons lemon juice

1 small shallot, minced

¼ teaspoon white sugar

¼ cup extra-virgin olive oil

2 to 3 small vine-ripened tomatoes, diced

4 cups lightly packed flat-leaf parsley leaves, well dried then minced

1 cup lightly packed mint leaves, well dried then minced

Israeli-born British chef Yotam Ottolenghi is clear about tabbouleh. It should be "all about the parsley." But in the U.S., the Middle Eastern salad often goes heavy on the bulgur, a wheat that has been cooked, dried and cracked. The result is a salad that is mealy, bland and stubbornly soggy. That's because the bulgur sponges up all the juices from the tomatoes. Our solution was to barely cook the bulgur—essentially underhydrating it— allowing it to soak up those juices without becoming waterlogged. We added generous helpings of herbs, livening up the parsley with some mint. Wet herbs will dilute the dressing and make the bulgur gummy. Be sure to dry them thoroughly with a spinner and paper towels before mincing. Some type of onion is traditional; we used shallots, preferring their gentler bite, and soaked them in lemon juice to soften their flavor and texture. While the sumac is optional, we loved its fruity complexity and light acidity.

Don't use coarse-grain bulgur; it won't hydrate evenly. If you can't find fine-grain bulgur, process medium- or coarse-grain in short pulses until fine, light and fluffy, five to 10 pulses.

1. In a medium bowl, combine the water, bulgur, sumac, if using, allspice and ½ teaspoon of salt. Cover with plastic wrap and let sit for 10 minutes. In a large bowl, stir together the lemon juice, shallot, sugar and ¾ teaspoon of salt; let sit for 10 minutes.

2. Whisk the oil into the lemon juice mixture. Fluff the bulgur with a fork and add to the dressing along with the tomatoes; mix well. Fold the parsley and mint into the tabbouleh, then taste and season with salt, pepper and additional sumac, if needed.

CHANGE THE WAY YOU COOK:
UNDERHYDRATE GRAINS FOR GREATER FLAVOR

Underhydrating starchy ingredients such as bulgur is a quick and easy way to boost flavor. The underhydrated grains better absorb seasonings and sauces, resulting in a more vibrantly flavored dish.

Apple, Celery Root and Fennel Salad with Hazelnuts

Start to finish: **20 minutes** / Servings: 6

1 small shallot, grated

1½ tablespoons cider vinegar

3 tablespoons lightly packed grated fresh horseradish

3 tablespoons extra-virgin olive oil

1 teaspoon honey

Kosher salt and ground black pepper

1 Granny Smith apple, cored and cut into matchsticks

½ small celery root (about 8 ounces), peeled and cut into matchsticks

1 medium fennel bulb, trimmed and thinly sliced

½ cup chopped fresh parsley leaves

¼ cup chopped fresh mint leaves

½ cup hazelnuts, toasted and coarsely chopped

A winter salad needs to stand up to hearty stews and roasts, and that calls for bold, bright flavors. We started with tart apples and thin slices of fennel bulb, the latter adding a pleasant anise flavor. Celery root added a fresh crispness while grated fresh horseradish gave the dish kick. Grating the horseradish triggers a chemical reaction that enhances the root's bite. Tossing it with vinegar and salt helps preserve that heat, which otherwise dissipates quickly. Make sure you grate horseradish in an open and well-ventilated space.

Don't use prepared horseradish in this recipe. It's bottled with vinegar and salt that would alter the balance of flavors.

In a large bowl, combine the shallot and vinegar. Let sit for 10 minutes. Whisk in the horseradish, oil, honey, 1 teaspoon salt and ½ teaspoon pepper. Add the apple, celery root and fennel, then toss. Stir in the parsley and mint, then sprinkle with hazelnuts.

Thai-Style Napa Coleslaw with Mint and Cilantro

Start to finish: **25 minutes** / Servings: **6**

3 tablespoons lime juice

4 teaspoons white sugar

1 tablespoon fish sauce

1 medium serrano chili,
seeded and minced

5 tablespoons coconut milk

1 pound napa cabbage
(1 small head), thinly sliced
crosswise (about 8 cups)

6 radishes, trimmed, halved
and thinly sliced

4 ounces sugar snap peas,
strings removed, thinly
sliced on diagonal

½ cup coarsely chopped
fresh cilantro

½ cup coarsely chopped
fresh mint

½ cup roasted, salted cashews,
coarsely chopped

In rethinking the classic American coleslaw we took our inspiration from San Antonio chef Quealy Watson, whose slaw world changed when he traveled to Asia. Watson, the former chef at San Antonio's funky Tex-Asian barbecue joint Hot Joy, created a slaw inspired by traditional Burmese lahpet, fermented tea leaves that are eaten. For our slaw, we used tender napa cabbage with red radishes and snap peas for crunch, with fresh mint and cilantro to tie it all together. Coconut milk—instead of mayonnaise—had the right balance of richness and fresh flavor. For heat, we used a fresh chili "cooked" in lime juice, which mellowed the bite and helped disperse the heat evenly. Fish sauce added a savory pungency.

Don't use "light" coconut milk or sweetened "cream of coconut" for this recipe. The former is too thin, and the latter is too sweet (think pina coladas). And don't forget to vigorously shake the can before opening to ensure the fat and liquid are fully emulsified.

In a liquid measuring cup, mix together the lime juice, sugar, fish sauce and chili. Let sit for 10 minutes. Whisk in the coconut milk until combined, then adjust seasoning with additional fish sauce, if desired. In a large bowl, combine the cabbage, radishes, peas, cilantro and mint. Add the dressing and toss until evenly coated. Stir in the cashews and serve.

Kale Salad with Smoked Almonds and Picada Crumbs

Start to finish: **15 minutes** / Servings: 6

2 shallots, thinly sliced

5 tablespoons sherry vinegar

Kosher salt

2 tablespoons honey

8 tablespoons extra-virgin olive oil, divided

Ground black pepper

1 cup smoked almonds

4 ounces chewy white bread, cut into 1-inch cubes

2 teaspoons fresh thyme

1 tablespoon sweet paprika

2 bunches lacinato kale, stemmed, washed, spun dry and thinly sliced crosswise (10 cups)

1 cup lightly packed fresh mint, chopped

Kale can make a flavorful and seasonal winter salad, but to be eaten raw it needs to be treated right. Otherwise, the greens can be unpleasantly tough. We started with lacinato kale, also known as dinosaur or Tuscan kale. Its long blue-green leaves are sweeter and more tender than curly kale. Slicing the greens thinly was the first step to making them more salad-friendly. Then, to soften them further, we borrowed a Japanese technique used on raw cabbage—massaging the leaves. In this case, we do it with ground smoked almonds, which help tenderize the kale and add crunch and flavor to the finished salad. An acidic shallot-sherry vinaigrette also helped soften and brighten the kale (look for a sherry vinegar aged at least 3 years). Intensely flavorful paprika breadcrumbs, inspired by the Catalan sauce picada, tied everything together.

Don't slice the kale until you're ready to make the salad; it will wilt. You can, however, stem, wash and dry it ahead of time.

1. In a small bowl, whisk together the shallots, vinegar and ½ teaspoon salt. Let sit for 10 minutes. Whisk in the honey, 5 tablespoons of the oil and ½ teaspoon pepper; set aside.

2. In a food processor, process the almonds until coarsely chopped, about 8 pulses; transfer to a large bowl. Add the bread to the processor and process to rough crumbs, about 20 seconds. Add the thyme, the remaining 3 table-spoons oil, the paprika, ½ teaspoon salt and ½ teaspoon pepper. Process until incorporated, about 10 seconds.

3. Transfer the crumb mixture to a large skillet over medium and cook, stirring frequently, until crisp and browned, 8 to 10 minutes. Transfer to a plate to cool.

4. Add the kale and mint to the bowl with the almonds and massage the greens until the kale softens and darkens, 10 to 20 seconds. Add the dressing and crumbs and toss to combine. Taste, then season with salt and pepper.

CHANGE THE WAY YOU COOK:
TENDERIZE TOUGH GREENS WITH SALT

Raw kale can be off-puttingly tough; massaging the leaves with kosher salt tenderizes them. Rubbing the leaves breaks down the plant's rigid cell walls, while salt draws out the cells' moisture. The combined effect makes the firm, raw leaves supple and easy to chew.

Eventide Green Salad
with Nori Vinaigrette

Start to finish: 30 minutes, plus cooling and chilling
Servings: 6

4 ounces red radishes, sliced into thin rounds

1 medium carrot, peeled and shaved into long, thin strips (see note)

½ small red onion, thinly sliced

1½ cups plus 2 tablespoons unseasoned rice vinegar, divided

⅓ cup white sugar

¼-ounce (7-gram) package roasted seaweed snacks, torn into small pieces (about 1 cup packed)

2 tablespoons soy sauce

2 tablespoons mirin

2 tablespoons grapeseed or other neutral oil

10 ounces spring mix or other delicate greens

Kosher salt

This is our adaptation of a salad created by Eventide Oyster Co. in Portland, Maine. Roasted seaweed (also called nori) is pulverized to a coarse powder and added to the dressing, lending the dish deep, umami-rich flavor notes reinforced with soy sauce and mirin. Instead of using full-sized sheets of plain nori (the variety used for sushi), we opted for the convenience of an individual package of seasoned seaweed snacks that are available in most grocery stores. Quick-pickled vegetables give the salad texture and bright flavor, but keep in mind that they need to pickle for at least two hours before they're ready to use. To shave the carrot, run a sharp vegetable peeler down the length of the vegetable.

Don't use a reactive bowl to make the pickles or the vegetables and liquid may take on an "off" metallic flavor. It's best to use glass, ceramic or stainless steel. Don't dress the salad until you're ready to serve so that the greens stay fresh and crisp (if left to stand after dressing, they'll wilt from the pickles' acidity and weight).

1. In a medium heatproof bowl, combine the radishes, carrot and onion. In a small saucepan over medium-high, combine 1½ cups vinegar, the sugar and ¾ cup water. Bring to a rapid boil, stirring to dissolve the sugar, then pour over the vegetables. Cool to room temperature, then cover and refrigerate for at least 2 hours or for up to 1 week.

2. In a spice grinder, process the seaweed until finely chopped, gently shaking the grinder, about 30 seconds; check under the blade for clumps and break up any. You should have about 2 tablespoons pulverized seaweed. In a large bowl, whisk together the seaweed, soy sauce, mirin, oil and the remaining 2 tablespoons vinegar; the dressing will thicken slightly.

3. Drain the pickles in a fine mesh strainer. Add half of the drained pickles to the bowl with the dressing along with the salad greens. Toss to combine, then taste and season with salt. Transfer to a platter or bowl and top with the remaining drained pickles.

Smashed Cucumber Salad

Start to finish: 40 minutes (15 minutes active) / Servings: 6

2 pounds English cucumbers (about 2 large)

4 teaspoons white sugar

1 tablespoon kosher salt

4 teaspoons unseasoned rice vinegar

1 medium garlic clove, smashed and peeled

2 tablespoons grapeseed or other neutral oil

½ teaspoon red pepper flakes

1½ tablespoons soy sauce

1 tablespoon toasted sesame oil

1 tablespoon grated fresh ginger

Cilantro leaves, sliced scallions and toasted sesame seeds, to serve (optional)

Seasoning watery vegetables such as sliced cucumbers can be a challenge; dressings won't adhere to the slick surfaces. Yet across Asia there is a whole class of boldly flavored salads made entirely of cucumber. What do they know that we don't? Our answer came from China's pai huang gua, or smashed cucumber salad. In this case, it's the prep work—not the dressing—that sets the dish apart. The cucumbers are smashed, banged and whacked. This works for two reasons. First, it ruptures more cell walls than slicing and dicing, making it easier to remove the seeds, the main culprit in watery cucumbers. Second, it creates craggy, porous surfaces that absorb more dressing. The easiest way to smash cucumbers is to place a rolling pin or the flat side of a chef's knife over them and smack it sharply with your hand. To draw out even more moisture from the cucumbers, we borrowed another Asian technique, salting and sugaring. In China, dressings vary by region. We blurred regional lines, combining garlic, soy sauce, fresh ginger and pepper-infused oil.

Don't substitute conventional, thick-sliced cucumbers for English. The ratio of seeds to flesh is higher and the skins are too tough.

1. Trim the ends off the cucumbers, then halve lengthwise. Place each half cut side down, then press a rolling pin or the flat side of a broad knife against the cucumber and hit firmly with the heel of your hand. Repeat along the length of the cucumbers until they crack. Pull the sections apart, scraping and discarding the seeds. Cut into rough ¾-inch pieces and set in a large bowl.

2. In a small bowl, combine the sugar and salt; toss the cucumbers with 5 teaspoons of the mixture. Transfer to a colander set over a bowl. Refrigerate for 30 to 60 minutes, tossing occasionally. Meanwhile, stir the vinegar and garlic into the remaining sugar-salt mixture. Set aside.

3. In a small skillet over medium-low, combine the grapeseed oil and pepper flakes. Cook, stirring, until sizzling and the pepper flakes begin to darken, 2 to 4 minutes. Strain the oil, discarding the solids.

4. Remove and discard the garlic from the vinegar mixture. Stir in the soy sauce, sesame oil and ginger. Transfer the drained cucumbers to a kitchen towel and pat dry. In a bowl, stir together the cucumbers and dressing, then stir in half of the chili oil. Serve drizzled with more chili oil and sprinkled with cilantro, scallions and sesame seeds, if desired.

CHANGE THE WAY YOU COOK:
FOR DRESSING THAT STICKS, SALT YOUR VEGETABLES

Slick and watery vegetables can be hard to flavor; dressings and seasonings slide right off. Salting them first draws out moisture, leaving behind firmer, drier flesh to which seasonings can stick.

Greens with Walnuts, Parmesan and Pancetta Vinaigrette

Start to finish: **15 minutes** / Servings: **6**

12 ounces (12 cups) mixed bitter greens, torn

2 tablespoons sherry vinegar

1 tablespoon Dijon mustard

Kosher salt

6 ounces thinly sliced pancetta, chopped

1 medium shallot, finely chopped

3 tablespoons extra-virgin olive oil

1 cup walnuts, toasted and roughly chopped

1 teaspoon ground black pepper

1 ounce Parmesan cheese, shaved (about ½ cup)

The bistro classic known as salade frisée aux lardons typically is made with lacy frisée and crisped salt pork, with a poached egg on top. For our version, we use pancetta and you can choose any combination of bitter greens, such as frisée, endive, radicchio, escarole or arugula. To toast the walnuts, spread them evenly on a rimmed baking sheet and bake at 350°F until lightly browned and fragrant, 5 to 7 minutes. A sharp Y-shaped vegetable peeler is the perfect tool for shaving the Parmesan cheese. For a heartier meal, and one that evokes the salad's bistro beginnings, top with a fried egg.

Don't allow the dressing to cool down before adding it to the greens. Its consistency is best when warm, and its heat slightly softens the sturdy greens. By the same token, make sure the greens are not cold when dressed so the dressing doesn't congeal on contact.

1. Place the greens in a large bowl and set aside. In a separate bowl, whisk together the vinegar, mustard and ½ teaspoon salt.

2. In a medium skillet over medium, cook the pancetta, stirring occasionally, until crisp, about 7 minutes. Using a slotted spoon, transfer the pancetta to a paper towel–lined plate. Pour off all but 1 tablespoon pancetta fat from the skillet, then return it to medium heat.

Add the shallot and cook, stirring, until light golden brown, about 2 minutes. Add the oil and the vinegar mixture, then remove from the heat and whisk until combined. Let stand for 30 seconds to warm through.

3. Add the warm dressing, walnuts and pepper to the greens and toss well. Taste and season with salt. Divide the salad among plates and top each portion with pancetta and Parmesan.

French Carrot Salad

Start to finish: 20 minutes
Servings: 6

---

2 tablespoons white balsamic
vinegar

2 tablespoons chopped
fresh tarragon

1 tablespoon minced shallot

1 teaspoon honey

⅛ teaspoon cayenne pepper

Kosher salt

¼ cup extra-virgin olive oil

1¼ pounds carrots, peeled
and shredded

1 cup chopped fresh parsley

Carrots tend to be a woody afterthought on U.S. salad bars. Here, we transform them into a lively side dish by taking a tip from France, where grated carrots stand alone as an iconic side dish—salade de carottes râpées. Grating fresh carrots releases their sugars and aromas, creating an earthy sweetness that just needs a bit of acid for balance. Using relatively mild white balsamic vinegar allowed us to up the vinegar-to-oil ratio (1:2) for a punchy but not overwhelming flavor. White balsamic also paired well with a touch of honey, which heightened the carrots' natural sweetness. The French have long favored handheld rotary graters to make this salad, but we found the food processor was the fastest and easiest way to shred carrots. We also liked the meatier shreds it produces, though a box grater works fine, too. No tarragon? Use 1½ teaspoons chopped fresh thyme instead.

Don't use old bagged carrots. This salad is all about the earthy, sweet carrot flavor. Large carrots can be woody, dry and bitter; small baby carrots are too juicy. Look for bunches of medium carrots with the greens still attached.

In a large bowl, whisk together the vinegar, tarragon, shallot, honey, cayenne and 1 teaspoon of salt. Let sit for 10 minutes. Whisk in the oil until emulsified, then add the carrots and parsley. Stir until evenly coated. Season with salt. Serve or refrigerate for up to 24 hours.

CHANGE THE WAY YOU COOK:
FOR SWEETER ROOT VEGETABLES, GRAB YOUR GRATER

When root vegetables are cut, their cells are ruptured, releasing sugars and volatile hydrocarbons, the source of their sweetness and aromas. The more cells are ruptured, the sweeter the vegetables taste. So for the sweetest, freshest tasting carrots, we grate them rather than chop.

Japanese Potato Salad

Start to finish: **1 hour (15 minutes active)**
Servings: 4

1 Persian cucumber, halved
lengthwise and thinly sliced
crosswise

1 medium carrot, peeled
and shredded

¼ cup minced red onion

Kosher salt and ground
black pepper

1½ pounds Yukon Gold potatoes,
peeled and cut into ¾-inch pieces

3 tablespoons unseasoned
rice vinegar

½ cup mayonnaise

2 ounces thick-cut smoked
deli ham, diced (about ⅓ cup)

1 hard-cooked egg plus
1 hard-cooked egg yolk, diced

1 teaspoon white sugar

2 scallions, finely sliced

Getting potato salad right is no picnic. Too often the salad lacks the acidity or piquancy needed to cut through the richness of the mayonnaise. Our search for a better option led us to Japan, where potato salads are partially mashed to create a creamier texture. And they balance that texture with crumbled hard-boiled egg and the crisp bite of vegetables, such as cucumber and carrots. Tying everything together is Kewpie, a Japanese mayonnaise made with rice vinegar and egg yolks. It is smoother and richer than American mayonnaise. We started by looking for the right potatoes, which turned out to be Yukon Gold. Salting the cooking water ensured even seasoning, as did sprinkling them with vinegar and black pepper as they cooled. Waiting until the potatoes were at room temperature before adding mayonnaise was important to avoid oiliness. We used American mayonnaise but approximated the Kewpie flavor by increasing the vinegar and adding an extra hard-cooked egg yolk and 1 teaspoon of sugar. For a savory touch, we added diced ham and finished with scallions.

Don't substitute starchy russet or waxy new potatoes. The smooth texture of partly mashed Yukon Golds gave us the creamy consistency we wanted.

1. In a medium bowl, combine the cucumber, carrot, onion and 2 teaspoons of salt. Set aside. In a large saucepan over medium-high, combine the potatoes with enough water to cover by 1 inch. Add 1 teaspoon of salt and bring to a boil. Reduce heat to medium-high and simmer until tender, 12 to 15 minutes.

2. Drain the potatoes, then transfer to a large bowl. Using a fork, coarsely mash half of them. Sprinkle with the vinegar and ¾ teaspoon pepper. Stir to combine, then spread in an even layer along the bottom and sides of the bowl. Let cool for at least 20 minutes.

3. Transfer the vegetable mixture to a fine mesh strainer and rinse well. Working in batches, use your hands to squeeze the vegetables, removing as much liquid as possible, then add to the potatoes. Add the mayonnaise, ham, diced egg and yolk and sugar. Fold until thoroughly combined. Taste and season with salt and pepper, if necessary. Sprinkle with scallions, then serve chilled or at room temperature.

Fattoush

Start to finish: **30 minutes** / Servings: 6

___

1 pound seedless red grapes, halved

¼ cup cider vinegar

Kosher salt and ground black pepper

½ cup extra-virgin olive oil, divided

3 medium garlic cloves, finely grated

2 teaspoons ground cumin

½ to ¾ teaspoon red pepper flakes

Two 8-inch pita bread rounds, each split into 2 rounds

½ cup plain whole-milk yogurt

½ cup finely chopped fresh dill

1 tablespoon pomegranate molasses (optional)

2 teaspoons ground sumac (optional)

1 English cucumber, quartered lengthwise, thinly sliced

6- to 7-ounce romaine heart, chopped into bite-size pieces

1 cup lightly packed fresh mint, finely chopped

This take on a Middle Eastern bread salad gets crunch and texture from pita bread split into rounds and brushed generously with seasoned olive oil before toasting to produce thin, crisp pieces packed with flavor. Pickled grapes are not a common fattoush ingredient, but we loved their sweet-tart flavor and succulent texture—they're an idea we borrowed from chef Ana Sortun of Oleana in Cambridge, Massachusetts. Both the pita and the grapes can be prepared a day in advance; store the pita in an airtight container to keep it fresh. Sumac, a fruity, lemony Levantine spice, has earthy, citrusy notes, and pomegranate molasses is tangy and lightly fruity. Both ingredients are optional, but they give the fattoush complexity and a distinct Middle Eastern character.

Don't combine the salad ingredients until just before serving or the pita chips will get soggy.

1. Heat the oven to 400°F with a rack in the middle position. In a medium bowl, stir together the grapes, vinegar and ½ teaspoon salt. Cover and refrigerate.

2. In a small bowl, stir together ¼ cup of oil, the garlic, cumin and pepper flakes. Arrange the pita rounds rough side up on a rimmed baking sheet, then brush each with the flavored oil, using all of it. Sprinkle with salt and black pepper. Bake until browned and crisp, 10 to 12 minutes. Set aside to cool. When cool enough to handle, break into bite-size pieces.

3. Drain the grapes, reserving the pickling liquid. In a large bowl, combine the remaining ¼ cup oil, the yogurt, dill, molasses and sumac, if using, and 1 teaspoon each of salt and pepper. Add the reserved pickling liquid and whisk well. Add the cucumber, romaine, mint, pickled grapes and pita pieces. Toss until evenly coated.

Shaved Zucchini and Herb Salad with Parmesan

Start to finish: **10 minutes** / Servings: 4

1 teaspoon grated lemon zest, plus 3 tablespoons juice

3 tablespoons extra-virgin olive oil

¼ teaspoon honey

Kosher salt and ground black pepper

1 pound zucchini (2 medium)

1 ounce Parmesan cheese, finely grated (about ½ cup), plus extra, shaved, to serve

½ cup lightly packed fresh mint, torn

½ cup lightly packed fresh basil, torn

¼ cup hazelnuts, toasted, skinned and coarsely chopped

For this vibrant salad, we adopted the Italian technique of slicing raw zucchini into thin ribbons. The zucchini really shines here, balanced with the clean, sharp flavors of lemon along with Parmesan and hazelnuts. A Y-style peeler makes it easy to shave the zucchini, or you can use a mandoline. Don't worry if the ribbons vary in width; this adds to the visual appeal of the dish. Toasted sliced, slivered or chopped whole almonds can be used in place of the hazelnuts.

Don't dress the salad until you are ready to serve. The zucchini and herbs are delicate and quickly wilt.

1. In a large bowl, whisk together the lemon zest and juice, oil, honey, ½ teaspoon salt and ¼ teaspoon pepper. Set aside.

2. Use a Y-style peeler or mandoline to shave the zucchini from top to bottom, rotating as you go. Stop shaving when you reach the seedy core. Discard the cores.

3. To the dressing, add the shaved zucchini, cheese, mint and basil. Gently toss until evenly coated. Transfer to a serving plate and sprinkle with shaved Parmesan and hazelnuts.

Bulgur-Tomato Salad with Herbs and Pomegranate Molasses (*Eetch*)

Start to finish: **30 minutes** / Servings: 4

3 tablespoons tomato paste

2 tablespoons extra-virgin olive oil

1 medium red bell pepper, stemmed, seeded and finely chopped

6 scallions (4 finely chopped, 2 thinly sliced, reserved separately)

Kosher salt and ground black pepper

3 medium garlic cloves, finely chopped

1½ teaspoons ground cumin

1 teaspoon Aleppo pepper or see substitute, p. 7

1 cup coarse bulgur

1 tablespoon pomegranate molasses, plus more if needed

1 pint grape tomatoes, halved

¾ cup chopped fresh mint or flat-leaf parsley

This Armenian salad, known as eetch, is heartier and more substantial than tabbouleh, the better-known bulgur salad. Instead of soaking the bulgur in water—as is done for tabbouleh—the bulgur here is cooked in a mixture of tomato paste and water, so the grains take on a red-orange hue. If you want to make the salad more tart and tangy, mix in a splash of lemon juice. For a more substantial meal, add blanched green beans and crumbled feta cheese.

Don't use fine or medium bulgur. These varieties have different liquid-absorption rates than coarse bulgur, the type called for in this recipe. They also don't have the same hearty chew.

1. In a small bowl, whisk together 1⅓ cups water and the tomato paste. Set aside. In a 10-inch skillet over medium, heat the oil until shimmering. Add the bell pepper, chopped scallions and ½ teaspoon salt. Cover and cook, stirring occasionally, until the bell pepper is tender, about 5 minutes. Stir in the garlic, cumin and Aleppo pepper, then cook until fragrant, about 1 minute.

2. Stir in the bulgur, the tomato paste mixture and 1¼ teaspoons salt. Bring to a boil over medium-high. Cover, reduce to low and cook until the bulgur has absorbed the liquid, 12 to 15 minutes. Remove from the heat and let stand, covered, for 5 minutes.

3. Transfer to a wide, shallow bowl and let cool until just warm, about 5 minutes. Drizzle the pomegranate molasses over the bulgur, then fold until combined. Fold in the tomatoes, mint and sliced scallions. Taste and season with salt, black pepper and additional pomegranate molasses.

Austrian Potato Salad

Start to finish: **30 minutes** / Servings: 4

2 pounds Yukon Gold potatoes, peeled, halved and sliced ¼-inch thick

2 cups low-sodium chicken broth

Kosher salt

¼ cup finely chopped cornichons, plus 1 tablespoon brine

2 tablespoons red wine vinegar, divided

Ground black pepper

½ cup diced red onion (about ½ medium)

½ teaspoon caraway seeds

¼ cup grapeseed or other neutral oil

1 tablespoon Dijon mustard

½ cup diced celery (about 2 medium stalks)

2 hard-boiled eggs, chopped (optional)

¼ cup chopped fresh dill

Our ongoing quest for better potato salad took us to Austria, where they don't drown their potato salads in mayonnaise. In this version, the flavor starts early as the potatoes are simmered in a mixture of chicken broth and water. Onions and caraway seeds also go into the pot, softening the flavors of both. Always loath to pour flavor down the drain, we save some of the seasoned, starchy cooking liquid to help thicken a dressing made tangy with mustard, oil and vinegar. If your potatoes are quite large, quarter them instead of halving before slicing. To add crunch, we used celery; you also could add chopped hard-boiled eggs. A handful of fresh dill made for a bright finish.

Don't overcook—or undercook—the potatoes. They should be firm but not grainy, creamy in the center and just starting to fall apart at the edges. This texture is important, as some of the potatoes will break down into the salad. But if they're too soft, they will turn into mashed potatoes.

1. In a medium saucepan, combine the potatoes, broth and 2 teaspoons salt. Add enough water to just cover the potatoes. Bring to a boil over medium-high. Reduce heat to medium-low and simmer until just tender, 8 to 10 minutes. Drain, reserving ½ cup of the cooking liquid, and transfer to a large bowl. Sprinkle with the cornichon brine, 1 tablespoon of the vinegar and ½ teaspoon pepper.

2. In the empty pan, combine the reserved cooking liquid with the onion and caraway seeds and bring to a simmer over medium-high. Pour the mixture over the potatoes and stir well. Let sit, stirring occasionally, until the liquid is absorbed and thickened, about 10 minutes.

3. Meanwhile, in a liquid measuring cup, whisk together the oil, mustard, the remaining 1 tablespoon of vinegar, ¾ teaspoon salt and ½ teaspoon pepper until emulsified. To the potatoes, add the dressing, celery, eggs, if using, cornichons and dill, then fold until evenly coated. Taste and season with salt and pepper. Serve at room temperature.

Senegalese Avocado and Mango Salad with Rof

Start to finish: **30 minutes** / Servings: **4**

2 cups lightly packed fresh
flat-leaf parsley

4 scallions, roughly chopped

2 medium garlic cloves, peeled

1 habanero chili, stemmed and seeded

Kosher salt and ground black pepper

1 teaspoon grated lime zest,
plus ¼ cup lime juice

¼ cup roasted peanut oil

Two 14- to 16-ounce ripe mangoes,
peeled, pitted and thinly sliced

2 ripe avocados

1 cup grape tomatoes, chopped

This spicy yet refreshing salad—adapted from a recipe in Pierre Thiam's cookbook "Yolele!"—combines sweet, sour and salty flavors, accented by fresh parsley. We learned this lesson while traveling to Dakar with Thiam. The dressing is based on the Senagalese condiment known as rof, an aromatic blend of parsley, garlic, onion and chilies. It's worth seeking out roasted peanut oil for the dressing, as it adds deep, nutty notes and a rich aroma, but regular peanut oil or extra-virgin olive oil worked, too. If you have flaky sea salt, use instead of kosher salt for sprinkling on the mangoes and avocados; the crunch adds dimension to the dish.

Don't prep the avocados until you're ready to assemble the salad so that the fruit remains vibrant green for serving.

1. In a food processor, combine the parsley, scallions, garlic, habanero, 1 teaspoon salt and ½ teaspoon pepper. Process until finely chopped, about 1 minute, scraping the sides of the bowl as needed. Add the lime zest and juice and peanut oil and process until smooth, about 30 seconds.

2. In a medium bowl, combine the mango slices with 3 tablespoons of the dressing and gently toss. Marinate at room temperature for 30 minutes.

3. Lay the mango slices on a serving platter; do not wash the bowl. Halve, pit, peel and thinly slice the avocados. Arrange the avocados on top of the mangoes. Sprinkle lightly with salt and drizzle with 3 tablespoons of the remaining dressing.

4. In the same bowl used for the mangos, toss together the tomatoes and 1 tablespoon of the remaining dressing. Scatter the mixture over the mangoes and avocados. Serve with the remaining dressing on the side.

Skillet-Charred Brussels Sprouts
with Garlic, Anchovy and Chili

Start to finish: **25 minutes** / Servings: 4

---

1 pound small to medium Brussels sprouts, trimmed and halved

4 tablespoons extra-virgin olive oil, divided

4 teaspoons honey, divided

Kosher salt

4 garlic cloves, minced

4 oil-packed anchovy fillets, minced

Red pepper flakes

2 teaspoons lemon juice

We loved the Brussels sprouts at Gjelina, a Los Angeles restaurant. Chef Travis Lett serves them with chili-lime vinaigrette, and they are both wonderfully charred and tender. We assumed they'd been roasted in a very hot oven. In fact, Lett had used a cast-iron skillet, a quicker and more efficient way to transfer heat. We tried it and loved the way the searing-hot skillet gave the sprouts a delicious char we'd never achieved in the oven. For the sauce, we were inspired by bagna càuda, the warm garlic- and anchovy-infused dip from Northern Italy, with red pepper flakes and a splash of lemon juice. A drizzle of honey in the dressing added a note of sweetness.

Don't use a stainless steel skillet. A well-seasoned cast-iron pan was key to this recipe. Stainless steel didn't hold the heat well enough to properly char. To comfortably accommodate the recipe, the pan needed to be at least 12 inches. And stick to small or medium sprouts; large ones didn't taste as good, containing a higher concentration of the compounds that lead to bitterness. Even smaller sprouts were best when cut in half, creating more surface area and contact with the skillet and therefore more charring.

1. In a large bowl, toss the sprouts with 1 tablespoon of the oil, 2 teaspoons of the honey and ½ teaspoon of salt. Set aside.

2. In a 12- to 14-inch cast-iron skillet over high, combine the remaining 3 tablespoons of oil, the garlic, anchovies and ¼ teaspoon pepper flakes. Cook, stirring, until the garlic begins to color, 3 to 4 minutes. Scrape the mixture, including the oil, into a bowl and set aside.

3. Return the skillet to high heat. Add the sprouts (reserve the bowl) and use tongs to arrange them cut side down in a single layer. Cook, without moving, until deeply browned and blackened in spots, 3 to 7 minutes, depending on your skillet. Use the tongs to flip the sprouts cut-side up and cook until charred and just tender, another 3 to 5 minutes.

4. As they finish, return the sprouts to the bowl and toss with the garlic mixture, the remaining 2 teaspoons of honey and the lemon juice. Season with salt and additional pepper flakes.

Roasted Cauliflower with Miso Glaze

Start to finish: 30 minutes
Servings: 4

2-pound head cauliflower, trimmed, cored and cut into 1½- to 2-inch florets

3 tablespoons peanut oil

Ground white pepper

⅓ cup red or white miso

4 teaspoons unseasoned rice vinegar

2 teaspoons sake

1 teaspoon honey

1 teaspoon finely grated fresh ginger

¼ cup shelled roasted pistachios, chopped

1 bunch scallions, thinly sliced

¼ cup chopped fresh cilantro

This recipe—inspired by a dish at Fujisaki, a Japanese restaurant along the Sydney waterfront—coats chunks of cauliflower with a thick, miso-based glaze that is sweet and savory. We roast the cauliflower before tossing the richly browned florets with miso blended with vinegar and ginger, then top it with toasted pistachios, scallions and cilantro. The result is fresh, warm and rich.

Don't forget to heat the baking sheet while preparing the cauliflower. A heated baking sheet—along with allowing the cauliflower to roast without stirring—ensures flavor-building caramelization.

1. Heat the oven to 500°F with a rack in the lowest position. Line a rimmed baking sheet with foil and place the baking sheet in the oven.

2. Place the cauliflower in a large bowl. Add the oil and ¼ teaspoon pepper, then toss to coat. When the oven is at temperature, quickly remove the baking sheet and distribute the cauliflower in an even layer; reserve the bowl. Roast until the cauliflower is just tender and browned in spots, 15 to 18 minutes; do not stir.

3. Meanwhile, in the reserved bowl, whisk together the miso, vinegar, sake, honey, ginger and 2 tablespoons water. As soon as the cauliflower is done, transfer to the bowl with the miso mixture and gently toss. Carefully stir in the pistachios, scallions and cilantro. Transfer to a serving platter.

Cumin-Coriander Potatoes with Cilantro (*Patates Mekhalel*)

Start to finish: **20 minutes (10 minutes active)** / Servings: 4

2½ pounds Yukon Gold potatoes, peeled and cut into 1-inch chunks

½ cup white vinegar, divided

Kosher salt and ground black pepper

¼ cup grapeseed or other neutral oil

4 teaspoons cumin seeds, lightly crushed

4 teaspoons coriander seeds, lightly crushed

4 medium garlic cloves, minced

2 teaspoons hot paprika (see note)

2 teaspoons honey

1½ cups lightly packed fresh cilantro, roughly chopped

In Cairo, patates mekhalel are served by street vendors as a side to liver sandwiches, their gentle acidity and crunchy spices balancing the richness of the liver. For our version, we peel, cut and cook the potatoes in water seasoned with both salt and vinegar, then dress the hot, just-drained potatoes with additional vinegar. To lightly crush the cumin and coriander seeds, use a mortar and pestle or the back of a heavy pan, or pulse them several times in a spice grinder. If you can't find hot paprika, use 2 teaspoons sweet paprika plus ¼ teaspoon cayenne pepper.

Don't overcook the potatoes; the chunks should be tender but not fall apart. Also, don't allow the garlic to brown in the oil or its flavor may be acrid and bitter. Remove the pan from the heat as soon as the garlic begins to turn golden and immediately add the paprika and honey, which lower the oil's temperature.

1. In a large saucepan over high, combine the potatoes, ¼ cup of vinegar, 2 tablespoons salt and 6 cups water. Bring to a boil and cook, stirring occasionally, until a skewer inserted into the potatoes meets no resistance, 6 to 8 minutes. Drain, then transfer to a large bowl. Drizzle with the remaining ¼ cup vinegar and toss; set aside.

2. In a small saucepan over medium-high, combine the oil, cumin and coriander, then cook, frequently swirling the pan, until sizzling, 45 to 90 seconds. Add the garlic and cook, stirring, until it just begins to turn golden, about 30 seconds. Off heat, stir in the paprika and honey, then pour the mixture over the potatoes. Add the cilantro, 1 teaspoon salt and ½ teaspoon pepper and toss. Let stand at room temperature for at least 10 minutes or up to 45 minutes. Serve warm or at room temperature.

Hot Oil–Flashed Chard with Ginger, Scallions and Chili

Start to finish: **20 minutes** / Servings: **4**

¼ teaspoon kosher salt

2 large bunches Swiss chard
(1½ to 2 pounds), stems removed,
leaves sliced crosswise into
3-inch pieces

2 scallions, thinly sliced on diagonal

1 tablespoon finely grated
fresh ginger

1 serrano chili, thinly sliced

2 tablespoons grapeseed or other
neutral oil

1 tablespoon toasted sesame oil

1 tablespoon unseasoned
rice vinegar

1 tablespoon soy sauce

2 teaspoons toasted
sesame seeds (optional)

Most hearty greens are naturally tough and bitter, requiring extended cooking. So we tamed and tenderized Swiss chard with sizzling oil, a technique we learned from cookbook author and Chinese cuisine expert Fuchsia Dunlop. Her recipe is modeled on a classic Cantonese method in which hot oil is poured over lightly blanched greens. We scattered fresh ginger, scallions and serrano chilies over our greens and found the hot oil bloomed the flavors beautifully. Instead of julienning the ginger, as is traditional, we used a wand-style grater to finely grate it, which distributed it better, was faster and released more of the aromatics. Bonus: No fibrous pieces in the finished dish. For the oil, we found the clean flavor and light texture of grapeseed oil was ideal, but vegetable oil worked well, too. We added toasted sesame oil for a savory touch. To finish the dish, soy sauce alone is fine, but even better was a blend of soy sauce and unseasoned rice vinegar, which added a gentle acidity and light sweetness.

Don't use the chard stems, but also don't throw them away. The stems are tougher than the leaves and won't cook through in the short time it takes to wilt the leaves. Chard stems do have good flavor, however, and can be sauteed, pickled or added to soups and stews.

1. In a large skillet over medium-high, bring ¼ cup water and salt to a boil. Pile the chard into the pan and cover (the lid may not close completely). Cook until the chard is wilted, about 5 minutes, stirring halfway through. Remove the lid and cook, stirring occasionally, until most of the liquid has evaporated, 1 to 3 minutes. Transfer the chard to a serving platter and wipe out the skillet.

2. Distribute the scallions, ginger and chili evenly over the chard. Add both oils to the skillet and return to medium-high heat until very hot, 1 to 2 minutes. Pour the oils directly over the greens and aromatics (you should hear them sizzle) and toss to distribute. Drizzle the vinegar and soy sauce over the chard and toss again. Sprinkle with the sesame seeds, if using.

CHANGE THE WAY YOU COOK:
ADD SIZZLING FLAVOR TO GREENS WITH HOT OIL

For flavor so big you can hear it, pile aromatics such as scallions and fresh ginger onto lightly cooked greens, then drizzle with hot oil (you should hear them sizzling) and toss. This also works on shredded carrots and julienned sugar snap peas, as well as on hardier vegetables, such as green beans and asparagus (blanch them first in salted water until just tender, then drain and thoroughly pat dry).

CHINESE VEGETABLE CLEAVERS

American home cooks typically are told the triangular Western chef's knife is the one knife to rule them all. But most of Asia favors rectangular cleaver-like knives, such as the Chinese cai dao. They typically have blades about 8 inches long and 4 inches deep and are surprisingly light. Though proficiency with them involves a learning curve, we were impressed with the way they sliced, diced, chopped, smashed, pulverized and pounded. They also were arguably the most effective bench scraper we've used.

If you're game to try one, keep a few things in mind:

• The forward weight of the blade is different from the neutral balance of a Western knife. The knife leads you rather than you leading it.

• The blade's height changes the spatial relationship between the hand you keep on the knife and the hand you keep on the cutting board. With Western knives, both hands operate on similar planes. It can be disconcerting for them to be so far apart.

• Western blades work best with a rocking motion. Asian cleaver blades are mostly flat and require more of a push or chop.

• Handle a cai dao similar to a Western chef's knife. For the best control you should pinch the blade between your thumb and forefinger while the rest of your fingers wrap around the handle.

Cracked Potatoes with Vermouth, Coriander and Fennel

Start to finish: **35 minutes (10 minutes active)** / Servings: 4

1½ pounds small Yukon Gold potatoes (1½ to 2 inches in diameter)

2 tablespoons extra-virgin olive oil, divided

1 teaspoon kosher salt

¼ teaspoon ground black pepper

1 tablespoon salted butter

2 teaspoons coriander seeds, cracked

1 teaspoon fennel seeds, cracked

1 cup dry vermouth

As much as we like them, crispy, smashed potatoes are a bother. First you boil, then flatten, then crisp in fat. And half the time our potatoes fall apart. We wanted a one-stroke solution, which we found in potatoes afelia, a Cypriot dish that calls for cracking the potatoes when raw, then braising them. Our starting point was a recipe from London chefs Sam and Sam Clark of Moro. They whack raw potatoes, causing them to split and fracture slightly, but not break apart. Next, they cook them in a covered pan with oil and coriander seeds, a traditional afelia flavoring. Red wine, added at the end, simmers into a flavorful sauce. Back at Milk Street we got cracking. Hit too hard and the potatoes break; too gently and they're merely dented. A firm, controlled hit with a meat mallet was the answer. We preferred dry vermouth to red wine. We hate opening a bottle of wine just to cook with and almost always have an open bottle of dry vermouth, which as a fortified wine lasts longer and adds a clean, herbal flavor.

Don't use a skillet with an ill-fitting lid. If the moisture evaporates too quickly, the bottom of the pan can scorch. If the pan looks dry after 10 minutes, add water 2 tablespoons at a time.

1. Using a meat mallet or the bottom of a heavy skillet, whack the potatoes one at a time to crack them until slightly flattened but still intact. In a bowl, toss the potatoes with 1 tablespoon of the oil and the salt and pepper.

2. In a 12-inch stainless steel skillet over medium-high, heat the remaining 1 tablespoon of oil and the butter. Add the potatoes in a single layer, reduce heat to medium, then cook without moving until well browned, 6 to 8 minutes. Flip and cook until well browned on the other side, about 5 minutes.

3. Add the coriander and fennel. Cook, shaking the pan constantly, until fragrant, about 1 minute. Add the vermouth. Cover and reduce heat to medium-low. Cook until the potatoes are just tender and the liquid has nearly evaporated, 12 to 14 minutes, flipping the potatoes halfway through. Transfer to a serving bowl, scraping the sauce and seeds on top.

Thai Stir-Fried Spinach

Start to finish: **20 minutes** / Servings: 4

1 tablespoon fish sauce

1 tablespoon oyster sauce

2 teaspoons white sugar

¾ teaspoon red pepper flakes

3 tablespoons grapeseed or other neutral oil, divided

3 tablespoons roughly chopped garlic

1½ pounds bunch spinach, trimmed of bottom 1½ inches, washed and dried

This simple, bold stir-fry uses regular bunch spinach rather than the water spinach common in Thai cooking. The wilted leaves and crisp-tender stems combine for a pleasing contrast of textures. Be sure to dry the spinach well after washing; excess water will cause splattering and popping when the spinach is added to the hot oil. A salad spinner works well, or roll the spinach in kitchen towels and squeeze dry. We liked to serve this with steamed jasmine rice to soak up the sauce.

Don't use baby spinach, which can't handle high-heat cooking and doesn't have stems to offer textural contrast. And don't allow the spinach leaves to fully wilt in the pan; some leaves should still look fairly fresh, but will continue to cook after being transferred to the bowl.

1. In a small bowl, whisk together the fish sauce, oyster sauce, sugar and pepper flakes until the sugar dissolves. Set aside.

2. In a 14-inch wok over medium-high, heat 2 tablespoons of the oil until barely smoking. Remove the wok from the heat, add the garlic and cook, stirring, until just beginning to color, 20 to 30 seconds. Return the wok to high and immediately add ½ of the spinach. Using tongs, turn the spinach to coat with the oil and garlic. When the spinach is nearly wilted and the garlic has turned golden brown, after 30 seconds or less, transfer to a large bowl. The leaves will continue to wilt but the stems should remain crisp-tender.

3. Return the wok to high heat. Add the remaining 1 tablespoon oil, swirl to coat the wok and heat until just beginning to smoke. Add the remaining spinach and cook as before, for 20 to 30 seconds. Transfer to the bowl with the first batch of spinach.

4. Pour the fish sauce mixture over the spinach and toss. Transfer to a platter and drizzle with any accumulated liquid.

Sweet Potato Gratin with Vanilla Bean and Bay Leaves

Start to finish: **3 hours (50 minutes active), plus cooling** / Servings: **8**

5 pounds sweet potatoes

1 cup heavy cream

4 bay leaves

1 vanilla bean

⅓ cup plus 1 tablespoon packed dark brown sugar, divided

1¼ teaspoons kosher salt

¾ teaspoon ground black pepper

⅓ cup white sugar

Pinch cayenne pepper

Sweet potato casserole is a Thanksgiving staple, but our version is delicious all year. We start by ditching the marshmallows and upping the flavor with a dash of spice. For ease, we roasted the sweet potatoes, a hands-off process that can be done a day ahead. Roasting rather than boiling produces cleaner, deeper flavors and a better, less watery texture. In lieu of marshmallows we infuse cream with vanilla bean and bay leaves and add a dusting of black pepper. A crunchy topping of dark brown and white sugar with a touch of cayenne keeps the dish appropriate for the adults' table.

Don't get distracted while the gratin is broiling; all broilers are different, and the difference between browned and burnt can be a matter of seconds.

1. Heat the oven to 400°F with one rack in the middle and another 6 inches from the broiler. Pierce the sweet potatoes with a fork and arrange on a rimmed baking sheet. Bake on the middle rack, turning once, until tender, 1 to 1½ hours. Let cool. Increase oven to 425°F.

2. Meanwhile, in a medium saucepan, combine the cream and bay leaves. With a paring knife, split the vanilla bean lengthwise, then scrape out the seeds. Add the seeds and pod to the cream and bring to a simmer over medium-high. Set aside, covered, for 30 minutes. Strain out and discard the solids.

3. Once the potatoes have cooled, scrape the flesh from the skins; discard the skins. In a food processor, combine half the flesh and half the infused cream. Add 1 tablespoon of the brown sugar, the salt and pepper. Process until smooth, about 1 minute, scraping the bowl halfway through; transfer to a large bowl. Repeat with the remaining potatoes and cream, then add to the first batch. Mix well, then transfer to a 13-by-9-inch broiler safe baking dish. Smooth the top.

4. In a bowl, stir together the remaining ⅓ cup of brown sugar, the white sugar and the cayenne. Transfer to a medium mesh strainer, then evenly sift the mixture over the surface of the potatoes (or do by hand). Brush any sugar off the rim of the baking dish.

5. Bake on the middle rack until bubbling at the edges, about 20 minutes. Remove from the oven, then heat the broiler. When ready, place the dish on the upper rack and broil until deeply browned and crisp, 2 to 7 minutes. Let sit for 20 minutes before serving.

Spicy Egyptian Eggplant with Fresh Herbs

Start to finish: **40 minutes** / Servings: 4

1 tablespoon coriander seeds

1 tablespoon cumin seeds

2 pounds globe or
Italian eggplant, trimmed

6 tablespoons extra-virgin
olive oil

¼ cup harissa paste

¼ cup cider vinegar

3 tablespoons honey

1 medium garlic clove,
finely grated

¼ cup finely chopped
fresh mint

3 tablespoons finely
chopped fresh dill, divided

Kosher salt and ground
black pepper

This is an oven-friendly version of a dish typically deep-fried by street vendors in Cairo. Because broilers vary in heat output, check the eggplant for doneness after 10 minutes. For the same reason, it also may need longer than called for. The pieces should be tender and lightly charred, but not falling apart. Harissa is a North African red pepper paste seasoned with spices and other ingredients; our favorite brand is DEA, which is sold in a yellow tube. Or, see our recipe for homemade harissa, p. 496. Serve warm or at room temperature.

Don't allow the eggplant to cool before tossing it with the harissa mixture. As they cool, the chunks absorb the flavorings. Allow the mixture to stand for at least 10 minutes before serving.

1. In a small skillet over medium, toast the coriander and cumin, shaking the pan, until fragrant, about 2 minutes. Transfer to a spice grinder and let cool slightly, then pulse until coarsely ground; set aside.

2. Heat the oven to broil with a rack 6 inches from the element. Line a rimmed baking sheet with foil and mist with cooking spray. Cut each eggplant crosswise into 1½-inch-thick rounds, then cut each round into 1½-inch cubes. In a large bowl, toss the eggplant with the oil to coat. Distribute in an even layer on the prepared baking sheet; reserve the bowl. Broil without stirring until tender and lightly charred on top, 10 to 12 minutes.

3. Meanwhile, in the reserved bowl, whisk together the harissa, vinegar, honey, garlic, mint, 2 tablespoons of dill and the coriander and cumin. When the eggplant is done, immediately add it to the bowl, then gently toss to combine. Taste and season with salt and pepper. Let stand for 10 minutes. Transfer to a serving platter and sprinkle with the remaining 1 tablespoon dill.

Celery Root Puree

Start to finish: **45 minutes** / Servings: **8**

2 pounds celery root, peeled
and cut into 1-inch pieces

1 pound Yukon Gold potatoes,
peeled and cut into 1-inch pieces

2 cups half-and-half

2 cups whole milk

4 garlic cloves, smashed
and peeled

4 sprigs fresh thyme

Kosher salt

8 tablespoons (1 stick)
salted butter

Ground black pepper

Chopped fresh chives

HOW TO PREPARE CELERY ROOT

With its lumpy shape, thick skin
and gnarly tangle of roots, celery root
can be a real challenge, but not an
insurmountable one. To start, use
a strong knife to chop off the bottom
(root end) of the bulb. Use a Y-style
peeler to peel and discard the skin
(you may need to use a paring knife for
thicker skins). Cut out any discolored
veins that may be left. Once peeled, cut
the root into chunks to be used as is—
as we do in our celery puree—or thinly
slice using a mandolin or food processor to use fresh in a salad, such as a
classic French remoulade.

We give mashed potatoes a sophisticated spin with an unlikely candidate:
celery root. Also known as celeriac, this vegetable gets little attention in
American kitchens—perhaps because of its less than beautiful appearance.
When cooked and processed, however, the knobby, gnarled root transforms
into a subtler, version of mashed potatoes with a light, fresh celery flavor.
To balance that lightness, we paired celery root with Yukon Golds, producing
a medium-bodied puree. We cooked the vegetables in a mixture of milk
and half-and-half, a combination that won't dilute or mask celery root's
flavor. A stick of butter gave the puree a silky texture. We liked the flavors
of thyme and garlic, but small amounts of sage, rosemary and marjoram
worked, too. The cooled puree can be refrigerated for two days; rewarm in
a saucepan over low heat and check the seasoning before serving.

*Don't add too much cooking liquid right away as the moisture content of
starchy vegetables can vary. If your puree is loose, start with just a splash and
go from there.*

1. In a large saucepan over high,
combine the celery root, potatoes,
half-and-half, milk, garlic, thyme and
1½ teaspoons salt. Bring to a boil,
then cover, leaving the lid slightly ajar,
and reduce heat to low. Simmer,
stirring occasionally, until the vegetables are tender, about 25 minutes.
The mixture will froth and foam and
may appear curdled; watch carefully
to prevent boiling over.

2. Drain the vegetables, reserving the
liquid. Remove and discard the thyme
sprigs, then transfer the solids to a food
processor. Process until smooth, about
1 minute. Return to the pan along with
the butter. Set over low heat and cook,
stirring occasionally, until the butter is
melted. Starting with ½ cup, gradually
stir in the reserved cooking liquid until
the puree reaches the desired consistency. The puree should be not quite
pourable. Taste and season with salt
and pepper. Sprinkle with chives.

Sweet-and-Spicy **Ginger Green Beans**

Start to finish: **10 minutes** / Servings: **4**

2 tablespoons packed
light brown sugar

1 tablespoon fish sauce

1 tablespoon soy sauce

3 tablespoons grapeseed
or other neutral oil, divided

1 pound green beans, stemmed
and halved crosswise on diagonal

1 tablespoon finely grated
fresh ginger

½ teaspoon red pepper flakes

2 tablespoons unseasoned
rice vinegar

Ground white pepper

The challenge of stir-frying green beans is that, more often than not, the frills slide off and you're left biting into a bland bean. The key is cooking them in a sauce that actually sticks. Chef Charles Phan, owner of The Slanted Door, a popular Vietnamese restaurant in San Francisco, caramelizes sugar, then stir-fries string beans in the blistering heat of a wok. A final toss with sake and fish sauce coats the charred beans with a dark, bittersweet sauce. We adjusted the recipe to work without a wok. Phan's recipe calls for blanching the beans first. We simplified by adding the beans to a very hot pan with a small amount of oil, then making a sauce around them as they cooked. We found a Dutch oven worked best to control splattering—drying the beans thoroughly also helped (though a large skillet works in a pinch). Cutting the beans on a bias gave us more surface area for better browning. To re-create Phan's flavorful sauce—itself a take on nuoc mau, or Vietnamese caramel sauce—we used brown sugar instead of taking the time to caramelize white sugar. It gave us comparable depth and flavor.

Don't use an ill-fitting lid. A proper seal is key to this recipe, whether you cook the beans in a Dutch oven or a skillet. Have the lid ready as soon as you add the water.

1. In a small bowl, stir together the sugar, fish and soy sauces. Set aside.

2. In a large Dutch oven or 12-inch skillet over medium-high, heat 2 tablespoons of the oil until beginning to smoke. Add the beans and cook, without stirring, until beginning to color, about 3 minutes. Add ¼ cup water and immediately cover the pan. Cook until the beans are bright green and barely tender, about 2 minutes.

3. Clear a space in the center of the pan, then add the remaining 1 tablespoon of oil to the clearing. Stir in the ginger and pepper flakes, then cook until fragrant, about 30 seconds. Stir the sugar-fish sauce mixture then pour it into the skillet and cook, stirring occasionally, until the liquid has thickened and coats the beans, about 1 minute. Off heat, stir in the vinegar. Taste and season with pepper.

Mashed Potatoes with Caraway-Mustard Butter

Start to finish: 40 minutes (10 minutes active) / Servings: 8

4 pounds Yukon Gold potatoes, peeled and quartered

Kosher salt

5 bay leaves

4 medium garlic cloves, smashed and peeled

10 tablespoons (1¼ sticks) salted butter, divided

1¾ cups half-and-half, warmed

½ cup drained prepared white horseradish, liquid reserved

1 tablespoon caraway seeds, lightly crushed

1 tablespoon yellow mustard seeds

2 tablespoons finely chopped chives

These mashed potatoes are classically creamy, but get a kick of sweet heat from horseradish. Infusing browned butter with caraway and mustard seeds and drizzling the mixture onto the mashed potatoes is a technique we picked up from Indian cooking. The spices add a complexity that balances the richness of the dish. We preferred buttery Yukon Gold potatoes; use potatoes of approximately the same size to ensure even cooking. Any brand of refrigerated prepared horseradish worked well.

Don't rush browning the butter. It needs to cook slowly over medium heat to properly brown (you'll see brown spots on the bottom of the saucepan).

1. In a large pot, combine the potatoes, 1 tablespoon salt, the bay leaves and garlic. Add enough water to cover by 2 inches and bring to a boil over high. Reduce to medium, then cook until a skewer inserted into the potatoes meets no resistance, 20 to 25 minutes. Drain the potatoes in a colander set in the sink. Discard the bay leaves, then return the potatoes to the pot.

2. In a small saucepan over medium-low, melt 6 tablespoons of the butter. Add the melted butter to the potatoes. Using a potato masher, mash until smooth. Stir in the half-and-half, horse-radish and 3 tablespoons of the reserved horseradish liquid. Taste and season with salt. Cover and set over low heat to keep warm.

3. Return the saucepan to medium and add the remaining 4 tablespoons butter and the caraway and mustard seeds. Cook, gently swirling the pan, until the butter is browned and the seeds are fragrant and toasted, 2 to 3 minutes. Pour the mixture into fine mesh strainer set over a small liquid measuring cup.

4. Transfer the potatoes to a serving bowl, then drizzle with the flavored butter and sprinkle with chives.

Cauliflower with Tahini and Egyptian Nut-and-Seed Seasoning (*Dukkah*)

Start to finish: **35 minutes** / Servings: **4**

½ cup tahini

1 teaspoon grated lemon zest, plus 2 tablespoons lemon juice, divided

2 tablespoons extra-virgin olive oil, plus more to serve

2 garlic cloves, grated

1½ teaspoons kosher salt

1 teaspoon sweet paprika

¼ to ½ teaspoon cayenne pepper

1 large head cauliflower (about 2½ pounds), cut into 1½- to 2-inch florets

⅓ cup roasted, salted cashews, chopped

⅓ cup chopped fresh cilantro

Cauliflower's been getting the celebrity treatment lately, but we liked it before it was cool for its mild, nutty flavor. In this take, we roasted florets with a tahini sauce brightened with lemon juice and cayenne. We used cilantro in our sauce, but flat-leaf parsley worked as a substitute. When buying cauliflower, look for a head with densely packed florets. Medium florets, about 1½ to 2 inches, were best in this dish; smaller pieces became mushy. And a hot oven and heated baking sheet were key to browning the cauliflower before it overcooked. For a crunchy, nutty alternative, substitute ⅓ cup dukkah (see sidebar) for the cashews.

Don't forget to line the baking sheet with foil before heating. The tahini mixture makes a mess of an unlined pan.

1. Heat the oven to 500°F with a rack in the lowest position. Line a rimmed baking sheet with foil and set on the rack to heat. In a large bowl, whisk together the tahini, lemon zest, 1 tablespoon of the lemon juice, the oil, garlic, salt, paprika and cayenne. Add the cauliflower and toss, massaging the dressing into the florets.

2. Working quickly, remove the baking sheet from the oven and carefully spread the cauliflower on it in an even layer, scraping any remaining tahini onto the florets. Reserve the bowl. Roast until well browned in spots and just tender, 15 to 18 minutes, stirring and turning the florets and rotating the pan halfway through.

3. Transfer the roasted florets to the reserved bowl. Add the remaining 1 tablespoon of lemon juice and toss. Add half of the nuts and the cilantro and toss. Sprinkle with the remaining cashews and serve drizzled with more oil, if desired.

EGYPTIAN NUT-AND-SEED SEASONING (DUKKAH)

The Egyptian seasoning mixture known as dukkah—a rich blend of seeds, nuts and spices—adds welcome texture and complexity to dips and salads, and even can be used as a rub for meat or fish. It began as peasant fare, used to give flavor to coarse bread. In the U.S., dukkah has found popularity with restaurant chefs. It can be bought ready-made from spice shops (and Trader Joe's), but the best way to enjoy it is to make your own. Store in an airtight container at room temperature for up to a week. Freeze for longer use.

Start to finish: **15 minutes**
Makes **about 1 cup**

½ cup raw cashews

2 tablespoons sesame seeds

2 tablespoons coriander seeds

2 tablespoons cumin seeds

1 tablespoon caraway seeds

1 teaspoon dried oregano

½ teaspoon kosher salt

½ teaspoon ground black pepper

In a large skillet over medium, toast the cashews, stirring, until beginning to brown, 3 to 4 minutes. Add the sesame seeds and toast, stirring, until golden, 1 to 2 minutes. Add the coriander, cumin and caraway, and toast, stirring, until fragrant, about 1 minute. Transfer to a food processor and let cool for 5 minutes. Add the oregano, salt and pepper. Pulse until coarsely ground, 12 to 15 pulses.

Harissa Roasted Potatoes

Start to finish: **1 hour** (10 minutes active)
Servings: 4

___

2 pounds Yukon Gold potatoes, peeled and cut into 1½-inch pieces

4 ounces shallots (about 4 small), peeled and quartered

2 tablespoons extra-virgin olive oil

1 teaspoon kosher salt

½ teaspoon ground black pepper

6 tablespoons harissa, divided (recipe p. 496)

⅓ cup chopped flat-leaf fresh parsley

1 tablespoon lemon juice, plus lemon wedges to serve

Harissa (pronounced ha-REE-sah) may well be one of the original hot sauces. It's generally believed to have originated in Tunisia, where it's often served with couscous and brik, a tuna-and-egg turnover. This recipe uses our piquant, homemade harissa sauce (p. 496) to give potatoes a sweet-spicy kick, but harissa also can be found online and in the grocer's international aisle. Tossing the raw potatoes with harissa before roasting muted the chili paste's flavor, so we crisped "naked" potatoes on the bottom rack first, then tossed them with a portion of the harissa and returned them to the oven. That gave the potatoes the right texture and a spicy crust. A final hit of the remaining harissa, along with parsley and lemon juice, kept the flavors bright.

Don't forget to taste your harissa for heat and pungency before tossing the potatoes. A harissa with gentle heat and smooth texture, like Milk Street's recipe, worked best here. If your variety is particularly spicy, you may want to reduce the total amount to ¼ cup, reserving 1 tablespoon to finish the dish.

1. Heat the oven to 400°F with racks in the middle and lowest positions and a rimmed baking sheet on the bottom rack. In a large bowl, toss the potatoes and shallots with the oil, salt and pepper.

2. Working quickly, remove the baking sheet from the oven, add the potato-shallot mixture and spread in an even layer; reserve the bowl. Roast on the bottom rack until the potatoes are well browned on the bottoms, about 20 minutes, rotating the sheet halfway through.

3. Use a thin metal spatula to transfer the potatoes to the reserved bowl, scraping up any browned bits. Add 4 tablespoons of the harissa and toss until evenly coated. Return the potatoes to the sheet, spreading in an even layer and reserving the bowl. Roast on the middle rack until tender, 18 to 22 minutes, rotating the sheet halfway through.

4. Return the potatoes to the reserved bowl, scraping up any browned bits from the pan. Add the parsley, the remaining 2 tablespoons of harissa and the lemon juice. Toss to coat. Serve with lemon wedges.

Stir-Fried Broccoli
with Sichuan Peppercorns

Start to finish: 30 minutes / Servings: 4

2 tablespoons unseasoned
rice vinegar, divided

1½ tablespoons soy sauce

1 teaspoon white sugar

3 medium garlic cloves, finely grated

1½ teaspoons finely grated
fresh ginger

1 teaspoon Sichuan peppercorns,
finely ground

¼ to ½ teaspoon red pepper flakes

2 scallions, white and pale green
parts minced, dark green parts thinly
sliced on the diagonal

3 tablespoons peanut or grapeseed oil

1¼ pounds broccoli, florets
cut into 1-inch pieces, stems peeled
and sliced ¼-inch thick

Kosher salt

2 teaspoons toasted sesame oil

Sichuan peppercorns don't provide heat so much as an intriguing, slightly resinous flavor and tingling sensation on your lips and tongue. The spice in this stir-fry instead comes from red pepper flakes. Use a spice grinder to grind the Sichuan peppercorns to as fine a powder as possible; if using an electric grinder, it helps to shake the grinder as it whirs. Pouring the vinegar-soy mixture down the sides of the wok rather than directly over the broccoli quickly heats and concentrates the mixture so the liquid doesn't cause the broccoli to overcook.

Don't be slow to cover the wok after adding the water or too much moisture may evaporate and the broccoli won't cook through properly. If your wok doesn't have a lid, improvise with a baking sheet or a lid from a large pot, such as a Dutch oven (the lid does not need to sit on the rim of wok—it can sit slightly inside).

1. In a small bowl, stir together 1 tablespoon of vinegar, the soy sauce and sugar. In another small bowl, stir together the garlic, ginger, Sichuan pepper, pepper flakes and minced scallions.

2. Heat a 12- to 14-inch wok over medium-high for 1 to 2 minutes; a drop of water should evaporate within 1 to 2 seconds. Add the peanut oil and swirl to coat the wok. Add the garlic-ginger mixture and stir-fry until fragrant, about 30 seconds. Add the broccoli and stir-fry for 30 seconds, then add ¼ teaspoon salt and 3 tablespoons water. Cover and cook for 1 minute. Uncover and cook, stirring, until the broccoli is crisp-tender, 3 to 5 minutes.

3. Drizzle the vinegar-soy mixture around the wok, down its sides. Cook, stirring and scraping up any browned bits, until the liquid is slightly reduced, about 1 minute. Off heat, stir in the sesame oil and remaining 1 tablespoon vinegar. Transfer to a platter and sprinkle with the sliced scallions.

Grains

Soft Polenta / 139

Quinoa Pilaf with Dates,
Almonds and Carrot Juice / 140

Thai Fried Rice / 142

Coconut Rice / 144

Japanese-Style Rice with
Flaked Salmon and Shiitake Mushrooms
(*Sake to Kinoko Takikomi Gohan*) / 146

Middle Eastern Rice
with Toasted Pasta and Herbs / 149

Coconut-Ginger Rice / 151

Herb-and-Pistachio Couscous / 153

Indian Tomato Rice / 155

Risotto with Fresh Herbs / 156

Lebanese Lentils and Rice with Crisped
Onions (*Mujaddara*) / 159

5

Soft Polenta

Start to finish: 1¾ hours (10 minutes active)
Servings: 6

2 cups coarse stoneground yellow cornmeal (see note)

Kosher salt and ground black pepper

Polenta, a savory cornmeal porridge, can be a disappointment in the U.S., tasting mostly of the cheese and fat that weigh it down. Not to mention it requires near-constant whisking to get a lump-free consistency. But in Cossano Belbo, Italy, we found a better way with no cheese, no butter and not much stirring. The porridge was light and fresh and the taste of the corn shined through. We followed that lead, using more water than called for in conventional recipes—11 cups. Combining the cornmeal with cold, not boiling, water, then bringing the entire pot to a simmer, prevented clumping. We finished cooking the polenta in the oven rather than the stovetop, which gave us more consistent, gentle heat. For the best flavor and texture, use coarse stone-ground cornmeal; fine cornmeal produced pasty, gluey polenta, while steel-ground cornmeal had less flavor. We liked Bob's Red Mill coarse-grind cornmeal and its polenta corn grits, but found that different brands can cook up with slightly different consistencies. The finished polenta should be pourable; if it's too thick, thin it with water as needed. It's good on its own or as a side to braised meats.

Don't use white cornmeal. Its flavor is milder than yellow cornmeal. In Italy, it is used mostly for sweet preparations. And don't skip the whisk for stirring the polenta as it cooks; its wires are more effective than a wooden spoon for breaking up lumps.

1. Heat the oven to 375°F with a rack in the lower-middle position. In a large Dutch oven, whisk together the cornmeal, 1 tablespoon salt and 11 cups water. Bring to a gentle simmer over medium-high, stirring frequently to prevent clumping. Transfer the pot, uncovered, to the oven and bake for 1 hour.

2. Remove the pot from the oven. Carefully whisk until smooth and use a wooden spoon to scrape along the bottom and into corners of the pot to loosen any stuck bits. Return the pot, uncovered, to the oven and cook until the cornmeal is thick and creamy and the granules are tender, another 10 to 30 minutes, depending on the cornmeal used.

3. Remove the pot from the oven. Vigorously whisk the polenta until smooth and use the wooden spoon to scrape the bottom, sides and corners of the pot. Let stand for 5 minutes. The polenta should thicken just enough for a spoon to leave a brief trail when drawn through; whisk in additional water, if needed, to thin the consistency. Taste and season with salt and pepper. Serve immediately.

CHANGE THE WAY YOU COOK:
STOP STIRRING YOUR POLENTA

For the creamiest, easiest polenta, all you need is an oven, a couple vigorous stirs and no endless whisking.

Quinoa Pilaf with Dates, Almonds and Carrot Juice

Start to finish: 40 minutes (15 minutes active) / Servings: 4

---

2 tablespoons salted butter

1 medium carrot, peeled and diced (about ½ cup)

1 small yellow onion, diced (about ½ cup)

Kosher salt

1 cup white quinoa

1 tablespoon finely grated fresh ginger

1 teaspoon ground cumin

½ cup carrot juice

4 medjool dates, pitted and diced

⅓ cup chopped almonds or cashews, toasted

2 scallions, trimmed and chopped

3 tablespoons chopped fresh dill, plus more to garnish

1 teaspoon grated lemon zest, plus 1 tablespoon lemon juice

Ground black pepper

Extra-virgin olive oil, for drizzling (optional)

We like the nutty, earthy flavor and gentle crunch of quinoa, but too often salads made with this seed—it's technically not a grain—end up mushy and flavorless. For a better way, we looked to Deborah Madison, author of "Vegetarian Cooking for Everyone." She cooks her quinoa in carrot juice, a winning combination that perked up its natural sweetness and tempered its tendency to muddiness. We also liked a quinoa by Erik Ramirez of Brooklyn's Llama Inn. He makes a famously madcap quinoa pilaf studded with bananas, bacon, cashews and avocado, which showed us that texture and contrast can make the often insipid seed exciting. We liked a simple combo of chewy-sweet dates and crunchy almonds. We took a three-step approach to keeping our pilaf light and fluffy: first toasting the quinoa, then cooking it with less liquid than typically called for, and finally letting the cooked quinoa rest before fluffing. For texture, we added dates and almonds or cashews; both worked. Finishing with scallions, lemon and fresh dill brightened the final dish. Eat this as is or pair it with sautéed shrimp, broiled salmon or fried tofu.

Don't worry about rinsing the quinoa. Most varieties sold in the U.S. are pre-rinsed. Just check the packaging.

1. In a medium saucepan over medium, melt the butter. Add the carrot, onion and ¼ teaspoon salt. Cook, stirring, until softened, 3 to 5 minutes. Add the quinoa and cook, stirring, until fragrant and beginning to pop, about 5 minutes. Stir in the ginger and cumin. Cook, stirring, for 1 minute. Add the carrot juice, ¾ cup water and ½ teaspoon salt. Bring to a boil. Cover, reduce to medium-low and cook until the liquid is absorbed, 11 to 13 minutes.

2. Remove the pan from the heat and uncover. Sprinkle in the dates, cover the pan with a kitchen towel and replace the lid. Let sit for 10 minutes. Fluff the quinoa with a fork, then add the almonds or cashews, scallions, dill, lemon zest and juice. Stir gently to combine, season with salt and pepper, then garnish with dill and a drizzle of olive oil, if desired.

CHANGE THE WAY YOU COOK:
ADD FLAVOR, NOT WATER, WHEN COOKING GRAINS

Substituting another, more flavorful liquid for the water typically used to cook grains is a simple way to boost flavor. We cook quinoa in diluted carrot juice, which mitigates its subtle bitterness.

Thai Fried Rice

Start to finish: 20 minutes / Servings: 4

1 tablespoon fish sauce

1 teaspoon soy sauce

1 teaspoon white sugar

4 cups cooked and chilled
jasmine rice

1 tablespoon peanut or
vegetable oil

2 eggs, lightly beaten

4 ounces thinly sliced
pancetta, chopped

4 scallions, white and green
parts thinly sliced, reserved
separately

1 large shallot, minced

1 garlic clove, minced

¼ cup chopped fresh cilantro

Sliced cucumber and lime
wedges, to serve

Cooked in under five minutes in the open-air kitchen of his home in Thailand, chef Andy Ricker's fried rice was speedy, simple—and delicious. Pork belly, shallot and garlic added bold flavors. Soy and fish sauces added savory depth. Fresh herbs kept everything bright and light. We returned to Milk Street and got to work deconstructing Thai cooking. Ricker prefers to use a wok because it allows him to move food away from the hot oil at the center to the cooler sides of the pan. In a nod to the Western kitchen, we began with a large nonstick skillet, though you can use a wok if you have one (and a burner powerful enough to heat it). Pork belly can be hard to find in the U.S. Looking for a substitute we found ground pork too greasy and bacon too smoky. Pancetta—if culturally odd—was just right, which makes sense since it's cured pork belly. In a skillet, we had to reverse-engineer the process and move foods in and out, starting with the eggs, then the pancetta. We liked the aromatic flavor of jasmine rice, but long-grain white or basmati work, too. If you have no leftover rice, follow our recipe (see sidebar). Thai restaurants offer condiments for fried rice, including sliced green chilies in white vinegar. We came up with our own (p. 523). Use it with the fried rice or any dish that needs a hit of gentle heat and acid.

Don't use hot or warm rice. The fried rice will be clumpy and gummy (see sidebar).

1. In a bowl, stir together the fish sauce, soy sauce, 1 teaspoon water and sugar. Set aside. Use your hands to break up the rice so no clumps remain. Set aside.

2. In a 12-inch nonstick skillet over medium-high, heat the oil until barely smoking. Pour in the eggs and cook, stirring, until just set. Transfer the eggs to a plate. Add the pancetta to the skillet and cook over medium until crisp. Using a slotted spoon, transfer to the plate with the eggs.

3. Pour off all but 1 tablespoon of the fat from the skillet and return to medium-high. Add the scallion whites, shallot and garlic and cook until softened, about 1 minute. Add the rice and cook, stirring occasionally, until heated through, about 2 minutes.

4. Stir the fish sauce mixture, then pour over the rice. Cook, stirring, until well mixed. Stir in the egg and pancetta, breaking up the eggs. Transfer to a large platter and sprinkle with cilantro and scallion greens. Serve with cucumber, lime wedges and fish sauce–pickled chilies (p. 523), if desired.

RICE AT THE READY

While our Thai fried rice takes just minutes to prepare, it does require cooked-and-cooled plain rice. Warm, freshly cooked rice won't work; it sticks to the pan and turns gummy. For rice to fry, its starches must first cool and recrystallize. Fresh rice needed two hours minimum to chill adequately, but it can be prepared up to three days in advance and kept refrigerated. For real make-ahead convenience, cooked rice also can be frozen. Make a batch or two, then freeze in zip-close plastic bags.

Rice for Thai Fried Rice

Start to finish: 20 minutes, plus cooling
Makes 4 cups

2 cups water

1½ cups jasmine rice, rinsed

½ teaspoon kosher salt

Line a rimmed baking sheet with kitchen parchment and lightly coat it with vegetable oil. In a large saucepan, combine the water, rice and salt. Bring to a simmer, then reduce to low, cover and cook until tender and fluffy, 15 to 18 minutes. Fluff with a fork, then spread on the prepared baking sheet. Let cool, then cover and refrigerate until cold.

Coconut Rice

Start to finish: 35 minutes (10 minutes active)
Servings: 4

---

2 tablespoons coconut oil,
preferably unrefined

½ cup unsweetened shredded
coconut

1½ cups jasmine rice, rinsed

14-ounce can coconut milk, shaken

1 teaspoon kosher salt

Plain rice needs to be paired with a flavorful counterpoint, otherwise it's just a bowl of bland. Fiery curries, for example, are a great partner. But what if you're not into (or in the mood for) heat? We found our flavor in coconut rice, a dish popular in India and Southeast Asia, where it appears in many forms. It's quick and easy to assemble and has layers of flavor. We start by toasting unsweetened coconut in coconut oil, which gave us a pleasant texture as well as flavor. The rice went in next and we added unsweetened coconut milk at two stages: as the rice cooked and at the very end. We chose jasmine rice for its aromatic flavor. Gentle heat ensured the liquid wouldn't boil over and the rice wouldn't burn on the bottom. Our finished rice made the perfect accompaniment to grilled or roasted meats and fish. We like to cook extra and use leftovers in fried rice, salads or to pair with fried eggs for breakfast. It's even good as a sweet snack with a sprinkle of brown sugar or drizzle of honey.

Don't use a small saucepan. If the cooking liquid bubbles over, the sugar will cause it to smoke and burn. A medium or large heavy-bottomed saucepan was best.

1. In a medium saucepan over medium, combine the oil and shredded coconut. Cook, stirring, until lightly toasted, 1 to 2 minutes. Add the rice and cook, stirring, until some of the grains are translucent and a few begin to pop, about 2 minutes. Stir in ¾ cup water, all but 2 tablespoons of the coconut milk and the salt.

2. Bring to a simmer, stirring and scraping the bottom of the pan frequently. Reduce heat to low, cover and cook until the liquid is absorbed, 15 to 18 minutes. Remove from the heat and let sit, covered, for 5 minutes. Drizzle in the reserved coconut milk, then fluff and stir.

Japanese-Style Rice with Flaked Salmon and Shiitake Mushrooms (*Sake to Kinoko Takikomi Gohan*)

Start to finish: **50 minutes (20 minutes active)** / Servings: **4**

¼ cup soy sauce

3 tablespoons sake

1 tablespoon mirin

One 6-ounce skinless salmon fillet

2 cups Japanese-style short-grain white rice, rinsed well and drained

4 ounces fresh shiitake mushrooms, stemmed and thinly sliced

3 scallions, thinly sliced on diagonal, whites and greens reserved separately

Kosher salt

Lemon wedges, to serve

This recipe is our version of a dish we learned from Elizabeth Andoh. The salmon here is thinly sliced and marinated in a mixture of soy sauce, sake and mirin, and it serves more as a flavoring for the rice than as a feature protein. After the fish marinates, the soy mixture is repurposed as a seasoning for the rice as it steams. Layering the salmon slices onto the rice after cooking and giving the rice a final quick burst of medium-high heat ensures the fish doesn't dry out. If you like, serve the rice with lemon wedges and additional soy sauce.

Don't use a saucepan with a loose-fitting lid. For the rice to cook properly, the lid must fit securely. If the lid has a vent hole, plug it with a bit of foil to prevent steam from escaping.

1. In a small bowl, stir together the soy sauce, sake and mirin. Holding your knife at a 45-degree angle to the cutting board, cut the salmon crosswise into ⅛-inch-thick slices. Add to the soy sauce mixture and gently toss. Cover and refrigerate for at least 20 minutes or up to 1 hour.

2. In a medium saucepan, combine the rice, mushrooms, scallion whites, 1 teaspoon salt and 1¾ cups water. Drain the salmon marinade into the rice and stir to combine; return the salmon to the refrigerator. Cover the pan and bring to a boil over high; this should take about 5 minutes. Reduce to low and cook for another 5 minutes.

3. Without lifting the lid, remove the pot from the heat and let stand for at least 10 minutes or up to 30 minutes. Uncover and arrange the salmon slices in an even layer on the surface of the rice. Cover and cook over medium-high until the salmon begins to turn opaque at the edges, about 1 minute. Remove from heat and let stand, covered, until the salmon is fully opaque, another 1 to 2 minutes.

4. Run a silicone spatula around the edge of the pan to loosen the rice. Gently lift and fluff the grains, flaking the fish and mixing it into the rice. Make sure to scrape along the bottom of the pan. Spoon into bowls, sprinkle with the scallion greens and serve with lemon wedges.

Middle Eastern Rice
with Toasted Pasta and Herbs

Start to finish: **25 minutes** / Servings: 4

4 tablespoons (½ stick)
salted butter, divided

1 ounce vermicelli pasta, broken into
1-inch pieces (generous ⅓ cup)

1 cup basmati rice, rinsed and drained

1⅔ cups low-sodium chicken broth

4 tablespoons lightly packed
fresh dill, chopped, divided

4 tablespoons lightly packed
fresh parsley, chopped, divided

Kosher salt and ground black pepper

¼ cup toasted sliced almonds

The combination of rice and pasta, introduced to the U.S. in the mid-20th century as Rice-A-Roni, is based on a classic Middle Eastern pilaf often served as a side dish with meat. Toasting the dry pasta in butter is key; it caramelizes some of the starch molecules, adding color and forming nutty flavors. We prefer thin vermicelli pasta, but thin spaghetti or angel hair (capellini) work well, too. We add the vermicelli halfway through the cooking to make sure the noodles don't overcook. We finish the dish with herbs and toasted sliced almonds. Toast the almonds in a small skillet over medium, stirring often, until browned and fragrant, 3 to 5 minutes.

Don't forget to rinse and drain the rice. Rinsing removes excess starch that can make the cooked grains sticky instead of light and fluffy.

1. In a large saucepan over medium, melt 2 tablespoons of butter. Add the pasta and cook, stirring frequently, until the noodles are deeply browned, about 5 minutes. Transfer to a small bowl and set aside.

2. In the same pan, combine the rice and broth, then set over medium-high. Bring to a boil, then reduce to low, cover and cook for 8 minutes. Stir in the toasted pasta. Cover and continue to cook until all of the liquid has been absorbed, about another 7 minutes.

3. Off heat, stir in the remaining 2 tablespoons butter and 2 tablespoons each of dill and parsley. Taste and season with salt and pepper. Transfer to a bowl and sprinkle with the remaining herbs and the almonds.

CHANGE THE WAY YOU COOK:
CARAMELIZE PASTA FOR DEEPER, RICHER FLAVOR

Toasting dry pasta caramelizes some of the starches, producing nutty flavors similar to caramelized sugar.

Coconut-Ginger Rice

Start to finish: **30 minutes** / Servings: 4

1 tablespoon coconut oil
(preferably unrefined)

2 medium shallots, halved
and thinly sliced

1-inch piece fresh ginger, peeled,
sliced into thirds and lightly bruised

1 stalk lemon grass, trimmed to the
lower 6 inches, dry outer leaves
discarded, lightly bruised

1½ cups jasmine rice, rinsed
and drained

½ cup coconut milk

Kosher salt

Jasmine rice steamed with shallots, ginger, lemon grass and coconut yields a richly aromatic side dish that's perfect with Southeast Asian mains, such as seafood curries. Rice cooked with all coconut milk was too rich and heavy. A combination of water and coconut milk made for fluffy grains that were light yet robustly flavored. Using unrefined coconut oil reinforced the coconut flavor.

Don't use the rice without first rinsing and draining. Rinsing removes excess starch that would otherwise make the cooked grains heavy and gluey.

1. In a large saucepan over medium-high, heat the oil until barely smoking. Add the shallots and cook, stirring frequently, until lightly browned, 3 to 5 minutes. Stir in the ginger and lemon grass and cook until fragrant, about 30 seconds.

2. Stir in the rice, 1½ cups water, the coconut milk and 1 teaspoon salt, then bring to a simmer. Cover, reduce to low and cook until the rice absorbs the liquid, 15 to 20 minutes.

3. Remove and discard the ginger and lemon grass, then fluff the rice with a fork. Taste and season with salt.

Herb-and-Pistachio Couscous

Start to finish: **30 minutes** / Servings: 6

1 cup couscous

3 tablespoons dried currants

½ teaspoon ground cumin

Kosher salt and ground black pepper

¾ cup boiling water

6 tablespoons extra-virgin olive oil, divided, plus more for serving

2 cups lightly packed fresh cilantro leaves and tender stems

2 cups lightly packed fresh flat-leaf parsley leaves

2 tablespoons finely chopped pickled jalapeños, plus 2 teaspoons brine

2 ounces baby arugula, coarsely chopped (about 2 cups)

½ cup shelled pistachios, toasted and chopped

2 scallions, trimmed and thinly sliced

Couscous may be fast and convenient to prepare, but it's also pretty dull. And the traditional method of infusing it with flavor—steaming it in a special pot over a flavorful liquid—just isn't happening. We found a better way by undercooking—technically underhydrating—the couscous by preparing it with less water than typically called for. We then combine the couscous with a flavorful paste made from oil and pureed fresh herbs. The "thirsty" couscous absorbs tons of flavor as it finishes hydrating. Inspired by a recipe from Yotam Ottolenghi, we piled on the herbs—2 cups each of cilantro and flat-leaf parsley plus another 2 cups of arugula. We also added currants as we doused the couscous with boiling water, giving them time to plump. Jalapeños brought a spicy kick; we used pickled peppers, which have more consistent heat and contributed welcome piquancy. Toasted pistachios and thinly sliced scallions added a finishing crunch. The couscous pairs well with most any meat, though it is particularly good with salmon.

Don't use Israeli (also called pearl) couscous, which won't hydrate sufficiently in this recipe.

1. In a large bowl, combine the couscous, currants, cumin and ¼ teaspoon each salt and black pepper. Stir in the boiling water and 1 tablespoon of the oil, then cover and let sit for 10 minutes.

2. Meanwhile, in a food processor, combine the cilantro, parsley, the remaining 5 tablespoons of oil, the jalapeño brine and ¼ teaspoon salt. Process until a smooth paste forms, about 1 minute, scraping down the bowl 2 or 3 times.

3. Fluff the couscous with a fork, breaking up any large clumps, then stir in the herb paste until thoroughly combined. Fold in the jalapeños, arugula, pistachios and scallions, then let sit for 10 minutes. Season with salt and pepper. Serve at room temperature, drizzled with oil.

Indian Tomato Rice

Start to finish: **35 minutes (15 minutes active)**
Servings: 4

---

1 cup white basmati rice, rinsed and drained

2 tablespoons tomato paste

2 tablespoons grapeseed or other neutral oil

1 teaspoon cumin seeds

1 teaspoon coriander seeds

1 teaspoon brown or black mustard seeds

2 bird's eye chilies, stemmed and halved lengthwise (optional)

1 garlic clove, finely grated

1 teaspoon finely grated fresh ginger

1½ teaspoons kosher salt

½ pound cherry or grape tomatoes, quartered

¼ cup chopped fresh cilantro leaves

Robust tomato flavor is key to this popular southern Indian dish, typically prepared when there is an abundance of ripe, red tomatoes and leftover basmati rice. It can be eaten as a light meal with a dollop of yogurt or pairs well with seafood, poultry or even a simple fried egg. We needed a year-round recipe, so we concentrated on finding the best way to impart deep tomato flavor. A combination of cherry or grape tomatoes and tomato paste was best. We also focused on making sure the rice was cooked properly, fluffy and tender with each grain separate. We were inspired by Madhur Jaffrey's tomato rice recipe in "Vegetarian India," though we upped the intensity of both the spices and tomato flavor. We preferred brown or black mustard seeds for their pungency; if you substitute yellow mustard seeds, increase the volume to 1½ teaspoons. Serrano chilies can be used in place of bird's eye chilies, also called Thai bird or Thai chilies. Or you can leave them out entirely. If your pan does not have a tight-fitting lid, cover it with foil before putting the lid in place.

Don't skip soaking the rice. This traditional approach to cooking the rice gives it time to expand gently and cook up in tender, separate grains.

1. In a bowl, combine the rinsed rice with enough cold water to cover by 1 inch. Let soak for 15 minutes. Drain the rice very well. In a 2-cup liquid measuring cup, combine 1¼ cups water and the tomato paste and whisk until dissolved. Set aside.

2. In a large saucepan over medium, combine the oil, cumin, coriander, mustard seeds, chilies, garlic and ginger. Cook until the seeds begin to pop and the mixture is fragrant, about 1 minute.

3. Stir in the rice and salt and cook, stirring, until coated with oil, about 30 seconds. Stir in the water-tomato paste mixture and bring to a simmer. Cover, reduce heat to low and cook until the water has been absorbed, about 15 minutes. Remove from the heat, add the tomatoes and let sit, covered, for 5 minutes. Stir in the cilantro, fluffing the rice with a fork.

Risotto with Fresh Herbs

Start to finish: **25 minutes** / Servings: 4

3½ cups vegetable broth
(see recipe p. 157)

6 tablespoons (¾ stick) salted
butter, cut into 1-tablespoon
pieces, divided

1 cup carnaroli or Arborio rice

1 ounce Parmesan cheese,
finely grated (½ cup)

2 teaspoons minced fresh
thyme

⅓ cup thinly sliced scallions

¼ cup finely chopped parsley

½ teaspoon grated lemon zest

Kosher salt

4 teaspoons white
balsamic vinegar

Medium-grain Italian rice has the ideal starch content for achieving the rich, creamy consistency that is the hallmark of risotto. Arborio rice is the most common choice for risotto in the U.S., but cooks in Milan—and at Milk Street—preferred carnaroli. We found that the grains better retained their structure and resisted overcooking. With careful cooking, however, Arborio will yield delicious results. A quick six-ingredient homemade vegetable broth is the best cooking liquid for this risotto; its fresh, clean flavor won't compete with the delicate herbs. Serve in warmed, shallow bowls to prevent the rice from cooling too quickly. If you want to try Milan's signature saffron version, which pairs well with roasted and braised meats, see the following variation.

Don't cook the rice to the ideal al dente texture before removing the pan from the burner. The grains will continue to cook with residual heat as the cheese and butter are stirred in.

1. In a small saucepan over medium, bring the broth, covered, to a simmer. Reduce to low to keep warm.

2. In a large saucepan over medium-high, melt 2 tablespoons of butter. Add the rice and cook, stirring constantly, until translucent at the edges, 1 to 2 minutes. Add 2½ cups of the remaining hot broth and bring to a boil, then reduce to medium and cook, stirring frequently and briskly, until the grains are almost tender but still quite firm at the core it will be quite soupy), 8 to 10 minutes; adjust the heat as needed to maintain a vigorous simmer.

3. Add ½ cup broth and cook, stirring frequently and briskly, until the rice is just shy of al dente but still soupy, 3 to 5 minutes. If the rice is thick and dry but the grains are still too firm, add the remaining hot broth in ¼-cup increments and continue to cook, stirring, until the rice is just shy of al dente.

4. Off heat, stir in the Parmesan, thyme, scallions, parsley, lemon zest, ½ teaspoon salt and the remaining 4 tablespoons butter, 1 piece at a time. Taste and season with salt, then stir in the vinegar. Serve immediately.

SAFFRON VARIATION
(RISOTTO MILANESE):

Prepare the vegetable-Parmesan broth for risotto, substituting 2 medium carrots (peeled and chopped) for the Parmesan rind, decreasing the garlic to 1 clove, and omitting the parsley. Follow the risotto recipe, adding 1 teaspoon saffron threads to the reserved ½ cup hot broth. When adding the Parmesan at the end, omit the thyme, scallions and chopped parsley.

EASY VEGETABLE-
PARMESAN BROTH

This simple vegetarian broth can be made in about 30 minutes. Use immediately after straining or cool to room temperature, cover and refrigerate for up to five days.

Don't simmer the broth uncovered. Partially covering the pan prevents excessive evaporation, but allows for some concentration of flavors.

Start to finish: **30 minutes**
Makes **about 1 quart**

One 1-ounce chunk of Parmesan rind

2 large celery stalks, chopped

1 medium yellow onion, chopped

1 medium tomato, roughly chopped

3 large garlic cloves, smashed and peeled

1 cup lightly packed fresh flat-leaf parsley

In a large saucepan over high, combine all ingredients with 5 cups water and bring to a boil. Partially cover, then reduce to medium and cook for 20 minutes, adjusting the heat to maintain a lively simmer.

Pour the broth through a fine mesh stainer into a large bowl; discard the solids. You should have about 1 quart of broth.

Lebanese Lentils and Rice
with Crisped Onions (*Mujaddara*)

Start to finish: **50 minutes** / Servings: 4

4 medium garlic cloves, smashed and peeled

4 bay leaves

2½ teaspoons ground cumin

½ teaspoon ground allspice

Kosher salt and ground black pepper

1 cup brown lentils, rinsed and drained

1 cup basmati rice, rinsed and drained

⅓ cup extra-virgin olive oil

2 medium yellow onions, halved and thinly sliced

1 bunch scallions, thinly sliced

Plain whole-milk yogurt, to serve

Rice and lentils with caramelized onions is a much-loved food in the Middle East. This is our take on the version we tasted in Lebanon, where the dish is called mujaddara. The rice and lentils are simmered together in the same pot, with the lentils getting a 10-minute head start so both finish at the same time. Meanwhile, the onions are fried until crisp and deeply caramelized—almost burnt, really—to coax out a savory bittersweet flavor. Serve hot, warm or at room temperature with a dollop of plain yogurt. It's a delicious accompaniment to grilled or roasted meats, but it's also hearty enough to be the center of a vegetarian meal.

Don't use French green lentils (lentils du Puy) in place of the brown lentils called for. Even when fully cooked, green lentils retain a firm, almost al dente texture, while brown lentils take on a softness that combines well with the rice. Don't worry if the onions turn quite dark at the edge of the skillet; deep browning is desirable. But do stir the browned bits into the mix to ensure the onions color evenly. However, if the onions brown deeply before they soften, lower the heat a notch or two and keep stirring until the pan cools slightly.

1. In a large Dutch oven over medium-high, combine 5 cups water, the garlic, bay, cumin, allspice, 1 tablespoon salt and 1 teaspoon pepper. Bring to a boil, then stir in the lentils and reduce to medium. Cover and cook, stirring occasionally and adjusting the heat to maintain a simmer, until the lentils are softened but still quite firm at the center, about 10 minutes.

2. Stir in the rice and return to a simmer. Cover, reduce to medium-low and cook until the liquid is absorbed and the lentils and rice are tender, about 25 minutes.

3. Meanwhile, in a 12-inch skillet over medium-high, heat the oil until shimmering. Add the onions and cook, stirring only occasionally at the start then more frequently once browning begins at the edges of the pan, until

the onions are deeply caramelized and crisped, 10 to 15 minutes; adjust the heat if the onions brown too quickly. Using a slotted spoon, transfer the onions to a paper towel–lined plate and spread evenly. Sprinkle with ¼ teaspoon salt and set aside; the onions will crisp as they cool.

4. When the lentils and rice are tender, remove the pot from the heat. Uncover and lay a kitchen towel across the pan, then replace the lid and let stand for 10 minutes.

5. Using a fork, fluff the lentils and rice, removing and discarding the bay. Taste and season with salt and pepper. Stir in half the scallions, then transfer to a serving bowl. Top with the fried onions and remaining scallions. Serve hot, warm or at room temperature with yogurt on the side.

CHANGE THE WAY YOU COOK:
FRY ONIONS FOR CARAMELIZED FLAVOR AND CRISP TEXTURE

Frying onions in a small amount of oil until crisp and deeply caramelized is an easy way to add bittersweet flavor and contrasting texture to grain and vegetable dishes. Also try crisped onions as a garnish for soups, salads and noodles.

Noodles

Campanelle Pasta with
Sweet Corn, Tomatoes and Basil / 163

Yakiudon with Pickled Ginger / 164

Spaghetti al Limone / 167

Chinese Chili-and-Scallion Noodles / 169

Pasta con Fagioli / 170

Gemelli Pasta with Chévre,
Arugula and Walnuts / 173

Pasta all'Amatriciana / 175

Pasta with Pistachios,
Tomatoes and Mint / 177

Pasta with Peruvian Pesto
(*Tallarines Verdes*) / 178

Soba Noodles with Asparagus,
Miso Butter and Egg / 180

Potato Gnocchi with Butter,
Sage and Chives / 182

Pasta with Trapanese Pesto / 185

Pasta with Pesto alla Genovese / 186

Spaghetti with Anchovies,
Pine Nuts and Raisins / 189

Whole-Wheat Pasta with
Yogurt and Tahini / 191

Spaghetti with Lemon,
Anchovies and Capers / 193

Cacio e Pepe / 195

Spaghetti with Pancetta
(*Pasta alla Gricia*) / 196

Roman Spaghetti Carbonara / 199

6

Campanelle Pasta with Sweet Corn, Tomatoes and Basil

Start to finish: **30 minutes** / Servings: 4

1 pint grape or cherry tomatoes, halved

Kosher salt and ground black pepper

4 ears corn, husked

4 tablespoons (½ stick) salted butter, cut in 1-tablespoon pieces, divided

2 medium shallots, minced

1 habanero chili, stemmed, seeded and minced

12 ounces campanelle or other short pasta

1 cup lightly packed fresh basil, sliced

The ingredients in this summery pasta dish are few, so using fresh corn and ripe tomatoes is key. To create a creamy sauce without cream, we grate the corn kernels from the cobs. To reinforce the corn flavor, we boil the grated cobs in a minimal amount of water—just 2½ quarts—that's also used to cook the pasta, concentrating the flavors and starches in the corn-infused liquid. We put some of that liquid to further use by stirring it into a corn-shallot sauce. Yellow corn gives the dish a golden hue, but white corn works, too. Whichever you use, make sure to remove as much of the silk as possible before grating.

Don't fear the habanero in this dish. It does add a little heat, but seeding the chili removes much of its burn. It's here as a fruity complement to the corn, tomatoes and basil.

1. In a small bowl, stir together the tomatoes and ½ teaspoon salt; set aside. Set a box grater in a large bowl or pie plate. Using the grater's large holes, grate the corn down to the cobs; reserve the cobs.

2. In a large pot, bring 2½ quarts water to a boil. Add the corn cobs and 1 tablespoon salt, reduce to medium and cook, covered, for 10 minutes. Using tongs, remove and discard the cobs, then remove the pot from the heat.

3. In a 12-inch nonstick skillet over medium, melt 2 tablespoons of butter. Add the grated corn, shallots, habanero and 1 teaspoon salt. Cook, stirring, until the shallots have softened, about 5 minutes. Stir in 1½ cups of the cooking liquid. Cook over medium-low, uncovered and stirring occasionally, until slightly thickened (a spatula should leave a trail when drawn through the mixture), 10 to 15 minutes.

4. Meanwhile, return the remaining corn-infused water to a boil. Add the pasta and cook, stirring occasionally, until al dente. Reserve 1 cup of the cooking water, then drain the pasta. Add the pasta to the skillet and cook over medium, stirring constantly, until the pasta is coated and the sauce is creamy, about 2 minutes; if needed, add the reserved cooking water 2 tablespoons at a time to reach proper consistency.

5. Off heat, add the remaining 2 tablespoons butter, basil and tomatoes with their juice, then toss until the butter has melted. Taste and season with salt and pepper.

CHANGE THE WAY YOU COOK:
CREATE CREAMINESS WITHOUT CREAM

A creamy sauce doesn't have to be made with cream. Grating corn kernels releases their milky pulp and starches to create the base of a rich sauce, as in our pasta with sweet corn, tomatoes and basil.

Yakiudon with Pickled Ginger

Start to finish: 45 minutes / Servings: 4

12 ounces dried udon noodles

2 tablespoons plus 2 teaspoons grapeseed or other neutral oil, divided

¼ cup soy sauce

2 tablespoons mirin

1 teaspoon white sugar

3 small dried shiitake mushrooms, broken in half

8 ounces fresh shiitake mushrooms, stemmed, halved if large, thinly sliced

1 small yellow onion, halved and thinly sliced

2 medium garlic cloves, minced

12 ounces baby bok choy, trimmed and sliced crosswise ½ inch thick

Ground white pepper

2 scallions, thinly sliced on diagonal

1 tablespoon sesame seeds, toasted

Shichimi togarashi, to serve (optional)

Pickled ginger, to serve (see recipe page 165)

This Japanese stir-fried noodle dish is largely about the chew, which comes from hearty wheat udon noodles. We got the dense chewiness we wanted by using the Italian technique of cooking until al dente—still quite firm. Japanese noodles often are rinsed after cooking, and chilling helps prevent them from turning soggy. We streamlined the process by adding ice to the strainer as we rinsed the udon under cold running water. Fresh udon is sold frozen, refrigerated and in shelf-stable packages, but for this recipe we used dried noodles, which are more widely available. The sharp bite of pickled ginger complements the salty, savory noodles. If you're not up to making your own, look for jars of it in the grocery store's Asian section. Also in that section: shichimi togarashi, a Japanese spice blend for sprinkling on at the table to add a little heat.

Don't fully cook the udon. *Check for doneness well before the cooking time suggested on the package.*

1. In a large pot, bring 4 quarts of water to a boil. Add the udon, stir well and cook until al dente. Drain in a colander, then add 2 cups ice to the noodles. Run under cool water, tossing, until chilled. Drain well, then transfer to a large bowl. Toss with 2 teaspoons of oil; set aside.

2. In a small saucepan over medium, combine the soy sauce, ¼ cup water, the mirin and sugar. Bring to a simmer, stirring, then add the dried mushrooms, pushing them into the liquid. Remove from the heat, cover and set aside until the mushrooms have softened and cooled, 20 to 30 minutes.

3. Remove the mushrooms from the soy sauce mixture, squeezing them to allow any liquid to drip back into the pan. Remove and discard the stems, then finely chop. Transfer to a medium bowl and set aside.

4. In a large nonstick skillet over medium-high, heat 1 tablespoon of the remaining oil. Add the fresh mushrooms and cook, stirring occasionally, until lightly browned and slightly shrunken, about 3 minutes. Add the onion, drizzle with the remaining 1 tablespoon oil and cook, stirring occasionally, until softened, about 3 minutes. Stir in the garlic and cook until fragrant, about 30 seconds. Add the bok choy and cook, stirring, until the leaves are wilted and the stem pieces are crisp-tender, about 2 minutes. Transfer to the bowl with the chopped dried shiitakes.

5. Set the now-empty skillet over medium and add the udon, gently tossing with tongs. Add the vegetable mixture, gently toss, then add the soy sauce mixture and ½ teaspoon pepper. Cook, tossing constantly, until the noodles are heated and have absorbed most of the liquid, about 2 minutes. Transfer to serving bowls and sprinkle with scallions and sesame seeds. Serve with shichimi togarashi, if using, and pickled ginger.

PICKLED GINGER

Look for large, plump, chunky pieces of fresh ginger without many nubs; they will be easier to peel and slice. A mandoline works well for slicing, but a Y-style peeler works, too.

Don't cut thick slices of ginger. They can be tough and chewy.

Start to finish: **40 minutes (10 minutes active)** Makes 1⅓ cup

¾ cup unseasoned rice vinegar

¼ cup water

2 tablespoons white sugar

1 teaspoon kosher salt

4 ounces fresh ginger, peeled and sliced paper thin

In a small bowl, stir together the vinegar, water, sugar and salt. Stir in the ginger. Cover and refrigerate for 30 minutes or for up to 1 week.

Spaghetti al Limone

Start to finish: **15 minutes** / Servings: 4

5 tablespoons salted butter, divided

8 medium garlic cloves, minced

1 teaspoon red pepper flakes

¾ cup dry white wine

12 ounces spaghetti

Kosher salt and ground black pepper

¾ cup finely chopped fresh flat-leaf parsley or basil

2 tablespoons grated lemon zest, plus 3 tablespoons lemon juice

Grated Parmesan cheese, to serve

This simple dish may have few ingredients, but it boasts bold, bright flavors. Many versions include cream, but we preferred to use a little butter and some of the starchy spaghetti-cooking water; this gave the pasta a saucy consistency and light creaminess that didn't mute the freshness of the lemon. Feel free to switch out linguine for the spaghetti and adjust the lemon zest and juice to your taste.

Don't cook the pasta until al dente. Drain it when it's a minute or two shy of al dente; it will continue to cook in the skillet.

1. In a 12-inch skillet over medium, melt 3 tablespoons of the butter. Add the garlic and cook, stirring constantly, until fragrant, about 30 seconds. Add the pepper flakes and cook, stirring constantly, until the garlic begins to turn golden, about 1 minute. Pour in the wine and cook until reduced to about ½ cup, about 3 minutes. Remove from the heat and set aside.

2. In a large pot, bring 2 quarts of water to a boil. Stir in 1 tablespoon salt and the pasta; cook until just shy of al dente. Reserve 2 cups of the cooking water, then drain and set aside.

3. Set the skillet with the garlic mixture over medium-high, stir in 1½ cups of the reserved pasta water and bring to a simmer. Add the drained pasta and toss. Cook, stirring, until most of the liquid has been absorbed, 2 to 3 minutes.

4. Off heat, stir in the remaining 2 tablespoons butter, 1 teaspoon black pepper, the lemon juice and zest, and the parsley. Taste and season with salt and, if needed, adjust the consistency ~by ading additional pasta water a few tablespoons at a time. Transfer to a serving bowl and serve with grated Parmesan.

CHANGE THE WAY YOU COOK:
PUT PASTA WATER TO WORK

Don't throw pasta water down the drain. The starchy liquid is a great way to create sauces that coat and cling to the cooked noodles.

Chinese Chili-and-Scallion **Noodles**

Start to finish: **40 minutes (20 minutes active)**
Servings: 4

---

12 ounces udon noodles,
lo mein or spaghetti

5 tablespoons soy sauce

3 tablespoons unseasoned
rice vinegar

3 tablespoons packed dark
brown sugar

1 tablespoon toasted sesame oil

¼ cup grapeseed or other
neutral oil

5 teaspoons sesame seeds

1¼ teaspoons red pepper flakes

12 scallions, white and green parts
thinly sliced on diagonal, reserved
separately

4 fried eggs, to serve (optional)

Every cook needs a few back-pocket recipes that can be thrown together quickly from pantry staples. Think spaghetti carbonara, the Italian pasta dish of bacon and eggs. Or Fuchsia Dunlop's game-changing "midnight noodles," a fresh spin on a Chinese staple. The simple sauce comes together in the time it takes the noodles to cook. Our version swaps out some of the hard-to-find Chinese ingredients and creates a simple chili oil that can be adjusted to taste. We cooked scallion whites in the hot oil to soften their bite and used the milder green parts to add brightness at the end. While we preferred udon noodles, chewy Chinese wheat noodles such as lo mein were fine substitutes. Even spaghetti worked in a pinch. These noodles also are great topped with a fried egg, see our recipe (p. 23).

Don't walk away while heating the oil. The sesame seeds can burn in an instant, and the red pepper flakes will blacken and become bitter. The seeds should be just turning golden, and the pepper flakes should be pleasantly fragrant.

1. Bring a large pot of well-salted water to a boil. Add the noodles and cook until al dente, then drain. Meanwhile, in a large bowl whisk together the soy sauce, vinegar, sugar and sesame oil.

2. In a large nonstick skillet over medium, heat the grapeseed oil, sesame seeds and pepper flakes until the pepper flakes are fragrant and the sesame seeds begin to brown, 3 to 5 minutes. Off heat, stir in the scallion whites, then transfer the oil mixture to the bowl with the soy sauce mixture.

3. Add the cooked pasta to the sauce and toss. Add the scallion greens, reserving some for garnish, and toss. Divide among 4 serving bowls and top each with more scallion greens and a fried egg, if desired.

Pasta con Fagioli

Start to finish: **35 minutes** / Servings: 6

8 ounces campanelle or
other short pasta

Kosher salt and ground black pepper

5 tablespoons extra-virgin olive oil,
divided, plus more to serve

2 pints grape or cherry tomatoes

1 large red onion, chopped

1 large fennel bulb, halved, cored
and thinly sliced

4 medium garlic cloves, minced

1 tablespoon minced fresh rosemary

1 teaspoon fennel seeds

¾ teaspoon red pepper flakes

Two 15½-ounce cans Roman
(borlotti) beans, drained but not
rinsed (see note)

2 cups low-sodium chicken broth

2 teaspoons grated lemon zest,
plus 2 tablespoons lemon juice

2 ounces Pecorino romano cheese,
grated (1 cup)

We thought this rustic pasta and bean dish from Sicily would feel heavy, but the starches are lightened by tomatoes, rosemary and lemon. In Italy, dried borlotti beans (often called cranberry beans in the U.S.) are used. For weeknight ease, we opted for canned beans. Some producers label canned borlotti beans as "Roman beans." If you cannot find them, use pink or kidney beans, which have a similar creaminess and mildly sweet flavor. Don't use cannellini beans, which are too tender. The pasta is boiled only until very slightly softened, then drained and rinsed to stop the cooking. It finishes cooking when combined with the beans and vegetables.

Don't rinse the canned beans after draining them; the starchy liquid clinging to them adds body to the sauce.

1. In a large Dutch oven over medium-high, bring 2 quarts water to a boil. Add the pasta and 1 tablespoon salt. Cook, stirring occasionally, until just shy of al dente. Reserve 2 cups of cooking water, then drain and rinse with cold water until cool; set aside.

2. In the same pot over medium-high, heat 3 tablespoons of oil until barely smoking. Add the tomatoes, cover, reduce to medium and cook, stirring occasionally, until lightly charred, about 5 minutes. Add the onion, sliced fennel and ½ teaspoon salt, then cook on medium-high, stirring occasionally, until the vegetables begin to soften, about 5 minutes.

3. Add the garlic, rosemary, fennel seeds and pepper flakes, then cook, stirring, until fragrant, about 30 seconds. Add the beans, broth and ½ cup of the reserved cooking water. Bring to a simmer over medium-high. Cover, reduce to medium and cook, stirring once or twice, until the vegetables are tender, about 10 minutes.

4. Add the pasta and cook, stirring frequently, until the pasta is al dente and the sauce is creamy, 3 to 5 minutes. If needed, add additional cooking water, 1 tablespoon at a time, to reach the proper consistency. Off heat, stir in the lemon zest and juice and the remaining 2 tablespoons oil. Taste and season with salt and pepper. Serve with the cheese and additional oil for drizzling.

Gemelli Pasta with Chèvre, Arugula and Walnuts

Start to finish: **45 minutes** / Servings: **4**

12 ounces gemelli or casarecce pasta

Kosher salt

4 ounces chèvre (fresh goat cheese)

5 tablespoons extra-virgin olive oil

Red pepper flakes

4 ounces baby arugula (about 4 cups)

¾ cup walnuts, toasted and chopped

⅓ cup finely chopped fresh chives

Creamy pasta sauces pose two problems: They are finicky to make and they quickly decompose into a stringy or grainy mess. So when we came across a recipe that suggested using fresh goat cheese instead of the Parmesan called for in classic Alfredo and carbonara, we were intrigued. The notion was simple. The heat of freshly cooked pasta and a splash of its cooking water would dissolve the soft chèvre into a rich, smooth sauce in no time. Except it didn't work. The ingredients quickly broke down into a chalky mess. Then we discovered a technique by Marcella Hazan in which you first mix the cheese with oil. It worked wonderfully, but why? Goat's milk has more fat than cow's milk, so turning it into cheese requires the addition of acid. The acid forms the cheese curds but also creates strong water-insoluble bonds between the proteins. Hence our clumpy mess. But add oil to the chevre and those bonds slip apart, and the cheese melts easily. The same trick works for any acid-set cheese, such as ricotta, cottage and feta.

1. In a large pot, bring 4 quarts of water to a boil. Add the pasta and 2 tablespoons salt, then cook until al dente. Meanwhile, in a medium bowl, combine the cheese, oil and ¼ teaspoon each salt and red pepper flakes, stirring and mashing with a fork until smooth. Drain the pasta, reserving ¾ cup of the cooking water, then return the pasta to the pot.

2. Add the arugula, the goat cheese mixture and the reserved pasta cooking water, then toss until the cheese mixture is evenly distributed and the arugula begins to wilt.

3. Stir in the walnuts and chives, reserving a tablespoon of each for garnish, if desired, then season with additional salt and red pepper flakes. Transfer the pasta to a warmed serving bowl, then garnish with the remaining walnuts and chives.

Pasta all'Amatriciana

Start to finish: **30 minutes** / Servings: 4

3 tablespoons extra-virgin olive oil, divided

3 ounces thinly sliced pancetta, finely chopped

10 medium garlic cloves, thinly sliced

½ teaspoon red pepper flakes

¾ cup dry white wine

14½-ounce can whole peeled tomatoes, drained, juices reserved, tomatoes crushed by hand into small pieces

1-ounce chunk pecorino Romano cheese, plus more finely grated, to serve

Kosher salt and ground black pepper

12 ounces spaghetti

Amatriciana is a minimalist equation of pasta, tomatoes, guanciale and pecorino Romano cheese, and in Rome it's served with barely any sauce. The cooking method—using as little liquid as possible when cooking the sauce—concentrates flavors in the sauce, which coats the pasta nicely. We apply that principle for the pasta in this recipe, as well, cooking spaghetti in half the amount of water (2 quarts) we usually use. To that we add a chunk of pecorino Romano, which infuses the noodles with rich, savory flavor. We also undercook the pasta, allowing it to finish cooking in the sauce. One 14½-ounce can of whole tomatoes, drained and cooked down, is plenty to dress four servings. Likewise, just 3 ounces of pancetta—more widely available than guanciale—provides ample flavor. Be sure to purchase thinly sliced pancetta and chop it finely to ensure the pieces crisp well.

Don't boil the pasta until it's done. Drain it a minute or two shy of al dente; it will continue to cook when added to the sauce in the skillet.

1. In a 12-inch skillet over medium, heat 1 tablespoon of the oil until shimmering. Add the pancetta and cook, stirring, until well browned and crisp, 5 to 7 minutes. Using a slotted spoon, transfer to a paper towel-lined plate and set aside.

2. Return the skillet to medium and add the garlic; cook, stirring, until light golden brown, about 2 minutes. Stir in the pepper flakes and cook until fragrant, about 30 seconds. Add the wine, increase to medium-high and cook, stirring, until most of the liquid has evaporated, 5 to 7 minutes. Add the drained tomatoes and cook, stirring, until heated, about 2 minutes. Stir in 3 tablespoons of the reserved tomato juice, then remove from the heat.

3. Meanwhile, in a large pot, bring 2 quarts of water and the pecorino chunk to a boil, stirring occasionally to prevent the cheese from sticking to the pot. Stir in the pasta and 2 teaspoons salt. Cook, stirring often, until the pasta is just shy of al dente. Discard the pecorino, then drain the pasta in a colander set in a large heat-safe bowl; reserve the cooking water.

4. Set the skillet over medium-high, stir in 1½ cups of the reserved pasta water and bring to a simmer. Add the drained pasta, tossing with tongs. Cook, stirring occasionally, until most of the liquid has been absorbed, 3 to 6 minutes.

5. Off heat, stir in the remaining 2 table-spoons oil, 2 teaspoons black pepper and the pancetta. Transfer to a serving bowl and serve with grated pecorino on the side.

CHANGE THE WAY YOU COOK:
SUPER-STARCH YOUR PASTA

Create silkier, thicker sauces by cooking pasta and noodles in less water than typically called for, concentrating the starches that leach out of the flour and into the cooking water.

Pasta with Pistachios, Tomatoes and Mint

Start to finish: **20 minutes** / Servings: 4

12 ounces long pasta (see note)

Kosher salt and ground black pepper

¼ cup extra-virgin olive oil, plus more to serve

1 pint grape or cherry tomatoes, halved

½ cup shelled roasted pistachios, finely chopped

1 tablespoon grated lemon zest

2 tablespoons roughly chopped fresh mint

Grated Parmesan or pecorino Romano cheese, to serve

Sicily is known for its pistachios, so it's no surprise that the colorful, subtly sweet nuts feature heavily in the region's cuisine. This recipe is our take on a pistachio- and tomato-dressed pasta we tasted in Siracusa. With lemon zest and mint as accent ingredients, the flavors are fresh and bright. Just about any pasta shape worked well, but we particularly liked long strands, such as linguine and spaghetti.

Don't use raw pistachios; opt for roasted, as they don't require toasting before chopping. Either salted or unsalted worked well.

1. In a large pot, bring 4 quarts water to a boil. Add the pasta and 2 tablespoons salt, then cook, stirring occasionally, until just shy of al dente. Reserve about 2 cups of the cooking water, then drain the pasta.

2. In a 12-inch skillet over medium, combine the oil and tomatoes. Cook, stirring only once or twice, until the tomatoes have softened and the oil has taken on a reddish hue, 4 to 6 minutes. Stir in half the pistachios, 1½ cups of the reserved cooking water, ½ teaspoon salt and ¼ teaspoon pepper. Bring to a simmer and cook, stirring occasionally, until the mixture is slightly reduced and the tomatoes are completely softened, about 2 minutes.

3. Add the pasta and lemon zest, then cook, stirring frequently, until the pasta is al dente and has absorbed most of the liquid but is still quite saucy, 2 to 4 minutes. Off heat, stir in the mint, then taste and season with salt and pepper. If the pasta is dry, add more cooking water, 1 tablespoon at a time. Transfer to a serving bowl, then sprinkle with the remaining pistachios and drizzle with additional oil. Serve with cheese.

CHANGE THE WAY YOU COOK:
SOME PASTA NEEDS NUTS

Pasta can suffer from a singular, soft texture. So we borrow a trick from Sicily, where cooks add textural contrast—plus sweet and savory notes—with nuts, such as crushed pistachios and almonds.

Pasta with **Peruvian Pesto**
(*Tallarines Verdes*)

Start to finish: **45 minutes** / Servings: 4

---

12 ounces linguine or fettuccine

Kosher salt and ground
black pepper

1 yellow onion chopped (1 cup)

½ cup extra-virgin olive oil

¼ cup water

3 garlic cloves, smashed and peeled

12 ounces baby spinach
(about 12 cups)

¼ cup heavy cream

2 ounces Parmesan cheese, grated
(about 1 cup)

4 ounces queso fresco, crumbled
(about 1 cup)

Lime wedges, to serve

The origin of Peruvian pesto, or tallarines verdes, dates to the 19th century, when a wave of Italian immigrants settled in Peru. Many came from Genoa—the birthplace of pesto—and they adapted the recipe to the available ingredients. A shocking amount of spinach replaces the basil, and crumbled queso fresco supplements (and sometimes entirely replaces) salty Parmesan cheese. "It became a kind of dialogue or maybe a love story" between two worlds, says Gastón Acurio, Peruvian culinary star, founder of the La Mar restaurants, and champion of his country's food. For bright color and fresh flavor, we pureed ¾ pound of spinach for this pesto, along with onion and garlic. A quick simmer in a skillet took the raw edge off the onion and spinach, giving a depth and complexity lacking in traditional raw Italian pestos. Once the sauce thickened, we added reserved pasta cooking water, followed by undercooked pasta. The starch-infused water gave the pesto body, and the pasta finished cooking in the sauce, absorbing more of its flavor.

Don't be alarmed if the skillet seems very full after adding the pasta. Use tongs to gently lift and stir the noodles, and a silicone spatula to scrape the edges of the pan.

1. In a large pot, bring 4 quarts of water to a boil. Add the pasta and 2 tablespoons salt, then cook until just tender but not fully cooked, about 2 minutes less than package directions. Drain the pasta, reserving 1½ cups of the cooking water.

2. Meanwhile, in a food processor, combine the onion, oil, ¼ cup water, garlic and 1 teaspoon each salt and pepper. Add a third of the spinach and process until smooth, about 30 seconds. Add the remaining spinach in 2 batches, processing until smooth after each.

3. Transfer the spinach mixture to a 12-inch nonstick skillet over medium-high. Bring to a boil and cook, stirring occasionally, until it begins to thicken, 3 to 5 minutes. Add the reserved pasta water and return to a simmer, then add the pasta and stir to coat. Simmer, stirring occasionally, until the pasta is al dente and the pesto no longer appears watery, 3 to 5 minutes. Stir in the cream. Off the heat, stir in the Parmesan, then taste and season with salt and pepper. Transfer to a serving dish, sprinkle with the queso fresco and serve with lime wedges.

PISCO SOUR

Start to finish: **5 minutes**
Makes **2 drinks**

This Peruvian staple is traditionally made with lime juice, but we preferred a brighter blend of lemon and lime. "Dry shaking" the cocktail with one ice cube (to seal the shaker) helps create the sour's signature foam.

3½ ounces pisco

1 egg white

½ ounce lemon juice

½ ounce lime juice

½ ounce simple syrup

Angostura bitters

In a cocktail shaker, combine the pisco, egg white, both juices and the syrup. Add 1 ice cube and shake vigorously for 15 seconds. Fill the shaker with ice, then shake vigorously for 15 seconds. Strain into chilled glasses and sprinkle 3 to 4 dashes of bitters over each.

Soba Noodles with Asparagus, Miso Butter and Egg

Start to finish: **25 minutes** / Servings: 4

1 pound medium asparagus, tough ends trimmed

5 tablespoons white miso

4 tablespoons (½ stick) salted butter, room temperature

1½ tablespoons finely grated fresh ginger

12 ounces soba noodles

3 scallions, chopped, plus thinly sliced scallions to garnish

4 fried eggs (p. 23)

Shichimi togarashi rice seasoning, to serve (optional)

Lemon wedges, to serve

Asparagus has a built-in challenge; the sturdy, fibrous stalks need to be cooked to a different degree than the feathery tips. How to handle both? We cut the spears in two—stalks and tips—and simply toss the stalks into the noodle cooking water first, and a minute later add the tips. Stalks that measured about ½ inch at the thickest end were best. To flavor our asparagus and noodles, we liked savory-sweet miso, but we needed a fat to draw out the flavors. We turned to Momofuku's David Chang, who famously blends miso and butter. We liked that combination, particularly when balanced with grated fresh ginger. For the noodles, we preferred those made from a blend of whole-wheat and buckwheat flours; 100 percent buckwheat noodles were fragile and expensive. A sunny-side up egg proved the perfect topper (p. 23). Most soba noodles cook in 4 minutes. For noodles that need longer, adjust the timing for adding the asparagus. Assembling and preparing all the ingredients before cooking the noodles was essential for proper timing. While the soba cooks, heat the skillet, then fry the eggs while tossing the noodles with the miso butter. To finish, we liked a sprinkle of shichimi togarashi, the Asian rice seasoning (p. 9).

Don't add salt to the soba cooking water. While we usually salt our pasta water, miso can be quite salty and sodium levels vary widely by brand. Skipping the salt gave us better control over seasoning.

1. Bring a large pot of water to a boil. Meanwhile, snap or cut off the tender tips of the asparagus. Set aside. Slice the stalks on diagonal into ½-inch pieces. Set aside separately. In a large bowl, combine the miso, butter and ginger, stirring and mashing.

2. Add the noodles to the boiling water. Cook for about 1 minute. Add the asparagus stalks and cook for another minute. Add the tips, then cook for 2 minutes. Drain the noodles and asparagus, reserving ½ of the cup cooking water. The noodles should be just tender. Add the noodles, asparagus and minced scallions to the miso butter. Add enough reserved cooking water to reach a creamy consistency, using tongs to toss until the butter melts and coats the noodles.

3. Divide the noodles among 4 serving bowls and top each with a fried egg. Sprinkle with sliced scallions and shichimi togarashi, if using. Serve with lemon wedges.

Potato Gnocchi with Butter, Sage and Chives

Start to finish: 1¾ hours, plus cooling / Servings: 4 to 6

2¾ to 3 pounds russet potatoes, peeled and cut into 1-inch chunks

Kosher salt

146 grams (1 cup plus 2 tablespoons) all-purpose flour, plus more for shaping

½ teaspoon baking powder

3 tablespoons extra-virgin olive oil, divided

1 large egg, lightly beaten

Our take on classic potato gnocchi was inspired by a cooking lesson we got in Paris from chef Peter Orr at his Robert restaurant in the 11th arrondissement. To process the cooked potatoes, a ricer or food mill works best for obtaining the smooth texture needed for light, fine gnocchi. A potato masher works, too, but the gnocchi will be slightly denser (but still delicious). The gnocchi can be cooked, cooled completely, covered with plastic wrap and refrigerated for up to a day. For longer storage, after covering with plastic, freeze the gnocchi until solid, about 2 hours, then transfer to a zip-close bag and freeze for up to a month. To thaw, spread the gnocchi in an even layer on a lightly oiled baking sheet and let stand at room temperature until soft to the touch, about 1 hour. Heat the chilled or thawed gnocchi by adding them to a skilletful of hot sauce, tossing with a silicone spatula until warmed.

Don't use Yukon Gold potatoes. The high starch content of russets is needed for light, tender gnocchi. Also, don't mash the potatoes without first drying them in the pot on the stovetop, then letting them cool on the rack-lined baking sheet. The drier the potatoes, the lighter the gnocchi. Finally, don't sauce the gnocchi immediately after removing them from the water. Give them 15 minutes to cool and firm up a bit.

1. In a large pot, combine the potatoes and 4 quarts water. Bring to a boil over high, then stir in 2 tablespoons salt. Reduce to medium-high and cook, stirring occasionally, until the potatoes break apart when pierced with a knife, 15 to 20 minutes. Meanwhile, set a wire rack in a rimmed baking sheet and line the rack with kitchen parchment.

2. Drain the potatoes in a colander, shaking the colander to remove excess water. Return the potatoes to the pot and cook over low, gently folding with a silicone spatula, until the potatoes look dry and slightly powdery and the bottom of the pot is coated with a thin film of potato starch, 3 to 4 minutes. Transfer the potatoes to the prepared cooling rack in an even layer. Cool to room temperature. Meanwhile, in a small

bowl, whisk together the flour, baking powder and 1 teaspoon salt.

3. Weigh out 1¼ pounds (about 4 cups) of the cooked potatoes into a large bowl; save the remainder for another use. Discard the parchment from the baking sheet, then line with fresh parchment and coat with 1 tablespoon of oil; set aside. Add 1 teaspoon salt to the potatoes and pass the potatoes through a ricer or a food mill fitted with the fine disk back into the bowl, or mash with a potato masher until smooth.

4. Sprinkle the flour mixture evenly over the potatoes. Using your hands, lightly toss the potatoes to distribute the flour mixture. Add the egg and gently mix with your hands until incorporated. Turn the dough out onto a lightly floured counter and gently knead just until

BUTTER, SAGE AND CHIVES SAUCE

Start to finish: **20 minutes**
Servings: **4 to 6**

A combination of lightly browned butter and fresh herbs creates a simple sauce that pairs perfectly with the delicate gnocchi.

4 tablespoons (½ stick) salted butter, cut into 4 pieces, divided

⅓ cup chopped fresh sage

1 recipe potato gnocchi

¼ cup finely chopped fresh chives

2 tablespoons lemon juice

Kosher salt and ground black pepper

In a nonstick 12-inch skillet over medium, melt 2 tablespoons of butter. Add the sage and cook, stirring, until fragrant and the butter just begins to brown, about 1 minute. Add the gnocchi and ½ cup water and bring to a simmer over medium-high, gently tossing with a silicone spatula.

Add the remaining 2 tablespoons butter and cook, swirling the pan to melt the butter, until the sauce has thickened slightly, about 1 minute. Off heat, stir in the lemon juice and chives. Taste and season with salt and pepper.

smooth; do not overknead. Using a bench scraper or knife, divide the dough into 4 pieces.

5. Roll 1 piece of dough into a rope about 16 inches long, then use the dough scraper to cut it into 16 pieces. Place the pieces in a single layer on the prepared baking sheet. Dip the back of the tines of a fork into flour, then gently press into each piece to create a ridged surface. Repeat with the remaining pieces of dough.

6. Set a wire rack in another rimmed baking sheet and line the rack with kitchen parchment. Coat the parchment evenly with the remaining 2 tablespoons oil. In a large pot, bring 4 quarts water to a boil and stir in 3 tablespoons salt. Add half of the gnocchi, return to a boil and cook, stirring gently and occasionally, until the gnocchi float to the surface. Cook for 1 minute, then use a slotted spoon to transfer the gnocchi, letting excess water drain, to the prepared rack. Return the water to a boil and repeat with the remaining gnocchi. Let the gnocchi cool for at least 15 minutes before using.

Pasta with **Trapanese Pesto**

Start to finish: **30 minutes** / Servings: 4

4 ounces slivered almonds
(about 1 cup), toasted

1 small garlic clove

¼ teaspoon red pepper flakes

1 pound cherry tomatoes

¾ ounce fresh basil leaves
(1 cup lightly packed)

Kosher salt

½ cup extra-virgin olive oil

1 ounce grated pecorino Romano
cheese (½ cup), plus more to serve

12 ounces short, sturdy pasta, such
as gemelli, casarecce or rigatoni

Ground black pepper

We hear "pesto" and see shades of green, but the word refers to prep, not pigment. It stems from pestare, to pound—this Italian sauce traditionally was made with a mortar and pestle. The basil-heavy, and therefore green, version we know best comes from northwestern Italy. In Sicily, you'll find pesto Trapanese (named for the town of Trapani), a sauce also known as mataroccu. It has less basil than the northern version and adds tomatoes, garlic and almonds, the latter a nod to Sicily's Arabic heritage. To make this a truly year-round recipe we ruled out standard winter tomatoes and instead settled on cherry tomatoes, though grape or small plum tomatoes worked, too. For ease, we used a food processor, though we found it was best to incorporate the olive oil or cheese (pecorino) by hand at the end. Raw almonds are common, but we found them a little dull. When we toasted them, however, we were wowed by how they brought out the sweetness of the tomato, added a crispier crunch and improved the balance of the dish. We preferred blanched, slivered almonds, which were easiest to toast and grind, but any variety is fine.

Don't add the cooking water to the sauce right away. While we always reserve some starchy cooking water before draining pasta, this sauce has so much moisture from the tomatoes that it wasn't always necessary.

1. In a large pot, bring 4 quarts of water to a boil. Meanwhile, in a food processor, combine the almonds, garlic and pepper flakes. Process until coarsely ground, 20 to 30 seconds. Add the tomatoes, basil and ¾ teaspoon salt. Pulse until uniformly ground but still chunky, 10 to 12 pulses. Transfer to a large bowl and stir in the oil and cheese.

2. To the boiling water, add the pasta and 2 tablespoons salt. Cook until al dente. Drain, reserving 1 cup of the cooking water. Add the pasta to the bowl with the pesto and toss. If the sauce is too thick, add a bit of the reserved pasta water. Taste and season with salt, pepper, red pepper flakes and more cheese.

Pasta with Pesto alla Genovese

Start to finish: 30 minutes / Servings: 4

1¾ ounces Parmesan cheese (without rind), chopped into rough 1-inch pieces

1 ounce pecorino Sardo cheese (without rind), chopped into rough 1-inch pieces (see note)

¼ cup pine nuts

2 medium garlic cloves, smashed and peeled

Kosher salt

⅓ cup extra-virgin olive oil

2½ ounces fresh basil leaves (about 5 cups lightly packed)

12 ounces dried pasta

We learned to make pesto alla Genovese in its birthplace—Genoa, Italy. It traditionally is made in a mortar and pestle of nothing more than basil, pine nuts, cheese, garlic, salt and olive oil, emphasis on the basil. Back at Milk Street, we felt a mortar and pestle simply weren't practical for U.S. home cooks. But we do follow the tradition of processing ingredients separately to ensure we preserve the appropriate texture of each. Good-quality cheese is essential for a rich, full-flavored pesto. Seek out true Italian Parmesan cheese, as well as pecorino Sardo, a sheep's milk cheese from Sardinia. If you can't find pecorino Sardo, don't use pecorino Romano, which is too strong. The best substitute is Manchego, a Spanish sheep's milk cheese. To store pesto, press a piece of plastic wrap against its surface and refrigerate for up to three days.

Don't toast the pine nuts. In Italy, the pine nuts for pesto are used raw. Don't be tempted to add all the ingredients at once to the food processor. Adding them in stages ensures the pesto has the correct consistency and texture, and that it won't end up thin and watery, the result of over-processing.

1. In a food processor, process both cheeses until broken into rough marble-sized pieces, about 10 seconds, then pulse until they have the texture of coarse sand, 5 to 10 pulses, scraping the bowl as needed. Transfer to a small bowl and set aside.

2. In the food processor, combine the pine nuts, garlic and ¾ teaspoon salt. Process until a smooth, peanut butter–like paste forms, about 1 minute, scraping the bowl as needed. Add the cheeses and about ½ of the oil, then process until mostly smooth, 10 to 20 seconds, scraping the bowl as needed; the mixture should hold together when pressed against the bowl with a rubber spatula.

3. Using a chef's knife, roughly chop the basil, then add to the food processor. Pulse about 10 times, scraping the bowl several times, until the basil is finely chopped and well combined with the cheese mixture. Add the remaining oil and pulse just until incorporated, about 2 pulses. The pesto should be thick, creamy and spreadable. Set the pesto aside.

4. In a large pot, bring 4 quarts water to a boil. Add the pasta and 2 tablespoons salt, then cook, stirring occasionally, until just shy of al dente. Reserve about ½ cup of the cooking water, then drain the pasta. Transfer the pasta to a large warmed bowl and top with the pesto. Pour in ⅓ cup of the reserved cooking water for long pasta shapes (such as spaghetti and linguine) or ¼ cup cooking water for short pasta shapes (such as penne and fusilli). Toss to combine.

CHANGE THE WAY YOU COOK:
STOP PUREEING YOUR PESTO

Processing the ingredients in a particular order—and only until grainy, not pureed—produces a dramatically better pesto with layers of texture and flavor.

HOW TO PROPERLY
SAUCE PASTA WITH PESTO

Cook 12 ounces dried pasta in 4 quarts boiling water seasoned with 2 tablespoons kosher salt until al dente. Reserve ½ cup of the pasta cooking water, then drain the pasta. Transfer to a warmed large bowl and add ⅓ cup of the reserved cooking water for long pasta shapes (such as linguine and spaghetti) or ¼ cup water for short pasta shapes (such as fusilli and penne). Top with 1 recipe (1 cup) pesto alla Genovese. Toss to combine at the table.

Spaghetti with Anchovies, Pine Nuts and Raisins

Start to finish: 30 minutes / Servings: 4

12 ounces spaghetti

Kosher salt and ground black pepper

6 tablespoons extra-virgin olive oil, divided, plus more to serve

⅓ cup panko breadcrumbs, finely crushed or chopped (see note)

¼ cup pine nuts, finely chopped

3 tablespoons golden raisins, finely chopped

10 oil-packed anchovy fillets, patted dry

8 medium garlic cloves, finely chopped

2 tablespoons white wine vinegar

½ cup lightly packed fresh flat-leaf parsley, chopped

This pasta dish features the classic Sicilian flavor combination of savory, sweet and sour, while getting richness from a handful of pine nuts. Toasted breadcrumbs, sprinkled on just before serving, cling to the strands of pasta and provide pleasant crispness. We preferred fluffy panko breadcrumbs over regular powder-fine breadcrumbs, but crushing or chopping the panko before toasting ensured better blending with the pasta. Crush the panko in a zip-close plastic bag with a meat pounder or rolling pin, or simply chop with a chef's knife on a cutting board. To be efficient, pile the pine nuts, raisins and garlic together on the cutting board and chop them all at once.

Don't overcook the pasta after adding it to the sauce. The noodles should be al dente and slippery, not fully tender and dry. If needed, loosen them by tossing with additional reserved pasta water.

1. **In a large pot,** bring 4 quarts water to a boil. Add the spaghetti and 2 tablespoons salt, then cook, stirring occasionally, until just shy of al dente. Reserve about 1½ cups of the cooking water, then drain the pasta.

2. **While the pasta cooks,** in a 12-inch skillet over medium, combine 2 tablespoons of oil and the panko. Cook, stirring frequently, until golden brown, 3 to 5 minutes. Transfer to a small bowl and set aside; wipe out the skillet.

3. **Set the skillet** over medium-high and add the remaining 4 tablespoons oil, the pine nuts, raisins, anchovies and garlic. Cook, stirring frequently, until the anchovies have broken up and the garlic is golden brown, about 2 minutes. Stir in the vinegar and cook until syrupy, 30 to 60 seconds. Add 1 cup of the reserved pasta water, ½ teaspoon salt and ¼ teaspoon pepper and bring to a simmer.

4. **Add the pasta,** reduce to medium, and cook, occasionally tossing to combine, until the pasta is al dente and has absorbed most of the moisture but is still a little saucy, about 2 minutes. Remove from the heat. If the pasta is dry, add more cooking water, 1 tablespoon at a time. Stir in the parsley, then taste and season with salt and pepper. Transfer to a serving bowl. Sprinkle with the panko and top with additional oil and pepper.

CHANGE THE WAY YOU COOK:
PARCOOK PASTA FOR BETTER FLAVOR

Boiling pasta until just shy of al dente, then finishing it directly in the sauce (fortified with some of the starchy cooking water), allows the pasta to better absorb other flavors. It's a good middle ground for when cooking the pasta entirely in the sauce isn't practical.

Whole-Wheat Pasta
with Yogurt and Tahini

Start to finish: **25 minutes** / Servings: 4

2 garlic cloves, finely grated

1 teaspoon grated lemon zest, plus 3 tablespoons lemon juice

½ cup walnuts, finely chopped

1½ teaspoons cumin seeds

2 scallions, trimmed and finely chopped

Kosher salt

12 ounces whole-wheat pasta

1 cup plain whole-milk Greek-style yogurt

⅓ cup tahini

2 tablespoons extra-virgin olive oil

With its earthy flavor and dense chew, whole-wheat pasta often gets passed over. But with the right ingredients it can be a star. Take our Greek-inspired pasta tossed with a simple, creamy sauce of thick yogurt and nutty tahini. While we recommend whole-grain, the dish also is delicious with traditional pasta. Chunky pastas such as orecchiette, farfalle and penne worked as well as long noodles, such as fettuccine and tagliatelle. To add interest to our sauce we toasted cumin seeds and finely chopped walnuts—they also provided the basis for a garnish. The ratio of tahini to yogurt—1:3 as it turned out—was key to a full-flavored, creamy sauce; a bit of olive oil helped with emulsification. For a tangy touch, we added lemon zest to both the toasted walnuts and the tahini sauce, giving us a double layer of flavor.

Don't substitute traditional yogurt for Greek-style or the sauce will be too thin.

1. In a large pot bring 4 quarts of water to a boil. Meanwhile, in a medium bowl combine the garlic and lemon juice and let sit for 10 minutes. In a small skillet over medium-low, toast the walnuts and cumin seeds, stirring frequently, until golden brown and fragrant, 3 to 5 minutes. Transfer to a small bowl and stir in the scallions, ½ teaspoon of the lemon zest and ¼ teaspoon salt.

2. Stir in the pasta and 2 tablespons salt and cook until al dente. Drain, reserving 1 cup of the cooking water, then return the pasta to the pot. To the lemon juice–garlic mixture, whisk in the yogurt, tahini, oil, the remaining ½ teaspoon of lemon zest, ½ teaspoon salt and ½ cup of the reserved pasta water. Add the sauce to the pasta and toss until evenly coated. Stir in half of the walnut mixture. Transfer the pasta to a platter or individual bowls, then garnish with the remaining walnut mixture.

Spaghetti with Lemon, Anchovies and Capers

Start to finish: 30 minutes / (15 minutes active) Servings: 4

12 ounces spaghetti

Kosher salt and ground
black pepper

¼ cup extra-virgin olive oil

6 garlic cloves, thinly sliced

¾ teaspoon red pepper flakes

12 anchovies, minced (2-ounce can)

3 tablespoons drained capers,
chopped, plus 2 tablespoons
caper brine

2 teaspoons lemon zest, plus
3 tablespoons lemon juice

¾ cup chopped fresh
parsley leaves

2 ounces grated Parmesan
cheese (about 1 cup)

Lidia Bastianich reminds us that the water we cook our pasta in is worth saving. She uses the starchy liquid to thicken quick, flavorful sauces made from potent pantry staples such as anchovies and capers. Our quick pasta dish, inspired by Bastianich, draws its intense flavor from anchovies, capers, garlic, lemon and red pepper flakes. We intentionally undercooked the pasta to leave it underhydrated and ready to absorb more flavor when cooking in the sauce.

Don't salt the pasta water as much as usual; the other ingredients provide plenty of salt. One tablespoon kosher salt for 4 quarts of water worked for this recipe.

1. In a large pot, bring 4 quarts of water to a boil. Add the pasta and 2 tablespoons salt, then cook until just tender but not fully cooked, about 2 minutes less than package directions. Reserve 2 cups of the cooking water, then drain.

2. In a large skillet over medium, combine the oil, garlic, pepper flakes, anchovies and capers. Cook, stirring occasionally, until fragrant and the garlic is golden, about 5 minutes. Add the reserved pasta water and bring to a simmer. Add the pasta and stir. Cook, stirring occasionally, until the pasta is al dente, 3 to 5 minutes.

3. Off heat, stir in the lemon zest and juice, the caper brine, parsley and half of the cheese. Taste, then season with salt and pepper. Serve topped with the remaining cheese.

Cacio e Pepe

Start to finish: **20 minutes** / Servings: 4

2 teaspoons cornstarch

6 ounces pecorino Romano cheese, finely grated (3 cups), plus more to serve

12 ounces linguini or spaghetti

Kosher salt and ground black pepper

Made of just pasta, cheese and plenty of freshly ground black pepper, cacio e pepe (literally, "cheese and pepper") is a study in the power of letting a few ingredients shine. The origins of the dish are debated—one theory is cheese and black pepper were the only ingredients shepherds could carry into the mountains. But it's widely accepted as the mother of classic Roman pastas. Add pancetta and you have pasta alla gricia (recipe p. 196). Add eggs and it becomes carbonara (recipe p. 199). The pepper in cacio e pepe is key, cutting through the richness of the cheese and bringing balance to the dish. Pecorino Romano, a salty hard sheep's milk cheese, is traditional. The addition of cornstarch allowed us to overcome the tendency of pecorino cheese in the U.S. to clump (even imported varieties). But for best flavor, we still recommend using cheese imported from Italy.

Don't use pre-grated cheese, even if it's true pecorino Romano. Make sure to grate the cheese on a wand-style grater; larger shreds won't melt. Don't pour the pecorino mixture onto the piping-hot, just drained pasta; letting the pasta cool for a minute or so ensures the mixture won't break from overheating.

1. In a large pot, bring 4 quarts water to a boil. Meanwhile, in a large saucepan, whisk 1½ cups water and the cornstarch until smooth. Add the pecorino and stir until evenly moistened. Set the pan over medium-low and cook, whisking constantly, until the cheese melts and the mixture comes to a gentle simmer and thickens slightly, about 5 minutes. Remove from heat and set aside.

2. Stir the pasta and 2 tablespoons salt into the boiling water and cook until al dente. Reserve about ½ cup of the cooking water, then drain the pasta very well. Return the pasta to the pot and let cool for about 1 minute.

3. Pour the pecorino mixture over the pasta and toss with tongs until combined, then toss in 2 teaspoons pepper. Let stand, tossing 2 or 3 times, until most of the liquid has been absorbed, about 3 minutes. The pasta should be creamy but not loose. If needed, toss in reserved pasta water 1 tablespoon at a time to adjust the consistency. Transfer to a warmed serving bowl and serve with additional pecorino and pepper on the side.

CHANGE THE WAY YOU COOK:
USE CORNSTARCH TO SMOOTH OUT LUMPY SAUCES

Some cheese-based sauces are notoriously difficult to make without clumping. Adding cornstarch to the mixture stabilizes the cheese as it melts, creating a silky-smooth sauce.

Spaghetti with Pancetta
(*Pasta alla Gricia*)

Start to finish: **20 minutes** / Servings: 4

3 ounces pancetta, finely chopped

2 teaspoons cornstarch

6 ounces pecorino Romano cheese, finely grated (3 cups), plus extra to serve

12 ounces linguini or spaghetti

Kosher salt and ground black pepper

This classic Roman pasta dish depends on the quality of the pecorino Romano, a salty, hard sheep's milk cheese. The addition of cornstarch allowed us to overcome the tendency of this cheese to clump. For best flavor we recommend seeking out pecorino imported from Italy. Guanciale (cured pork cheek) is traditional for gricia, but we used more widely available pancetta.

Don't use pre-grated cheese, even if it's true pecorino Romano. Make sure to grate it on a wand-style grater; larger shreds won't melt. Don't pour the pecorino mixture onto the piping-hot, just-drained pasta; letting the pasta cool for a minute or so ensures the mixture won't break from overheating.

1. In a large pot, bring 4 quarts water to a boil. Meanwhile, in a 10-inch skillet over medium, cook the pancetta, stirring occasionally, until crisp, about 5 minutes. Using a slotted spoon, transfer the pancetta to a paper towel-lined plate; reserve 2 tablespoons of the rendered fat.

2. In a large saucepan, whisk 1½ cups cold water and the cornstarch until smooth. Add the pecorino and stir until evenly moistened. Set the pan over medium-low and cook, whisking constantly, until the cheese melts and the mixture comes to a gentle simmer and thickens slightly, about 5 minutes. Remove from the heat, whisk in reserved pancetta fat and set aside.

3. Stir the pasta and 2 tablespoons salt into the boiling water and cook until al dente. Reserve about ½ cup of the cooking water, then drain the pasta very well. Return the pasta to the pot and let cool for about 1 minute.

4. Pour the pecorino mixture over the pasta and toss with tongs until combined, then toss in 2 teaspoons pepper and the crisped pancetta. Let stand, tossing 2 or 3 times, until most of the liquid has been absorbed, about 3 minutes. The pasta should be creamy but not loose. If needed, toss in reserved pasta water 1 tablespoon at a time to adjust the consistency. Transfer to a warmed serving bowl and serve, offering additional pecorino and pepper on the side.

Roman Spaghetti Carbonara

Start to finish: **25 minutes** / Servings: 4

3 ounces thinly sliced
pancetta, chopped

6 large egg yolks

2 teaspoons cornstarch

6 ounces pecorino Romano
cheese, finely grated (3 cups),
plus more to serve

12 ounces spaghetti

Kosher salt and ground
black pepper

This brighter take on carbonara came from Pipero Roma in Rome. Their secret: The egg yolks are whisked until cooked and slightly foamy, creating a sauce that is much lighter in texture than most carbonara recipes. Mixing the yolks with water and cornstarch ensures the cheese won't clump when tossed with the pasta.

Don't substitute bacon for the pancetta. The smokiness of the bacon will overwhelm the cleaner flavors of the egg-based sauce.

1. In a 10-inch skillet over medium, cook the pancetta, stirring, until crisp, about 5 minutes. Using a slotted spoon, transfer to a paper towel-lined plate. Measure out and reserve 3 tablespoons of the rendered fat; if needed, supplement with olive oil. Set the pancetta and fat aside.

2. In a large pot, bring 4 quarts water to a boil. Meanwhile, in a large saucepan, whisk 1¾ cups water, the egg yolks and cornstarch until smooth. Add the cheese and stir until evenly moistened. Set the pan over medium-low and cook, whisking constantly, until the mixture comes to a gentle simmer and is airy and thickened, 5 to 7 minutes; use a silicone spatula to occasionally get into the corners of the pan. Off heat, whisk in the reserved pancetta fat. Set aside.

3. Stir the pasta and 2 tablespoons salt into the boiling water and cook until al dente. Reserve about ½ cup of the cooking water, then drain the pasta very well. Return the pasta to the pot and let cool for about 1 minute.

4. Pour the pecorino-egg mixture over the pasta and toss with tongs until well combined, then toss in 2 teaspoons pepper. Let stand, tossing 2 or 3 times, until most of the liquid has been absorbed, about 3 minutes. Crumble in the pancetta, then toss again. The pasta should be creamy but not loose. If needed, toss in up to 2 tablespoons reserved pasta water to adjust the consistency. Transfer to a warmed serving bowl and serve with additional pecorino and pepper on the side.

CHANGE THE WAY YOU COOK:
ADD AIR TO YOUR CARBONARA

Classic carbonara can be heavy and dense. Whisking the egg-and-cheese sauce as it cooks slowly over gentle heat lightens it by pumping air into it.

Suppers

Pita and Chickpea Salad
with Yogurt and Mint (*Fatteh*) / 203

Beef Kibbeh / 205

Punjabi Chickpeas with Potato (*Chole*) / 206

Spanish Spice-Crusted Pork Tenderloin
Bites (*Pinchos Morunos*) / 208

Chicken Teriyaki Rice Bowls
(*Teriyaki Donburi*) / 211

Hot-Smoked Salmon Salad with Arugula,
Avocado and Pepitas / 213

Tlayudas / 214

Molletes with Pico de Gallo / 216

Skirt Steak Salad with Arugula
and Peppadews / 218

Taiwanese Five-Spice Pork with Rice
(*Lu Rou Fan*) / 221

Three-Cup Chicken / 223

Spicy Beef Salad with Mint and Cilantro
(*Larb Neua*) / 225

Thai Braised Pork and Eggs with Star Anise
and Cinnamon (*Moo Palo*) / 226

Salmon Chraimeh / 229

Spanish Ratatouille (*Pisto Manchego*) / 230

Shrimp with Feta Cheese
(*Garides Saganaki*) / 233

Lomo Saltado / 235

Ginger-Scallion Steamed Cod / 237

Singapore Chicken Satay / 238

Singapore Sling / 241

Roasted Mushroom Pizza
with Fontina and Scallions / 242

Orange-Guajillo Chili Pulled Chicken / 246

Vietnamese Shaking Beef (*Bô Lúc Lắc*) / 249

Oaxacan Green Mole with Chicken / 251

Pork and Chorizo
with Piquillo Peppers (*Carcamusa*) / 253

Stir-Fried Chicken
with Snap Peas and Basil / 255

Turkish Beans with Pickled Tomatoes / 256

Spicy Stir-Fried Cumin Beef / 258

Carnitas / 260

Oaxacan Refried Black Beans / 262

Sesame Stir-Fried Pork with Shiitakes / 265

Lentil Salad with Gorgonzola / 266

Sichuan Chicken Salad / 268

Turkish Meatballs
with Lime-Yogurt Sauce / 270

Green Enchiladas with Chicken
and Cheese (*Enchiladas Verdes*) / 272

Quick Refried Beans / 275

Israeli Hummus (*Hummus Masabacha*)
with Spiced Beef Topping (*Kawarma*) / 276

Curry-Coconut Braised Fish / 279

Za'atar Chicken Cutlets
and Lemon-Parsley Salad / 280

Mussels with Chorizo
and Slow-Roasted Tomatoes / 282

Burmese Chicken / 285

Vietnamese Caramel Fish / 287

Shrimp in Chipotle Sauce
(*Camarones Enchipotlados*) / 289

7

Pita and Chickpea Salad
with Yogurt and Mint (*Fatteh*)

Start to finish: **25 minutes** / Servings: 4

1 cup plain whole-milk yogurt

¼ cup tahini

2 medium garlic cloves, finely grated

1 teaspoon grated lemon zest, plus 1 tablespoon lemon juice

Kosher salt and ground black pepper

Two 8-inch pita breads, each split into 2 rounds

2½ teaspoons ground cumin, divided

5 tablespoons salted butter, melted, divided

¼ cup pine nuts

⅛ to ¼ teaspoon cayenne pepper (optional)

Two 15½-ounce cans chickpeas, rinsed and drained

1½ teaspoons za'atar, plus more to serve (optional)

1½ cups lightly packed fresh mint, torn if large

CHANGE THE WAY YOU COOK:
TREAT HERBS AS GREENS, NOT GARNISH

For full-flavored but still simple salads, add herbs by the cupful rather than as a delicate sprinkle. But be sure to wait until serving before dressing the salads. Like any delicate green, fresh herbs will wilt once dressed.

This dish is known as fatteh in the Levant, where it often is eaten for breakfast. It's a way to turn stale pita bread into a hearty meal. We, however, start with fresh pita, brush it with butter, crisp it in the oven, then break it into shards before topping the pieces with warmed chickpeas. Yogurt spiked with garlic, tahini and lemon ties everything together. Za'atar, a Middle Eastern spice blend that usually includes sesame seeds, sumac, thyme and oregano, adds complex flavor. But the za'atar is optional; even without it, the salad is delicious and satisfying. If you like, instead of mint, use flat-leaf parsley or a combination.

Don't cut back on the butter that's tossed with the toasted pine nuts. It may seem like a lot, but the butter adds a sweetness that balances the tang of the yogurt and makes the dish taste full and deep.

1. Heat the oven to 400°F with a rack in the middle position. In a small bowl, whisk together the yogurt, tahini, garlic, lemon zest and juice, ½ teaspoon salt and ¼ teaspoon black pepper. Set aside.

2. Arrange the pita on a rimmed baking sheet. Use 2 tablespoons of the butter to brush both sides of each round, then sprinkle evenly with 2 teaspoons of the cumin. Bake for 5 minutes, then flip each round and continue to bake until browned and crisp, 5 to 6 minutes. Transfer to a wire rack and let cool; reserve the baking sheet.

3. While the pita cools, distribute the pine nuts on the reserved baking sheet and toast until golden brown, 3 to 5 minutes, stirring once about halfway through. Immediately transfer to a small bowl and toss with the remaining 3 tablespoons butter, the remaining ½ teaspoon cumin, cayenne (if using) and ¼ teaspoon each salt and black pepper. Set aside.

4. In a medium microwave-safe bowl, toss the chickpeas with the za'atar (if using), 1 teaspoon salt and 3 tablespoons water. Cover and microwave on high until hot, 3 to 3½ minutes, stirring once halfway through. Meanwhile, break the pita into bite-size pieces and place in a wide, shallow serving bowl or divide among 4 individual bowls.

5. Using a slotted spoon, scoop the warmed chickpeas onto the pita. Spoon on the yogurt mixture, top with mint and spoon on the pine nut–butter mixture. Sprinkle with additional za'atar (if using).

Beef Kibbeh

Start to finish: 50 minutes (20 minutes active)
Servings: 4

1 medium yellow onion, peeled

½ cup fine bulgur (see note)

Kosher salt and ground black pepper

12 ounces 85 percent lean ground beef

1 large egg, beaten

¼ cup pine nuts, toasted and chopped

¾ teaspoon ground allspice

¾ teaspoon ground cardamom

¾ teaspoon ground cinnamon

¼ teaspoon cayenne pepper

6 medium garlic cloves, finely grated

1 cup whole-milk plain yogurt

1 cup lightly packed fresh flat-leaf parsley, chopped

¼ cup tahini

4 tablespoons grapeseed or other neutral oil, divided

Lemon wedges, to serve

Kibbeh, a popular dish throughout the Levant, is a spiced mixture of bulgur and ground meat. It may be layered with stuffing in a baking dish and baked, or shaped into small portions, filled and fried, with the goal of getting a toasty, browned crust that brings out the nuttiness of the bulgur. In this version, we skip the stuffing and form the mixture into patties, then pan-fry them, rather than deep-fry, for ease. We use ground beef, but you could substitute 12 ounces of ground lamb. Pine nuts add their distinct, slightly resinous flavor to the mix. Toast them in a small skillet over medium-low, shaking the pan frequently, until light golden brown and fragrant, about 4 minutes. Serve the kibbeh, yogurt-tahini sauce and lemon wedges for squeezing with warmed flatbread.

Don't use coarse or medium bulgur. Fine bulgur, with particles that are very small and flaky, is key for yielding a mixture that holds together when formed into patties. If you can't find fine bulgur, process medium or coarse bulgur in a spice grinder for 10 to 30 seconds. Don't rinse the bulgur before use because the added moisture will make the meat mixture difficult to shape. If your mixture is very sticky or wet when you attempt to shape it, refrigerate for an additional 10 minutes or so to allow the bulgur to soak up more moisture.

1. Grate the onion on the large holes of a box grater, catching the pulp and liquid in a medium bowl. Stir in the bulgur and 2 teaspoons salt. Set aside for 10 minutes, until the bulgur has absorbed the onion liquid and is slightly softened.

2. Add the beef, egg, pine nuts, allspice, cardamom, cinnamon, cayenne, 1 teaspoon black pepper and ⅔ of the grated garlic. Knead with your hands or mix vigorously with a wooden spoon until well combined, then cover and refrigerate for 20 minutes.

3. Meanwhile, in a small bowl, whisk together the yogurt, parsley, tahini, ½ teaspoon salt, ¼ teaspoon black pepper and the remaining garlic. Set aside until ready to serve.

4. Line a rimmed baking sheet with kitchen parchment. Using your hands, form the bulgur-beef mixture into 12 balls (about 2 heaping tablespoons each) and place on the prepared baking sheet. Using your hands, flatten the balls into ½-inch-thick patties about 2½ inches in diameter.

5. In a 12-inch skillet over medium, heat 2 tablespoons of oil until barely smoking. Add half the patties and cook undisturbed until browned and crisp on the bottoms, about 4 minutes. Flip and continue to cook until the second sides are browned and crisp, about another 4 minutes, then transfer to a plate. Wipe out the skillet with paper towels and repeat with the remaining oil and patties. Serve with the yogurt-tahini sauce and lemon wedges.

Punjabi Chickpeas with Potato (*Chole*)

Start to finish: 45 minutes / Servings: 4

1 large red onion

4 tablespoons grapeseed or other neutral oil, divided

1½ teaspoons ground coriander

1 teaspoon ground cardamom

1 teaspoon sweet paprika

½ teaspoon cinnamon

¼ teaspoon ground cloves

¼ teaspoon nutmeg

⅛ teaspoon cayenne pepper

Kosher salt and ground black pepper

1 teaspoon cumin seeds

¾ pound russet potatoes (about 2 medium potatoes), peeled and cut into ½-inch cubes

1 tablespoon finely grated fresh ginger

3 garlic cloves, finely grated

1 tablespoon tomato paste

Two 15½-ounce cans chickpeas, drained

1 tablespoon lime juice, plus lime wedges, to serve

¼ cup coarsely chopped cilantro leaves, plus more to garnish

Chopped fresh tomato, thinly sliced bird's eye or serrano chilies and whole-milk Greek-style yogurt, to serve (optional)

Seasoning blends known as masalas are the backbone of much of Indian cooking. But they often involve intimidatingly long lists of spices, each requiring toasting and grinding. Buying prepared blends is easier, but they can taste faded and stale. For our chole (pronounced CHO-lay)—a chickpea curry popular in India and Pakistan—we mix our own garam masala, a warm seasoning blend that features cayenne pepper and cinnamon. To make the sauce, we started with onion cooked until it practically melted. Grating the onion before browning helped it cook faster and gave it a better texture. Amchoor powder made from dried green mangoes gives traditional chole its characteristic tang, but we found lime juice was a good—and more convenient—substitute. When preparing this dish, make sure your potato pieces are no larger than ½ inch thick so they cook in time. Chole typically is eaten with flatbread, such as roti or naan.

Don't use a nonstick skillet for this recipe; the fond (browned bits on the bottom of the pan) won't form, which will alter the chole's flavor. And don't be deterred by the lengthy list of spices here. Most are pantry staples and are key to producing the dish's complex flavor.

1. Using the large holes of a box grater, grate the onion, then transfer to a mesh strainer and drain. In a small bowl, stir together 1 tablespoon of the oil with the coriander, cardamom, paprika, cinnamon, cloves, nutmeg, cayenne, 1¼ teaspoons salt and ½ teaspoon pepper.

2. In a 12-inch skillet over medium-high, heat the remaining 3 tablespoons of oil. Add the cumin seeds and cook, shaking the pan, until the seeds are fragrant and darken, 30 to 60 seconds. Add the drained onion and cook, stirring frequently, until the moisture has evaporated, 1 to 3 minutes. Add the potatoes, reduce heat to medium and cook, stirring frequently, until the onions begin to brown and a fond forms on the bottom of the pan, 6 to 8 minutes. Add the ginger, garlic and tomato paste, then cook for 1 minute, stirring constantly.

3. Clear the center of the pan, then add the spice paste to the clearing and cook, mashing and stirring until fragrant, about 15 seconds. Stir into the vegetables. Add 1½ cups water and bring to a boil, scraping up all the browned bits. Add the chickpeas and return to a boil, then cover, reduce heat to low and cook until the potatoes are tender and the oil separates from the sauce at the edges of the pan, 13 to 15 minutes.

4. Off the heat, stir in the lime juice and cilantro. Taste and season with salt and pepper. Serve with lime wedges, chopped tomato, chilies and yogurt, if desired.

Spanish Spice-Crusted Pork Tenderloin Bites (*Pinchos Morunos*)

Start to finish: **50 minutes (25 minutes active)** / Servings: **4**

1½ teaspoons ground coriander

1½ teaspoons ground cumin

1½ teaspoons smoked paprika

¾ teaspoon each kosher salt and coarsely ground black pepper

1-pound pork tenderloin, trimmed of silver skin and cut into 1- to 1½-inch pieces

1 tablespoon lemon juice, plus lemon wedges for serving

1 tablespoon honey

1 medium garlic clove, finely grated

2 tablespoons extra-virgin olive oil, divided

1 tablespoon chopped fresh oregano

Loosely translated as "Moorish bites impaled on thorns or small pointed sticks," pinchos morunos is a Basque dish of seared pork tenderloin rubbed with a blend of spices, garlic, herbs and olive oil. The recipe dates back generations, boasting influences from Spain and North Africa. Classic versions skewer the meat, which is seasoned with ras el hanout, a Moroccan spice blend, among other flavorings. We streamlined, nixing the skewers. And since ras al hanout can be hard to find, we went with a blend of cumin, coriander and black pepper. A bit of smoked paprika added the requisite Basque touch. We finished with a drizzle of honey, which heightened the flavor of the pork and seasonings.

Don't cut the tenderloin too small. Cutting it into 1- to 1½-inch pieces produced more surface area, allowing the spice rub to quickly penetrate and season the meat. Any smaller and the meat cooked too quickly.

1. In a medium bowl, combine the coriander, cumin, paprika, salt and pepper. Add the pork and toss to coat evenly, massaging the spices into the meat until no dry rub remains. Let the pork sit at room temperature for at least 30 minutes and up to 1 hour. Meanwhile, in another bowl, combine the lemon juice, honey and garlic. Set aside.

2. In a large skillet over high, heat 1 tablespoon of the oil until barely smoking. Add the meat in a single layer and cook without moving until deeply browned on one side, about 3 minutes. Using tongs, flip the pork and cook, turning occasionally, until cooked through and browned all over, another 2 to 3 minutes. Off the heat, pour the lemon juice-garlic mixture over the meat and toss to evenly coat, then transfer to a serving platter. Sprinkle the oregano over the pork and drizzle with the remaining 1 tablespoon of oil. Serve with lemon wedges.

Chicken Teriyaki Rice Bowls
(*Teriyaki Donburi*)

Start to finish: **40 minutes** / Servings: **4**

4 tablespoons sake, divided

4 tablespoons plus 1 teaspoon soy sauce, divided

1½ pounds boneless, skinless chicken thighs, trimmed and cut into 1-inch pieces

¼ cup mirin

2 teaspoons white sugar

1 tablespoon finely grated fresh ginger

1½ cups finely shredded green cabbage

3 medium scallions, thinly sliced on diagonal

2 teaspoons unseasoned rice vinegar

¼ teaspoon toasted sesame oil

2 tablespoons cornstarch

4 teaspoons grapeseed or other neutral oil, divided

3 cups cooked Japanese-style short-grain rice, hot

Contrary to popular belief, "teriyaki" refers not to a sauce, but a technique. Meat is seared, broiled or grilled then lacquered with a glaze of soy, mirin and sugar. In this recipe, our adaptation of one taught to us by Japanese cooking expert Elizabeth Andoh, chicken thighs are briefly marinated to become tender. A coating of cornstarch gives the pieces just a hint of crispness. "Donburi" refers to individual one-bowl meals of rice with various toppings, as well as to the deep bowls that are used for serving. To our chicken teriyaki donburi, a simple slaw adds texture and freshness, rounding out the dish beautifully.

Don't forget to drain the chicken before coating it with cornstarch. Excess liquid will cause splattering during cooking.

1. In a medium bowl, whisk together 3 tablespoons of sake and 1 teaspoon of soy sauce. Add the chicken and toss. Let stand at room temperature for 20 minutes or cover and refrigerate for up to 2 hours. Meanwhile, in a small saucepan over medium, combine the remaining 1 tablespoon sake, 3 tablespoons of the remaining soy sauce, the mirin and sugar. Cook, stirring, until the sugar is dissolved, about 1 minute. Off heat, stir in the ginger; set aside.

2. In a medium bowl, toss the cabbage and scallions with the remaining 1 tablespoon soy sauce, the rice vinegar and sesame oil. Set aside. Drain the chicken in a fine mesh strainer. Wipe out the bowl, then return the chicken to it. Sprinkle with the cornstarch and toss to coat.

3. In a 12-inch nonstick skillet over medium-high, heat 2 teaspoons of grapeseed oil until barely smoking. Add half the chicken in an even layer and cook without stirring until well browned on the bottom and the edges turn opaque, 3 to 4 minutes. Flip and cook without stirring until well browned on the second side, about another 3 minutes. Transfer to a clean bowl and repeat with the remaining 2 teaspoons oil and remaining chicken.

4. Wipe out the skillet, then return the chicken to the pan. Pour in the soy sauce–ginger mixture and stir to coat. Cook over medium-high, stirring, until the liquid is syrupy and the chicken is glazed, about 2 minutes. Remove from the heat. Divide the rice among 4 bowls. Top with the cabbage mixture and chicken.

Hot-Smoked Salmon Salad with Arugula, Avocado and Pepitas

Start to finish: **15 minutes** / Servings: 4

¼ cup lemon juice (about 1 lemon)

2 tablespoons whole-grain mustard

1 tablespoon honey

Kosher salt and ground black pepper

6 tablespoons extra-virgin olive oil

8 ounces hot-smoked salmon, plain or black pepper, skin removed

½ cup toasted, salted pepitas, coarsely chopped

2 avocados

10 ounces baby arugula or stemmed watercress (about 10 cups)

Ingredients with contrasting flavors and textures are an easy way to elevate everyday meals. And it's key to one of Nigella Lawson's go-to Tuesday night dinners, which upsells basic poached salmon by pairing it with crunchy and tangy ingredients. Lawson simply flakes the salmon into a salad with some watercress, avocado, pumpkin seeds and tangy vinegar. The lush avocado complements the rich salmon, both of which are balanced by the vinegar and pumpkin seeds. The greens add freshness, while the pepitas lend texture. Our Milk Street version saves time by using hot-smoked salmon, which has a texture similar to cooked salmon, but with an intensely smoky flavor and sweet and salty overtones. We made our dressing with lemon juice and whole-grain mustard. Eat this dish indulgently, as Lawson would want you to. "You know, the whole guilt thing I never quite get," she said. "One of the things I'm asked most often when I'm interviewed is, 'What is your guilty pleasure?' And I get rather prissy and I always say to everyone, 'Look, if you feel guilty about pleasure, you don't deserve to have pleasure.'"

Don't assemble the salad until just before serving. Otherwise, the avocado will brown and the greens will begin to wilt.

1. In a large bowl, whisk together the lemon juice, mustard, honey and ½ teaspoon each salt and pepper. Whisking constantly, add the oil in a stream until emulsified. Into another large bowl, flake the salmon into large chunks. Add half of the chopped pepitas and 2 tablespoons of the dressing. Toss lightly.

2. Halve the avocado lengthwise and discard the pit. Using a paring knife, cut the flesh into ½-inch pieces while still in the skin. Scoop the avocado chunks into the bowl with the salmon. Stir gently to combine. Taste, then season with salt and pepper.

3. Add the greens to the bowl with the remaining dressing and toss. Transfer the arugula to a serving dish and top with the salmon mixture and remaining pepitas.

Tlayudas

Start to finish: **20 minutes** / Servings: **4**

3 tablespoons grapeseed or other neutral oil, divided

8 ounces fresh Mexican chorizo sausage (see note), casing removed, crumbled

4 large jalapeño chilies, stemmed, seeded and thinly sliced

1 bunch scallions, cut into 1-inch pieces

Four 8-inch flour tortillas

1 cup black bean puree (p. 215)

4 ounces whole-milk mozzarella cheese, shredded (1 cup)

Shredded lettuce, to serve

Pickled red onions (p. 261), to serve

Sliced tomato, to serve

Green chili and tomatillo hot sauce (p. 215) to serve

Oaxaca, Mexico, is home to the antojito (street food) known as the tlayuda, an oversized corn tortilla topped with black beans, cheese, meats and a spate of other ingredients, then toasted on a grill. Since fresh, extra-large corn tortillas are difficult to find in much of the U.S., we use flour tortillas instead. And we do as some Oaxacans do and fold them in half to enclose the fillings. For ease, we bake them in a hot oven rather than cook them over a live fire. Fill the tlayudas to your liking and cut into wedges just before serving.

Don't use Spanish chorizo, which is dry-cured and firm, like salami. Mexican chorizo, which is soft and fresh, is the variety to use here.

1. Heat the oven to 450°F with a rack in the middle position. In a 12-inch cast-iron or other heavy skillet over medium-high, heat 1 tablespoon of oil until barely smoking. Add the chorizo and cook, stirring occasionally and breaking the meat into small bits, until well browned, about 5 minutes. Using a slotted spoon, transfer the chorizo to a paper towel–lined plate; set aside. Add the jalapeños and scallions to the pan, then cook, stirring occasionally, until the vegetables are lightly charred, 3 to 5 minutes. Transfer to the plate with the chorizo; set aside.

2. Pour the remaining 2 tablespoons oil onto a rimmed baking sheet and brush to coat the entire surface. Place 2 tortillas on the baking sheet to coat the bottoms with oil, then flip them and coat the second sides. Spread ¼ cup of the bean mixture evenly on half of each tortilla, all the way to the edges. Top the beans on each with ¼ of the cheese, then fold the unfilled half over to cover and press gently to seal. Transfer to a plate. Repeat with the remaining tortillas, beans and cheese.

3. Place the filled and folded tortillas in a single layer on the baking sheet. Bake until the cheese has melted and the bottoms of the tortillas are golden brown, about 10 minutes.

4. Using a metal spatula, transfer the tlayudas to a wire rack and cool for 5 minutes. Carefully open each and fill as desired with the chorizo-jalapeño-scallion mixture, lettuce, pickled onions, tomato and hot sauce. Re-fold, then cut into wedges. Serve warm.

BLACK BEAN PUREE

Start to finish: 15 minutes
Makes 3 cups

This bean puree is quick and simple to make. Keep some on hand for use as a filling for tacos, quesadillas or molletes; serve it warm as a side dish to any Mexican-inspired meal; or use it as a dip for tortilla chips. Leftovers can be thinned with water or broth to the desired consistency.

Don't forget to reserve ¼ cup of the bean liquid when you drain the cans. And don't rinse the beans after draining them; the liquid left clinging to them helps create a puree with a silky consistency.

1 tablespoon ground cumin

1 tablespoon ground coriander

Two 15½-ounce cans black beans, drained (do not rinse), ¼ cup liquid reserved

2 chipotle chilies in adobo sauce, plus 2 teaspoons adobo sauce

2 tablespoons lime juice

Kosher salt and ground black pepper

½ cup finely chopped fresh cilantro

In a small skillet over medium, toast the cumin and coriander, stirring often, until fragrant, about 1 minute. Transfer to a food processor and add the beans and reserved liquid, chipotle chilies and adobo sauce, lime juice and 1 teaspoon salt. Process until smooth, scraping the bowl as needed. Transfer to a medium bowl. Stir in the cilantro, then taste and season with salt and pepper.

GREEN CHILI AND TOMATILLO HOT SAUCE

Start to finish: 45 minutes (15 minutes active)
Makes 1 cup

This brightly acidic, cumin-spiked hot sauce is an excellent condiment for any Mexican-inspired meal. To give the sauce kick, we use a serrano chili with its seeds, but you could remove the seeds for less heat. For an even milder sauce, replace the serrano with a seeded jalapeño. Stored in an airtight container in the refrigerator, the sauce will keep for up to a week.

Don't worry if the vegetables broil somewhat unevenly. The chilies may brown the most and the tomatillos should be fully softened, but be careful not to scorch the garlic. And don't worry about removing the charred skins before processing—they add a subtly smoky flavor.

3 medium tomatillos (about 6 ounces), husked, cored and halved lengthwise

1 medium poblano chili (about 4 ounces), stemmed, halved lengthwise and seeded

1 serrano chili, stemmed and halved lengthwise

1 medium garlic clove, smashed and peeled

2 teaspoons white vinegar

1 teaspoon ground cumin

Kosher salt

Heat the broiler with a rack about 6 inches from the element. Line a rimmed baking sheet with foil. Place the tomatillos and both chilies cut sides down on the prepared baking sheet, then add the garlic. Broil until the chilies are deeply charred and the tomatillos are softened, 5 to 8 minutes, rotating the baking sheet about halfway through. Remove from the oven and cool for about 5 minutes.

In a food processor, combine the broiled vegetables, vinegar, cumin, 1 teaspoon salt and ¼ cup water. Process until smooth, scraping down the bowl as needed, about 1 minute. Transfer to a small bowl, then taste and season with salt. Cover and let stand at room temperature for 30 minutes before serving

Molletes with Pico de Gallo

Start to finish: **15 minutes** / Servings: 4

___

Eight ½-inch-thick slices
crusty bread (see note)

¼ cup extra-virgin olive oil

Kosher salt and ground black pepper

2 cups black bean puree (p. 215)

1 pound whole-milk mozzarella
cheese, shredded

½ cup finely chopped fresh cilantro

Pico de gallo (p. 217), to serve

Sliced avocado, to serve (optional)

Pickled sliced jalapeños, to serve
(optional)

Mexican molletes are not unlike Italian bruschetti, but the bread is topped with pureed beans and cheese, then toasted until the cheese is melted and browned. They make a great breakfast, light lunch or midday snack. In Mexico, the bread of choice typically is soft-crumbed, thin-crusted rolls called bolillos that are split open before they're topped. We opted for ½-inch-thick slices of supermarket bakery bread with a soft crumb; look for a loaf that measures about 10-by-5 inches and weighs about 1 pound. Pico de gallo (fresh tomato salsa) adds color and fresh flavor to the molletes, so we consider it a necessary embellishment; sliced avocado and pickled jalapeños are delicious, but optional.

Don't walk away from the bread as it broils. Broilers vary in heat output, so keep a close eye on the slices to make sure they don't scorch.

1. Heat the broiler with a rack about 6 inches from the element. Line a rimmed baking sheet with foil and mist with cooking spray. Arrange the bread in a single layer on the baking sheet and brush the tops with the oil. Season with salt and pepper. Broil until the bread is golden brown, 3 to 5 minutes. Flip each slice and broil until the second sides are golden brown, 1 to 2 minutes. Remove from the broiler.

2. Flip each slice once again. Spread ¼ cup bean puree on each slice, then top each with some of the cheese, dividing it evenly (½ cup each). Broil until the cheese is melted and begins to brown, 4 to 6 minutes. Transfer the baking sheet to a wire rack and cool for 5 minutes. Sprinkle with cilantro, then transfer to a platter. Serve with pico de gallo, sliced avocado (if using) and pickled jalapeños (if using).

PICO DE GALLO

Start to finish: **30 minutes**
Makes about **2 cups**

Pico de gallo is a bright, fresh tomato salsa. We use grape or cherry tomatoes because they tend to be dependably sweet and flavorful even when regular tomatoes are dull, mealy and out of season. For a spicier salsa, leave the seeds in the jalapeño.

Don't make the pico de gallo too far ahead. Even after the tomatoes are transferred to a serving bowl with a slotted spoon, they will continue to release liquid and their texture will soften.

1 pint grape or cherry tomatoes, roughly chopped

¼ small red onion, finely chopped (about 3 tablespoons)

¼ cup lightly packed fresh cilantro, chopped

½ jalapeño chili, stemmed, seeded and minced

2 teaspoons white vinegar

1½ teaspoons extra-virgin olive oil

Kosher salt

In a medium bowl, stir together the tomatoes, onion, cilantro, chili, vinegar, oil and 1 teaspoon salt. Cover and let stand at room temperature for 15 minutes. Using a slotted spoon, transfer to a serving bowl, letting the liquid drip away. Taste and season with salt.

Skirt Steak Salad with Arugula and Peppadews

Start to finish: **30 minutes** / Servings: 4

2 teaspoons ground fennel

Kosher salt and ground black pepper

1 pound skirt steak, trimmed

7 tablespoons extra-virgin olive oil, divided

3 tablespoons lemon juice

½ cup chopped Peppadew peppers, drained

1 large garlic clove, thinly sliced

8 cups baby arugula

1½ ounces Parmesan cheese, shaved (¾ cup)

Our steak salad takes inspiration from classic Italian tagliata, then skips across continents with the addition of Peppadews, tangy peppers from South Africa. A popular dish in Tuscany, tagliata is a simple presentation of thinly sliced, rare steak, extra-virgin olive oil, arugula and shaved Parmesan. We made ours work with an inexpensive skirt steak seasoned with a dry rub of salt, pepper and ground fennel. We then whipped up a simple lemon juice–olive oil vinaigrette. The steak got a quick sear. Then, while it rested, we added thinly sliced garlic and chopped Peppadew peppers to the pan. In an unusual touch, we used half the vinaigrette to dress the arugula and the other half to deglaze the pan, creating a warm, sweet-and-sour garlicky sauce that blended with the steak's juices. Pay attention to how you slice the steak. Cuts like skirt steak have longer, thicker muscle fibers than sirloin and tenderloin; they are relatively tough unless cut against the grain, which results in shorter fibers. Skirt steaks can sometimes come as long pieces; if needed, cut the meat in half to fit the pan. If you can't find skirt steak, flank, flat iron and bavette steaks all work well.

Don't cook the steak beyond medium-rare or it will be tough.

1. In a small bowl, combine the fennel, 1 teaspoon salt and 2 teaspoons pepper. Coat the steak with the seasoning, then let sit for 15 minutes. Meanwhile, in a liquid measuring cup, whisk together 6 tablespoons of the oil, the lemon juice, ¾ teaspoon salt and ½ teaspoon pepper. Set aside.

2. In a large skillet over medium-high, heat the remaining tablespoon of oil until beginning to smoke. Add the steak and sear, without moving, until well browned, about 3 minutes. Flip and brown on the second side, about another 2 minutes for rare to medium-rare.

3. Transfer to a plate and let rest for 10 minutes. Return the skillet to the heat. Add the Peppadews and garlic, then cook for 30 seconds. Stir the dressing, then add half of it to the skillet, along with any juices from the meat on the plate, scraping the pan to deglaze.

4. In a large bowl, toss the arugula with the remaining dressing and half of the Parmesan, then divide among serving plates. Thinly slice the steak against the grain, then arrange slices over the arugula. Spoon some warm pan sauce over each serving. Top with the remaining Parmesan.

Taiwanese Five-Spice Pork
with Rice (*Lu Rou Fan*)

Start to finish: **40 minutes** / Servings: 6

1½ pounds ground pork

1 cup low-sodium soy sauce, divided, plus more, as needed

¼ cup grapeseed or other neutral oil

12 ounces shallots, halved and thinly sliced

10 medium garlic cloves, minced

1¼ cups dry sherry

⅓ cup packed dark brown sugar

2 tablespoons five-spice powder

1 tablespoon unseasoned rice vinegar

Steamed rice, to serve

3 scallions, thinly sliced on diagonal

This Taiwanese dish is a one-bowl meal consisting of richly flavored, soy-simmered pork served over steamed rice. Pork belly is traditional, but we found ground pork faster to cook and just as delicious. Hard-cooked eggs are a common garnish, but we preferred soft-cooked eggs for their runny yolks. To make soft-cooked eggs, bring 2 cups of water to a simmer in a large saucepan fitted with a steamer basket. Add the eggs, cover and steam over medium for 7 minutes. Transfer the eggs to ice water to stop the cooking, then shell and halve the eggs before serving. We liked serving steamed or stir-fried bok choy or broccoli alongside, a nice balance to the richness of the pork.

Don't use regular soy sauce; it will become too salty because the sauce is reduced during cooking. And don't use cooking sherry, which contains added salt; use an inexpensive dry sherry.

1. In a medium bowl, mix the pork with ¼ cup of the soy sauce. Cover and refrigerate until needed. In a large Dutch oven over medium, heat the oil until barely smoking. Add the shallots and cook, stirring, until deeply browned, 15 to 20 minutes. Add the garlic and cook, stirring constantly, until the garlic is fragrant and just beginning to brown, about 1 minute.

2. Add the sherry, sugar, five-spice and remaining ¾ cup soy sauce. Stir until the sugar has dissolved, then increase to high and bring to a boil. Cook, stirring, until reduced and syrupy and a spoon leaves a clear trail, about 5 minutes.

3. Reduce to low and allow the simmering to subside. Add the pork, breaking it into small pieces. Cook, stirring, until the meat is no longer pink, 5 to 7 minutes. Stir in the vinegar, then taste and add more soy sauce, if needed. Spoon steamed rice into 6 bowls, top with the pork and sprinkle with the scallions.

Three-Cup **Chicken**

Start to finish: **35 minutes (15 minutes active)**
Servings: 4

---

2 teaspoons cornstarch

3 tablespoons soy sauce

¾ cup sake

2 tablespoons packed brown sugar

1 tablespoon grapeseed or other neutral oil

2 pounds boneless, skinless chicken thighs, trimmed, patted dry and cut into 1-inch-wide strips

12 medium garlic cloves, halved lengthwise

1 bunch scallions, cut into 1-inch lengths

1 serrano chili, stemmed and sliced into thin rounds

¼ cup minced fresh ginger

2 tablespoons toasted sesame oil

3 cups lightly packed fresh basil, torn if large

Sesame seeds, to serve

Taiwanese three-cup chicken is named for the formula once used to prepare the dish: 1 cup each of sesame oil, soy sauce and rice wine. Not surprisingly, recipes no longer adhere to that ratio, but the name has stuck. Bone-in chicken legs that have been hacked into pieces are traditional for this one-pan dish; we opted for boneless, skinless chicken thighs for easier prep and eating. Though we prefer to use a wok, this recipe also works in a 12-inch skillet. Serve with rice and steamed or stir-fried vegetables.

Don't begin cooking until all ingredients are prepared; the dish comes together quickly. Don't stir the chicken for about 5 minutes after adding it to the skillet. This helps the chicken brown and develop flavor.

1. In a small bowl, stir together the cornstarch and soy sauce, then stir in the sake and sugar until the sugar has dissolved. Set aside. Heat a 14-inch wok over medium-high for about 3 minutes, or until a drop of water evaporates within 1 to 2 seconds of contact. Add the grapeseed oil and swirl to coat. Add the chicken in an even layer and cook without stirring until browned, about 5 minutes.

2. Add the garlic and cook, stirring occasionally, until the garlic is well-browned and softened, about 4 minutes. Add the scallions, chili, ginger and sesame oil, then cook, stirring constantly, until the scallions begin to wilt, about 1 minute.

3. Stir the sake-cornstarch mixture to recombine, then add to the wok. Cook, stirring constantly, until the sauce has thickened, about 3 minutes. Off heat, dd the basil and stir until it begins to wilt, about 30 seconds. Sprinkle woth sesame seeds.

Spicy Beef Salad with
Mint and Cilantro (*Larb Neua*)

Start to finish: **20 minutes** / Servings: 4

---

2 tablespoons jasmine rice

3 tablespoons lime juice

2 tablespoons fish sauce

2 teaspoons white sugar, divided

Kosher salt and ground black pepper

2 medium shallots, sliced
into thin rings

2 Fresno chilies, stemmed
and sliced into thin rings

2 teaspoons grapeseed or
other neutral oil

1 pound 85 percent lean ground beef

1 cup lightly packed fresh mint, torn

1 cup lightly packed fresh cilantro
leaves

Larb is a minced-meat salad from northern Thailand. This beef version was inspired by the spicy, tangy Isaan style from the northeast that's also popular in neighboring Laos. Easy-to-make toasted rice powder, called khao kua, is an essential ingredient here—it imparts a unique flavor, absorbs a small amount of the liquid and adds a subtle crunch. Cabbage leaves and sticky rice are the traditional accompaniments, but lettuce leaves and steamed jasmine rice are equally good. If you like, for more spiciness, add another chili or two.

Don't use extra-lean ground beef. A little fat keeps the meat moist, adds flavor and balances the acidity of the dressing.

1. In a 12-inch skillet over medium-low, toast the rice, stirring often, until browned and fragrant, 6 to 7 minutes. Transfer to a small bowl and let cool, about 10 minutes; set the skillet aside.

2. Meanwhile, in a medium bowl, whisk together the lime juice, fish sauce, 1 teaspoon of sugar, 1 teaspoon salt and ½ teaspoon pepper. Stir in the shallots and chilies. Let stand for at least 10 minutes or up to 20 minutes while you prepare the rest of the dish.

3. Using a spice grinder or mortar and pestle, pulverize the toasted rice to a coarse powder. Return the powder to the bowl and set aside.

4. In the same skillet over medium-high, heat the oil until shimmering. Add the beef, the remaining 1 teaspoon sugar and ½ teaspoon salt and cook, breaking the meat into very small bits, until no longer pink, 4 to 5 minutes. Immediately add the beef and any juices to the shallot-chili mixture, along with the mint, cilantro and half of the rice powder, then toss to combine. Let stand for 5 minutes. Taste and season with salt and pepper, then transfer to a serving platter and sprinkle with the remaining rice powder.

CHANGE THE WAY YOU COOK:
FOR BOLD, FRESH FLAVOR, SAUCE AFTER COOKING

We often skip marinades for meat. Instead we focus on adding bold flavorings after cooking. As meat rests after cooking, it is better able to absorb seasonings.

Thai Braised Pork and Eggs with Star Anise and Cinnamon (*Moo Palo*)

Start to finish: **1 hour 40 minutes (30 minutes active)** / Servings: 6

---

1 bunch cilantro, stems chopped, leaves roughly chopped, reserved separately

8 medium garlic cloves, smashed and peeled

1 tablespoon whole white peppercorns

3 whole cloves

6 tablespoons low-sodium soy sauce, plus more as needed

⅓ cup fish sauce

⅓ cup packed dark brown sugar, plus more as needed

5 star anise pods

Three 3-inch cinnamon sticks

4 pounds boneless pork shoulder, trimmed and cut into 1½-inch chunks

6 large eggs

Moo palo is a classic Thai braise that combines the richness of pork belly and eggs in savory-sweet broth flavored with Chinese five-spice powder. For our version, we opted for easier-to-source pork shoulder; it's a leaner cut but it cooks up equally flavorful. Traditionally, hard-cooked eggs are simmered with the pork and take on a brown hue from the braising liquid, along with a firm texture from long cooking. We opted instead to simply garnish with hard-cooked eggs so their color is brighter and texture more tender. And rather than use five-spice powder, which can give the braise a muddled, overspiced flavor, we preferred the cleaner, purer notes of whole cloves, star anise and cinnamon sticks. Serve the pork and eggs with steamed jasmine rice. As with most braises, this dish tastes even better the next day.

Don't use preground white pepper. Whole white peppercorns have far more flavor and aroma. Black peppercorns would be a better substitute than preground white pepper, but its flavor is sharper and more pungent and will slightly alter the flavor profile of the dish. And don't use regular soy sauce, which is too salty.

1. In a blender, combine the cilantro stems, garlic, peppercorns, cloves, soy sauce, fish sauce and 6 tablespoons water. Puree until almost smooth, about 20 seconds. Set aside.

2. In a large Dutch oven over medium-high, stir together the sugar and 1 tablespoon water. Bring to a simmer and cook, stirring often, until the sugar turns foamy, then dry and begins to smoke lightly, 3 to 4 minutes. Stir in the cilantro stem–garlic mixture, then add 7 cups water to the blender, swirl to rinse it, then add the water to the pot. Stir, scraping up any caramelized sugar from the bottom and sides of the pot.

3. Add the star anise, cinnamon sticks and pork, distributing the meat in an even layer. Bring to a boil, then cover and reduce to medium-low and cook, adjusting the heat as needed to maintain a gentle simmer, for 50 minutes.

4. Meanwhile, place a folding steamer basket in a large saucepan and add enough water to skim the bottom of the basket. Bring to a boil over medium-high. Add the eggs to the steamer basket, cover and cook for 12 minutes. While the eggs cook, fill a medium bowl with ice water. When the eggs are done, immediately transfer them to the ice water and let stand until cooled. Crack and peel the eggs, then set aside.

5. After the pork has simmered for 50 minutes, uncover, increase to heat medium and cook until a skewer inserted into the pork meets no resistance, 20 to 30 minutes. Remove and discard the star anise and cinnamon sticks, then let stand for about 5 minutes. Tilt the pot to pool the liquid to one side, then use a wide spoon to skim off and discard as much fat as possible from the surface of the liquid. Taste and season with additional soy sauce, then return to a simmer over medium.

6. Spoon the pork and broth into bowls. Cut the eggs lengthwise in halves or quarters and place 2 or 4 pieces in each bowl, then top with cilantro leaves.

Salmon Chraimeh

Start to finish: **20 minutes** / Servings: 4

Four 6-ounce center-cut salmon fillets, 1 to 1½ inches thick

Kosher salt and ground black pepper

1 tablespoon extra-virgin olive oil, plus more to serve

4 scallions, thinly sliced, dark green parts reserved separately

3 medium garlic cloves, thinly sliced

1 jalapeño pepper, stemmed, halved, seeded and thinly sliced

1 teaspoon coriander seeds

1 teaspoon cumin seeds

¾ teaspoon smoked paprika

14½-ounce can diced tomatoes, with juices

2 tablespoons finely chopped fresh mint

¼ cup lightly packed fresh cilantro, chopped

Lemon wedges, to serve

Center-cut salmon fillets deliver weeknight ease with vibrant flavor in this recipe inspired by the Sephardic dish chraimeh, or fish braised in a mildly spicy tomato sauce. The name comes from the word for thief and refers to the way the spice comes at the end of the sauce, sneaking up on the diner. We tailored ours to work with pantry staples and scaled down the amount of garlic typically used. Whole cumin and coriander, paprika, jalapeño and scallions rounded out the aromatics. Look for salmon pieces that are evenly thick, about 1 to 1½ inches. We liked our salmon cooked between 115°F and 120°F, which leaves the thickest part with some translucency. If you like yours more thoroughly cooked, after simmering remove the skillet from the heat and leave the fillets in the covered pan until cooked to desired doneness.

Don't use fillets of widely varying thicknesses; they will require different cooking times. If unavoidable, begin checking the thinner fillets ahead of the thicker ones.

1. Season the salmon fillets on both sides with salt and pepper. In a 10-inch skillet over medium-high, heat the oil until shimmering. Add the white and light green scallion parts, the garlic and jalapeño. Cook, stirring occasionally, until lightly browned, about 2 minutes. Stir in the coriander, cumin and paprika, then cook until fragrant, about 30 seconds.

2. Stir in the tomatoes, ½ teaspoon salt and ¼ teaspoon pepper. Bring to a simmer, then nestle the fillets skin side up in the sauce. Reduce to medium, cover and simmer for 6 to 8 minutes, until only the center of the thickest parts of the fillets are translucent or until they reach 115°F to 120°F.

3. Using tongs, carefully peel off and discard the skin from each fillet, then use a spatula to transfer to serving plates flesh side up. If the sauce is watery, continue to simmer over medium-high until slightly thickened, 1 to 2 minutes.

4. Off heat, stir in the mint and cilantro. Taste and season with salt and pepper. Spoon the sauce over the salmon, sprinkle with the scallion greens, drizzle with oil and serve with lemon wedges.

Spanish Ratatouille (*Pisto Manchego*)

Start to finish: **40 minutes** / Servings: 4

One 12-ounce zucchini

Two 8-ounce Chinese or Japanese eggplants, peeled and cut into 1-inch cubes

Kosher salt and ground black pepper

8 tablespoons extra-virgin olive oil, divided

1 large yellow onion, quartered lengthwise and thinly sliced

2 medium bell peppers, stemmed, seeded and cut into ½-inch pieces

8 medium garlic cloves, thinly sliced

¾ teaspoon ground cumin

1½ teaspoons dried oregano

14½-ounce can diced tomatoes, with juices

¼ cup chopped fresh flat-leaf parsley

2 ounces manchego cheese, shaved

Pisto manchego, Spain's colorful combination of sautéed summer vegetables, is similar to France's ratatouille. As is, it makes a wonderful side. When topped with a poached or fried egg, it becomes a delicious main course. The flavorful tomato juices make crusty bread almost obligatory, but the dish would also pair wonderfully with rice or a baked potato. We liked the effect of using one each of red and yellow bell peppers, but you could use just one color. If you can't find Japanese or Chinese eggplant, a pound of globe eggplant will do, but you may need to increase the covered cooking time by a few minutes.

Don't use the seedy core of the zucchini; it turns soft and mushy with cooking. And don't skip the manchego cheese; its buttery, grassy flavor is a key component.

1. Trim off the ends of the zucchini, then slice lengthwise into planks, leaving behind and discarding the seedy core. Cut the zucchini planks into ½-inch cubes and set aside. In a medium bowl, toss the eggplant with 1 teaspoon salt and ½ teaspoon pepper.

2. In a large Dutch oven over medium-high, heat 6 tablespoons of oil until shimmering. Add the eggplant in an even layer and cook without stirring until golden brown, 3 to 5 minutes. Stir, cover and reduce to medium. Continue to cook, stirring occasionally, until tender but not falling apart, another 3 to 5 minutes. Using a slotted spoon, transfer to a paper towel-lined medium bowl and set aside.

3. To the same pot, add 1 tablespoon of the remaining oil and heat over medium-high until shimering. Add the zucchini in an even layer and cook without stirring until well-browned, about 4 minutes. Continue to cook, stirring occasionally, until browned on all sides and tender when pierced with a fork, another 1 to 2 minutes. Using the slotted spoon, transfer to the bowl with the eggplant.

4. To the same pot, add the remaining 1 tablespoon oil and heat over medium-high until shimmering. Add the onion and ½ teaspoon salt. Cook, stirring occasionally, until golden brown, 3 to 5 minutes. Stir in the bell peppers, 1 teaspoon salt and ½ teaspoon pepper. Cover and cook, stirring, until the peppers soften, 3 to 5 minutes. Stir in the garlic, cumin and oregano, then cook until fragrant, about 30 seconds. Stir in the tomatoes, then cover and simmer over medium for 5 to 7 minutes.

5. Reduce to low and stir in the eggplant-zucchini mixture. Cook until heated through, 1 to 2 minutes. Stir in the parsley, then taste and season with salt and pepper. Transfer to a platter and top with the manchego.

Shrimp with Feta Cheese
(*Garides Saganaki*)

Start to finish: **30 minutes** / Servings: 4

3 tablespoons extra-virgin olive oil, divided

1¼ pounds jumbo shrimp, 16/20 per pound, peeled, deveined, tails removed, patted dry

4 large garlic cloves, finely chopped

4 teaspoons fennel seeds, finely ground

¼ teaspoon red pepper flakes

⅓ cup dry white wine

1½ pounds small tomatoes, such as Campari, chopped, plus ¼ cup finely diced

⅓ cup pitted Kalamata olives, chopped

2 tablespoons plus 2 teaspoons chopped fresh oregano

Kosher salt and ground black pepper

4 ounces feta cheese, coarsely crumbled (1 cup)

¼ cup chopped Peppadew peppers (optional)

This classic Greek dish pairs plump, sweet shrimp with briny feta cheese. We added chopped Kalamata olives for added savory flavor, as well as ground fennel seed for a hint of licorice. Our preferred tomatoes for this recipe are Campari (or cocktail) tomatoes, as they tend to be sweet and flavorful year-round; they're larger than cherry tomatoes but smaller than standard round tomatoes and usually are sold on the vine in plastic containers. We tried cherry and grape tomatoes but found their skins to be tough and unpleasant in the finished sauce. Chopped Peppadew peppers are an unconventional ingredient, but their mild, sweet heat makes them a welcome addition. Serve with crusty bread to sop up the sauce.

Don't use pre-crumbled feta. The cheese plays a prominent role in this dish, so good-quality feta sold in blocks is important.

1. In a 12-inch nonstick skillet over medium-high, heat 1 tablespoon of the oil until shimmering. Add half the shrimp in an even layer and cook without disturbing until deep golden brown on the bottoms, 1 to 2 minutes. Stir and cook until the shrimp are pink and opaque on all sides, another 20 to 30 seconds. Transfer to a medium bowl. Repeat with 1 tablespoon of the remaining oil and the remaining shrimp. Set aside.

2. Add the remaining 1 tablespoon oil to the pan and heat over medium-high until shimmering. Add the garlic, fennel and red pepper flakes and cook, stirring constantly, until the garlic is light golden brown, about 20 seconds. Add the wine and cook, stirring, until the liquid is almost evaporated, 30 to 60 seconds. Add the chopped tomatoes, olives and 1½ teaspoons salt. Cook, stirring, until the tomatoes have broken down into a sauce, 6 to 7 minutes.

3. Remove the pan from heat. Stir in 2 tablespoons of the oregano, then taste and season with salt and pepper. Return the shrimp to the skillet, along with the accumulated juices. Cover the pan and let stand until the shrimp are heated through, about 1 minute.

4. Transfer to a serving dish. Sprinkle with the feta, finely diced tomatoes, the Peppadews (if using) and the remaining 2 teaspoons oregano.

Lomo Saltado

Start to finish: **35 minutes** / Servings: **4**

1½ pounds beef sirloin tips, trimmed, cut with the grain into 3-inch pieces and sliced ½ inch thick against the grain

1½ teaspoons ground cumin

Kosher salt and ground black pepper

5 tablespoons soy sauce, divided

3 tablespoons grapeseed or other neutral oil, divided

1 large red onion, halved and cut into ½-inch half-rings

¼ cup red wine vinegar

2 medium garlic cloves, minced

1 jalapeño chili, stemmed and sliced into thin rounds

1½ cups grape tomatoes, halved

Peru's lomo saltado, a quick stir-fry of soy-marinated beef, tomatoes and onions, is fusion cooking at its easiest and most approachable. It's part of chifa cuisine—Asian-influenced dishes created by indentured Chinese workers in the late 19th century. For our take, we developed deeper flavor by mixing ground cumin into the soy sauce marinade. Tenderloin is often used here, but we preferred sirloin tips (also called flap meat) for their meatier flavor as well as lower price. And we seared the meat instead of stir-frying. Readily available jalapeño peppers made a good substitute for the traditional yellow ají peppers. If you prefer little to no spiciness, halve and seed the jalapeño before slicing it into half rings. Classic lomo saltado is frequently served over french fries; your favorite, frozen or otherwise, would be a good choice here. Steamed rice is an equally good accompaniment.

Don't cook the beef without patting it dry. Marinating in soy sauce adds flavor, but also moisture. Drying the beef helps ensure that the slices sear nicely, rather than steam. Also, cook it in two batches; crowding the pan inhibits browning.

1. In a medium bowl, combine the beef, cumin, 1 teaspoon each salt and pepper, and 2 tablespoons of soy sauce. Marinate at room temperature for 10 minutes. Pat the meat dry and set aside.

2. In a 12-inch skillet over high, heat 1 tablespoon of oil until barely smoking. Add half of the meat in a single layer and cook, turning once, until well browned on both sides, 2 to 3 minutes total. Transfer to a plate. Repeat with 1 tablespoon of the remaining oil and the remaining meat.

3. In the same pan over medium-high, heat the remaining 1 tablespoon oil over medium-high until shimmering. Add the onion and cook, stirring, until just starting to soften, about 2 minutes.

4. Stir in the vinegar and the remaining 3 tablespoons soy sauce, scraping up any browned bits on the bottom of the pan. Cook for about 1 minute, or until the sauce thickens slightly. Stir in the garlic and jalapeño and cook until fragrant, about 30 seconds. Add the tomatoes and the meat, along with any accumulated juices. Cook until the meat is just warmed through, about 30 seconds. Taste and season with salt and pepper.

Ginger-Scallion **Steamed Cod**

Start to finish: 45 minutes / Servings: 4

3 tablespoons chopped fresh cilantro, plus ¼ cup whole leaves, divided

6 scallions, 3 minced and 3 thinly sliced on diagonal, reserved separately

2 tablespoons finely grated fresh ginger

6 tablespoons soy sauce, divided

3 tablespoons grapeseed or other neutral oil, divided

6 large green cabbage leaves, plus 2 cups thinly sliced green cabbage

Four 6-ounce skinless cod, haddock or halibut fillets

2 tablespoons unseasoned rice vinegar

2 teaspoons white sugar

1 teaspoon ground white pepper

1 serrano chili, stemmed and sliced into thin rings

1 tablespoon toasted sesame oil

In southern China, cooks have a worry-free method for cooking delicate, flaky white fish to perfection: steaming the fish whole with aromatic-spiked water. The mild heat slowly firms the protein, allowing it to stay moist. We adapted the technique, using skinless cod fillets for convenience and lining our steamer basket with cabbage leaves to mimic the skin of the whole fish. Rubbing the fillets with a seasoning paste of ginger, cilantro, scallions and soy sauce produced deep flavor in the mild-tasting fish. We drew on another classic Chinese technique for a flavorful finish—topping the fillets with raw chopped scallions and serrano chilies, then pouring sizzling-hot oil over them to bring out the flavors and aromas. Though this recipe calls for cod, haddock and halibut—or any firm, thick white fish fillets—also work. Because fillets vary in thickness, a general guide is to steam them for about 8 minutes per 1-inch thickness.

Don't let the steaming water reach a full boil. A gentle heat cooks the fish slowly and evenly, helping it stay moist.

1. In a wide, shallow bowl, stir together the chopped cilantro, the minced scallions, ginger, 2 tablespoons of soy sauce and 1 tablespoon of grapeseed oil. Add the fish and coat well. Let stand at room temperature for 10 minutes.

2. Place a steamer basket in a large pot. Add enough water to fill without reaching the basket. Remove the basket. Cover the pot and bring to a simmer over medium-high. Line the basket with 4 of the cabbage leaves. Place the fish fillets on the leaves, then cover with the remaining 2 leaves. Turn off the heat under the pot, then set the basket in the pot. Cover and return to a simmer over medium. Steam until the fish flakes easily, 8 to 12 minutes.

3. Meanwhile, in a small bowl, whisk the remaining 4 tablespoons soy sauce, the rice vinegar, sugar and pepper. Transfer 3 tablespoons to a medium bowl, add the sliced cabbage and toss. Arrange on a serving platter. Reserve the remaining dressing.

4. When the fish is ready, discard the cabbage leaves covering it. Use a spatula to transfer the fillets to the platter, placing them on the sliced cabbage. Sprinkle with the sliced scallions and the serrano.

5. In a small skillet over medium-high, heat the remaining 2 tablespoons grapeseed oil until barely smoking. Carefully pour the oil over the fillets. Drizzle with the sesame oil and sprinkle with the cilantro leaves. Serve with the reserved dressing on the side.

Singapore Chicken Satay

Start to finish: 35 minutes, plus marinating
Servings: 4

For the chicken:

2 tablespoons grated fresh ginger

6 medium garlic cloves, finely grated

¼ cup white sugar

3 tablespoons toasted peanut oil

2 tablespoons ground turmeric

4 teaspoons ground cumin

Kosher salt

2 pounds boneless, skinless chicken
thighs, trimmed and cut lengthwise
into 1-inch-wide strips

For the sauce:

¼ cup boiling water

1 tablespoon creamy peanut butter

¼ cup soy sauce

¼ cup unseasoned rice vinegar

2 tablespoons white sugar

2 tablespoons toasted peanut oil

2 teaspoons grated fresh ginger

1 medium garlic clove, finely grated

2 teaspoons chili-garlic sauce

½ teaspoon ground turmeric

¼ cup finely chopped salted
dry-roasted peanuts

In Singapore, satay—thin strips of boldly seasoned and skewered meat—is cooked quickly over long beds of hot coals. The skewers are flipped frequently to ensure even cooking and plenty of delicious charred bits at the edges. It typically is served with a thin vinegar-based sauce that includes a scant amount of peanut butter and chopped peanuts for flavor and texture. In our recipe, the skewers are broiled on a wire rack set over a baking sheet lined with foil and sprinkled with 1 cup of kosher salt. The salt absorbs the fat when drips hit the pan, preventing the fat from smoking.

Don't marinate the chicken for more than three hours or it will be too salty. And don't substitute chicken breasts. Under the high heat of the broiler, they easily overcook and dry out.

1. To prepare the chicken, in a large bowl, combine the ginger, garlic, sugar, oil, turmeric, cumin, 1 tablespoon salt and ½ cup water. Stir until the sugar dissolves, then stir in the chicken. Cover and refrigerate for 2 to 3 hours.

2. To make the sauce, in a medium bowl, whisk the boiling water and peanut butter until smooth. Whisk in the soy sauce, vinegar and sugar, then set aside. In a small skillet over medium, heat the oil, ginger and garlic. Cook, stirring constantly, until fragrant, about 1 minute. Stir in the chili-garlic sauce and turmeric, then cook until fragrant, about 30 seconds. Whisk the garlic mixture into the soy sauce mixture. Reserve ¼ cup for basting the chicken. Cover and refrigerate the remaining sauce for serving.

3. About 30 minutes before skewering and cooking the chicken, remove the sauce from the refrigerator. Stir in the chopped peanuts. Heat the broiler with a rack about 4 inches from the element. Line a rimmed baking sheet with foil and spread 1 cup salt in an even layer over it. Set a wire rack in the baking sheet over the salt and mist with cooking spray.

4. Drain the chicken in a colander. Thread 2 or 3 pieces of chicken onto each of eight 8-inch metal skewers, evenly dividing the meat and pushing the pieces together, but not tightly packing them. Evenly space the skewers on the wire rack.

5. Broil the chicken until beginning to brown, 5 to 7 minutes. Flip the skewers and continue to broil until the second sides begin to brown, another 4 to 6 minutes. Remove from the oven and brush the surface of each skewer with 1 to 2 tablespoons of the reserved sauce. Continue to broil until well-charred, 2 to 4 minutes. Remove from the oven once again, flip the skewers and brush with another 1 to 2 tablespoons of the reserved sauce. Continue to broil until the second sides begin to char and the chicken is cooked through, another 2 to 4 minutes. Serve with the dipping sauce.

Singapore Sling

Start to finish: **5 minutes**
Servings: **1**

1½ ounces rye whiskey

¾ ounce orange juice

⅓ ounce cassis liqueur

⅓ ounce simple syrup

3 dashes angostura bitters

Prosecco

2-inch strip orange zest

At Smoke & Mirrors bar in Singapore, this lightly fruity update to the original Singapore sling is topped with pineapple juice bubbles. We found a strip of orange zest was similarly tropical and more practical.

In a cocktail shaker, combine the rye, orange juice, cassis, simple syrup and bitters. Add 1 cup ice, then shake for 15 to 20 seconds, or until the sides of the shaker are quite cold. Strain into a chilled coupe glass. Top with a splash of prosecco and the orange zest.

Roasted Mushroom Pizza
with Fontina and Scallions

Start to finish: 35 minutes, plus heating the oven
Makes one 12-inch pizza

1 pound portobello mushroom caps

⅓ cup extra-virgin olive oil

Kosher salt and ground black pepper

1 tablespoon finely chopped
fresh thyme

3 medium garlic cloves, minced

1 portion pizza dough (see recipe
p. 245), warmed to 75°F

Bread flour, for dusting

1 tablespoon semolina flour,
for dusting

1 cup fontina-Parmesan cream
(see recipe p. 243)

2 scallions, thinly sliced on diagonal

¼ teaspoon red pepper flakes

Heating the oven and pizza steel or stone for pizza-baking takes about an hour. We use this time to roast portobello mushrooms, which we combine with our fontina-Parmesan cream sauce. The mushrooms can also be prepared and refrigerated up to 24 hours beforehand. When shaping the pizza dough, make sure that the edges are thicker than the center so they will contain the sauce, which becomes runny during baking. We found that pizza bakes best at 550°F; if your oven heats only to 500°F, the pie will need to bake for an extra two minutes. If you don't have a pizza steel or stone, use an overturned rimmed baking sheet.

Don't undercook the mushrooms. Roasting them until they are well browned removes moisture that would otherwise make the pizza crust soggy.

1. One hour before baking, heat the oven to 550°F with a baking steel or stone on the upper-middle rack and a second rack in the lower-middle position.

2. Using a spoon, scrape off and discard the gills on the undersides of the mushroom caps. Halve any caps that are 5 inches or larger in diameter, then cut the caps into ¼-inch slices. In a large bowl, toss the mushrooms, olive oil and ½ teaspoon salt.

3. Spread the mushrooms in an even layer on a rimmed baking sheet. Roast on the lower oven rack, stirring once, until they have released their moisture, the moisture evaporates and the mushrooms begin to brown, about 15 minutes. Stir in the thyme and garlic, then roast until the mushrooms have browned and the garlic is no longer raw, another 3 to 4 minutes. Let cool completely on a wire rack. Leave the oven on.

4. Turn the dough out onto a counter dusted with bread flour. Flour your hands and, using your fingers, press the dough, starting at the center and working out to the edges, into a 12-inch round, turning the dough over once. The round should be thin at the center, with slightly thicker edges. Lightly dust a baking peel, inverted baking sheet or rimless cookie sheet with the semolina. Transfer the dough to the peel and, if needed, reshape into a round.

5. Using the back of a spoon, spread the fontina-Parmesan cream evenly on the dough, leaving a ½-inch border at the edge. Scatter the mushrooms over it and season with pepper. Slide the pizza onto the baking steel or stone and bake until the crust is well browned, 7 to 9 minutes.

6. Using the peel, transfer the pizza to a wire rack. Let cool for a couple of minutes, then sprinkle with the scallions and red pepper flakes.

FONTINA-PARMESAN CREAM

Start to finish: **10 minutes**
Makes **2 cups** (enough for 2 pizzas)

This cream-based pizza sauce—inspired by Nancy Silverton, who in turn picked it up at Pellicano, a pizzeria in Umbria—pairs well with roasted portobello mushrooms. We also liked it with sausage and hot peppers (but make sure the peppers are cooked first so they don't leak moisture into the sauce).

¾ cup heavy cream, cold

2 ounces (1 cup) shredded fontina cheese

¼ cup grated Parmesan cheese

1 tablespoon minced fresh rosemary

½ teaspoon ground black pepper

In a stand mixer fitted with the whisk attachment, whip the cream on medium until stiff peaks form, about 2½ minutes. Using a rubber spatula, fold in the fontina, Parmesan, rosemary and pepper. Refrigerate in an airtight container for up to 3 days.

548 grams (4 cups) bread flour, plus more for dusting

1 tablespoon white sugar

¾ teaspoon instant yeast

1½ cups cool (65°F) water

2 teaspoons kosher salt

PIZZA DOUGH

Start to finish: **1½ days (20 minutes active)**
Makes **four 8-ounce portions of dough**

Though any brand of bread flour will work in this recipe, we liked King Arthur Flour best. It has a higher protein content, producing crusts with good flavor, nicely crisped surfaces and a satisfying chew. We found that making the dough with cool or cold water helped prolong the fermentation process, which developed better flavor. For fermenting the dough, quart-size zip-close plastic bags coated on the inside with cooking spray are easiest, but well-oiled bowls or plastic containers with lids work well, too. Following the overnight fermentation, the dough can be frozen for longer storage; to use, allow to thaw overnight in the refrigerator, then proceed with the recipe.

Don't shorten the fermentation and room-temperature warming times. The dough requires at least 24 hours in the refrigerator to ferment, then needs to come up to 75°F before shaping.

1. In a stand mixer fitted with the dough hook, combine the flour, sugar and yeast. Mix on low to combine, about 15 seconds. With the mixer running, slowly add the water, then mix on low until a slightly bumpy dough forms and clears the sides of the bowl, about 5 minutes. Cover the bowl with plastic wrap and let rest for 20 minutes.

2. Uncover the bowl, sprinkle the salt over the dough and mix on low until smooth and elastic, 5 to 7 minutes. If the dough climbs up the hook, stop the mixer, push it down and continue kneading.

3. Scrape the dough onto a well-floured counter and divide it into 4 pieces. With floured hands, form each into a taut ball and dust with flour. Mist the insides of 4 quart-size zip-close plastic bags with cooking spray, then add 1 ball to each. Seal and refrigerate for 24 to 72 hours.

4. About 1 hour before making pizza, mist 4 small bowls with cooking spray. Transfer the dough balls to the bowls. Cover with plastic wrap, then set each bowl into a larger bowl of 100°F water for 30 minutes, or until the dough reaches 75°F, changing the water as needed. Shape according to directions.

Orange–Guajillo Chili Pulled Chicken

Start to finish: 45 minutes / Servings: 4

---

1 ounce guajillo chilies (5 medium), stemmed, seeded and torn into 1-inch pieces

1½ cups orange juice

5 medium garlic cloves, smashed and peeled

2 tablespoons white vinegar

2 teaspoons ground coriander

2 teaspoons honey

1 teaspoon dried oregano

Kosher salt

2 pounds boneless, skinless chicken thighs, trimmed

Chilorio, a pulled pork from the Mexican state of Sinaloa, inspired this dish, but instead of pork shoulder, we used faster-cooking chicken thighs. Fresh orange juice amplified the fruity notes of the guajillo chilies while giving the sauce a natural sweetness; a little vinegar and honey helped the balance. Serve with Mexican rice or tortillas, or use it as a filling for tacos. Diced white onion, sliced radishes and/or crumbled queso fresco are excellent garnishes.

Don't forget to trim any excess fat from the chicken thighs before cooking to prevent the dish from being greasy.

1. In a 12-inch skillet over medium-high, toast the chilies, pressing with a wide metal spatula and flipping halfway through, until fragrant, about 1 minute. Transfer to a small bowl and pour in the juice; press on the chilies to submerge. Let stand until the chilies have softened, about 10 minutes. Set the skillet aside.

2. In a blender, combine the chilies and juice, garlic, vinegar, coriander, honey, oregano and 1 teaspoon salt. Puree until smooth, about 30 seconds. Pour the puree into the same skillet and bring to a boil over medium-high. Nestle the chicken into the sauce, cover and cook over medium-low, stirring and flipping the chicken halfway through, until a skewer inserted into the chicken meets no resistance, about 20 minutes.

3. Using tongs, transfer the chicken to a large plate and set aside until cool enough to handle, 10 to 15 minutes. Using 2 forks, shred into bite-size pieces. While the chicken cools, bring the sauce to a simmer over medium-high and cook, stirring, until thickened and reduced to 1 cup, about 10 minutes. Stir the shredded chicken into the sauce, then taste and season with salt.

Vietnamese Shaking Beef
(*Bò Lúc Lắc*)

Start to finish: **30 minutes**/ Servings: 4

1½ pounds beef sirloin tips or tri-tip, trimmed, patted dry and cut into 1½-inch pieces

3 tablespoons soy sauce, divided

Kosher salt and ground black pepper

5 tablespoons lime juice, divided, plus lime wedges, to serve

3 tablespoons fish sauce

2 tablespoons white sugar

2 tablespoons grapeseed or other neutral oil, divided

8 medium garlic cloves, finely chopped

1 small red onion, halved and sliced ¼ inch thick

1 bunch watercress, stemmed

The name of this Vietnamese dish refers to the way the pan is shaken while the beef cooks. We, however, prefer to minimize the meat's movement so the pieces achieve a nice dark, flavor-building sear. Sirloin tips (also called flap meat) or tri-tip are excellent cuts for this recipe—both are meaty, tender and reasonably priced (many recipes for shaking beef call for pricier beef tenderloin). If you can find baby watercress, use a 4-ounce container in place of the regular watercress; baby cress has a particularly peppery bite that pairs well with the beef. Serve with steamed jasmine rice.

Don't cut the beef into pieces smaller than 1½ inches or they may overcook. And don't forget the lime wedges for serving. A squeeze of fresh lime juice brightens the other flavors.

1. In a medium bowl, combine the beef, 2 tablespoons of the soy sauce and ½ teaspoon pepper. Toss and set aside. In a small bowl, stir together 4 tablespoons of the lime juice, the fish sauce, sugar and remaining 1 tablespoon soy sauce.

2. In a 12-inch skillet over medium-high, heat 1 tablespoon of the oil until barely smoking. Swirl to coat the pan, then add the beef in a single layer. Cook without stirring until well browned, about 1½ minutes. Flip each piece and cook until the second sides are well browned, about another 1½ minutes. Transfer to a medium bowl.

3. To the same skillet, add the remaining 1 tablespoon oil, the garlic and 1 teaspoon pepper. Cook over low, stirring constantly, until fragrant and the garlic is no longer raw, about 30 seconds. Pour in the lime juice mixture and any accumulated meat juices (don't add the meat), increase to medium-high and cook, stirring constantly, until a spoon leaves a trail when drawn across the skillet, 2 to 4 minutes.

4. Add the beef and cook, stirring and scraping up any browned bits, until the sauce clings lightly to the meat, about 2 minutes. Add the onion and stir until slightly softened, about 1 minute. Remove from the heat.

5. In a bowl, toss the watercress with the remaining 1 tablespoon lime juice and ½ teaspoon salt. Make a bed of the watercress on a serving platter. Top with the beef mixture and its juices. Serve with lime wedges.

Oaxacan Green Mole with Chicken

Start to finish: **1 hour 10 minutes** / Servings: 4

2 pounds boneless, skinless chicken thighs, trimmed and halved

Kosher salt and ground black pepper

Seven 6-inch corn tortillas

1 quart low-sodium chicken broth

4 medium garlic cloves, peeled

2 medium tomatillos, husked and halved

1 medium poblano chili (about 4 ounces), stemmed, seeded and quartered lengthwise

1 small white onion, root end intact, quartered lengthwise

1 bunch cilantro, leaves and tender stems

1 cup lightly packed fresh flat-leaf parsley

½ cup lightly packed fresh mint

1 teaspoon fennel seeds

1 teaspoon cumin seeds

8 ounces small Yukon Gold potatoes (1 to 1½ inches in diameter), halved

6 ounces green beans, trimmed and cut into 1-inch pieces

1 medium yellow zucchini, cut into 1-inch pieces (about 2 cups)

When we think of mole, we most often think of mahogany-colored mole negro. But as we learned in Oaxaca, there is a wide variety of moles, each with a unique character. Mole verde—or green mole—traditionally is made with pork and gets its bright, fresh flavor from a blend of fresh chilies, tomatillos and herbs. For our version, we opted for quicker-cooking but equally tasty chicken thighs, and we sought out supermarket substitutes for hard-to-find epazote and hoja santa, two herbs that are standard ingredients in Mexico (we mimicked their flavors with mint and fennel seeds). Oaxacans thicken this stew-like soup with masa, the corn dough used to make tortillas and tamales. For ease, we opted to use what we were taught is the second-best option: corn tortillas themselves softened in liquid then blended until smooth.

Don't brown the vegetables too darkly under the broiler. Light charring provides complexity, but too much will muddle the fresh herbal notes.

1. Season the chicken thighs with salt and pepper. In a large pot over medium-high, combine the tortillas and broth, then bring to a boil. Using a slotted spoon, transfer the tortillas (they will have softened) to a blender, add ¼ cup water and blend until smooth, about 1 minute.

2. Pour the puree into the boiling broth and stir to combine; rinse out the blender and reserve. Add the chicken to the pot, cover and reduce to low. Cook, stirring occasionally and adjusting the heat as needed to maintain a gentle simmer, until a skewer inserted into the chicken meets just a little resistance, 30 to 35 minutes.

3. Meanwhile, heat the broiler with a rack about 4 inches from the element. Line a rimmed baking sheet with foil. Arrange the garlic, tomatillos, poblano chili and onion in an even layer on the baking sheet. Broil until the vegetables are lightly charred, about 4 minutes, then flip them and continue to broil until the second sides are lightly charred, 3 to 5 minutes. Let cool for about 5 minutes, then transfer to the blender.

4. Add ½ cup water to the blender, then puree until smooth, about 30 seconds. Add the cilantro, parsley, mint, fennel, cumin, 2 teaspoons salt and ¾ teaspoon pepper. Blend until smooth and bright green, about 2 minutes, scraping the sides as needed. You should have about 2 cups of puree; set aside.

5. When the chicken is ready, stir the potatoes, green beans and zucchini into the pot. Bring to a simmer over medium and cook, uncovered and stirring occasionally, until the skewer inserted into a potato meets no resistance, about 15 minutes. Stir in the puree, then taste and season with salt and pepper.

Pork and Chorizo with Piquillo Peppers (*Carcamusa*)

Start to finish: **1 hour (35 minutes active)** / Servings: 4

6 ounces Spanish chorizo, halved lengthwise and thinly sliced

8 medium garlic cloves, peeled

2½ teaspoons dried oregano

2½ teaspoons ground cumin

Kosher salt and ground black pepper

28-ounce can whole peeled tomatoes, drained, juices reserved

1¼-pound pork tenderloin, trimmed of silver skin and cut into ½-inch pieces

3 tablespoons grapeseed or other neutral oil, divided

1 large yellow onion, finely chopped

½ cup dry sherry

10.4-ounce jar piquillo peppers (see note), drained and cut into ½-inch pieces (1 cup)

1 cup roughly chopped flat-leaf parsley

Carcamusa, a Spanish tapas dish, traditionally calls for three different types of pork—fresh pork, cured ham and chorizo—all simmered with seasonal vegetables in tomato sauce. To simplify, we skipped the ham and opted for jarred roasted piquillo peppers, which are heat-free, meaty red peppers from Spain. If you can't find them, jarred roasted red bell peppers are a fine substitute. Serve the dish with slices of toasted rustic bread.

Don't use Mexican chorizo, which is a fresh sausage, in place of the Spanish chorizo called for here. Spanish chorizo is dry-cured and has a firm, sliceable texture similar to salami. If the chorizo you purchased has a tough casing, peel it off before cooking.

1. In a food processor, combine half the chorizo, the garlic, oregano, cumin, 1 teaspoon pepper and 3 tablespoons of the tomato juices. Process until smooth, about 2 minutes, scraping down the bowl as needed. Transfer 3 tablespoons of the chorizo paste to a medium bowl and stir in 1 teaspoon salt and another 1 tablespoon of the tomato juices. Add the pork and toss, then marinate at room temperature for 15 minutes. Meanwhile, add the drained tomatoes to the chorizo paste in the processor and process until smooth, about 1 minute; set aside.

2. In a 12-inch skillet over medium-high, heat 1 tablespoon of the oil until barely smoking. Add the pork in a single layer and cook without stirring until well-browned, 4 to 6 minutes. Return the pork to the bowl. Add the remaining 2 tablespoons oil to the skillet and heat over medium until shimmering. Add the onion, cover and cook, stirring occasionally, until softened, about 8 minutes.

3. Add the sherry and cook, scraping up any browned bits, until most of the liquid evaporates, 2 to 4 minutes. Stir in the tomato-chorizo mixture and the remaining tomato juice. Bring to a simmer, then reduce to medium-low. Cover and cook for 10 minutes.

4. Uncover and continue to cook, stirring occasionally, until the mixture is slightly thickened, another 5 minutes. Return the pork and any accumulated juices to the skillet and add the remaining chorizo and the piquillo peppers. Cook, stirring occasionally, until the pork is heated through, about 5 minutes. Stir in the parsley, then taste and season with salt and pepper.

Stir-Fried Chicken with Snap Peas and Basil

Start to finish: **30 minutes** / Servings: 4

1 pound boneless, skinless chicken breasts, cut into 1-inch chunks

3 tablespoons fish sauce, divided

1 tablespoon soy sauce

Ground white pepper

2 tablespoons peanut oil, divided

¼ cup chopped fresh basil, plus 3 cups torn and lightly packed

2 tablespoons white vinegar

4 ounces sugar snap peas, strings removed, halved on diagonal

8 scallions, white and light green parts finely chopped, dark green parts cut into 1-inch pieces, reserved separately

2 or 3 serrano chilies, stemmed and sliced into thin rings

4 medium garlic cloves, thinly sliced

1 tablespoon white sugar

A double dose of basil adds herbal flavor and fragrance to this stir-fry. Inspired by Thailand's popular chicken-and-basil dish known as kai pad krapow, we follow the Thai approach of using herbs by the fistful. Using both chopped basil (mixed with the cooked chicken) and torn basil leaves (stirred in at the end) provided the full herbal flavor and fragrance we were looking for. Serve with steamed white or brown jasmine rice.

Don't begin cooking until all ingredients are prepared. The stir-fry comes together quickly, so make sure everything is ready and close at hand.

1. In a medium bowl, stir together the chicken, 1 tablespoon of fish sauce, the soy sauce and ½ teaspoon white pepper. Let stand at room temperature for 15 minutes, then drain and pat dry with paper towels.

2. Heat a 14-inch wok over medium-high for about 3 minutes, or until a drop of water evaporates within 1 to 2 seconds of contact. Add 1 tablespoon of oil and swirl to coat. Add the chicken in an even layer and cook without stirring until it begins to brown, about 1 minute. Stir and continue to cook, stirring occasionally, until well browned and cooked through, about 4 minutes. Transfer to a clean bowl, then stir in the chopped basil and vinegar.

3. Return the wok to medium-high and add the remaining 1 tablespoon oil. Swirl to coat and heat until barely smoking. Add the snap peas, the finely chopped scallion parts and the chilies. Cook, stirring, until the peas are lightly browned, about 2 minutes. Add the garlic and stir-fry until fragrant, about 30 seconds. Stir in the sugar, the scallion greens and chicken, along with any accumulated juices. Stir-fry until most of the juices have evaporated, about 1 minute.

4. Off heat, add the remaining 2 tablespoons fish sauce and the torn basil. Stir until the basil is wilted, about 30 seconds. Taste and season with white pepper.

Turkish Beans with Pickled Tomatoes

Start to finish: **3 hours (15 minutes active)**
Servings: 6

---

1 pound dried cannellini beans, soaked overnight and drained

12- to 16-ounce beef or lamb shank

1 large yellow onion, chopped (about 2 cups)

4 tablespoons (½ stick) salted butter

8 garlic cloves, smashed and peeled

4 sprigs fresh thyme

2 bay leaves

1 teaspoon sweet paprika

1 teaspoon red pepper flakes

14½-ounce can diced tomatoes, drained

Kosher salt

½ cup chopped fresh parsley

2 tablespoons chopped fresh dill, plus more to serve

2 tablespoons pomegranate molasses, plus more to serve

Ground black pepper

Whole-milk yogurt and extra-virgin olive oil, to serve

Pickled tomatoes (see sidebar), to serve

This hearty white bean stew was inspired by the Turkish dish kuru fasulye, basically beans stewed in a spicy tomato sauce. We also borrowed a bit of flavor from the Middle Eastern pantry, using pomegranate molasses, a syrup of boiled pomegranate juice, to add a unique and fruity sweetness. You'll find it in the grocer's international section or near the honey, maple syrup and molasses. This dish calls for dried beans, which means an overnight soak for evenly cooked beans. We found the creamy texture of dried cannellini beans was best, but Great Northern beans worked, too. We maximized meaty flavor—without using a lot of meat—by using a collagen-rich beef or lamb shank. Serve these beans as is or with a drizzle of extra-virgin olive oil and a spoonful of whole-milk yogurt. We also loved the bright contrast provided by pickled tomatoes (see sidebar). The beans can be made up to two days ahead. Reheat over low, adding water to reach your desired consistency.

Don't forget to salt the beans' soaking water. The salt tenderizes and seasons the beans. We liked a ratio of 1½ tablespoons kosher salt to 3 quarts water.

1. Heat the oven to 325°F with a rack in the lower middle position. In a large oven-safe pot or Dutch oven over high, combine 5½ cups water, the beans, shank, onion, butter, garlic, thyme, bay leaves, paprika and red pepper flakes. Bring to a boil, then cover and transfer to the oven. Bake for 1 hour 15 minutes.

2. Remove the pot from the oven. Stir in the tomatoes and 2 teaspoons salt. Return, uncovered, to the oven and bake until the beans are fully tender and creamy and the liquid is slightly thickened, another 1 hour 15 minutes.

Transfer the pot to a rack. Remove the shank and set aside. Discard the thyme sprigs and bay leaves.

3. When cool enough to handle, remove the meat from the bone, discarding fat, gristle and bone. Finely chop the meat and stir into the beans. Stir in the parsley, dill and molasses. Taste and season with salt and pepper. Serve with yogurt, oil, pickled tomatoes and additional pomegranate molasses and dill.

PICKLED TOMATOES

Start to finish: 5 minutes,
plus chilling
Servings: 1½ cups

These pickled tomatoes are delicious with our Turkish beans, but also can be used on sandwiches or in hearty soups. Make them up to two days ahead. Be sure to seed the tomatoes. Seeds gave the final product an unpleasant texture.

3 plum tomatoes (12 ounces), cored, seeded and diced

3 tablespoons cider vinegar

1 tablespoon chopped fresh dill

1 teaspoon crushed Aleppo pepper or see substitute, p. 7

1 teaspoon white sugar

½ teaspoon kosher salt

In a medium bowl, stir together all ingredients. Refrigerate for at least 1 hour. Will keep, refrigerated, for 3 days.

Spicy Stir-Fried Cumin Beef

Start to finish: 1 hour (35 minutes active)
Servings: 4

---

1 pound beef sirloin tips, trimmed, cut with the grain into 2-inch pieces and sliced thinly against the grain

3½ tablespoons soy sauce, divided

Ground black pepper

4 teaspoons unseasoned rice vinegar

1 teaspoon white sugar

12 dried red chilies (such as árbol or japones), stemmed

1½ tablespoons cumin seeds, toasted

5 medium garlic cloves, minced

6 teaspoons grapeseed or other neutral oil, divided

1 large yellow onion, thinly sliced lengthwise

2 teaspoons toasted sesame oil

1½ cups roughly chopped fresh cilantro

Cumin is not thought of as a traditionally Chinese spice, but it is used in some regional cuisines, including in Hunan where an abundance of whole cumin seeds is combined with whole chilies and aromatics to great effect in Hunan beef. We also loved this dish made with boneless lamb leg or shoulder, trimmed and thinly sliced; if using lamb, start with about 1½ pounds, as more weight is lost with trimming than with beef. Toasted cumin seeds add both earthy flavor and crunchy texture to this stir-fry. Breaking some of the chilies in half releases the seeds, giving the dish an assertive spiciness; leave all of the chilies whole for a milder version. The chili pods are edible, but we advise eating around them. Serve with steamed white rice.

Don't start cooking until all ingredients are prepared, as things move along quickly at the stove. Also, make sure to turn on your hood vent or open a window or two. Toasting the chilies and searing the meat produces a fair amount of smoke and fumes.

1. In a medium bowl, combine the beef, 1 tablespoon of soy sauce and ½ teaspoon black pepper. Stir to coat, then set aside at room temperature. In a small bowl, stir together the remaining 2½ tablespoons soy sauce, the vinegar and sugar.

2. Meanwhile, break open about half of the chilies, then transfer all of them to a 14-inch wok. Toast over medium, pressing the pods against the wok, until fragrant and darkened in spots, 1 to 3 minutes. Transfer to a large bowl and add the cumin. In a small bowl, stir together the garlic and 2 teaspoons of grapeseed oil to form a paste.

3. Heat the wok over medium-high for about 3 minutes, or until a drop of water evaporates within 1 to 2 seconds of contact. Add 2 teaspoons of the remaining grapeseed oil and swirl to coat. Add the onion and cook, stirring, until charred in spots and partially softened, 3 to 5 minutes. Transfer to the bowl with the cumin seeds and chilies.

4. Return the wok to high, add 1 teaspoon of the remaining grapeseed oil and arrange half of the beef in a single layer. Cook without stirring until deeply browned, 1 to 2 minutes. Stir, scraping the bottom and sides of the wok, and continue to cook until no pink remains, 60 to 90 seconds. Transfer to the bowl with the onion. Repeat with the remaining 1 teaspoon grapeseed oil and the remaining beef.

5. Set the wok over medium-high, add the garlic paste and cook, mashing the paste against the pan, until fragrant, about 30 seconds. Add the contents of the bowl and stir to combine. Pour the soy sauce–vinegar mixture in a thin stream down the sides of the wok, then cook, scraping up any browned bits, until the liquid is slightly thickened, about 1 minute. Off heat, stir in the sesame oil and cilantro.

Carnitas

Start to finish: 4 hours (45 minutes active)
Servings: 4 to 6

5 to 6 pounds boneless pork butt, not trimmed, cut into 2-inch cubes

1 large yellow onion, halved and thinly sliced

10 medium garlic cloves, smashed and peeled

2 tablespoons ground cumin

2 tablespoons ground coriander

2 teaspoons dried oregano

½ teaspoon dried thyme

1 teaspoon red pepper flakes

Kosher salt and ground black pepper

1 cup grapeseed or other neutral oil

Authentic Mexican carnitas involve slow-cooking pork in lard until fall-apart tender, then increasing the heat so the meat fries and crisps. The fried pork then is broken into smaller pieces for eating. In the U.S., however, carnitas usually is made by simmering pork in liquid, then shredding the meat. The result is moist and tender, but lacks intense porkiness as well the crisping traditional to carnitas. Our method melds the two techniques. We cook cubes of pork shoulder in 1 cup each of neutral oil and water, along with spices and aromatics, until the meat is fork-tender. We then break the pork into smaller pieces, moisten it with its own juices, and fry it in a hot skillet. The pork gets to keep its flavor and develop crisp bits. If you have a fat separator, it makes quick work of removing the fat from the cooking liquid: pour the liquid into it after removing the pork from the pot, then return the defatted cooking liquid to the pot, but remember to reserve the fat. You can cook, shred and moisten the pork with the reduced cooking liquid up to three days in advance; try the pork just before serving so it's hot and crisp. And if you like your carnitas extra-crisp, after browning the first side, use the spatula to flip the pork and cook until the second side is well-browned and crisp, another 5 to 7 minutes. You can serve carnitas simply with rice and beans or make tacos with warmed corn tortillas. Either way, pickled red onions (recipe follows) are a must—their sharp acidity balances perfectly the richness of the pork. Also offer sliced radishes and a salsa, such as our tomatillo-avocado salsa (p. 493).

Don't trim the fat from the pork shoulder. The pork should render its fat in the oven and so the meat cooks slowly in it and the juices. And after cooking, don't discard the fat you skim off the cooking liquid—you'll need some of it to crisp the shredded pork in a hot skillet.

1. Heat the oven to 325°F with a rack in the lower-middle position. In a large (at least 7-quart) Dutch oven, stir together the pork, onion, garlic, cumin, coriander, oregano, thyme, pepper flakes and 2 teaspoons salt. Stir in the oil and 1 cup water. Cover, transfer to the oven and cook for 3 hours.

2. Remove the pot from the oven. Stir the pork and return the pot, uncovered, to the oven. Cook until a skewer inserted into the meat meets no resistance, another 30 minutes. Using a slotted spoon, transfer the meat to a rimmed baking sheet in an even layer to cool. Tilt the pot to pool the cooking liquid to one side, then use a wide spoon to skim off as much fat as possible; reserve the fat. Bring the defatted cooking liquid to a simmer over medium-high and cook, stirring occasionally, until reduced to about ⅓ cup, about 5 minutes. Set aside.

3. When the meat is cool enough to handle, break the chunks into ¾- to 1-inch pieces, discarding any large pieces of fat. Add the pork back to the

pot and stir until evenly moistened with the reduced cooking liquid.

4. In a nonstick 12-inch skillet over medium-high, heat 1 teaspoon of the reserved fat until barely smoking. Add the pork in an even layer and cook without stirring, pressing the meat against the skillet with a spatula, until the bottom begins to brown and the pork is heated through, 3 to 5 minutes. Taste and season with salt and pepper.

PICKLED RED ONIONS

Start to finish: 10 minutes, plus chilling

Makes about 2 cups

1 cup white vinegar

2 teaspoons white sugar

Kosher salt

2 medium red onions, halved and thinly sliced

1 jalapeño chili, stemmed, halved lengthwise and seeded

In a medium bowl, combine the vinegar, sugar and 2 teaspoons salt, then stir until the salt and sugar dissolve. Stir in the onions and jalapeño. Cover and refrigerate for at least 1 hour or up to 24 hours.

Oaxacan Refried Black Beans

Start to finish: 2¾ hours (35 minutes active)
Servings: 6

4 tablespoons lard or refined coconut oil, divided

5 guajillo chilies, stemmed and seeded

1 pint grape or cherry tomatoes

1 large white onion, chopped

1 pound dried black beans, rinsed and drained

10 medium garlic cloves, peeled and kept whole, plus 5 medium garlic cloves, minced

3 bay leaves

1 teaspoon aniseed

Kosher salt and ground black pepper

4 teaspoons ground cumin

4 teaspoons ground coriander

1 tablespoon ancho chili powder

1 teaspoon dried oregano

In Oaxaca, black beans are part of almost every meal. Though they sometimes are served whole, we especially liked the balanced, complex flavor and smooth, velvety consistency of refried black beans. Lard gives these beans a rich meatiness, but coconut oil is a good vegetarian substitute. The beans can be stored in an airtight container in the refrigerator for up to a week. We liked these topped with crumbled cotija cheese and fresh cilantro.

Don't soak the beans before cooking. Unlike other types of dried beans, black beans soften readily without soaking. And don't forget to reserve the bean cooking liquid; you'll need 2 cups when pureeing the beans in the food processor. And if you'll be making black bean soup (p. 263), you'll need 3 cups to thin the beans. The liquid also is useful for thinning the beans when reheating (they thicken as they stand).

1. In a large pot over medium-high, heat 1 tablespoon of the lard until barely smoking. Add the onion, tomatoes and guajillo chilies, then cook, stirring occasionally, until the onion is well browned, 5 to 7 minutes. Add the beans, whole garlic cloves, bay and aniseed, then stir in 10 cups water. Bring to a boil, then cover partially and reduce to low. Cook, stirring occasionally, until the beans are completely tender, 1½ hours to 2 hours.

2. Stir in 2 teaspoons salt. Set a colander in a large bowl and drain the beans, reserving the cooking liquid. Remove and discard the bay leaves from the beans. Transfer the drained beans to a food processor and pulse a few times to break them up. With the machine running, add 1½ cups of the reserved cooking liquid and process until smooth, 2 to 3 minutes, scraping the bowl as needed. Taste and season with salt, then set aside.

3. In a 12-inch nonstick skillet over medium, heat 2 tablespoons of the remaining lard until shimmering. Add the minced garlic, cumin, coriander, chili powder and oregano, then cook, stirring, until fragrant, about 30 seconds.

4. Stir in the pureed beans and cook, stirring frequently, until beginning to brown on the bottom, 8 to 10 minutes. Continue to cook and stir, adding reserved cooking water as needed, until the mixture has the consistency of mashed potatoes, 5 to 7 minutes. Off heat, stir in the remaining 1 tablespoon lard, then taste and season with salt and pepper.

CHANGE THE WAY YOU COOK:

LARD IT UP

Lard fell out of fashion a while back, but it's coming back because it's an easy way to add deep, rich meaty flavors to a dish. It can boost flavor stirred into a pot of beans or help baked goods achieve a delicious flakiness. "Leaf" lard has the lightest flavor.

MORE WAYS WITH REFRIED BEANS

Our recipe for Oaxacan refried black beans makes about 5 cups of beans, enough for one meal, plus leftovers that easily can be turned into lunch or a light dinner. In Oaxaca, the beans are spread onto tortillas, then folded into half-rounds and triangles to make tlayudas and tetelas, respectively. Here are a couple more of our favorite ways to use them. Be sure to save your bean cooking liquid, which you'll need for the soup, but which also is perfect for using to reheat the refried beans.

BLACK BEAN SOUP: In a large sauce-pan over medium, heat 3 cups cooking liquid from refried beans, stirring occasionally, until hot. Add 3 cups refried beans and cook, whisking frequently, until the mixture is well combined and heated through, about 5 minutes. Off heat, stir in ½ cup finely chopped fresh cilantro and ¼ cup lime juice. Taste and season with salt and pepper. Serve with lime wedges, diced avocado, sour cream, sliced scallions and tortilla chips.

HONDURAN BALEADAS: Heat the oven to 450°F with racks in the upper- and lower-middle positions. In a medium microwave-safe bowl, microwave 2 cups refried beans, covered, until hot, about 2 minutes. Stir in 2 tablespoons finely chopped fresh cilantro and 1 tablespoon lime juice, then taste and season with salt and pepper. Place three 8-inch flour tortillas in a single layer on each of 2 baking sheets lined with kitchen parchment. Spread ⅓ cup of the bean mixture onto each tortilla. Use ½ cup shredded cheddar cheese to sprinkle over the tortillas, dividing it evenly. Bake until the cheese melts, 6 to 8 minutes, switching and rotating the baking sheets halfway through. Sprinkle with ½ cup crumbled cotija cheese, dividing it evenly, then top with diced avocado, pickled jalapeños and thinly sliced scallions. Fold each tortilla in half and serve.

Sesame Stir-Fried Pork with Shiitakes

Start to finish: **30 minutes** / Servings: **6**

1-pound pork tenderloin, trimmed of silver skin

2½ tablespoons soy sauce, divided

Kosher salt and ground black pepper

3 tablespoons grapeseed or other neutral oil, divided

8 ounces shiitake mushrooms, stems discarded, caps sliced ¼ inch thick

3 medium garlic cloves, thinly sliced

2½ cups well-drained napa cabbage kimchi, roughly chopped, plus 2 tablespoons kimchi juice

3 tablespoons mirin

1 tablespoon toasted sesame oil

2 tablespoons sesame seeds, toasted

1 bunch scallions, thinly sliced

Kimchi—Korea's spicy, fermented cabbage—most often is eaten raw as a small plate or as a side. But this recipe cooks kimchi, turning it into a one-ingredient way to add complex flavors and vegetables to a simple dish. Fresh shiitake mushrooms, a full bunch of scallions and sesame (both oil and seeds) add to its richness. Serve with steamed short- or medium-grain rice.

Don't finely chop the kimchi. Larger pieces retain a slightly crisp texture and have more presence in the stir-fry.

1. Cut the tenderloin in half lengthwise, then slice each half crosswise about ¼ inch thick. In a medium bowl, toss the pork with 1 tablespoon of soy sauce and ½ teaspoon pepper.

2. Heat a 12- to 14-inch wok over high until a drop of water evaporates within 1 to 2 seconds of contact, about 2 minutes. Add 1½ teaspoons of grapeseed oil and swirl to coat the wok, then distribute half the pork in an even layer. Cook without stirring until well browned, 1 to 2 minutes, then stir and continue to cook, stirring often, until no longer pink, 1 to 2 minutes. Transfer to a clean medium bowl. Repeat using another 1½ teaspoons oil and the remaining pork.

3. Set the wok over medium-high and heat 1 tablespoon grapeseed oil until barely smoking. Add the mushrooms and ½ teaspoon salt. Cook, stirring occasionally, until the moisture released by the mushrooms has mostly evaporated, about 4 minutes. Stir in the remaining 1 tablespoon oil and the garlic and cook until fragrant, about 1 minute. Return the pork and any juices to the wok and cook, stirring, until the juices evaporate, 30 to 60 seconds.

4. Add the kimchi and kimchi juice, mirin and remaining 1½ tablespoons soy sauce. Cook, stirring and scraping up any browned bits, until the kimchi is heated through, about 3 minutes. Stir in the sesame oil, half the sesame seeds and half the scallions. Transfer to a platter and sprinkle with remaining scallions and sesame seeds.

Lentil Salad with Gorgonzola

Start to finish: 1½ hours (30 minutes active)
Servings: 6

½ cup white balsamic vinegar

2 medium shallots, thinly sliced

Kosher salt and ground black pepper

1 garlic head, outer papery skins removed

2 medium carrots, halved crosswise

1 celery stalk, halved crosswise

1 tablespoon yellow mustard seeds

6 sprigs thyme, tied together

2 bay leaves

1½ cups French green lentils, sorted, rinsed and drained

1 tablespoon extra-virgin olive oil

2 ounces Gorgonzola cheese, crumbled (about ¾ cup)

½ cup chopped fresh flat-leaf parsley leaves

½ cup walnuts, toasted and chopped

Green lentils du Puy, also known as French lentils, cook quickly, hold their shape well and do a great job at soaking up flavors in a rich broth or stew. But it can be a bit of a race to develop that flavor before the lentils overcook and become mushy. Our solution: Simmer vegetables and aromatics in advance, then add lentils. To really punch up the flavor we turned to one of our favorite seasoning shortcuts and simmered a whole head of garlic with the herbs until it was mellow and tender; the cloves became soft enough to be mashed and formed the basis of a richly savory dressing. Pungent Gorgonzola cheese gave the salad sharp contrast, while toasted walnuts added crunch.

Don't use brown lentils here. They are larger and have a different cooking time from peppery green lentils.

1. In a liquid measuring cup, combine the vinegar, shallots and 1 teaspoon salt. Let sit for 10 minutes. Meanwhile, cut off and discard the top third of the garlic head, leaving the head intact. In a 2-quart saucepan over medium-high, combine the garlic, 6 cups water, carrots, celery, mustard seeds, thyme, bay leaves and 1 teaspoon salt. Bring to a boil, then cover, reduce heat to low and simmer for 30 minutes. Remove and discard the carrots, celery, thyme and bay leaves.

2. Return the pot to medium-high and stir in the lentils. Return to a boil, then cover and reduce heat to low. Simmer until the lentils are tender but still hold their shape, 30 to 35 minutes. Remove the garlic and set aside. Drain the lentils, reserving the liquid, and transfer to a large bowl. Stir in the vinegar-shallot mixture and let cool to room temperature.

3. Squeeze the pulp from the garlic into a bowl and mash with a fork. Stir in ¼ cup of the reserved cooking water, the oil and ½ teaspoon salt. Stir the garlic mixture, half of the cheese, the parsley and half of the walnuts into the lentils. Taste and season with salt and pepper. Transfer to a platter and top with the remaining cheese and walnuts.

Sichuan Chicken Salad

Start to finish: **1 hour 20 minutes (20 minutes active)**
Servings: 4

Two 10- to 12-ounce bone-in,
skin-on split chicken breasts

6 scallions, white parts coarsely
chopped, green parts thinly sliced
on diagonal, reserved separately

1-inch piece fresh ginger,
cut into 4 pieces and smashed

2 medium garlic cloves, smashed
and peeled

Kosher salt

¼ cup dry sherry (optional)

2 tablespoons chili oil

2 tablespoons tahini

1½ tablespoons white sugar

1½ tablespoons toasted sesame oil

1 tablespoon soy sauce

2 tablespoons unseasoned
rice vinegar

⅛ to ¼ teaspoon cayenne pepper

1 teaspoon Sichuan peppercorns,
toasted and finely ground

1 large English cucumber, halved
lengthwise, seeded and thinly sliced
crosswise on diagonal

⅓ cup dry-roasted peanuts, chopped

Traditionally, the meat for this salad is pounded to shreds to better absorb the flavorful dressing. We got similar results by mashing it with a sturdy wooden spoon in a bowl; make sure the bowl you use is not fragile. We loved the tongue-tingling, piney notes of Sichuan peppercorns in the dressing. Toast them over medium heat until aromatic, about 2 minutes, then grind them to a fine powder with a spice grinder or mortar and pestle.

Don't boil the chicken; keep the liquid at a bare simmer so the meat stays moist and tender.

1. In a large saucepan, place the chicken skin side down, then add the scallion whites, ginger, garlic and 1½ teaspoons salt. Add 4 cups water and the sherry, if using. Bring to a boil over medium-high, then cover, reduce to low and cook at a bare simmer until a skewer inserted into the thickest part of the chicken meets no resistance, or the thickest part of the chicken reaches 160°F, 20 to 25 minutes. Uncover the pan and let the chicken cool in the liquid for 15 minutes.

2. Meanwhile, in a small bowl, whisk together the chili oil, tahini, sugar, sesame oil, soy sauce, vinegar, cayenne, Sichuan pepper and 1½ teaspoons salt.

3. Using tongs, remove the chicken from the cooking liquid. Remove and discard the skin and bones, then transfer the meat to a large bowl. Add 2 tablespoons of the tahini dressing, then use a wooden spoon to smash the meat, shredding it and working in the dressing. Use your fingers to pull the shreds into bite-size pieces.

4. Add the cucumber and ¾ each of the peanuts and scallion greens. Drizzle with the remaining dressing and toss until evenly coated. Transfer to a serving bowl and sprinkle with the remaining peanuts and scallions.

CHANGE THE WAY YOU COOK:
FOR BOLDER FLAVOR, SHRED YOUR CHICKEN

Shredding cooked chicken not only makes the meat more tender, it also can result in better flavor. Shredded chicken has more surface area to better absorb seasonings and sauces.

Turkish Meatballs with Lime-Yogurt Sauce

Start to finish: 20 minutes, plus cooling / Servings: 6

3 tablespoons extra-virgin olive oil, divided

1 medium shallot, finely chopped

1 garlic clove, grated

½ teaspoon ground cumin

½ teaspoon cinnamon

½ teaspoon dried oregano

One 8-inch pita bread, torn into small pieces (about 3 ounces)

¼ cup plain whole-milk yogurt

1 cup packed fresh mint leaves, finely chopped

1½ pounds 90-percent lean ground beef

1½ teaspoons kosher salt

1 teaspoon ground black pepper

Lime-yogurt sauce, to serve (see sidebar)

There are many variations (and spellings) of kofta across the Middle East and North Africa, but essentially they're seasoned patties, often made from ground lamb or a blend of beef and lamb. It's the rest of the world's answer to the Italian meatball. We particularly liked Turkish kofta, which sometimes are squashed flat and can be grilled, fried or even cooked on a skewer. We went with an all-beef version using 90 percent lean beef, though this recipe also works with a blend of lamb and beef. We pan-fried our patties, which gave us a deliciously crispy crust. To stop our meat mixture from getting tough in the middle we borrowed the French technique known as panade. It involves mixing a bread and dairy paste into the ground meat to bind it together and keep it moist during cooking. Since we already were serving pita bread with the patties, we used crumbled pita for our panade. We served the cooked patties in pita pockets with sliced tomato, cucumber, red onion and parsley. They also would be good over rice pilaf and served with a simple salad.

Don't use stale bread for the meatballs. The fresh pita added a lighter texture and fresh flavor. Likewise, use plain whole-milk yogurt, not Greek-style, to get the right consistency in both the meatballs and the sauce.

1. In a small bowl, stir together 2 tablespoons of the oil, the shallot, garlic, cumin, cinnamon and oregano. Microwave until fragrant, about 30 seconds, then set aside to cool.

2. In a large bowl, combine the pita bread, yogurt and ¼ cup water. Use your hands to mash the mixture to a smooth paste. Add the reserved oil mixture, the mint, beef, salt and pepper. Use your hands to thoroughly mix. Divide the meat into 12 portions, then use your hands to roll each into a smooth ball. Refrigerate for 15 minutes.

3. In a 12-inch nonstick skillet, heat the remaining tablespoon of oil over medium-high until just beginning to smoke. Add the meatballs and use a metal spatula to press them into ½-inch-thick patties. Cook over medium, adjusting the heat as necessary, until the meatballs register 140°F at the center and are cooked through and well browned on both sides, 5 to 7 minutes per side. Transfer to a platter, tent with foil and let rest for 5 minutes.

LIME-YOGURT SAUCE

Start to finish: **5 minutes**
Servings: **1½ cups**

1 cup plain whole-milk yogurt

3 tablespoons tahini

3 tablespoons lime juice

½ teaspoon kosher salt

¼ teaspoon cayenne pepper

In a small bowl, whisk together all ingredients until smooth.

Green Enchiladas with Chicken and Cheese (*Enchiladas Verdes*)

Start to finish: **45 minutes** / Servings: 4

3 tablespoons extra-virgin olive oil, divided

3 medium poblano chilies (about 12 ounces), stemmed, seeded and chopped

1 pound tomatillos, husked, cored and chopped

1 medium white onion, chopped

6 medium garlic cloves, peeled

1 tablespoon ground cumin

½ cup low-sodium chicken broth or water

1 cup lightly packed cilantro leaves and stems

Kosher salt and ground black pepper

1½ cups finely chopped cooked chicken (see note)

6 ounces whole-milk mozzarella cheese, shredded (1½ cups)

2 tablespoons hot sauce (see note)

Eight 6-inch corn tortillas

Lime wedges, to serve

To make the filling for these enchiladas, use leftover roasted or grilled chicken or meat from a store-bought rotisserie bird. You also can poach your own chicken. To do so, place 1 pound boneless, skinless chicken breasts in a medium saucepan, cover with water or chicken broth, bring to a simmer over medium-high, then reduce to low, cover and cook until the thickest part of the meat registers 160°F, about 20 minutes. Let the chicken cool in the liquid until just warm to the touch, then finely chop the meat. Our homemade green chili and tomatillo hot sauce (p. 215) is especially good here, but any bottled hot sauce that's not too vinegary (such as Tapatío or Cholula) will work. Chopped white onion and sour cream or Mexican crema are great garnishes.

Don't skip the step of brushing the tortillas with oil and briefly warming them in the oven. If the tortillas are filled and rolled straight from the package, they will crack and tear. But take care not to overheat them, which will dry them out and make them too brittle to roll.

1. Heat the oven to 475°F with a rack in the middle position. In a large pot over medium-high, combine 1 tablespoon of the oil, the poblanos, tomatillos, onion and garlic. Cook, stirring occasionally, until the vegetables are well-browned and beginning to soften, 5 to 8 minutes. Stir in the cumin and cook until fragrant, about 30 seconds. Add the broth and cook, stirring occasionally, until the vegetables have softened, about 5 minutes. Remove from the heat and let cool for 5 minutes.

2. Transfer the mixture to a food processor and process until smooth, about 1 minute. Add the cilantro and continue to process until smooth, about 1 minute. Taste and season with salt and pepper. Spread 1 cup of the sauce in the bottom of a 13-by-9-inch baking dish; set aside.

3. In a medium bowl, toss together the chicken, cheese, hot sauce, 1½ teaspoons salt and 1 teaspoon pepper; set aside.

4. Brush both sides of the tortillas with the remaining 2 tablespoons oil, then arrange them on a rimmed baking sheet (it's fine to overlap them slightly). Cover tightly with foil and warm in the oven just until soft and pliable, about 3 minutes.

5. Uncover the tortillas; reserve the foil. Lay the tortillas out on a large cutting board or clean counter. Divide the chicken mixture evenly among the tortillas (about 3 heaping tablespoons each), arranging and pressing the filling in a line along the bottom edge of each tortilla.

6. Working one at a time, roll up the tortillas to enclose the filling and place seam side down in a tight row down the center of the prepared baking dish. Spoon ½ cup of the sauce over the enchiladas. Cover tightly with the reserved foil and bake until the cheese begins to melt out of the ends, about 15 minutes.

7. Uncover and spread ½ cup of the remaining sauce over the enchiladas. Re-cover and let stand for 5 minutes. Serve with lime wedges and the remaining sauce.

Quick Refried Beans

Start to finish: **15 minutes** / Servings: 4

Two 15½-ounce cans pinto
or black beans, drained

4 tablespoons lard, olive oil
or vegetable oil, divided

1 large yellow onion, quartered
and thinly sliced

2 garlic cloves, thinly sliced

Kosher salt

1 teaspoon ground cumin

1 teaspoon ground coriander

¾ teaspoon dried oregano

2 chipotle chilies in adobo sauce,
plus 1 tablespoon adobo sauce

⅓ cup water, plus extra for
thinning beans as needed

½ cup minced fresh cilantro leaves

1 tablespoon lime juice

Traditional refried beans involve an overnight soak followed by cooking, stirring and mashing the beans to the desired consistency. It is a bit more of a commitment than most of us can make on a weeknight. So we came up with a fast—as in 15 minutes—and simple approach that uses canned beans and lets the food processor do most of the work. We found pinto beans slightly sweeter and creamier than black beans, but both worked in this recipe. We loved the rich flavor lard gave the beans, but if you'd rather keep this vegetarian, olive or vegetable oil worked, too. For a smoother texture, process the beans longer after removing 1 cup in the first step. For a thinner consistency, stir in more water. Serve as a side with shredded cheese, sliced scallions or chopped onion, or spread into a torta, folded into a quesadilla or burrito, or spooned over nachos.

Don't remove the remaining beans from the food processor after measuring out 1 cup. Set aside until needed later.

1. In a food processor, pulse the beans until coarsely chopped, about 7 pulses. Transfer 1 cup of the beans to a bowl and set aside. In a 12-inch nonstick skillet over medium, heat 2 tablespoons of the lard until shimmering. Add the onion, garlic and 1 teaspoon salt. Cook until the onion is lightly browned, about 5 minutes. Stir in the cumin, coriander and oregano; cook until fragrant, about 30 seconds. Stir in the chilies and adobo sauce and cook, breaking up the chilies with a spatula, until fragrant, about 30 seconds.

2. Transfer the onion mixture to the processor, reserving the skillet; pulse until coarsely chopped, about 7 pulses. Add the water and pulse until the onions and beans are coarsely pureed, 7 to 12 more pulses. Set aside.

3. Add the remaining 2 tablespoons of lard to the empty skillet and heat over medium until barely smoking. Add the reserved cup of beans and cook until they begin to brown and most of the lard has been absorbed, 1 to 2 minutes. Stir in the pureed beans, then spread the mixture to the edges of the skillet. Cook, without stirring, until the beans begin to brown at the edges, 1 to 2 minutes. Stir the beans well and repeat the process twice more. Off heat, stir in the cilantro and lime juice. Taste and season with salt. Adjust the consistency with additional water.

Israeli Hummus (*Hummus Masabacha*)

Start to finish: 1 hour (15 minutes active), plus soaking / Makes 4 cups

---

8 ounces (227 grams) dried chickpeas

2 tablespoons plus 1 teaspoon kosher salt

½ teaspoon baking soda

¾ cup sesame tahini, room temperature

3½ tablespoons lemon juice

1 to 2 tablespoons extra-virgin olive oil

1 tablespoon chopped fresh parsley

½ teaspoon ground cumin

½ teaspoon sweet paprika

In Israel, hummus is breakfast, not a party dip. Our education began in Tel Aviv at Abu Hassan, the country's premier hummus shop, where customers get wide, shallow bowls of hummus topped with whole chickpeas, a sprinkle of parsley, pops of red paprika and amber cumin. The hummus is light, almost sour cream smooth—and warm. Back at Milk Street, we found small chickpeas worked best. The Whole Foods Market 365 Everyday Value brand worked very well. Cook larger chickpeas for 10 to 15 minutes longer, or until almost starting to break down. Soak the chickpeas for at least 12 hours. We liked the Kevala brand tahini, but Soom and Aleppo were good, too. Processing the chickpeas while warm ensures the smoothest, lightest hummus, as will processing it for a full three minutes in the first stage. Hummus traditionally is served warm and garnished with paprika, cumin, chopped fresh parsley and a drizzle of extra-virgin olive oil. Sometimes a sliced hard-boiled egg is added. Leftover hummus can be refrigerated for up to five days. To reheat, transfer to a microwave-safe bowl, cover and gently heat, adding a few tablespoons of tap water as needed to reach the proper consistency, 1 to 2 minutes.

Don't forget to stir the tahini very well. Some brands separate and can become quite thick at the bottom of the container.

1. In a large bowl, combine 8 cups water, the chickpeas and 2 tablespoons of salt. Soak for at least 12 hours.

2. In a stockpot over high, bring another 10 cups water and the baking soda to a boil. Drain the soaked chickpeas, discarding the soaking water, and add to the pot. Return to a simmer, then reduce heat to medium and cook until the skins are falling off and the chickpeas are very tender, 40 to 50 minutes.

3. Set a mesh strainer over a large bowl and drain the chickpeas into it; reserve ¾ cup of the chickpea cooking water. Let sit for 1 minute to let all liquid drain. Set aside about 2 tablespoons of the chickpeas, then transfer the rest to the food processor. Add the remaining 1 teaspoon of salt, then process for 3 minutes.

4. Add the tahini. Continue to process until the mixture has lightened and is very smooth, about 1 minute. Use a rubber spatula to scrape the sides and bottom of the processor bowl. With the machine running, add the reserved cooking liquid and the lemon juice. Process until combined. Taste and season with salt.

5. Transfer the hummus to a shallow serving bowl and use a large spoon to make a swirled well in the center. Drizzle with olive oil, then top with the reserved chickpeas, the parsley, cumin and paprika.

SPICED BEEF TOPPING (KAWARMA)

Start to finish: **25 minutes**
Makes **about 2 cups**

Warm ground meat toppings lend rich, savory notes to hummus, and make it a more robust meal.

½ pound lean ground beef

2 teaspoons sweet paprika

¾ teaspoon kosher salt

½ teaspoon cinnamon

½ teaspoon ground cumin

½ teaspoon dried oregano

½ teaspoon cayenne pepper

2 garlic cloves, grated

¾ cup water

½ small yellow onion, chopped

1 tablespoon extra-virgin olive oil

2 tablespoons tomato paste

2 tablespoons chopped fresh parsley or mint

1½ teaspoons lemon juice

Tahini, to serve

1. In a medium bowl, mix together the beef, paprika, salt, cinnamon, cumin, oregano, cayenne, garlic and 2 tablespoons of the water.

2. In a 10-inch skillet over medium-high, add the ground beef mixture, the onion and oil. Cook until the onion is softened and the beef is no longer pink, 6 to 8 minutes. Stir in the tomato paste and cook until fragrant, about 30 seconds.

3. Add the remaining water and cook, scraping the pan, until the water has evaporated and the mixture sizzles, about 5 minutes. Off heat, stir in the parsley and lemon juice. salt. Spoon over hummus, then drizzle with tahini.

Curry-Coconut Braised Fish

Start to finish: **20 minutes** / Servings: 4

14-ounce can coconut milk

2 medium carrots, peeled, halved lengthwise and cut into ½-inch pieces

1 medium yellow onion, halved and thinly sliced

6 garlic cloves, finely grated

2 teaspoons turmeric

2 teaspoons curry powder

½ teaspoon red pepper flakes

1 cup low-sodium chicken broth

1½ pounds firm whitefish, cut into 2-inch chunks

Kosher salt and ground white pepper

Steamed white rice, to serve

Lime wedges, to serve

Comfortingly creamy with a little hit of heat, this easy weeknight dish was inspired by chef Edward Lee, author of "Smoke & Pickles," which explores his philosophy of finding innovative ways to blend Southern cuisine and Asian flavors. The coconut milk curry evokes traditional Thai flavors as well as fish amok, the Cambodian classic fish curry often served steamed in a banana leaf. And assembly couldn't be simpler—dump everything but the fish into a pot for about 10 minutes, then add the fish to gently cook for another 10. Any thick, firm whitefish, such as cod, hake or Chilean sea bass, will work. Avoid a thin fillet such as sole or tilapia, which will break down in the braising liquid. Using full-fat coconut milk was important, as it will not break as the vegetables cook. Low-sodium chicken broth gave us better control over the dish's final seasoning.

Don't cook the fish too long or it will fall apart.

1. In a large Dutch oven over medium-high, combine the coconut milk, carrots, onion, garlic, turmeric, curry powder and pepper flakes. Cook over medium heat, uncovered and stirring occasionally, until thickened and the vegetables are softened, about 10 minutes.

2. Stir in the broth and bring to a simmer. Season the fish with salt and white pepper, then stir into the pot. Cover and cook over low until the fish flakes easily when poked with a fork but remains intact, 7 to 10 minutes. Taste and season with salt and pepper. Serve over steamed white rice with lime wedges.

Za'atar Chicken Cutlets
and Lemon-Parsley Salad

Start to finish: **30 minutes** / Servings: 4

1½ pounds boneless, skinless chicken breast cutlets (4 cutlets), pounded to ¼-inch thickness

Kosher salt

¼ cup plus 1 teaspoon za'atar, divided

3 tablespoons all-purpose flour

¾ teaspoon Aleppo pepper

2 tablespoons plus 1 teaspoon olive oil, divided

¾ cup lightly packed fresh flat-leaf parsley

2 scallions, trimmed and thinly sliced on diagonal

½ teaspoon lemon zest, plus 1 tablespoon lemon juice

2 tablespoons pomegranate molasses

3 tablespoons finely chopped walnuts

Our search for ways to spice up weeknight chicken took us to the Middle East where za'atar is a popular seasoning blend that often includes sesame seeds, sumac, thyme, oregano, marjoram and salt. We were influenced by Ana Sortun, who often uses za'atar at her Oleana restaurant in Cambridge, Massachusetts. She calls za'atar "craveable" and jokes, "I can imagine it as the next Doritos flavor." Her recipe for crispy lemon chicken with za'atar calls for making a lemon confit and stuffing it under the skin of whole halves of deboned chicken along with cubes of butter. We took a simpler tack and coated chicken cutlets in a flour-za'atar mixture. We also used lemon zest and juice in our sauce along with tart and smoky Aleppo pepper, which has a fruity, moderate heat. If you can't find Aleppo pepper, see substitute, p. 7.

Don't substitute chicken breasts here without pounding the meat first. Boneless, skinless chicken cutlets were ideal for fast cooking and are widely available at grocers. If you have only chicken breasts, use a meat mallet or heavy skillet to flatten them to an even ¼ inch.

1. Season the chicken all over with salt. In a wide, shallow dish, combine ¼ cup of the za'atar, the flour and pepper. In a 12-inch stainless steel skillet over medium-high, heat 2 tablespoons of the oil until shimmering. One cutlet at a time, transfer the chicken to the za'atar mixture, coating and pressing onto all sides. Add the cutlets to the pan and cook until well browned, about 3 minutes per side. Transfer to a platter.

2. In a medium bowl, mix together the parsley, scallions, lemon zest and juice, the remaining 1 teaspoon of oil and a pinch of salt. Drizzle the molasses evenly over the chicken, then mound the greens over the cutlets. Sprinkle with walnuts and the remaining za'atar.

MAKING CHICKEN CUTLETS

1. Start with boneless, skinless chicken breasts that weigh 6½ to 7 ounces each. (If breasts are larger than 8 ounces, halve horizontally after removing the tenderloin. Cutlets will require less pounding but will be smaller.)

2. Remove the tenderloin from the breast using kitchen shears and save for another use, such as chicken fingers.

3. Use a sharp knife or kitchen shears to trim away any fat, then, if necessary, trim the breasts to 6 ounces each.

4. Working with 1 breast at a time, place on a cutting board and lay a sheet of plastic wrap on top. Use a meat mallet or small, heavy skillet to gently but firmly pound the breast to an even, ¼-inch thickness.

Mussels with Chorizo and Slow-Roasted Tomatoes

Start to finish: **20 minutes** / Servings: 4

4 ounces Spanish chorizo, halved lengthwise and sliced into ½-inch pieces

3 tablespoons extra-virgin olive oil

1 small red onion, thinly sliced

1 small fennel bulb, halved, cored and thinly sliced crosswise

8 garlic cloves, smashed and peeled

2 bay leaves

1 teaspoon fennel seeds

16 slow-roasted tomato halves, chopped

1½ cups dry vermouth

3 pounds blue mussels, scrubbed

4 tablespoons (½ stick) salted butter, chilled

½ cup chopped fresh flat-leaf parsley

1 tablespoon lemon juice

Kosher salt and ground black pepper

Mussels have a reputation as being tricky, but actually are quick and easy to cook. And as a bonus, they generate their own broth, producing maximum taste in minutes. Our take on mussels turns up the taste by adding Spanish chorizo, giving this dish its smoky, savory flavor. Then we took it a step further by adding our slow-roasted tomatoes (p. 509). Buy mussels from a reliable fishmonger and refrigerate them in a loosely covered colander set over a bowl. You may need to remove the "beard" from the mussels if they aren't cleaned already. Be sure to discard any mussels that are partially opened or broken. Larger black mussels will take a bit longer to cook than blue mussels. Keep a close eye on the mussels; once they start to open, take them off the burner to finish cooking in the residual heat. When buying chorizo for this recipe look for Spanish style, which is cured, smoked and quite firm. Mexican chorizo is soft and crumbles easily. Our favorite brand is Palacios, which is available at many grocers or online. If you can't find it, andouille or linguica are good alternatives. If you don't have any slow-roasted tomatoes, substitute a 14½-ounce can of fire-roasted tomatoes with juice. We liked this dish served with crusty bread and extra-virgin olive oil.

Don't fully cook the mussels on the stove. They continue to cook as they sit off the heat.

1. In a large pot over medium, cook the chorizo in the olive oil until the chorizo begins to brown, about 3 minutes. Stir in the onion, fennel, garlic, bay leaves and fennel seeds. Cover and cook until the onion softens, about 5 minutes. Stir in the tomatoes, vermouth and ½ cup water, then bring to a simmer. Cover and cook, stirring occasionally, until the fennel is tender, about 7 minutes.

2. Add the mussels and stir. Cover and cook until the mussels just begin to open, about 3 minutes. Remove the pot from the heat and let the mussels continue to cook, covered, until all mussels open, another 3 to 5 minutes, quickly stirring once halfway through.

3. Using a kitchen spider or slotted spoon, transfer the mussels to a serving platter, leaving the sauce in the pot. Return the sauce to a simmer over low, then remove from the heat. Whisk in the butter until melted. Stir in the parsley and lemon juice. Taste and season with salt and pepper. Pour the sauce over the mussels.

Burmese Chicken

Start to finish: **30 minutes** / Servings: 4

8 ounces plum tomatoes (2 large), quartered

4 tablespoons grapeseed or other neutral oil, divided

3 teaspoons kosher salt, divided

2 teaspoons ground turmeric

¼ teaspoon red pepper flakes

2 stalks lemon grass, trimmed to the lower 6 inches, dry outer layers discarded

2 large shallots, quartered

2 ounces fresh ginger, thinly sliced (about ¼ cup)

8 garlic cloves, peeled

1½ pounds boneless, skinless chicken thighs, trimmed and cut into 1½-inch pieces

½ cup chopped fresh cilantro

2 tablespoons lime juice, plus lime wedges, to serve

Food writer and photographer Naomi Duguid's stunning books provide keen insight into the people and foods of the countries she visits. One of our favorites, "Burma," includes a terrific recipe called Aromatic Chicken from the Shan Hills. It's simple, yet has deep flavor. We wanted to finesse things to make this even faster and easier for the home cook. We swapped in boneless thighs for Duguid's bone-in chicken and switched to a Dutch oven instead of a wok. She suggests a mortar and pestle, but we used a blender to make a paste of lemon grass, garlic, ginger and shallots. This meant we could skip a marinade and let the chicken season as it cooked. A dose of red pepper flakes added moderate heat, but traditional Burmese food can be fairly spicy; if you want more heat, increase the red pepper flakes or stir in a slivered jalapeño, serrano or bird's eye chili with the cilantro. We liked the chicken over steamed rice or thin rice noodles. It also would be excellent with our coconut rice (p. 144).

Don't use the fibrous outer layers of the lemon grass. You want only the white, slightly tender (but still firm) inner bulb. Trim the root and all but the bottom 5 inches of the stalk, then peel off the first few layers. If you buy lemon grass in a plastic clamshell container, it likely already has been trimmed.

1. In a blender, combine the tomatoes, 1 tablespoon of the oil, 1 teaspoon of the salt, the turmeric, pepper flakes, lemon grass, shallots, ginger and garlic. Blend until a thick paste forms, about 1 minute, scraping down the blender as needed.

2. In a large Dutch oven over medium-high, add the remaining 3 tablespoons of oil, the chicken and the remaining 2 teaspoons of salt. Cook, stirring occasionally, until the chicken is no longer pink, about 5 minutes. Add the spice paste and cook, stirring occasionally, until fragrant and the paste coats the chicken, 2 to 3 minutes.

3. Cover, reduce heat to medium-low and cook, stirring occasionally, for 10 minutes. Uncover, increase heat to medium-high and simmer until the chicken is cooked through and the sauce is thickened, 7 to 9 minutes. Off heat, stir in the cilantro and lime juice. Serve with lime wedges.

Vietnamese Caramel Fish

Start to finish: **30 minutes** / Servings: 4

1 tablespoon plus ½ cup coconut water, divided

¼ cup white sugar

3 tablespoons fish sauce

½ cup thinly sliced shallots

1½-inch piece fresh ginger, halved and smashed

Four 2-inch strips lime zest

Four 5- to 6-ounce cod fillets, about ¾-inch thick

Ground black pepper

¼ cup chopped fresh cilantro leaves

1 jalapeño or serrano chili, thinly sliced

We're always looking for ways to cook moist, flavorful fish with relatively little fuss. And we found a new, unusual way to do that via a sauce we usually associate with dessert. In Vietnam, fish is cooked in a savory-sweet caramel sauce, both seasoning the fish and keeping it moist. To ensure our sauce was dark and savory, not cloying, we cooked the sugar a little longer, creating a darker and slightly bitter caramel. We found that a tablespoon of coconut water helped the sugar caramelize faster, getting us the deep coffee color we were after in just minutes. Keep a close eye on the caramel to prevent it from burning and becoming too bitter. Dark, oily fish are common in this dish, but we liked it better with a firm whitefish. Note that cooking times are for fillets about ¾ inch thick.

Don't use canned coconut milk here. Coconut water is widely available and lends a light sweetness and subtle coconut flavor to the caramel. If you can't find it, use water.

1. In a large Dutch oven over medium-high, bring 1 tablespoon of the coconut water and the sugar to a boil. Cook, stirring occasionally, until the mixture begins to color at the edges, 2 to 3 minutes. Reduce heat to medium-low and cook, stirring often, until the sugar is mahogany-colored, another 1 to 3 minutes. Off heat, add the fish sauce and whisk until smooth (the mixture will steam and bubble vigorously). Add the remaining ½ cup of coconut water and whisk until fully incorporated. Add the shallots, ginger and lime zest. Return to a simmer over medium. Reduce heat to medium-low and simmer gently for 5 minutes.

2. Season the fish with pepper, then nestle it into the pot. Simmer for 3 minutes, then gently turn the fish and continue simmering until just cooked through, 3 to 5 minutes, scraping the edges of the pot as necessary to prevent burning and adjusting the heat to maintain a gentle simmer. (If the caramel darkens too quickly around the edges, reduce the heat to low.)

3. Carefully transfer the fish to a rimmed serving plate. The sauce should be thick and syrupy. If necessary, continue to simmer until the proper consistency is achieved. Off heat, remove and discard the ginger and zest. Drizzle the fish with the sauce, then sprinkle with cilantro and chili.

Shrimp in Chipotle Sauce (*Camarones Enchipotlados*)

Start to finish: **25 minutes** / Servings: 4

4 vine-ripened tomatoes
(1¼ pounds), quartered

4 chipotle chilies in adobo sauce
and the sauce clinging to them

Kosher salt and ground black pepper

4 tablespoons olive oil, divided

1½ pounds extra-large raw shrimp,
peeled, deveined, tails removed and
patted dry

4 tablespoons lime juice, divided

1 medium yellow onion, chopped

3 garlic cloves, thinly sliced

½ teaspoon dried oregano

¼ cup dry white wine

½ cup chopped fresh cilantro,
plus more to serve

Eight 6-inch corn tortillas, warmed

Avocado, sour cream and lime
wedges, to serve

A perfectly cooked shrimp—pink, firm but not tough, curved but not coiled—stymies most of us. The window between done and overdone is narrow. We solved that problem by giving the shrimp very little time over direct heat. Instead, we let the residual heat of a flavorful sauce cook them more gently. For the sauce, we used canned chipotle chilies and the adobo sauce in which they are packed, which give the dish pleasant, lingering heat and deep smoky flavor. The shrimp got a brief sear to start, then finished cooking off the burner in the warm sauce. Perfect results, effortlessly, every time. These shrimp made wonderful tacos when paired with diced avocado, fresh cilantro, lime wedges and sour cream. This dish also is delicious served alongside rice or cold as an appetizer.

Don't worry if your chipotles vary in size. Despite appearances, most weigh about half an ounce.

1. In a food processor, pulse the tomatoes, chilies and any sauce coating them and ¾ teaspoon salt until mostly smooth, 1 minute. Set aside.

2. In a 12-inch nonstick skillet over medium-high, heat 2 tablespoons of the oil until beginning to smoke. Add half the shrimp and cook, stirring, until golden, about 45 seconds. Transfer to a bowl. Repeat with the remaining shrimp, adding them to the bowl. Toss with 2 tablespoons of the lime juice. Set aside.

3. Return the skillet to medium-high and add the remaining 2 tablespoons of oil. Add the onion and cook for 3 to 4 minutes. Add the garlic and oregano and cook until just beginning to brown, 1 minute. Stir in the wine and any accumulated shrimp juice from the bowl. Cook until the liquid is nearly evaporated. Add the chipotle mixture and simmer, stirring, until thick enough to coat a spoon, 10 to 12 minutes.

4. Remove the skillet from the heat. Stir in the shrimp, cover and let sit until the shrimp are opaque and cooked through, 2 to 4 minutes. Stir in the cilantro and remaining lime juice. Taste, then season with salt and pepper. Serve with warmed tortillas, avocado, sour cream and lime wedges.

Dinners

Chicken Traybake with
Roasted Poblano and Tomato Salsa / 293

Chinese White-Cooked Chicken
with Ginger-Soy Dressing / 296

Colombian Braised Beef (*Posta Negra*) / 298

Brown-Ale Turkey with Gravy / 300

Easy-Bake Herbed Dressing / 303

Japanese Fried Chicken (*Karaage*) / 304

No-Sear Lamb or Beef
and Chickpea Stew / 306

Argentinian-Style Stuffed
Pork Loin with Chimichurri / 308

Miso-Gochujang Pulled Pork / 312

Crispy Chicken Under a Brick
(*Tsitsila Tabaka*) / 314

Prune, Peppercorn and Fresh Herb–Rubbed
Roast Beef with Horseradish Sauce / 318

Piri Piri Chicken / 320

Cuban-Style Pork Shoulder
with Mojo Sauce / 322

Za'atar-Roasted Chicken / 327

Thai Beef Salad (*Yam Neua*) / 328

Tacos al Pastor / 331

Cape Malay Chicken Curry / 333

Austrian Beef Stew with Paprika
and Caraway (*Rindsgulasch*) / 335

Crispy Sichuan-Chili Chicken / 336

North African Chicken Couscous / 338

Oven-Poached Salmon with
Thyme, Dill and Vermouth / 341

Beef, Orange and Olive Stew
(*Boeuf à la Gardiane*) / 343

Lemon-Saffron Chicken (*Tangia*) / 345

Salmon Packets with Chermoula / 346

Senegalese Braised Chicken
with Onions and Lime (*Yassa Ginaar*) / 349

Tuscan Beef and Black Pepper Stew
(*Peposo alla Fornacina*) / 350

Filipino Chicken Adobo
with Coconut Broth / 352

Caramelized Pork
with Orange and Sage / 354

Red Chili Spatchcocked
Roast Chicken / 356

Chiang Mai Chicken (*Kai Yang*) / 358

Fennel-Rosemary Porchetta / 360

Chicken Tagine with Apricots,
Butternut Squash and Spinach / 362

Carne Adovada / 365

Chicken en Cocotte / 367

Sumac-Spiced Chicken (*Musakhan*) / 369

Southern Thai-Style Fried Chicken / 370

8

Chicken Traybake with Roasted Poblano and Tomato Salsa

Start to finish: **50 minutes** / Servings: 4

1 tablespoon chili powder

Kosher salt and ground black pepper

2 poblano chilies, stemmed, seeded and roughly chopped

1 medium yellow onion, root end intact, cut into 8 wedges

1 pint cherry or grape tomatoes

1 habanero chili, stemmed halved and seeded (optional)

¼ cup extra-virgin olive oil

1 tablespoon firmly packed light or dark brown sugar

1 tablespoon dried oregano

3 pounds bone-in, skin-on chicken parts, trimmed and patted dry

10 medium garlic cloves, peeled

1 tablespoon white vinegar

¼ cup lightly packed fresh cilantro, roughly chopped

CHANGE THE WAY YOU COOK:
ROAST ON BAKING SHEETS, NOT ROASTING PANS

Cooking on a low-rimmed baking sheet rather than in a deep roasting pan allows for better air circulation around the food, accelerating cooking and boosting browning. To turn this into a whole meal, roast vegetables alongside the chicken and add sauce ingredients such as garlic cloves. Once the chicken parts are cooked, add water to the pan and scrape up the browned, crispy bits for a quick and flavorful sauce.

In Oaxaca, in southeastern Mexico, salsas start with charring chilies, tomatoes, onions and garlic on a steel or clay comal (a flat griddle used to make tortillas) to soften and deepen their flavors. We adapt that concept in this traybake, roasting chilies alongside chicken parts. Glossy, dark green poblano peppers have an earthy, minerally flavor and moderate heat level. Habanero adds a burst of bright, fruity heat that sharpens the tomatoes' flavor. The tomatoes release their juice during cooking, so deglazing the baking sheet with water after roasting isn't necessary. If you want a lot of heat in your salsa, include the optional habanero chili. The tomatoes release their juice during cooking, so deglazing the baking sheet with water after roasting isn't necessary.

Don't forget to leave the root end of the onion intact so the wedges don't separate into layers. If the layers separate, they tend to scorch during roasting.

1. Heat the oven to 450°F with a rack in the middle position. In a small bowl, stir together the chili powder and 2 teaspoons salt. In a large bowl, toss together the poblanos, onion wedges, tomatoes, habanero (if using), 1 tablespoon of the chili powder mixture and the oil. Into the remaining chili powder mixture, stir the sugar, oregano, 1 tablespoon salt and 2 teaspoons pepper.

2. On a rimmed baking sheet, evenly season both sides of the chicken parts with the chili powder mixture. Place the garlic cloves in the center of the baking sheet, then arrange the chicken parts, skin up, around the garlic; this prevents the garlic from scorching during roasting. Arrange the vegetables evenly around the chicken.

3. Roast until the thickest part of the breast (if using) reaches about 160°F and the thickest part of the largest thigh/leg (if using) reaches about 175°F, 30 to 40 minutes.

4. Using tongs, transfer the chicken to a platter and transfer the onion wedges and habanero to a cutting board. Pour the garlic, the remaining vegetables and any liquid on the baking sheet into a medium bowl. Roughly chop the onion and habanero, then add to the bowl. Using a fork or potato masher, mash the mixture until broken down but slightly chunky, then stir in half of the cilantro and the vinegar. Serve the salsa with the chicken and sprinkle with the remaining cilantro.

1. In a large bowl, toss together the poblanos, onion wedges, tomatoes, habanero, 1 tablespoon of the chili powder mixture and the oil.

2. Place the garlic cloves in the center of the baking sheet, then arrange the chicken parts, skin up, around the garlic; this prevents the garlic from scorching during roasting.

3. Arrange the vegetables around the chicken, taking care to not overlap for even cooking.

4. Tilt the pan to pour the garlic, the remaining vegetables and any liquid on the baking sheet into a medium bowl.

5. Using a fork or potato masher, mash the mixture until broken down but slightly chunky.

6. Stir in half of the cilantro and the vinegar, then serve the salsa with the chicken. Sprinkle with remaining cilantro.

Chinese White-Cooked **Chicken** with Ginger-Soy Dressing

Start to finish: **2 hours (30 minutes active)** / Servings: 4

For the chicken and poaching broth:

3½- to 4-pound chicken, giblets discarded

1 bunch fresh cilantro

6 scallions, trimmed and halved crosswise

4½ quarts water

2 cups dry sherry or mirin

4-inch piece fresh ginger, cut into 4 pieces and smashed

2 tablespoons kosher salt

For the dressing:

4 scallions, thinly sliced on diagonal

3 tablespoons soy sauce

2 tablespoons grapeseed or other neutral oil

4 teaspoons finely grated fresh ginger

1 tablespoon unseasoned rice vinegar

1 tablespoon toasted sesame oil

½ teaspoon white sugar

½ pound (½ small head) napa or savoy cabbage, thinly sliced (4 cups)

Cooked white rice, to serve (optional)

It's easy to take a skin-deep approach to chicken, paying lots of attention to getting a golden brown crust only to end up with dull, bland—and too often overcooked—meat. We avoid that trap by adopting the Chinese technique of whole-bird poaching to create a chicken with simple, clean flavors and a silky, tender-but-firm meat primed for a variety of vibrant sauces. Simmered without soy sauce (and therefore white), the classic Cantonese dish is known as white-cooked or white-cut chicken. Poaching—in which the chicken is slowly cooked in liquid just below a simmer—delivers heat evenly, so no worries about dry breasts or pink thighs. The whole process takes about the same amount of time as roasting, most of it hands-off. In fact, the last 30 minutes of cooking occurs off the heat entirely. Poaching results in blond skin that most Americans will want to discard (though Chinese cooks leave it on and consider it perfectly tasty). The bright aromatics of raw scallions and ginger worked best in a soy sauce–based dressing, which we thinned with some of the poaching liquid.

Don't use cooking sherry for this recipe; it usually has added sodium and little, if any, actual sherry flavor. Look for a high-quality (but affordable) dry sherry.

1. Remove the chicken from the refrigerator and let sit at room temperature while making the broth. Reserving a few sprigs for garnish, cut the cilantro bunch in half crosswise, separating the stems and leaves. Use kitchen twine to tie the stems and scallions into a bundle. Chop enough of the cilantro leaves to measure ½ cup and set aside. (The remaining cilantro leaves are not needed.)

2. In a large pot (at least 8 quarts) over high, combine the cilantro-scallion bundle with the remaining broth ingredients and bring to a boil. Using tongs, lower the chicken into the broth breast side up, letting the liquid flow into the cavity. If the chicken isn't fully submerged in the broth after flooding the cavity, weigh it down with a plate.

3. Allow the broth to return to a boil, then reduce heat to medium and cook for 25 minutes, adjusting the heat to maintain a bare simmer; flip the chicken to be breast side down after 15 minutes. Turn off the heat, remove the pot from the burner and let the chicken sit in the hot broth for 30 minutes. Transfer the chicken to a carving board and let rest for 15 minutes.

4. While the chicken rests, prepare the dressing. In a small bowl, stir together ¼ cup of the poaching broth, the scallions, soy sauce, grapeseed oil, ginger, vinegar, sesame oil and sugar.

DON'T TOSS YOUR POACHING BROTH

While the poached chicken cools before carving, use the hot, seasoned broth to cook rice to round out the meal. Use the broth 1:1 for any water called for by the variety of rice you use. For long-grain white rice, for example, combine 1½ cups rinsed rice with 2 cups of the broth. Bring to a simmer, then reduce heat to low, cover and cook until the rice is fluffy and tender, 15 to 18 minutes. And be sure to save any remaining broth for use in rice, soup, sauces and braises. We freeze it in 2-cup portions in zip-close freezer bags.

5. Using a sharp knife, remove the legs from the chicken by cutting through the thigh joints, then separate the thighs from the drumsticks. Carve the breast meat from the bone and slice each breast crosswise into 4 pieces. Discard the chicken skin, if desired. Spread the cabbage on a serving platter, then arrange the chicken pieces on top. Pour the dressing over the chicken and sprinkle with the reserved ½ cup chopped cilantro. Garnish with cilantro sprigs.

Colombian **Braised Beef** (*Posta Negra*)

Start to finish: **5 hours (30 minutes active)**
Servings: **4**

5-pound boneless beef chuck roast, trimmed and patted dry

Kosher salt and ground black pepper

2 tablespoons grapeseed or other neutral oil

1 large yellow onion, chopped

10 medium garlic cloves, peeled

2 tablespoons tomato paste

½ cup packed dark brown sugar

2 cinnamon sticks

1 tablespoon whole allspice

2 teaspoons whole black peppercorns

1 teaspoon whole cloves

1 cup dry red wine

¼ cup Worcestershire sauce

1 cup pitted prunes, roughly chopped

1 tablespoon cornstarch

3 tablespoons red wine vinegar

Named after its dark, sweet sauce, posta negra is a classic Colombian dish made by braising beef in a flavorful liquid seasoned with panela (a type of raw cane sugar) and spices. For our version, we call for a 5-pound beef chuck roast; it's a fat-rich cut, so trim it well before tying the roast. In the end, the meat will be superbly tender and succulent. In Colombia, the dish might be served with fried plantains, yucca fritters and a simple salad; we liked it with fresh pico de gallo and potatoes.

Don't carve the roast without first letting it rest. Resting makes the meat easier to cut into neat slices.

1. Heat the oven to 300°F with a rack in the lower-middle position. Using kitchen twine, tie the roast at 2-inch intervals. Season all over with salt and pepper.

2. In a large Dutch oven over medium-high, heat the oil until shimmering. Add the onion and ½ teaspoon salt, then cook, stirring occasionally, until well browned, 5 to 7 minutes. Stir in the garlic and cook until fragrant, about 30 seconds. Add the tomato paste and cook, stirring constantly, until it begins to brown, about 2 minutes. Stir in the sugar, cinnamon, allspice, peppercorns and cloves. Pour in the wine, bring to a simmer and cook until thick and syrupy, 3 to 5 minutes. Stir in the Worcestershire sauce and prunes.

3. Place the roast in the pot, then turn to coat with the liquid. Cover, place in the oven and cook until a paring knife inserted into the thickest part meets no resistance, 3½ to 4 hours. Transfer the roast to a shallow baking dish and tent with foil. Let rest for 30 minutes.

4. Meanwhile, set a fine mesh strainer over a medium bowl. Pour the contents of the pot into the strainer and press on the solids to extract as much liquid and pulp as possible, scraping the underside to collect the pulp. Discard the solids. Let the liquid settle for about 5 minutes (you should have about 1½ cups), then skim off the fat. Return the defatted liquid with pulp to the Dutch oven and bring to a simmer over medium.

5. In a small bowl, stir together 3 tablespoons water and the cornstarch. Whisk into the simmering liquid and cook, stirring constantly, until lightly thickened, about 2 minutes. Stir in the vinegar. Taste and season with salt and pepper.

6. Transfer the roast to a cutting board. Remove and discard the twine. Cut the meat against the grain into ½-inch slices and transfer to a platter. Pour about 1 cup of the sauce over the meat. Serve with the remaining sauce on the side.

QUICK PICO DE GALLO

Start to finish: 40 minutes
(10 minutes active)
Makes about 1 cup

3 medium plum tomatoes, cored,
seeded and finely chopped

1 jalapeño chili, stemmed, seeded
and sliced into thin half rings

¾ teaspoon kosher salt

3 tablespoons red wine vinegar

2 tablespoons finely chopped
fresh cilantro

In a small bowl, stir together all
ingredients. Cover and let stand,
stirring occasionally, for at least
30 minutes or up to 2 hours.

Brown Ale Turkey with Gravy

Start to finish: 3½ hours (30 minutes active), plus cooling
Servings: 10

2 medium yellow onions
(1 to 1¼ pounds), cut into
8 wedges each

4 large sprigs fresh thyme

2 large sprigs fresh rosemary

2 large sprigs fresh sage

2 bay leaves

2 garlic cloves, crushed

Two 12-ounce bottles brown ale,
such as Newcastle Brown Ale

4 tablespoons (½ stick) salted
butter, cut into 4 pieces

¼ cup fish sauce

Kosher salt and ground
black pepper

12- to 14-pound turkey, neck
and giblets discarded

2 stalks celery, quartered

Low-sodium chicken broth,
as needed

¼ cup instant flour, such
as Wondra

Roasting a turkey, whether for Thanksgiving, Christmas or just because, can be an ordeal. The debate over brining alone is enough to make one consider going vegetarian. And, of course, there is the finicky business of how to get the thigh and breast meat to cook to perfect—yet different— temperatures simultaneously. We skipped the culinary gymnastics in favor of a tried-and-true method—basting. Then we made it better with beer. We doused our turkey—but only twice, so no worries about having to babysit the bird—with a reduction of brown ale, onions, garlic and fresh herbs, which combined to form a rich, malty base. Avoid hoppy beers, which turned unpleasantly bitter when reduced. We also used a secret ingredient: fish sauce. It adds savory depth to the baste that is reflected in the umami-rich gravy made from pan drippings. Relax, it doesn't taste at all fishy.

1. Heat the oven to 350°F with a rack in the lower middle position. In a 12-inch skillet, combine the onions, thyme, rosemary, sage, bay leaves, garlic and beer. Bring to a boil, then reduce heat to medium and simmer until reduced to ⅔ cup, about 20 minutes.

2. Strain the mixture into a large bowl, pressing on the solids. Reserve the solids. The liquid should measure ⅔ cup. If not, either reduce further or add water. Return reduction to the skillet, add the butter, and whisk until melted. Stir in the fish sauce and ½ teaspoon each salt and pepper.

3. Pat the turkey dry inside and out with paper towels. Tuck the wings underneath. Spread the reserved solids and celery in a large roasting pan and place the turkey breast side up over the mixture. Pour half of the beer reduction over the turkey; use your hands to coat it evenly. Cover loosely with foil, then roast for 1½ hours.

4. Remove the foil. Whisk the remaining beer reduction, then pour over the turkey. Roast until the breast registers 160°F and the thigh registers 175°F, 1 to 1 hour 45 minutes. If the turkey gets too dark, cover with foil.

5. Transfer the turkey to a platter or carving board, letting the juices run into the pan, then tent with foil and let rest for 30 minutes. Strain the pan drippings into a 4-cup liquid measuring cup, pressing on the solids; discard the solids.

6. Skim the fat from the drippings. If you have less than 3 cups of defatted drippings, add stock to measure 3 cups, then return to the roasting pan. Whisk in the flour, then set the pan on the stovetop and bring to a boil over medium. Simmer, whisking constantly and scraping the bottom, until thickened, 1 to 3 minutes. Season with salt and pepper. Carve the turkey, adding any accumulated juices to the gravy, then serve with gravy.

Easy-Bake Herbed Dressing

Start to finish: 2 hours 15 minutes (30 minutes active), plus cooling
Servings: 8

1 cup finely chopped celery

8 tablespoons (1 stick) salted butter, melted

8 ounces shallots, peeled

⅓ cup lightly packed fresh sage leaves

2 tablespoons fresh thyme leaves

1½ teaspoons kosher salt

1 teaspoon ground black pepper

1½ pounds sturdy white sandwich bread, cut into ¾-inch cubes

3 cups low-sodium chicken broth

½ cup heavy cream

½ cup chopped fresh flat-leaf parsley leaves

Let's face it, stuffing is basically a flavorful sponge to soak up gravy and any stray melting butter that escapes a vegetable. But mincing and sauteing the aromatics that help turn bland bread tasty is a chore. We sped things up—and maximized flavor—by giving butter, fresh herbs and raw shallots a whiz in the food processor, then using the resulting paste to season bread cubes as they toast in the oven. We found that any sturdy, high-quality sliced sandwich bread worked well. As the bread bakes, the raw bite of the shallots cooks off, leaving behind a mellow tang. Chopped celery was tossed with melted butter and mixed into the bread, softening as the cubes toast. The mixture then was moistened with chicken broth and a touch of cream before being baked to create a relatively carefree stuffing that will satisfy even the strictest traditionalists.

Don't use regular chicken broth. Make sure to use low-sodium, otherwise you'll end up with an oversalted stuffing.

1. Heat the oven to 325°F with racks in the upper- and lower-middle positions. In a bowl, toss the celery with 1 tablespoon of the butter; set aside. In a food processor, combine the shallots, sage, thyme, salt, pepper and the remaining butter. Process to form a smooth paste, about 30 seconds.

2. In a large bowl, combine the bread and shallot-herb paste, tossing gently. Fold in the celery, then divide the mixture between 2 rimmed baking sheets. Bake until the celery is tender and the bread is crisp and golden, 50 to 60 minutes, stirring the bread and switching and rotating the pans halfway through. Let cool slightly. At this stage the bread mixture can be cooled, bagged and stored for a day.

3. When ready to proceed, increase the oven temperature to 400°F. Transfer the bread mixture to a large bowl, scraping any browned bits off the sheet pans. Fold in the broth, cream and parsley; let sit for 10 minutes, stirring occasionally. Transfer to a 13-by-9-inch baking dish and spread evenly. Bake on the upper- middle rack until well browned on top, 40 to 45 minutes, rotating the dish halfway through. Let sit for 20 minutes before serving.

Japanese Fried Chicken (*Karaage*)

Start to finish: 1 hour 45 minutes (15 minutes active), plus resting
Servings: 4

___

For the chicken:

3-ounce chunk unpeeled fresh ginger, coarsely grated

¼ cup sake

¼ cup tamari

1 tablespoon grated lemon zest

2 pounds boneless, skinless chicken thighs, trimmed and cut into thirds

264 grams (2 cups) cornstarch

1 tablespoon shichimi togarashi (or 1 teaspoon red pepper flakes)

1 teaspoon ground black pepper

2 quarts peanut or vegetable oil

For the dipping sauce:

¼ cup tamari

¼ cup unseasoned rice vinegar

1 teaspoon finely grated peeled fresh ginger

¼ teaspoon toasted sesame oil

We love crispy, juicy fried chicken, but getting it right can be hard. Too often, the breading is heavy and dull, masking the flavor of the meat. And coating the chicken can be a messy three-step process. We found a better way in karaage (kah-rah-ah-gay), the Japanese bite-sized fried chicken that starts with a zesty marinade and is coated with potato starch or potato flour, which creates a thin, crispy crust. We chose boneless, skinless chicken thighs and soaked them briefly in a slurry featuring fresh ginger. We also used tamari, a Japanese soy sauce. Tamari has a bolder flavor and darker color than Chinese-style soy sauces, but if you can't find it any soy sauce will work. For our coating, we tried potato starch, which was good but tricky to work with. Cornstarch proved easier to handle—and find at the store—and produced good results. A large Dutch oven, at least 7 quarts, was essential for frying. We finished with a dipping sauce that mirrored the marinade with tamari, unseasoned rice vinegar, grated fresh ginger and toasted sesame oil.

Don't let the chicken sit for longer than an hour after coating it before frying. It will get gummy.

1. To make the chicken, gather the ginger in your hands and squeeze as much juice as possible into a large bowl. Add the ginger solids to the bowl and stir in the sake, tamari and lemon zest. Add the chicken and stir to coat. Refrigerate for at least 30 minutes or up to 1 hour.

2. Set a wire rack in a rimmed baking sheet. In a large bowl, combine the cornstarch, shichimi togarashi and pepper. Working 1 piece at a time, remove the chicken from the marinade, letting excess drip off, then dredge in the cornstarch mixture, pressing evenly to adhere on all sides. Transfer to the rack and refrigerate, uncovered, for at least 30 minutes and up to 1 hour.

3. In a 7-quart Dutch oven, heat the oil to 375°F. Add a third of the chicken to the hot oil and fry, stirring to prevent sticking, until the chicken is deep golden brown, 5 to 7 minutes. Transfer the chicken to a clean wire rack, return the oil to 375°F and repeat twice with the remaining chicken.

4. For the dipping sauce, whisk together all ingredients.

No-Sear Lamb or Beef and Chickpea Stew

Start to finish: 2 hours 15 minutes (40 minutes active)
Servings: 4

1 tablespoon sweet paprika

2 teaspoons ground cumin

1 teaspoon ground cardamom

¼ teaspoon cinnamon

Kosher salt and ground black pepper

1¼ pounds boneless lamb shoulder, trimmed of fat and cut into ¾-inch pieces

1 head garlic

2 tablespoons salted butter

1 large yellow onion, diced (about 2 cups)

2 tablespoons tomato paste

½ pound carrots (2 to 3 medium), peeled, halved lengthwise and cut crosswise into ½-inch pieces

15½-ounce can chickpeas, drained

3 ounces baby spinach (about 3 cups)

1 cup chopped fresh cilantro, plus more to garnish

3 tablespoons lemon juice

Plain whole-milk yogurt, to serve (optional)

CHANGE THE WAY YOU COOK:
STOP SEARING YOUR MEAT

Skip the searing. It's easier to build flavor into a stew by adding handfuls of herbs and plenty of robust spices. You'll save the time and hassle.

The mess, time and trouble required to brown meat for a stew left us longing for a better way. Did we really need that step to get big flavor? Then we discovered a world of alternatives from cultures where cooks skip the browning and instead build layers of flavor with spices and condiments. For our no-sear, no-stock stew, based on the Yemeni dish known as maraq, we started with a dry seasoning mix—paprika, cumin, cardamom, cinnamon, salt and pepper. It did double duty, with half the mixture rubbed onto the meat and the rest briefly cooked in the pot with onion, butter and tomato paste. Cooking the seasonings with the fat and tomato paste bloomed their flavors and lightly browned the tomato paste. We wanted the savory sweetness of roasted whole garlic cloves (mincing releases aggressive sulfurous compounds) but not the trouble of roasting a head separately. So, we sliced off the top of the head, then added it whole to the stew to cook alongside the meat. We liked the flavor and texture of lamb shoulder. Boneless beef chuck worked, too (but needs an extra cup of water and must cook longer, 90 minutes total, before adding the carrots).

Don't use old spices. The backbone of the dish is the bold, vibrant spice mixture. Make sure yours are no more than a year old.

1. In a bowl, stir together the paprika, cumin, cardamom, cinnamon, 2 teaspoons salt and ½ teaspoon pepper. Reserve half of the spice mixture, then toss the lamb with the rest until well coated. Set aside. Cut off and discard the top third of the garlic head, leaving the head intact.

2. In a large Dutch oven over medium-high, melt the butter. Add the onion and cook, stirring often, until softened and just beginning to brown around the edges, 5 to 8 minutes. Add the tomato paste and the reserved spice mixture, then cook, stirring constantly, for 1 minute. Add 6 cups water and bring to a boil over high, then add the lamb and garlic head, cut side down. Cover, leaving the lid slightly ajar, and reduce heat to low.

3. Simmer for 1 hour, adjusting the heat as necessary to maintain a gentle bubble. Add the carrots and continue to simmer, partially covered, for another 30 minutes. Using tongs, remove the garlic head and squeeze over the stew to release the cloves. Stir in the chickpeas and spinach and cook until the spinach is wilted, about 5 minutes.

4. Stir in the cilantro and lemon juice, then season the stew with salt and pepper. Serve topped with yogurt and sprinkled with cilantro.

Argentinian-Style Stuffed Pork Loin with Chimichurri

Start to finish: **3 hours (1 hour active)** / Servings: **8**

For the Chimichurri:

3 cups lightly packed fresh flat-leaf parsley

⅓ to ½ cup lightly packed fresh oregano

7 medium garlic cloves, smashed and peeled

1½ teaspoons ground cumin

1½ teaspoons ground coriander

¾ teaspoon red pepper flakes

Kosher salt and ground black pepper

¼ cup red wine vinegar

¾ cup extra-virgin olive oil

For the Roast:

1 tablespoon ground cumin

1 tablespoon ground coriander

2 teaspoons packed light brown sugar

Kosher salt and ground black pepper

4-pound boneless center-cut pork loin

6 ounces thinly sliced capicola or mortadella

½ cup pitted green olives, roughly chopped

1½ cups drained roasted red peppers, patted dry and torn into large pieces

⅓ cup panko breadcrumbs

3 hard-cooked large eggs, peeled and halved crosswise

1½ tablespoons extra-virgin olive oil

Flaky sea salt, to serve (optional)

This holiday-worthy roast was inspired by Argentinian matambre arrollado, or beef that is stuffed with hard-cooked eggs, vegetables and sliced cured meats, then poached or roasted. We opted for a boneless pork loin roast because its uniform shape makes it easy to cut into a ½- to ¾-inch-thick slab ideal for filling and rolling. Herbal, garlicky and subtly spicy chimichurri is the perfect accompaniment to the sweet, mild pork; we use some inside the roast, too. You'll need a digital thermometer to test the roast for doneness. For convenience, the chimichurri can be made and refrigerated in an airtight container up to a day ahead. The seasonings for the roast can be combined and stored at room temperature and the pork loin can be butterflied and refrigerated a day in advance, too. Additionally, the roast rests for 30 to 60 minutes after cooking, so your oven will be free for last-minute sides.

Don't trim the fat off the pork loin. The fat cap lends richness to an otherwise lean cut and gives the roast an appealing burnished-brown appearance. Don't rush when butterflying the pork loin. Short, small cuts allow for the best control so you can maintain an even slice and adjust as you go. Don't worry if the surface of the butterflied meat is not perfectly flat or even; it won't matter in the finished dish.

1. To prepare the chimichurri, in a food processor, combine the parsley, oregano, garlic, cumin, coriander, pepper flakes, 1 teaspoon salt and ½ teaspoon black pepper. Process until finely chopped, 30 to 45 seconds. Scrape the bowl, add the vinegar and oil, then process until as smooth as possible, 45 to 60 seconds. Measure ¼ cup of the chimichurri into a small bowl and set aside; transfer the remainder to a serving bowl; cover and refrigerate until ready to serve.

2. To prepare the roast, heat the oven to 350°F with a rack in the lower-middle position. Line a rimmed baking sheet with foil, then fit with a wire rack. In a small bowl, stir together the cumin, coriander, brown sugar, 3½ teaspoons salt and 1½ teaspoons pepper. Set aside.

3. Cut eight 24-inch lengths of kitchen twine. Place the roast, fat side down, on a cutting board, positioning a short end facing you (see step-by-step photographs pp. 310-11). With a sharp boning or carving knife, cut along the length of the roast, slicing down its center, stopping about ½ inch from cutting through the roast.

4. Starting at the base of the cut and with the knife blade held as parallel as possible to the cutting board, slice along one side of the roast, unrolling the meat with your free hand as you go. Continue cutting and opening up the meat until the half is a flat, fairly even surface ½ to ¾ inch thick. Rotate the roast 180 degrees and repeat with the second side. If there are areas that are slightly too thick, use a meat mallet to pound those spots to the same thickness.

5. Season the pork on both sides with the spice mixture. Place the meat fat side down and with a short side nearest you. Spread the reserved ¼ cup chimichurri evenly on the meat. Shingle on the capicola slices, covering the entire surface, then sprinkle evenly with the olives. Lay the red peppers on top, tearing them as needed to cover the entire surface. Sprinkle the filling evenly with the panko. Place the egg halves cut sides down in a row about 3 inches from the bottom edge.

6. Lift the bottom edge of the roast over the eggs and slowly roll the meat into a tight cylinder. Position the cylinder seam side down and tie at even intervals with the twine, then snip off excess twine. If any bits of filling fall out, simply tuck them back in at the ends. Brush the roast on all sides with the oil.

7. Transfer the roast fat side up to the prepared baking sheet. Bake until the top is nicely browned and the center of the roast reaches 135°F, 1½ to 2 hours. Let rest on the wire rack for 30 to 60 minutes.

8. Remove the chimichurri from the refrigerator about 30 minutes before serving. Cut the roast into ½-inch-thick slices, removing the twine as you go. Arrange the slices on a platter, sprinkle with flaky salt (if using) and serve with the remaining chimichurri on the side.

BUTTERFLYING, STUFFING, ROLLING, AND TYING PORK LOIN

1. Position the roast on a cutting board with a short end facing you. Make a lengthwise cut, stopping about ½ inch from cutting all the way through the roast.

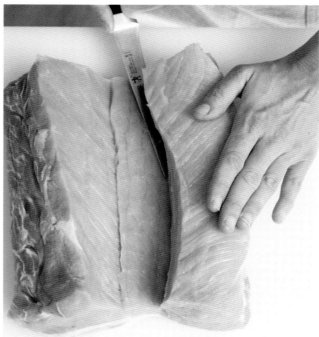

2. With the knife blade parallel to the meat surface, make small incisions into the meat, slicing lengthwise and opening the loin like a book as you slice.

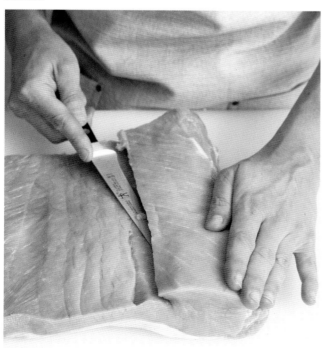

3. Rotate the roast 180 degrees to cut the second side, then repeat the cutting and opening to create a large, flat piece of meat with an even surface.

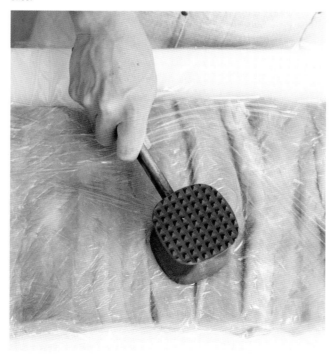

4. If there are spots in the meat that are thicker than desired, use a meat mallet to pound those spots to the same thickness—roughly ½ to ¾ inch thick.

5. With the roast positioned so the grain of the meat runs parallel to the cutting board, brush the reserved ¼ cup chimichurri sauce over the surface of the meat, then shingle the capicolla, olives, pepper and panko on the pork.

6. Using both hands, roll the edge of the meat up over the eggs, pressing down gently to keep the eggs in place. The panko will act as a binder for the filling.

7. Stabilizing the meat at either end, continue to roll the pork loin into a tight cylinder. Position the roast, seam side down, on a cutting board before tying.

8. Starting in the middle of the roast, tightly tie the roast in 1-inch intervals with kitchen twine. Tuck any filling that falls out back into the ends.

Miso-Gochujang Pulled Pork

Start to finish: 4 hours (1 hour active)
Servings: 6 to 8

___

5 pound boneless pork butt, trimmed and cut into 2-inch cubes

¾ cup gochujang, divided

6 tablespoons white miso, divided

1 bunch fresh cilantro, stems minced, leaves left whole, reserved separately

¼ cup hoisin sauce

3 ounces fresh ginger, peeled and cut into 3 chunks

2 tablespoons grapeseed or other neutral oil

2 large yellow onions, thinly sliced

Kosher salt and ground black pepper

3 tablespoons unseasoned rice vinegar

Pickled jalapeños, to serve

PULLED PORK TOPPINGS

We liked the miso-gochujang pulled pork piled onto soft potato rolls and topped with quick-pickled carrots, sliced pickled jalapeños and gochujang-spiked sour cream.

This Asian-inflected take on barbecue pulled pork was inspired by the "Pigalicious" wrap served at Bird & Ewe in Sydney. White miso and gochujang provide deep, savory-sweet notes and lots of complex flavor to oven-braised pork butt. Miso usually is sold in the refrigerator case; gochujang, or Korean red pepper paste, does not require refrigeration until the container is opened. Both are available in well-stocked supermarkets and Asian grocery stores. The pork cooks for about three hours; use this time to prep and cook the miso-seasoned onions that are combined with the meat after shredding.

Don't forget to skim the fat off the cooking liquid so the pulled pork doesn't end up greasy. But make sure to allow the liquid to settle before skimming so all the fat has time to rise to the surface.

1. Heat the oven to 325°F with a rack in the lower-middle position. In a large Dutch oven, combine the pork, ½ cup of gochujang, 2 tablespoons of miso, the cilantro stems, the hoisin, ginger and 1 cup water; stir to combine. Bring to a simmer over medium-high, then cover and place in the oven. Cook until a skewer inserted into the meat meets no resistance, about 3 hours.

2. Meanwhile, in a 12-inch nonstick skillet over medium-high, heat the oil until shimmering. Add the onions and ½ teaspoon salt, then reduce to medium. Cook, stirring occasionally, until the onions are golden brown, about 15 minutes. Stir in the remaining 4 tablespoons miso and cook, stirring frequently, until the miso begins to brown, about 5 minutes. Transfer to a plate and let cool, then cover and refrigerate until ready to use.

3. Using a slotted spoon, transfer the pork to a large bowl. When cool enough to handle, shred into bite-size pieces, discarding any fat; set aside. Remove and discard the ginger chunks from the cooking liquid. Tilt the pot to pool the liquid to one side and use a wide spoon to skim off and discard as much fat as possible from the surface. Bring to a simmer over medium-high and cook, stirring occasionally, until reduced by about half and a spatula drawn through the sauce leaves a trail, 5 to 7 minutes.

4. Whisk the remaining 4 tablespoons gochujang into the sauce. Stir in the pork and onions. Reduce to medium and cook, stirring frequently, until heated through, 5 to 10 minutes. Off heat, stir in the vinegar, then taste and season with pepper. Serve with cilantro leaves, pickled carrots and pickled jalapeños.

GINGERY PICKLED CARROTS

Start to finish: 10 minutes,
plus resting
Makes about 2 cups

1 cup unseasoned rice vinegar

1 tablespoon white sugar

Kosher salt

3 medium carrots, peeled and
shredded on the large holes of
a box grater

2-inch piece fresh ginger, peeled
and sliced into thin rounds

In a large bowl, stir together the
vinegar, sugar and 1 teaspoon salt.
Stir in the carrots and ginger. Cover
and refrigerate for at least 3 hours
or up to 24 hours.

GOCHUJANG SOUR CREAM

Start to finish: 5 minutes
Makes about ¾ cup

½ cup sour cream

4 to 6 tablespoons gochujang,
to taste

In a small bowl, whisk together the
sour cream and gochujang. Cover
and refrigerate for up to 1 week.

Crispy Chicken Under a Brick
(*Tsitsila Tabaka*)

Start to finish: 2 hours (50 minutes active) / Servings: 4

1½ teaspoons ground coriander

½ teaspoon granulated garlic

Kosher salt and ground black pepper

3½- to 4-pound whole chicken, spatchcocked (see instructions, pp. 316-17)

1 tablespoon grapeseed or other neutral oil

2 tablespoons salted butter

8 medium garlic cloves, peeled and chopped

2 cups low-sodium chicken broth

⅛ to ¼ teaspoon cayenne pepper

2 tablespoons lemon juice

¼ cup lightly packed fresh cilantro, chopped

CHANGE THE WAY YOU COOK:
FLAT BIRDS COOK FASTER, CRISP BETTER

Spatchcocking puts the breasts and thighs on an even plane so they cook at the same time. Flattening the bird also exposes all of the skin to heat, resulting in crisper skin.

For this recipe, we find inspiration in Georgia, set at the crossroads of Eastern Europe and Western Asia and known for dishes that benefit from both traditions. The chicken is spatchcocked, which puts thighs and breasts on the same plane for even cooking. Georgian cooks use a brick to keep their chickens truly flat (you'll find the same technique in Italy's pollo al mattone). The weight presses the chicken down, ensuring the bird makes good contact with the pan's hot surface, which renders the fat and ensures even browning. If crisp skin is what you're after, this is the way to get it. For the "brick," we use a second heavy skillet or a large, sturdy pot (such as a Dutch oven); it's easier and works just as well. However, if you have them on hand, you instead could use one or two clean bricks wrapped in heavy-duty foil. An easy pan sauce with garlic, lemon and cilantro perfectly complements the chicken.

Don't use a chicken much larger than 4 pounds, as it may not fit comfortably in the skillet. Don't forget to pat the chicken dry before searing (after it has stood for 45 minutes). The drier the skin, the better it crisps. After searing, drain off the fat in the pan before putting the bird in the oven; this helps reduce splatter. Finally, don't forget that the skillet's handle will be hot when taken out of oven.

1. In a small bowl, stir together the coriander, granulated garlic, 1 tablespoon salt and ½ teaspoon black pepper. Place the spatchcocked chicken, skin-side up, on a cutting board. Season the chicken all over with the spice mixture, rubbing it into the skin. Let stand uncovered at room temperature for 30 to 45 minutes.

2. Heat the oven to 450°F with a rack in the lowest position. Thoroughly pat the chicken dry with paper towels.

3. In a 12-inch oven-safe skillet over medium-high, heat the oil until barely smoking. Place the chicken breast down in the pan. Lay a small sheet of foil over the chicken, then place a second heavy skillet or pot on top. Reduce to medium and cook until the skin is golden brown,

10 to 15 minutes, removing the weight and foil and checking every 4 to 5 minutes to ensure even browning.

4. Using tongs, carefully transfer the chicken to a large plate, turning it breast up. Pour off and discard the fat in the skillet. Slide the chicken breast up back into the pan and place in the oven. Roast until the thickest part of the breast reaches 160°F, 25 to 35 minutes. Carefully transfer the chicken to a cutting board and let rest while you make the sauce.

5. Set the skillet (the handle will be hot) over medium-high and cook the butter and garlic, stirring occasionally, until the garlic is lightly browned, about 2 minutes. Add the broth and bring to a simmer, scraping up any browned bits, then cook until the garlic is softened and the mixture is lightly thickened and reduced to about ¾ cup, 10 to 15 minutes. Using a silicone spatula, mash the garlic until almost smooth and mix it into the sauce. Off heat, stir in the cayenne, lemon juice and cilantro, then transfer to a serving bowl. Carve, then serve with the sauce.

HOW TO SPATCHCOCK A CHICKEN

1. Set the chicken breast down on a cutting board. Using sturdy kitchen shears, cut along one side of the backbone from top to bottom.

2. Repeat the cut on the other side of the backbone, then remove and discard the backbone.

3. Spread the sides of the chicken, opening it like a book and flattening it as much as possible.

4. Flip the chicken breast up, then use your hands to press firmly on the highest point of the breast to flatten the bird. The breast bone may crack.

5. If desired, the skin of the thighs and breasts can be loosened from the edges to allow seasonings to be rubbed under the skin.

Prune, Peppercorn and Fresh Herb–Rubbed **Roast Beef**

Start to finish: 2 hours 45 minutes, plus 48 hours to marinate
Servings: 10

___

8 ounces pitted prunes
(about 1½ cups)

½ cup soy sauce

¼ cup ketchup

3 tablespoons kosher salt

2 tablespoons black peppercorns

2 tablespoons chopped
fresh rosemary

2 tablespoons fresh thyme leaves

3 oil-packed anchovy fillets

5- to 6-pound beef eye round
roast, trimmed

Fresh horseradish sauce,
(see sidebar) to serve (optional)

We challenged ourselves to transform a thrifty, low-cost cut of beef into a lush, celebratory meal. The answer was eye round, a roast often deemed too lean to be tender. The cut is taken from the hind leg of a steer, so there's little marbling, the usual key to keeping meat moist. To roast this tough cut and get succulent, perfectly cooked results, we marinated the meat in ingredients that would do the work for us. We started with a sticky, sweet puree of prunes. That may sound unusual, but prunes are high in hygroscopic sorbitol and fructose, which—along with salt and soy sauce—amplify the way the meat absorbs flavor. The puree also adhered well to the roast, promoting moisture retention and a caramelized crust without the trouble of browning. Ketchup and anchovies added rich umami, while rosemary, thyme and black peppercorns brought an herbal kick. To boost the marinade's effect, we poked the roast repeatedly with a fork. The roast beef tasted best after marinating for 48 hours, but 24 will work.

Don't check the roast too frequently. A succulent roast relied on even cooking at a low temperature; opening the oven door interrupted that process.

1. In a food processor, blend the prunes, soy sauce, ketchup, salt, peppercorns, rosemary, thyme and anchovies until smooth, about 1 minute. Transfer to a 2-gallon zip-close bag. Poke the roast all over with a fork, then place in the bag. Turn to coat, then refrigerate for 48 hours.

2. Heat the oven to 275°F with a rack in the middle position. Set a wire rack in a rimmed baking sheet. Remove the roast from the bag and transfer to the rack. Discard the marinade in the bag and

evenly brush any marinade sticking to the roast's surface. Roast until the meat registers 125°F, 1 hour 45 minutes to 2 hours.

3. Transfer the roast to a carving board, tent loosely with foil and let rest for 30 minutes. Thinly slice and serve with fresh horseradish sauce, if desired.

FRESH HORSERADISH SAUCE

Start to finish: **5 minutes**
Makes **about 1½ cups**

We preferred the brightness and intensity of fresh horseradish in this sauce, but bottled horseradish worked well, too. If you use bottled, reduce the vinegar to 1 tablespoon. Look for fresh horseradish root in the produce aisle, often near the fresh ginger. For maximum flavor, peel and finely grate the root with a wand-style grater. If you have extra horseradish, try grating it into mashed potatoes, or over a warm steak or pork chop.

1 cup sour cream

½ cup freshly grated horseradish root (3-inch piece)

2 tablespoons white wine vinegar

1 tablespoon water

2 teaspoons minced fresh rosemary

1 teaspoon kosher salt

In a bowl, stir together all the ingredients. The sauce can be refrigerated for up to 2 days.

Piri Piri Chicken

Start to finish: 2½ hours (30 minutes active)
Servings: 4

3 tablespoons New Mexico
or California chili powder

1 tablespoon ground cumin

1 tablespoon ground coriander

1 tablespoon sweet paprika

Kosher salt

4- to 4½-pound whole chicken,
spatchcocked (see instructions
on p. 317)

2 tablespoons white sugar

8 medium Fresno chilies, stemmed
and quartered

3 medium garlic cloves, peeled

⅓ cup lemon juice

¼ cup red wine vinegar

1 cup lightly packed fresh cilantro,
finely chopped

Piri piri can refer to a finger-staining chili pepper sauce—usually spiked with garlic, sugar and plenty of cayenne, lemon and paprika—or to whatever the sauce douses. Its origins are Portuguese, but today it is found in South Africa, Mozambique and Namibia. Ancho, chipotle and regular chili powders tasted off in this recipe, but New Mexico or California chili powders worked well. If you can't find either, purchase whole chilies, toast and seed them, then finely grind them. Or simply leave out the chili powder and increase the paprika to ¼ cup. Fresno chilies are fresh red chilies similar in size and shape to jalapeños, but with pointy tips; if they are unavailable, fresh cherry peppers work well, too.

Don't reduce the number of fresh chilies in the sauce; all eight were needed for flavor and color. For milder heat, remove some or all of the seeds and ribs before processing.

ON THE GRILL:

1. In a medium bowl, mix together the chili powder, cumin, coriander, paprika and 1½ tablespoons salt. Transfer 2 tablespoons of the mixture to a small bowl, setting the rest aside. Loosen the skin over the chicken's breast and thighs by gently working your fingers between the skin and flesh. Using a small spoon, evenly distribute the 2 tablespoons of spice mixture under the skin, then rub it into the flesh. Set the chicken on a baking sheet.

2. In a food processor, combine the reserved spice mixture, the sugar, chilies and garlic. Pulse until finely chopped, scraping the bowl as needed. With the machine running, add the lemon juice and vinegar; process until smooth, scraping the bowl once or twice. Measure out ¼ cup of the sauce, reserving the rest for later, and brush evenly over the chicken, including the bone side. Let stand at room temperature for 45 minutes to 1 hour.

3. Meanwhile, prepare a grill for indirect, high-heat cooking. For a charcoal grill, spread a large chimney of hot coals evenly over one side of the grill bed; open the bottom grill vents. For a gas grill, set half of the burners to high. Heat the grill, covered, for 5 to 10 minutes, then clean and oil the cooking grate.

4. Set the chicken skin side up on the cooler side of the grill. Cover and cook for 25 minutes. Using tongs, rotate the chicken 180 degrees to bring the far side of the chicken closest to the heat. Cover and continue to cook until a skewer inserted into the thickest part of the breast meets no resistance or until the thickest part of the breast reaches 160°F and the thighs reach 175°F, another 25 to 35 minutes.

5. Brush the chicken with 2 tablespoons of the reserved sauce, then use tongs to flip it skin side down onto the hot side of the grill. Cook until the skin is lightly charred, 1 to 2 minutes. Transfer skin side up to a cutting board and let rest for 10 minutes. Stir the cilantro into the remaining sauce, then baste the chicken once more. Serve with the sauce on the side.

OVEN-COOKING METHOD:

6. Heat the oven to 425°F with a rack in the middle position. Line a rimmed baking sheet with foil and spread 1 cup kosher salt over it. Mist a wire rack with cooking spray, then set over the salt. Arrange the seasoned, sauce-brushed chicken skin side up on the rack and let stand at room temperature for 45 minutes to 1 hour. Roast the chicken until well browned, 45 to 50 minutes. Brush with 2 tablespoons of the reserved sauce, then continue to roast until a skewer inserted into the thickest part of the breast meets no resistance or the thickest part of the breast reaches 160°F and the thighs reach 175°F, another 10 to 15 minutes. Remove from oven and let rest for 10 minutes. Stir the cilantro into the remaining sauce, then baste the chicken once more. Serve with the sauce on the side.

Cuban-Style Pork Shoulder
with Mojo Sauce

Start to finish: 4½ hours, plus marinating
Servings: 6

---

3 tablespoons kosher salt

1 tablespoon smoked sweet paprika

4- to 5-pound bone-in pork butt,
fat cap trimmed to ¼ to ½ inch

1 teaspoon grated orange zest, plus
⅔ cup orange juice (2 to 3 oranges)

1 teaspoon grated lime zest, plus
⅓ cup lime juice (2 to 3 limes)

⅓ cup fresh oregano leaves

8 garlic cloves, smashed and peeled

2 tablespoons extra-virgin olive oil

1 tablespoon ground cumin

1 teaspoon ground black pepper

½ cup coarsely chopped fresh cilantro

Lime wedges, to serve

A thick, well-marbled pork shoulder shines in pernil asado, a classic Cuban dish in which the meat marinates overnight in salt, spices and sour orange juice before being roasted for many hours. It's impressive, but most recipes call for repeated basting and flipping, or fiddling with oven temperatures, sometimes for five hours or more. We tried low, dry heat but it took too long and our meat was drying out on the surface before it finished cooking inside. So, we ratcheted the oven up to 400°F, put the pork on a roasting rack and surrounded it with a loose wrapping of parchment-lined foil. When we opened our foil packet after three and a half hours, the meat was practically falling off the bone. We sacrificed a crackly crust, but didn't miss it. That's partly because the cooking liquid—a mix of garlic, orange and lime juices, fresh oregano and cumin—gave the meat so much flavor. We also poked holes into the surface of the pork, then covered it with salt and paprika for at least eight hours before roasting. This tenderized the meat and promoted browning. Eight hours seasoning was best, but one hour will suffice. Be careful when forming the packet. Tears or openings will cause the meat to dry out. Flavorful juices pooled in the foil-parchment packet; we combined those with orange and lime juices (to replicate the taste of the sour Seville oranges typically used) and fresh cilantro to make a mojo sauce. Tossing the shredded pork with the sauce ensured every bite had a delicious, tangy flavor.

Don't let the pork or its juices come into contact with the foil during cooking; it can cause a metallic taste and discolor the juices. Make sure the parchment fully lines the bottom of the pan and covers the pork on top.

1. In a small bowl, mix together the salt and paprika. Using a paring knife and a twisting motion, make twelve 1-inch-deep cuts all over the pork. Rub with the salt mixture, then wrap tightly in plastic wrap and refrigerate for 8 to 24 hours.

2. Heat the oven to 400°F with a rack in the lower-middle position. In a liquid measuring cup, combine both juices. In a food processor, combine both zests, the oregano, garlic, oil, cumin and pepper. Process until the garlic is finely chopped, about 1 minute. Add ¼ cup of the juice and process until combined, about 10 seconds.

3. Using 18-inch-wide heavy-duty foil, make a sling in a large roasting pan. Leaving generous overhang on either side, gently press 1 sheet of foil into the pan lengthwise. Press a second sheet over that crosswise, again leaving ample overhang. Using kitchen parchment, repeat the process, setting the parchment sling over the foil. Set a wire roasting rack over the parchment.

4. Unwrap the pork and rub all over with the herb-garlic paste. Place fat side up on the rack in the prepared pan. Pour ¼ cup of the juice into the bottom of the pan. Loosely fold the excess parchment

around the pork, then fold the excess foil up over the pork. Crimp the foil to create a loose but sealed packet. Roast until the meat is tender and registers 190°F in the thickest part, about 3½ hours.

5. Transfer the pork to a carving board, tent loosely with foil and let rest for 30 minutes. Pour the accumulated juices from the pan into a medium saucepan over medium heat, then add the remaining ½ cup of citrus juice. When hot, remove from the heat and stir in the cilantro; cover and keep warm.

6. Using tongs and a knife or carving fork, cut and shred the meat into chunks, discarding the bone and any fat. Transfer to a bowl and toss with ¼ to ½ cup of the sauce. Serve with the remaining sauce and lime wedges.

STEAM COOKING WITH A FOIL-PARCHMENT PACKET

1. Leaving a generous amount of overhang on either side, gently press 1 sheet of 18-inch-wide foil lengthwise into a large roasting pan. Press a second sheet over that crosswise, again leaving ample overhang.

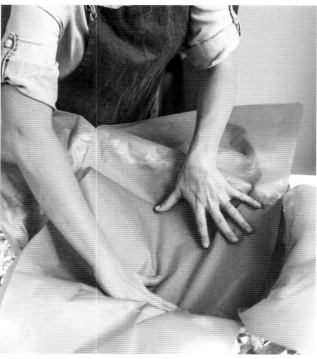

2. Using kitchen parchment, repeat this process, setting the sheets over the foil.

3. Set a wire roasting rack over the parchment.

4. Loosely fold the excess parchment around the pork.

5. Fold the excess foil up over the pork. Crimp the foil together to create a loose but sealed packet.

CHILI-PINEAPPLE MARGARITA

Start to finish: 1 hour 30 minutes
(20 minutes active)
Makes 2 drinks

The smooth, round flavor of reposado tequila worked best with the chilies in this cocktail.

1 cup plus 1½ teaspoons white sugar, divided

1 cup water

Four 1-inch strips lime zest

Four 1-inch strips orange zest, plus 1 orange wedge

1 jalapeño chili, halved

1 habanero chili, halved

1 tablespoon kosher salt

¾ teaspoon chili powder

4 ounces (½ cup) reposado tequila

2 ounces (¼ cup) pineapple juice

1½ ounces (3 tablespoons) lime juice (1 to 2 limes)

1. In a small saucepan, combine 1 cup of the sugar, the water, both zests and both chilies. Bring the mixture to a boil, stirring occasionally, then remove from the heat and steep for 15 minutes. Strain into a jar, discarding the solids. Let cool.

2. While the syrup cools, in a small bowl, stir together the salt, chili powder and the remaining 1½ teaspoons of sugar. Spread the mixture on a small plate. Use the orange wedge to moisten the rims of 2 rocks glasses, then dip in the chili salt, turning to coat.

3. In a cocktail shaker, combine the tequila, pineapple juice, lime juice and 1½ ounces (3 tablespoons) of the chili syrup. Add 2 cups of ice and shake vigorously until chilled, 10 to 15 seconds. Strain into the prepared glasses.

Za'atar-Roasted Chicken

Start to finish: **50 minutes**
Servings: **4**

3 tablespoons za'atar seasoning

2 teaspoons dried oregano

1¼ teaspoons white sugar

Kosher salt and ground black pepper

3 pounds bone-in, skin-on chicken parts, trimmed and patted dry

10 medium garlic cloves, peeled

1 tablespoon finely grated lemon zest, plus ¼ cup lemon juice

2 tablespoons extra-virgin olive oil

2 tablespoons minced fresh oregano

Za'atar is a Middle Eastern blend of herbs and sesame seeds; look for it in well-stocked markets, Middle Eastern grocery stores or online. We mix za'atar with dried oregano to boost its herbal flavor. Use chicken breasts, legs, thighs or a combination.

Don't use a roasting pan. The low sides of a sturdy rimmed baking sheet allow the chicken to cook quickly and brown evenly.

1. Heat the oven to 450°F with a rack in the middle position. In a small bowl, combine the za'atar, dried oregano, sugar, 1 tablespoon salt and 2 teaspoons pepper.

2. Place the chicken parts on a rimmed baking sheet and evenly season both sides with the za'atar mixture. Place the garlic cloves in a single layer down the center of the baking sheet, then arrange the chicken parts, skin up, around the garlic; this prevents the garlic from scorching during roasting.

3. Roast the chicken until the thickest part of the breast (if using) reaches 160°F and the thickest part of the largest thigh/leg (if using) reaches 175°F, 30 to 40 minutes. The meat should show no pink when cut into. Transfer the chicken to a platter; leave the garlic on the baking sheet.

4. Using a fork, mash the garlic to a paste on the baking sheet. Carefully pour ⅓ cup water onto the baking sheet and use a wooden spoon to scrape up any browned bits. Pour the mixture into a small bowl and whisk in the lemon zest and juice, oil and fresh oregano. Taste and season with salt and pepper. Serve the sauce with the chicken.

Thai Beef Salad (*Yam Neua*)

Start to finish: 40 minutes
Servings: 4

1 large shallot, sliced into very
thin rings

3 tablespoons lime juice
(about 2 limes)

4 teaspoons packed brown
sugar, divided

1½ teaspoons kosher salt

¾ teaspoon ground white pepper

1½ pounds skirt steak, trimmed
and cut into 2 or 3 pieces

Neutral oil (if using a skillet)

1 to 2 tablespoons fish sauce

1 teaspoon red pepper flakes

1½ cups (about 7 ounces) red or
yellow cherry tomatoes, halved

½ cup coarsely chopped fresh
cilantro, plus cilantro sprigs to
garnish (optional)

½ cup coarsely chopped
fresh mint

Thai beef salad, or yam neua, is a tangle of thinly sliced grilled steak, tossed with a hot, sour, salty and slightly sweet dressing, shallots and a heap of cilantro and fresh mint—and possibly some sliced cucumbers and chopped tomatoes. "Yam" refers to a style of salads that are spicy and slightly sour thanks to the classic Thai combination of fish sauce, lime juice, palm sugar and chilies. For our version of yam neua (pronounced yum n-UH), we started by choosing the right steak—skirt. The thin, well-marbled cut has big beefy flavor that can stand up to the salad's robust dressing. To season the meat, we used white pepper instead of black for its complexity. A couple teaspoons of brown sugar, balanced with salt, approximated the faint maple flavor of palm sugar. Rubbing the steak with sugar first increased the char.

Don't ignore the steak's grain. Cutting with the grain results in tough slices. Cutting against the grain shortens the muscle fibers, producing tender, juicy meat.

1. In a large bowl, combine the shallot and lime juice and let sit for 10 minutes, stirring occasionally. In a small bowl, combine 2 teaspoons of the sugar, the salt and white pepper. Pat the steak dry with paper towels, then rub all over with the sugar-salt mixture. If using a cast-iron or carbon-steel skillet, cut the steak into 4 to 6 pieces if needed to fit into the pan.

2. Prepare a grill or skillet for very high heat. For a charcoal grill, spread a full chimney of hot coals evenly over half of the grill bed. For a gas grill, set all burners to a high, even flame. Heat the grill for 5 minutes, then clean and oil the cooking grate. For a cast-iron or carbon-steel pan, heat 1 teaspoon canola oil over medium-high until smoking, about 5 minutes.

3. If using a grill, grill the steak (directly over the coals, if using a charcoal grill) until charred all over, 2 to 4 minutes per side. If using a skillet, sear the steak in

2 batches until charred, 2 to 4 minutes per side. Transfer the steak to a carving board and let rest for 10 minutes.

4. Meanwhile, add 1 tablespoon of the fish sauce, the pepper flakes and the remaining 2 teaspoons of sugar to the shallot–lime juice mixture and stir until the sugar has dissolved. Taste, then add additional fish sauce, if desired. Thinly slice the steak against the grain, then transfer to the bowl along with any accumulated juices. Add the tomatoes, cilantro and mint and stir. Transfer to a platter and garnish with cilantro sprigs, if desired.

Tacos al Pastor

Start to finish: **1 hour** / Servings: **4**

1 medium pineapple, peeled

¼ cup grapeseed or other neutral oil, plus more for the baking sheet and pineapple

¼ cup packed dark brown sugar

8 medium garlic cloves, peeled

4 chipotle chilies in adobo, plus 1 tablespoon adobo sauce

4 teaspoons ground cumin

4 teaspoons ancho chili powder

Kosher salt and ground black pepper

2 tablespoons lime juice, divided, plus lime wedges, to serve

1¼-pound pork tenderloin, trimmed of silver skin and halved lengthwise

⅓ cup lightly packed fresh cilantro, chopped

8 corn tortillas, warmed

Finely chopped white onion, to serve

We combine tender broiled pork, spicy chilies and the subtle smokiness of charred pineapple in this take on tacos al pastor. The dish is from Mexico but has Levantine roots, stemming from the 19th century when Lebanese immigrants arrived, bringing their tradition of vertical spits for roasting lamb shawarma. Not finding much lamb, cooks switched to pork and instead of sandwiching the meat in flatbread, they used tortillas. Subsequent generations added pineapple and dried chilies. For everyday ease, we use pork tenderloin that has been pounded, briefly marinated and broiled. Chopped pineapple, also broiled, and fresh finely chopped white onion complete the tacos. For extra color and crunch, offer finely shredded red cabbage for sprinkling. To simplify prep, you can buy fresh pineapple that has already been peeled, cored and sliced.

Don't substitute regular chili powder for the ancho chili powder. If you can't find ancho chili powder, pulverize whole ancho chilies (stemmed, seeded and torn) in a spice grinder.

1. Slice the pineapple into seven ½-inch-thick rounds. Quarter 2 rounds, discarding the core. In a food processor, puree the quartered pineapple slices, oil, brown sugar, garlic, chipotles and adobo, cumin, ancho powder and 4 teaspoons salt until smooth, about 1 minute. Pour ½ cup into a baking dish; pour the rest into a medium bowl and stir in 1 tablespoon of the lime juice. Set both aside.

2. Place the tenderloin halves between 2 large sheets of plastic wrap. Using a meat mallet, pound the pork to an even ½-inch thickness. Season both sides of each piece with salt and pepper, place in the baking dish and turn to coat with the puree. Let marinate at room temperature for 15 minutes.

3. Meanwhile, heat the broiler to high with a rack about 4 inches from the element. Line a rimmed baking sheet with extra-wide foil and mist with cooking spray. Arrange the 5 remaining pineapple slices in a single layer on the

prepared baking sheet. Brush the slices with oil and sprinkle with salt and pepper, then broil until charred in spots, 7 to 10 minutes. Transfer the pineapple to a cutting board and set aside; reserve the baking sheet.

4. Transfer the tenderloin halves to the same baking sheet and broil until charred in spots and the center reaches 140°F or is just barely pink when cut, 7 to 10 minutes. Let rest for 5 minutes.

5. While the pork rests, chop the pineapple into rough ½-inch cubes, discarding the core. Transfer to a small bowl and stir in the cilantro and the remaining 1 tablespoon lime juice, then taste and season with salt and pepper.

6. Cut the pork crosswise into thin slices on the diagonal. Transfer to a medium bowl, then stir in any accumulated pork juices along with 3 tablespoons of the reserved pineapple puree. Serve the pork, chopped pineapple and remaining pineapple puree with the tortillas, chopped onion and lime wedges.

Cape Malay **Chicken Curry**

Start to finish: **1 hour**
Servings: **6**

---

1 tablespoon fennel seeds

1 tablespoon cumin seeds

1 teaspoon ground turmeric

Kosher salt and ground black pepper

2 pounds boneless, skinless chicken thighs, trimmed

2 tablespoons grapeseed or other neutral oil

2 medium yellow onions, chopped

4-ounce piece fresh ginger, peeled and cut into 5 pieces

4 medium garlic cloves, minced

2 serrano chilies, stemmed and halved lengthwise

2 cups low-sodium chicken broth or water

1 pint grape or cherry tomatoes

Two 3-inch cinnamon sticks

2 bay leaves

1 pound Yukon Gold potatoes, cut into 1-inch cubes

2 tablespoons lemon juice, plus lemon wedges, to serve

½ cup lightly packed fresh mint, torn

Cooked basmati or jasmine rice, to serve

Lemony and richly savory, Cape Malay curry is a chicken and vegetable one-pot from South Africa. Its ingredients are similar to those in Indian curries, but the techniques are different, creating a refreshingly light curry. Spices aren't ground but are dropped whole into the broth and often discarded just before serving. We started our curry with a flavor base of lightly browned onions, then used whole fennel and cumin seeds to add texture and flavor. Fresh ginger and lemon juice kept flavors bright. A whole chicken is sometimes used for this dish, but we liked the ease of boneless, skinless thighs, which stay moist and taste richer than chicken breasts.

Don't forget to remove the ginger, cinnamon sticks, bay leaves and chili halves from the cooking liquid after removing the chicken. Also, don't cut the potatoes smaller than 1-inch chunks; smaller pieces will overcook and break apart. Finally, don't pull the chicken into fine shreds after simmering—the pieces should be bite-size.

1. In a bowl, mix the fennel, cumin, turmeric, 2 teaspoons salt and 1 teaspoon pepper. Using 1 tablespoon of this mixture, season the chicken on all sides.

2. In a large Dutch oven over medium-high, heat the oil until barely smoking. Add the onions and cook, stirring occasionally, until lightly browned, 8 to 10 minutes. Stir in the ginger, garlic and chilies, then cook, stirring, until fragrant, about 30 seconds. Stir in the broth or water, tomatoes, cinnamon sticks, bay leaves and remaining spice mixture, then add the chicken thighs, submerging them in the cooking liquid.

3. Bring to a simmer, then cover and cook for 25 minutes, adjusting the heat to maintain a steady but gentle simmer. Stir in the potatoes, cover and return to a simmer. Cook until the chicken and potatoes are tender, another 12 to 15 minutes.

4. Using tongs, transfer the chicken to a large plate. Remove and discard the ginger, cinnamon sticks, bay leaves and chili halves, then continue to simmer over medium until the liquid is slightly reduced, about 5 minutes.

5. Meanwhile, using 2 forks, pull the chicken into bite-size pieces. Return the chicken to the pot and stir to combine, taking care not to break up the potatoes. Stir in the lemon juice, then taste and season with salt and pepper. Transfer to a serving bowl and sprinkle with the mint. Serve with rice and lemon wedges.

Austrian Beef Stew with Paprika and Caraway (*Rindsgulasch*)

Start to finish: 4 hours (30 minutes active) / Servings: 4 to 6

5 pounds boneless beef chuck roast, trimmed, cut into 1½-inch pieces, patted dry

6 tablespoons Hungarian sweet paprika, divided

Kosher salt and ground black pepper

2 cups low-sodium beef broth

¼ cup tomato paste

4 tablespoons (½ stick) salted butter

1 large yellow onion, finely chopped

2 tablespoons caraway seeds, lightly crushed

⅓ cup all-purpose flour

1 tablespoon Hungarian hot paprika

3 bay leaves

2 teaspoons dried marjoram (optional)

¼ cup finely chopped fresh dill, plus dill sprigs to serve

1 tablespoon cider vinegar

Sour cream, to serve

This simple stew, inspired in part by classic Austrian iterations and in part by Kurt Gutenbrunner's recipe in "Neue Cuisine," derives much of its bold flavor and rich color from sweet and hot paprika, so make sure the paprika you use is fresh and fragrant. For the deepest, earthiest flavor, we recommend seeking out true Hungarian paprika; we use a combination of sweet and hot to achieve just the right degree of spice. Serve with egg noodles, Spätzle or mashed potatoes.

Don't be shy about trimming the chuck roast; removing as much fat as possible before cooking prevents the stew from being greasy. In our experience, the roast usually loses about 1 pound with trimming. Also, don't cut the beef into pieces smaller than 1½ inches or the meat will overcook.

1. Heat the oven to 325°F with a rack in the lower-middle position. Season the beef with 1 tablespoon of sweet paprika, 2 teaspoons salt and 1 teaspoon pepper; toss to coat. In a measuring cup or small bowl, whisk together the broth and tomato paste; set aside.

2. In a large Dutch oven over medium, melt the butter. Add the onion and 1 teaspoon salt, then cook, stirring occasionally, until the onion is lightly browned, 8 to 10 minutes. Stir in the caraway and flour, then cook, stirring frequently, until the flour begins to brown, 2 to 4 minutes. Stir in the hot paprika and the remaining 5 tablespoons sweet paprika and cook until fragrant, about 30 seconds. Slowly whisk in the broth mixture and bring to a simmer, stirring frequently. Stir in the beef, bay and marjoram (if using), then bring to a simmer over medium-high. Cover, place in the oven and cook for 2 hours.

3. Remove the pot from the oven. Uncover and stir, then return to the oven uncovered and continue to cook until a skewer inserted into the meat meets no resistance, another 1 to 1½ hours. Remove from the oven, stir and let stand, uncovered, at room temperature for 15 minutes. Stir in the dill and vinegar. Taste and season with salt and pepper. Ladle into bowls and garnish with dill sprigs. Serve with sour cream.

Crispy **Sichuan-Chili** Chicken

Start to finish: **1 hour** / Servings: 4

⅓ cup soy sauce

3 tablespoons unseasoned
rice vinegar

4 tablespoons white sugar, divided

2 large egg whites, lightly beaten

2 pounds boneless, skinless chicken
thighs, trimmed and cut into 1-inch
pieces

264 grams (2 cups) cornstarch

¼ cup Sichuan peppercorns, toasted
and finely ground

2 teaspoons kosher salt

2 quarts peanut oil

6 tablespoons Sichuan chili oil, plus
extra to serve (see recipe p. 337)

8 scallions, thinly sliced

1 tablespoon Sichuan seasoning salt,
plus extra to serve (see recipe p. 337)

1 cup lightly packed fresh cilantro

Sichuan peppercorns give crispy fried chicken a citrusy, floral note followed by tingling—but not eye-watering—heat. To toast the peppercorns, heat them in a small skillet over medium. Cook, shaking the pan, until fragrant, about 2 minutes. Transfer to a bowl and let cool, then finely grind. We used the peppercorns in a light, cornstarch-based coating that added crunch and flavor to briefly marinated chicken thighs. For additional heat, we made our own chili oil from Sichuan chili flakes, more peppercorns and whole dried red Sichuan chilies. Tailor the heat of this dish by using more or less of the chili oil.

Don't marinate the chicken longer than 30 minutes or it will be too salty.

1. In a large bowl, combine the soy sauce, vinegar, 2 tablespoons of sugar and the egg whites. Stir until the sugar dissolves. Stir in the chicken, cover and marinate at room temperature, 20 to 30 minutes. Meanwhile, set a wire rack in a rimmed baking sheet. In a large bowl, mix the remaining 2 tablespoons sugar, the cornstarch, Sichuan pepper and salt.

2. Drain the chicken in a colander. Add ⅓ of the chicken to the cornstarch mixture and toss to coat, pressing the pieces into the cornstarch. Transfer to a mesh strainer and shake to remove excess cornstarch. Transfer to the prepared rack in a single layer. Repeat with the remaining chicken and cornstarch mixture.

3. Set another wire rack in a rimmed baking sheet. In a large Dutch oven over medium-high, heat the peanut oil to 350°F. Add half of the coated chicken and cook, stirring occasionally, until well browned, about 5 minutes. Using a slotted spoon, transfer to the second rack. Allow the oil to return to 350°F, then repeat with the remaining chicken.

4. In a small microwave-safe bowl or glass measuring cup, microwave the Sichuan chili oil on high until just warm, about 30 seconds. Combine the chicken and scallions in a large bowl, sprinkle with the seasoning salt and drizzle with the warm chili oil, then toss to coat. Add the cilantro and toss again, then transfer to a platter. Serve with additional chili oil and seasoning salt at the table.

SICHUAN CHILI OIL

Start to finish: 5 minutes,
plus cooling
Makes about 1 cup

1 cup peanut oil

1 ounce whole dried red Sichuan
chilies (1 cup)

3 tablespoons Sichuan chili flakes

2 tablespoons Sichuan peppercorns

1. In a small saucepan over
medium-low, combine all ingredients. Heat until the oil reaches
275°F, 3 to 4 minutes. Remove
from the heat and let cool to room
temperature.

2. Pour the oil into a fine mesh
strainer set over a bowl or liquid
measuring cup; discard the solids.
Store in a tightly sealed jar in a
cool, dark place for up to 1 month.

SICHUAN SEASONING

Start to finish: 5 minutes
Makes about ¼ cup

3 tablespoons Sichuan peppercorns,
toasted and ground

2 teaspoons white sugar

1 teaspoon kosher salt

In a small bowl, stir together all
ingredients. Store in an airtight
container for up to 1 month.

North African **Chicken Couscous**

Start to finish: 1 hour 15 minutes (30 minutes active)
Servings: 6

2 cups couscous

4 tablespoons extra-virgin olive oil, divided, plus extra to serve

Kosher salt and ground black pepper

1½ tablespoons ground turmeric

2 pounds boneless, skinless chicken thighs, trimmed and halved crosswise

1 pound Yukon Gold potatoes, cut into 1½-inch chunks

6 medium carrots, peeled, halved lengthwise and cut into 2-inch pieces

1 large red onion, root end intact, peeled and cut into 8 wedges

2 jalapeño chilies, stemmed and sliced into thin rounds

6 medium garlic cloves, minced

2 tablespoons tomato paste

½ cup harissa, divided (see note)

Lemon wedges, to serve

In Tunisia, couscous is vibrant, bright, and topped with stews at once savory, spicy, earthy and sweet. Based on the couscous dishes we learned there, we developed this recipe using an 8-quart pot fitted with a stackable steamer insert that sits on top. If you don't own one, a large pot and a folding steamer basket worked well, too. Whisking the liquid from the stew into the steamed couscous is a key step, deeply flavoring the grain-like pasta and helping it stay light, fluffy and distinct. We especially liked this dish made with our homemade harissa (see recipe p. 496). Among store-bought brands, we preferred DEA, which is sold in a tube and in cans. We start the recipe using ¼ cup of harissa to flavor the stew, then finish by mixing another ¼ cup into the stew liquid just before whisking it with the steamed couscous. If your harissa is particularly spicy or you prefer less heat, reduce the second addition of harissa.

Don't worry about the couscous falling through the steamer basket holes. The lightly oiled, partially hydrated specks hold together enough that they won't fall through. Also, don't stir the stew during simmering. The vegetables better retain their shape and flavor when cooked on top of the chicken, rather than submerged in liquid.

1. In a medium bowl, combine the couscous and 2 tablespoons of oil, rubbing with your fingers until the couscous is evenly coated. Stir in 1¼ cups water and ¾ teaspoon salt. Let stand for 15 minutes.

2. Meanwhile, in a medium bowl, stir together the turmeric and 1 teaspoon each salt and pepper. Add the chicken and toss. Set aside for 15 minutes. In a large bowl, combine the potatoes, carrots, onion, 1 tablespoon of the remaining oil and 1 teaspoon each salt and pepper. Toss, then set aside.

3. Stir the couscous to separate the granules, then mound it in a steamer insert or basket that fits onto or into an 8-quart pot. Set aside. Set the pot over medium-high, then heat the remaining 1 tablespoon oil until barely smoking. Add the jalapeños and cook, stirring, until slightly softened, about 1 minute. Add the garlic, tomato paste and ¼ cup of the harissa and cook, stirring, until beginning to brown, 1 to 2 minutes.

4. Add 2 cups water and bring to a simmer. Place the chicken in the pot in an even layer, then top with the vegetables and any liquid in the bowl; do not stir. Bring to a simmer, then set the steamer insert with the couscous on the pot; if using a folding steamer basket, set it directly on the vegetables. Cover, reduce to low and cook at a gentle simmer until the chicken and vegetables are tender, about 45 minutes; do not stir the couscous or the stew.

5. Remove the steamer basket and transfer the couscous to a large bowl; cover with foil. Stir the vegetables and chicken, cover and let stand 5 minutes.

6. Use a slotted spoon to transfer the chicken and vegetables to a large bowl; taste and season with salt and pepper. Measure out 2 cups of the cooking liquid from the pot, add the remaining ¼ cup harissa to it and stir to combine.

7. Whisk the couscous until no clumps remain, then whisk in the cooking liquid–harissa mixture. Taste and season with salt and pepper. Transfer to a large, deep platter and make a well in the center. Spoon the chicken and vegetables into the well. Drizzle with oil and serve with lemon wedges.

Oven-Poached Salmon with Thyme, Dill and Vermouth

Start to finish: 1½ hours / Servings: 8

½ cup soy sauce

3½- to 4-pound salmon fillet, skin on, pin bones removed

2 medium carrots, finely chopped

1 celery stalk, finely chopped

1 shallot, thinly sliced

8 sprigs fresh thyme

8 sprigs fresh dill, plus 3 teaspoons minced, divided

Kosher salt

1 cup dry vermouth

Ground black pepper

2 tablespoons salted butter

1 tablespoon lemon juice

Lemon wedges, to serve

Ideal for a crowd, a side of salmon is an impressive main course that's as good at room temperature as it is hot from the oven. Trouble is, it can be difficult to cook without drying out and often is flavorless. Our inspiration for a better way came from an oven-poaching method we learned from French chef Michel Bras. He slow cooks smaller cuts of salmon in a 250°F oven over a water-filled baking pan. To adapt the technique for a larger side of salmon, we ratcheted up the heat; surrounded the fish with carrots, celery, shallot and a bit of vermouth; and covered it all tightly with foil. This allowed the salmon to steam and infuse with flavor while cooking faster and staying tender. And for even more flavor, we start by soaking the salmon briefly in soy sauce. A fillet between 1½ and 1¾ inches thick worked best. We found temperature was a better indicator for doneness than cooking time. To test the salmon's temperature, carefully peel back the foil just enough to insert a digital thermometer at the thickest end. The best way to perfectly cook this dish was to remove it from the oven a little before the salmon was fully cooked. The residual heat gently finished the cooking.

Don't marinate the salmon longer than 20 minutes. The soy sauce adds an earthy dimension to the salmon's flavor, but if left too long its saltiness will become overpowering.

1. Heat the oven to 500°F with a rack in the middle position. Pour the soy sauce into a baking dish large enough to fit the salmon. Add the fish, flesh side down. Marinate for 15 to 20 minutes.

2. Meanwhile, in a bowl toss the carrots, celery, shallot, thyme, 8 dill sprigs and 1 teaspoon salt. Set aside. Fold an 18-inch-long sheet of foil lengthwise into a strip wide enough for the salmon to fit on. Lightly coat the foil with oil, then place it, oiled side up, in the center of a rimmed baking sheet. Arrange the carrot-celery mixture around the outside edges of the foil. Drizzle the vegetables with the vermouth. Place the salmon on the foil, flesh side up. Season with pepper.

3. Cover the entire pan tightly with foil, allowing it to dome over the salmon. Roast until the salmon registers 120°F,

20 to 25 minutes. Remove the pan from the oven, keeping the foil in place, and let the salmon rest until it is between 125°F and 130°F, another 5 to 8 minutes. Remove the top foil, then use the foil under the salmon to lift and transfer it to a serving platter. Let cool for 5 minutes.

4. Meanwhile, strain the liquid and solids on the baking sheet into a saucepan. Discard the solids and all but ¾ cup of the liquid. Over medium heat, bring the liquid to a simmer. Off the heat, stir in the butter, lemon juice and 1 teaspoon of the minced dill. Season with salt and pepper. Pour 3 tablespoons of the sauce over the salmon. Sprinkle the remaining 2 teaspoons dill over the salmon. Serve with lemon wedges and the remaining sauce.

Beef, Orange and Olive Stew
(*Boeuf à la Gardiane*)

Start to finish: 4½ hours (1 hour active) / Servings: 6 to 8

---

6 to 7 pounds boneless beef chuck roast, trimmed and cut into 2-inch cubes

Kosher salt and ground black pepper

4 medium carrots, peeled and cut crosswise into ½-inch rounds, divided

3 oil-packed anchovy fillets, patted dry

2 tablespoons extra-virgin olive oil

2 medium garlic cloves, thinly sliced

1 medium yellow onion, chopped

1 cup pitted Kalamata olives, rinsed, patted dry and chopped, divided

2½ cups dry red wine

1 medium red bell pepper, stemmed, seeded and cut into 1-inch pieces

1 tablespoon grated orange zest, plus ⅓ cup orange juice

2 teaspoons red wine vinegar

1 cup lightly packed fresh flat-leaf parsley, roughly chopped

CHANGE THE WAY YOU COOK:
USE LESS LIQUID FOR MOISTER MEAT

Cooking in a lot of liquid does not lead to moister meat. In a covered pot, without additional liquid, the meat and aromatics cook gently, releasing only a scant amount of juice. The meat retains more of its natural moisture, giving us a more succulent braise. Removing the lid for the last hour of cooking concentrates the juices and allows for browning and flavor development.

Our version of this hearty stew from Camargue, in the south of France, uses chuck roast, a well-marbled cut. The dish gets robust flavor from Provençal ingredients—red wine, olives, anchovies and garlic. Orange is traditional, too; it lends the braise a balancing touch of brightness. Wine is key to this dish, and we wait until the beef is cooked before we add it, retaining more of the flavors. A bold, full-bodied dry red wine such as Côtes du Rhône or syrah is ideal, as it holds its own against the other big flavors. Serve with rice, egg noodles or potatoes.

Don't forget to zest the orange before juicing it—it's much easier to grate the zest from a whole orange than from one that's been halved and squeezed. Don't add all of the carrots to the pot with the beef. Adding some at the beginning gives the stew a subtle sweetness, but after hours of braising, these carrots are spent. We add more carrots near the end of cooking so that they are tender but still flavorful.

1. Heat the oven to 325°F with a rack in the lower-middle position. In a large Dutch oven, toss the beef with 2 tablespoons salt and 2 teaspoons pepper. Add ½ the carrots, the anchovies, oil, garlic and onion, then toss. Cover, transfer to the oven and cook for 2 hours.

2. Remove the pot from the oven and stir in ½ cup of the olives. Return to the oven uncovered and cook until a knife inserted into a piece of beef meets no resistance, 1 to 1½ hours.

3. Using a slotted spoon, transfer the meat to a large bowl, leaving the vegetables in the pot. Set a fine mesh strainer over a medium bowl. Pour the meat juices into the strainer, pressing on the solids to extract as much liquid as possible; discard the solids. You should have about 2½ cups liquid; if needed, add water.

4. Pour the wine into the now-empty pot and bring to a boil over medium-high, scraping up any browned bits.

Reduce to medium and simmer, stirring occasionally, until the wine is reduced by half, about 8 minutes. Meanwhile, use a spoon to skim off and discard the fat from the surface of the strained cooking liquid.

5. Pour the defatted cooking liquid into the pot and add the remaining carrots and the bell pepper. Return to a simmer and cook, uncovered and stirring occasionally, until the vegetables are tender and the sauce is slightly thickened, 10 to 15 minutes. Stir in the orange juice and beef. Continue to cook, stirring occasionally, until the sauce begins to cling to the meat, 3 to 6 minutes.

6. Off heat, stir in the remaining ½ cup olives, the orange zest, vinegar and half of the parsley. Taste and season with salt and pepper. Sprinkle with the remaining parsley.

Lemon-Saffron Chicken (*Tangia*)

Start to finish: **1 hour**
Servings: 4

---

5 teaspoons ground cumin, divided

Kosher salt and ground black pepper

3 pounds boneless, skinless chicken thighs, trimmed and patted dry

2 tablespoons extra-virgin olive oil

2 medium yellow onions, finely chopped

12 medium garlic cloves, chopped

2 teaspoons ground turmeric

2 teaspoons ground ginger

2 teaspoons ground coriander

1 teaspoon saffron threads, crumbled

3 tablespoons salted butter, cut into 3 pieces

½ cup pimento-stuffed green olives, chopped

3 tablespoons grated lemon zest, plus ¼ cup lemon juice

Tangia—which originates in Marrakech and often is slow-cooked in the community wood-fired ovens that heat bathhouses—traditionally is made with lamb. For a more approachable version, we used boneless, skinless chicken thighs, which have a similar richness. In Morocco, preserved lemons lend a gentle acidity, lightening the richness. For an easier version, we get similar flavor from lemon zest and juice—as well as chopped green olives for brininess—added at the end of cooking. Serve with warmed, halved pita bread for scooping up the meat and thickened sauce.

Don't reduce the amount of lemon zest or juice. The zest provides both flavor and fragrance, and the juice adds tang and acidity. You'll need 3 to 4 lemons to get 3 tablespoons grated zest; a wand-style grater works best.

1. In a small bowl, stir together 2 teaspoons of cumin and 2 teaspoons salt. Set aside. Season the chicken on both sides with salt and pepper.

2. In a large Dutch oven over medium-high, heat the oil until shimmering. Add the onions and garlic and cook, stirring occasionally, until softened, about 5 minutes. Add the remaining 3 teaspoons cumin, the turmeric, ginger and coriander, then cook, stirring, until fragrant, about 30 seconds. Stir in 1½ cups water and the saffron, scraping up any browned bits. Nestle the chicken in the liquid, turning to coat. Cover, reduce to medium-low and cook for 20 minutes at a gentle simmer.

3. Using tongs, turn the chicken. Cover and continue cooking until tender, another 25 minutes. Using tongs, transfer the chicken to a plate. Bring the liquid to a simmer over medium-high and cook, stirring, until thickened, 10 to 14 minutes.

4. Return the chicken to the pot and stir. The chicken will break up a bit. Off heat, add the butter, stirring until melted, then stir in the olives and lemon zest and juice. Taste and season with salt and pepper. Transfer to a platter and serve, sprinkling with the cumin-salt mixture to taste.

Salmon Packets with Chermoula

Start to finish: 50 minutes (15 minutes active)
Servings: 4

Four 6-ounce center-cut skinless salmon fillets (1 to 1¼ inches thick)

Kosher salt and ground black pepper

1 teaspoon extra-virgin olive oil

Chermoula sauce, to serve
(see sidebar)

Lemon wedges, to serve

Cooking salmon can be a conundrum. Cook it long enough to brown the skin and the inside becomes dry and overcooked. Take it off the heat sooner and the flesh is tender but wanly unappetizing. To get our salmon both browned and delectably moist we use the classic French method of cooking food in a sealed packet. The packet traps the natural moisture of the food inside, puffing impressively and steaming the dish in its own juices. Known as cooking en papillote, variations of the technique, such as cooking food wrapped in leaves, husks or even paper bags, exist around the world. But there's one drawback: The results can be bland because browning—the source of rich caramelized flavors—occurs only above 300°F. But steaming (which is the cooking that occurs inside a packet) never gets above 212°F. So we borrowed a variation we'd seen French chef and restaurateur Jean-Georges Vongerichten use—foil. Encasing a salmon fillet in a foil packet that is cooked on the stovetop allowed us to both brown (because of the direct heat beneath the fish) and steam (because of the trapped moisture) the fish. Six-ounce fillets were the perfect size; if the fillets were thinner than 1 inch or thicker than 1¼ inches, we needed to adjust the cooking time.

Don't hesitate to remove the packet from the skillet a little early if you think it's cooking too quickly. It's easy to return it to the skillet.

1. Remove the salmon from the refrigerator and let sit at room temperature for 20 to 30 minutes.

2. Pat the salmon dry with paper towels and season with salt and pepper. Place a 12-by-24-inch sheet of foil on the counter, shiny side down. Fold in half to form a 12-inch square. Unfold the foil and spread oil evenly over half of it (one 12-inch square), leaving a 3-inch border.

3. Arrange the salmon fillets over the oiled area, leaving at least ½ inch between them. Fold the top square of foil over the salmon and, without pressing down on the fillets, roll and crimp the open sides to create an airtight packet. Fold in the corners of the packet to help it fit in the pan.

4. Heat a 12-inch skillet over high heat for 5 minutes. Carefully place the packet in the skillet and cook 5 minutes for medium and 6 minutes for medium-well, rotating the pan frequently to ensure even cooking. The packet should begin puffing after 2 minutes and be fully inflated after 4 minutes. If the bottom edges of the packet start lifting up, reduce the heat slightly.

5. Using tongs, slide the packet onto a platter and let sit for 1 minute. Carefully open the packet. Spoon the accumulated juices over the salmon and serve topped with chermoula and lemon wedges.

CHERMOULA SAUCE

Start to finish: 10 minutes
Makes enough to top 4 salmon fillets

1 cup lightly packed flat-leaf parsley leaves

2 tablespoons pine nuts, toasted

2 teaspoons grated lemon zest

1 large garlic clove

1 teaspoon ground coriander

1 teaspoon sweet paprika

½ teaspoon kosher salt

½ teaspoon ground cardamom

¼ teaspoon red pepper flakes (optional)

3 tablespoons extra-virgin olive oil

In a food processor, combine all ingredients but the oil. Process until finely ground, about 20 seconds. Scrape down the bowl, add the oil, then process until incorporated, about 10 seconds.

Senegalese Braised Chicken with Onions and Lime (*Yassa Ginaar*)

Start to finish: 1 hour 15 minutes, plus marinating / Servings: 4

4 tablespoons peanut oil, divided

3 tablespoons grated lime zest, plus 6 tablespoons lime juice

1 habanero chili, seeded and minced

Kosher salt and ground black pepper

2 teaspoons chicken bouillon concentrate (see note)

2 pounds bone-in, skin-on chicken breasts, thighs or drumsticks, trimmed

3 medium yellow onions, halved and thinly sliced

Finely chopped fresh chives, to serve

With just a few ingredients, yassa ginaar delivers multiple layers of flavor—savory yet sweet with lightly caramelized onions, citrusy with lime zest and juice, meaty from deeply browned chicken, and spicy from the heat of a habanero chili. Our version is based on a recipe in "Yolele!" by Pierre Thiam, who marinates and sears the chicken, then uses the marinade as a base for the flavorful sauce. Bouillon concentrate adds to the savoriness of the dish; our preferred brand is Better than Bouillon. Serve with steamed rice.

Don't marinate the chicken for longer than two hours; the acidity of the lime juice will soften the meat. Don't use an uncoated cast-iron pot to cook this dish. The lime's acidity will react with the metal, causing the sauce to taste metallic.

1. In a large bowl, stir together 3 tablespoons of oil, the lime zest, habanero, 1 tablespoon salt and 1 teaspoon pepper. Transfer 2 teaspoons of the mixture to a small bowl and set aside. To the remaining oil-zest mixture, whisk in the lime juice, bouillon concentrate and ¼ cup water. Add the chicken and onions and toss. Cover and marinate at room temperature for 1 hour or refrigerate up to 2 hours, stirring once.

2. Remove the chicken from the marinade and pat dry with paper towels. Set a colander over a large bowl and drain the onions, reserving both the marinade and the onions.

3. In a large Dutch oven over medium-high, heat the remaining 1 tablespoon oil until barely smoking. Add the chicken, skin side down, and cook until well browned, about 4 minutes. Transfer to a plate and pour off and discard all but 1 tablespoon of the fat. Set the pot over medium heat and stir in the onions and ¼ cup water, scraping up any browned bits. Cover and cook, stirring frequently, until the onions are softened and lightly browned, 15 to 20 minutes.

4. Stir the reserved marinade into the onions. Return the chicken, skin side up, to the pot, nestling the pieces in the onions, then pour in any accumulated juices. Reduce to medium-low, cover and cook, stirring occasionally, until a skewer inserted into the thickest part of the meat meets no resistance, about 25 minutes.

5. Using a slotted spoon, transfer the chicken to a serving platter or shallow bowl. Off heat, stir the reserved oil-zest mixture into the onions, then taste and season with salt and pepper. Spoon the onions and sauce around the chicken and sprinkle with chives.

Tuscan Beef and Black Pepper Stew
(*Peposo alla Fornacina*)

Start to finish: 4 hours (30 minutes active) / Servings: 6

6½- to 7-pound boneless beef chuck roast, well trimmed and cut into 2-inch chunks

Kosher salt and coarsely ground black pepper

2 tablespoons extra-virgin olive oil

1 large yellow onion, halved and thinly sliced

12 medium garlic cloves, peeled

3 tablespoons tomato paste

2 sprigs rosemary, plus 1 tablespoon minced fresh rosemary

2 cups dry red wine

The simple, generously peppered beef stew known as peposo is said to have been created by 15th century kiln (fornacina) workers in Tuscany, Italy. Chianti is the best-known wine produced in that region and is the traditional choice for peposo, but any dry, medium-bodied red wine works well. Make sure to use coarsely ground black pepper, as it has more presence and better coats the beef. This recipe makes a generous amount of stew—about 2 quarts—so serve it one night with polenta (p. 139), mashed potatoes or braised beans. The stew keeps well, so it can be made up to three days ahead and reheated in the microwave or in a saucepan over low.

Don't be shy about trimming the fat from the chuck roast. Remove as much as you can, which may mean shedding about 1 pound. Pull the roast apart at the natural seams, then use a sharp knife to trim the fat and cut the meat into 2-inch chunks.

1. Heat the oven to 325°F with a rack in the lower-middle position. Place the beef in a large bowl, sprinkle with 1 tablespoon salt and 2 tablespoons pepper, then toss.

2. In a large Dutch oven over medium, heat the oil until shimmering. Add the onion and garlic and cook, stirring, until the onion is lightly browned, 7 to 9 minutes. Add the tomato paste and cook, stirring, until the paste begins to brown, 3 to 5 minutes. Nestle the beef and rosemary sprigs in the onion mixture, cover and transfer to the oven. Cook for 2 hours.

3. Remove the pot from the oven. Stir, then return to the oven uncovered. Cook until a metal skewer inserted into a piece of beef meets no resistance, another 1 to 1½ hours.

4. Using a slotted spoon, transfer the meat to a medium bowl. Set a fine mesh strainer over a fat separator or a medium bowl. Pour the meat juices into

the strainer and press on the solids to push them through the strainer; discard the solids.

5. Pour the wine into the empty pot and bring to a boil over medium-high, scraping up any browned bits. Reduce to medium and simmer until the wine is syrupy and reduced to 1 cup, 5 to 7 minutes. Meanwhile, if you strained the meat juices into a bowl, use a spoon to skim off and discard the fat from the surface.

6. Pour the defatted meat juices into the pot. Bring to a simmer over medium-high and cook, stirring occasionally, until thickened to the consistency of heavy cream, 5 to 7 minutes. Return the beef to the pot, add the minced rosemary and stir gently. Bring to a gentle simmer and cook, stirring occasionally, until the meat is heated through, 4 to 5 minutes. Stir in 2 teaspoons pepper, then taste and season with salt.

STEW TODAY, PASTA TOMORROW

If you have about 3 cups of leftover stew, you can transform it into an altogether different meal. We liked:

Pasta with beef ragu: In a large skillet, sauté 5 medium garlic cloves (minced) and 3 tablespoons tomato paste in 2 tablespoons extra-virgin olive oil for 1 to 3 minutes. Add a 28-ounce can whole peeled tomatoes (crushed) and simmer until thickened, 5 to 7 minutes. Add 3 cups of the Tuscan beef stew, cook for 5 to 7 minutes, then break up the beef into bite-size pieces. Add 12 ounces pappardelle or fettucine (cooked just shy of al dente) and ½ cup of pasta cooking liquid, toss, then cook for 3 minutes. Off heat, stir in ½ cup fresh basil. Serve with grated Parmesan.

Beef and broccoli rabe sandwiches: Blanch 1 pound broccoli rabe (trimmed) in a large pot of well-salted water for about 40 seconds; immediately transfer to an ice bath, then pat dry and cut into 1-inch pieces. Reheat 3 cups of the Tuscan beef stew, then shred the meat into bite-size pieces. In a large skillet, sauté the broccoli rabe in 3 tablespoons extra-virgin olive oil for 2 to 3 minutes. Add 5 medium garlic cloves (thinly sliced) and ¼ teaspoon red pepper flakes and cook for 1 minute. Off heat, toss with 2 tablespoons red wine vinegar. Place slices of provolone onto the cut sides for 4 crusty rolls and broil under the cheese melts. Divide the beef and broccoli rabe among the rolls, filling the sandwiches evenly.

Filipino Chicken Adobo with Coconut Broth

Start to finish: 1¾ minutes (30 minutes active)
Servings: 4

1½ cups unseasoned rice vinegar

¾ cup low-sodium soy sauce

6 medium garlic cloves, smashed

3 serrano chilies, halved lengthwise

4 bay leaves

1 teaspoon black peppercorns

3 pounds bone-in, skin-on
chicken thighs, trimmed

1 cup coconut milk

⅓ cup chopped fresh cilantro

Steamed white rice, to serve

Thousands of islands make up the Philippines. And there probably are as many recipes for chicken adobo, the classic Filipino dish that turns a handful of ingredients—loads of garlic, black pepper and vinegar—into a bright and tangy meal. We tailored our recipe for weeknight ease, using a hefty dose of rice vinegar blended with soy sauce and aromatics to create a potent marinade for bone-in thighs. For heat we used serrano chilies. Look for chicken thighs that are uniform in size; if some are smaller than others, begin to check them early and remove them as they come up to temperature.

Don't use regular soy sauce. As the chicken braises, the cooking liquid reduces, concentrating the flavor—and salt. Low-sodium soy sauce produced a broth that was well-seasoned.

1. In a large Dutch oven, combine the vinegar, soy sauce, garlic, chilies, bay leaves and peppercorns. Add the chicken thighs, submerging them. Cover and refrigerate for 30 to 60 minutes.

2. Bring the mixture to a boil over medium-high. Reduce to medium-low and cook, turning the thighs occasionally, until the chicken registers 170°F, 25 to 30 minutes, adjusting the heat as necessary to maintain a medium simmer.

3. Heat the broiler with an oven rack 6 inches from the element. Line a rimmed baking sheet with foil. Remove the chicken thighs from the pot and arrange skin side up on the baking sheet. Pat dry with paper towels and set aside.

4. Strain the cooking liquid, discarding the solids, then skim off the fat. Return 1 cup of the defatted liquid to the pot, stir in the coconut milk and bring to a simmer over medium. Take the pan off the heat, stir in the cilantro, then cover and set aside.

5. Broil the chicken until the skin is deeply browned and blackened in spots, 3 to 8 minutes. Serve in shallow bowls with steamed white rice, ladling the broth over the rice.

Caramelized Pork with Orange and Sage

Start to finish: **25 minutes** / Servings: 6

2 pounds pork tenderloin, silver skin trimmed, cut into 6 pieces

Kosher salt and ground black pepper

99 grams (½ cup) turbinado sugar

3 strips orange zest, chopped (1 tablespoon), plus ½ cup orange juice (1 to 2 oranges)

2 tablespoons chopped fresh sage, divided

¼ teaspoon cayenne pepper

2 tablespoons olive oil

2 tablespoons cider vinegar

Looking for a way to add flavor to all-too-often utilitarian pork tenderloin, we drew inspiration from Francis Mallmann, the Argentine chef best known for pushing the limits of browning—using live fire to cook vegetables, meat and fruit until they're almost burnt. Mallmann tops pork tenderloin with brown sugar, thyme and a fruity orange confit tinged by bay leaves and black peppercorns. The flavorful coating is seared onto the surface in a cast-iron griddle until the orange and thyme are crispy and charred. We loved the flavors, but the technique wasn't home cook friendly. To simplify and preserve the flavors, we started by streamlining the orange confit: Orange zest and fresh sage, coarsely chopped, gave a similar texture and fragrance. Gently pounding the tenderloin ensured a flat surface for a sugar mixture to adhere. Instead of searing the pork, we opted to broil it, making it easier to maintain the topping. Brown sugar became a sticky mess under the broiler, so we used coarse turbinado sugar, which kept its shape and crunch. If the sugar gets too dark before the meat comes to temperature, turn off the oven; the pork will finish cooking in the residual heat.

Don't tent the pork with foil after removing it from the oven. It will lose its candy-like crust. For the same reason, don't spoon the sauce over it.

1. Heat the broiler with a rack 6 inches from the element. Pat the pork dry, then use a meat mallet or a small heavy skillet to gently flatten the pieces to an even 1-inch thickness. Season with salt and pepper. In a small bowl, rub together the sugar, orange zest, 1 tablespoon of the sage and the cayenne. Set aside.

2. In a 12-inch oven-safe skillet over medium-high, heat the oil until just beginning to smoke. Add the pork and cook until deep golden brown on one side, about 3 minutes. Transfer the pork browned side up to large plate; reserve the skillet. Press the sugar mixture onto the tops of the pork pieces in an even layer. Return the meat to the skillet, sugar side up. Set under the broiler until the meat registers 135°F at the center and the sugar mixture is golden brown, 5 to 7 minutes, rotating the pan halfway through. Transfer to a carving board and let rest.

3. Meanwhile, return the skillet to medium-high heat on the stovetop. Add the orange juice and the remaining 1 tablespoon of sage. Cook, scraping up any browned bits, until the sauce is syrupy, 2 to 3 minutes. Stir in the vinegar. Taste and season with salt and pepper. Serve the pork over the sauce.

Red Chili Spatchcocked **Roast Chicken**

Start to finish: **1 hour 45 minutes (30 minutes active)**
Servings: 4

¼ cup grapeseed or other neutral oil

2 ounces whole dried ancho chilies, stemmed and seeded

1 tablespoon dried oregano, Mexican if available

2 garlic cloves, smashed and peeled

2 tablespoons packed light brown sugar

1 tablespoon cider vinegar

Kosher salt and ground black pepper

½ teaspoon ground cumin

¼ teaspoon cinnamon

3½- to 4-pound whole chicken, backbone cut out

¼ cup lime juice, plus lime wedges to serve

Warmed corn tortillas, to serve (optional)

How to cook a whole chicken quickly and evenly? Remove its backbone and flatten the bird—a technique called spatchcocking or butterflying. Our next challenge was adding flavor that doesn't stop at the skin. Our solution was to slide a chili-herb-spice mixture between the skin and meat. Our flavoring rub was based on a classic adobado, a seasoning common in Mexican cooking, revamped for indoor cooking without a long marination. Roasting and coarsely grinding the dried chilies before rehydrating them meant we could use less water, giving the resulting chili paste deeper flavor. If you prefer a milder heat, remove the seeds after stemming the chilies.

1. Heat the oven to 375°F with a rack in the middle position. In a 12-inch oven-safe heavy skillet over medium-high, heat the oil until shimmering. Add the chilies and toast until lightly browned, about 20 seconds per side. Transfer to a food processor, reserving the pan and oil. Process until coarsely chopped, about 30 seconds. In a small saucepan, bring ⅔ cup water to a boil. Add the chilies, oregano and garlic, then cover, remove from heat and let sit for 15 minutes.

2. In the food processor, combine the sugar, vinegar, 2½ teaspoons salt, ¼ teaspoon pepper, cumin, cinnamon and 2 tablespoons of the reserved chili oil from the skillet. Add the chili-water mixture and process until smooth, about 1 minute, scraping the bowl as needed. Reserve a third of the mixture, about 5 tablespoons.

3. With the breast side up, flatten the chicken by pressing on the center of the breast with your palms. Carefully lift the skin from the meat of the breasts and legs, avoiding tears. Spoon the remaining chili paste under the skin, massaging the skin to evenly distribute. Rub the skin of the chicken with the remaining reserved chili oil, then season with salt and pepper. Tuck the wing tips under the breasts, then place the chicken breast side up in the empty skillet. Transfer to the oven and roast until the breast registers 160°F, 45 to 50 minutes.

4. Transfer the chicken to a carving board, tent with foil and let rest for 15 minutes. Meanwhile, place the empty skillet over medium heat on the stove-top, then add the reserved chili paste and lime juice. Cook until warmed through. Taste and season with salt and pepper. Carve the chicken, adding any juices to the sauce, and serve with the sauce, lime wedges and warmed tortillas, if desired.

TEQUILA AT HIGH NOON

Start to finish: **5 minutes**
Makes **2 drinks**

For our take on the classic tequila sunrise, we substituted the mildly bittersweet Italian spirit Aperol for the typical (and often too sweet) grenadine. And we loved the way a dose of chocolate bitters—½ teaspoon's worth—complemented the orange juice.

4 ounces tequila blanco

4 ounces orange juice

1 ounce lemon juice

1 ounce Aperol

½ teaspoon chocolate bitters

In a cocktail shaker, combine all ingredients. Fill the shaker with ice, then shake vigorously for 15 seconds. Strain into chilled rocks glasses.

Chiang Mai Chicken (*Kai Yang*)

Start to finish: **3 hours (20 minutes active)**
Servings: 4

___

1 cup lightly packed fresh cilantro leaves and tender stems

½ cup fish sauce

½ cup soy sauce

¼ cup packed light brown sugar

1 stalk lemon grass, trimmed to lower 6 inches, dry outer layers discarded, chopped (optional)

4 garlic cloves, smashed and peeled

1 tablespoon coriander seeds

1 tablespoon black peppercorns

1 teaspoon white peppercorns

Two 10- to 12-ounce whole chicken legs

Two 10- to 12-ounce bone-in, skin-on chicken breasts, ribs trimmed

1 cup kosher salt

Lime wedges, to serve (optional)

We first tried this chicken at a sidewalk restaurant in Chiang Mai in northern Thailand. The spatchcocked birds were stuck with two bamboo skewers set in a V shape that were used first to turn the chicken, then to elevate it above the heat. The chicken had started the day before with a marinade of fish sauce, coconut milk, lemon grass, crushed coriander and peppercorns, garlic, cilantro root, palm sugar and, perhaps, a touch of MSG—a respectable ingredient in this part of the world. The marinade had actually flavored the chicken, a rare event. The barbecue sauce was another surprise, a tamarind-based concoction that included dried chilies, galangal (a relative of ginger), salt and more fish sauce. Our version uses brown sugar in place of harder-to-find palm sugar. We opted for the ease of chicken parts; you can buy leg quarters and breasts. Use four whole legs or four split breasts, or break down a whole chicken. It's optional, but lemon grass added bright, citrusy flavor that's characteristic of Thai food. The lemon grass paste sold in tubes near the fresh herbs worked in a pinch; substitute 2 tablespoons of paste for the fresh lemon grass. Cooking the chicken over a bed of salt prevented the marinade from burning as it dripped off the chicken. While a simple squeeze of lime was enough to dress the meat, we also liked dipping it in tangy tamarind (p. 504) or chili-lime sauce (see sidebar).

Don't marinate the chicken longer than two hours. The salt in the marinade can toughen the meat and overwhelm its flavor.

1. In a blender, combine the cilantro, fish sauce, soy sauce, sugar, lemon grass, if using, garlic, coriander and both peppercorns. Blend until smooth, about 1 minute. Reserve ¼ cup of the marinade for the glaze.

2. Place the chicken in a large zip-close plastic bag. Pour in the remaining marinade and seal. Set in a bowl and refrigerate for 2 hours.

3. Heat the oven to 400°F with the rack in the middle position. Line a rimmed baking sheet with foil and spread the salt over it. Mist a wire rack with cooking spray, then set over the salt. Arrange the chicken on the rack. Bake for 30 minutes. Brush the chicken with the reserved marinade and continue to bake until the thighs register 175°F and the breasts register 160°F, another 10 to 15 minutes. Transfer the chicken to a carving board and let rest for 15 minutes. Serve with lime wedges or dipping sauce, if desired.

CHILI-LIME DIPPING SAUCE

Start to finish: **5 minutes**
Makes **about ¾ cup**

Chili-garlic sauce has a coarser texture, fuller body and more pronounced garlic flavor than Sriracha. Look for it in the grocer's Asian foods aisle.

½ cup lime juice (4 to 6 limes)

3 tablespoons fish sauce

2 tablespoons packed light brown sugar

2 teaspoons chili-garlic sauce

In a bowl, stir together all ingredients until the sugar dissolves. Use immediately or refrigerate for up to 3 days.

Fennel-Rosemary **Porchetta**

Start to finish: 1½ days (30 minutes active)
Servings: 8

For the roast:

7- to 8-pound boneless pork butt

8 ounces pancetta, cut into ½-inch cubes

4 tablespoons salted butter, room temperature

1 cup (1½ ounces) lightly packed fresh rosemary

1 cup (1 ounce) lightly packed fresh oregano

20 medium garlic cloves, peeled

1 tablespoon red pepper flakes

½ cup plus 2 tablespoons ground fennel seed, divided

Kosher salt and ground black pepper

2 tablespoons packed light brown sugar

For the sauce:

¾ cup defatted pan juices

⅓ cup lemon juice

2 tablespoons extra-virgin olive oil

1 teaspoon ground fennel

Ground black pepper

Porchetta is a roasted whole hog tradition from the Italian region of Umbria. Turning it into a home cook–friendly pork roast proved challenging. After testing recipes with pork loin (too dry) and pork belly (too fatty), we settled on a boneless pork butt roast. Traditional porchetta is succulent and complex because almost all parts of the pig are used. For our scaled-down version, we added pancetta (seasoned and cured pork belly that has not been smoked), which lent a richness to the filling and helped baste the roast from the inside out. Fennel is a key flavor of the dish. We used ground fennel seeds in a seasoning rub and, while the roasted pork rested, we used the time (and the flavorful fond in the pan) to roast wedges of fresh fennel. Be sure to buy a boneless pork butt, not a boneless picnic roast; both are cut from the shoulder, but the butt comes from higher up on the animal and has a better shape for this recipe. Porchetta leftovers make great sandwiches, thinly sliced and served on crusty bread or ciabatta rolls. Leftover roasted fennel is perfect for sandwiches, as well.

Don't cut short the porchetta's one-hour resting time. The roast is much easier to slice after it rests for the full hour.

1. To prepare the roast, remove any twine or netting around the pork. Locate the cut made to remove the bone, then open up the roast. Using a sharp knife, continue the cut until the roast opens like a book; do not cut all the way through, as the meat must remain in one piece. Using the tip of a paring knife, make 1-inch-deep incisions into the pork spaced about 1 inch apart; do not cut all the way through the meat. Set aside.

2. In a food processor, pulse the pancetta until coarsely chopped, about 15 pulses. Add the butter, rosemary, oregano, garlic, pepper flakes, ½ cup of ground fennel and 2 teaspoons salt. Process until the mixture forms a spreadable paste, about 1 minute, scraping the bowl as needed. Spread the paste evenly over the interior of the pork, pressing it into the cuts. Roll the roast into a tight cylinder, then set it seam side down.

3. Cut 7 to 9 pieces of kitchen twine, each 28 to 30 inches long. In a small bowl, stir together the remaining 2 tablespoons ground fennel, 1 tablespoon salt, the brown sugar and 2 teaspoons black pepper. Rub this mixture over the top and sides of the roast. Using the twine, tie the roast at 1-inch intervals, seam side down; you may not need all of the twine. Trim the ends of the twine. Wrap the roast tightly in plastic, transfer to a large baking dish and refrigerate for at least 24 hours or up to 48 hours.

4. Heat the oven to 300°F with a rack in the middle position. Set a roasting rack in a roasting pan and pour 4 cups water into the pan. Unwrap the roast and set it fat side up on the rack. Roast until the center registers 195°F, 6 to 7 hours.

5. Transfer the roast to a carving board and let rest, uncovered, for 1 hour. Reserve the liquid in the pan.

6. Meanwhile, make the sauce. Pour the liquid from the roasting pan into a fat separator; if making roasted fennel (see recipe below), do not wash the pan. Let the liquid settle for 5 minutes, then measure out ¾ cup. In a medium bowl, whisk together the pan juices, the lemon juice, ¼ cup water, the oil, ground fennel and 2 teaspoons pepper.

7. Cut the pork into thin slices, removing the twine as you slice. Serve with the sauce.

ROASTED FENNEL

Start to finish: **50 minutes**
Servings: **8**

This side dish makes good use of the fond left in the porchetta's roasting pan.

4 large fennel bulbs, trimmed, halved, cored and cut lengthwise into 1-inch wedges

¼ cup extra-virgin olive oil

Kosher salt

1. Heat the oven to 450°F with a rack in the middle position. In the roasting pan used for the porchetta, combine the fennel, oil and 1 teaspoon salt; stir until evenly coated.

2. Roast for 20 minutes, then stir. Roast for another 10 minutes, then add ½ cup water and scrape up the browned bits on the bottom of the pan. Continue to roast until tender and lightly browned, another 10 minutes.

Chicken Tagine with Apricots, Butternut Squash and Spinach

Start to finish: **1 hour (30 minutes active)** / Servings: 4

4 tablespoons extra-virgin
olive oil, divided

Kosher salt and ground black pepper

2 teaspoons cinnamon

2 teaspoons ground cumin

2 teaspoons sweet paprika

1 teaspoon ground coriander

¼ teaspoon cayenne pepper

1½ pounds boneless, skinless
chicken thighs, trimmed and
cut into 1½-inch pieces

1 large yellow onion, thinly sliced
lengthwise

4 garlic cloves, smashed and peeled

4 teaspoons grated fresh ginger

2½ cups low-sodium chicken broth

14½-ounce can diced tomatoes

¾ cup dried apricots, quartered

8 ounces peeled butternut squash,
cut into ¾-inch cubes (about 2 cups)

1 cup Greek green olives, pitted
and halved

1 cup chopped fresh cilantro, divided

¼ cup pistachios, toasted and chopped

2 teaspoons grated lemon zest,
plus 3 tablespoons lemon juice

4 ounces baby spinach
(about 4 cups)

This spicy, fruity chicken stew is based on tagine, a classic North African dish that cooks meat, vegetables and fruit mostly in their natural juices. We love it because the richness of the dish comes from layers of flavor, not laborious browning. The word tagine refers to both the dish and the clay pot it typically is cooked in. The pot has a shallow pan and a conical top designed to collect condensation from the steam of the cooking food and return the moisture to it. We used a more commonly available Dutch oven, but kept to the spirit of the tagine, using a fragrant spice paste to season the chicken and act as a base for the stew. Apricots added sweetness (we preferred sulfured for their vibrant color) that was balanced by briny green olives. An equal amount of carrots can be substituted for the butternut squash. Serve the tagine with couscous, rice or warmed pita bread.

Don't drain the diced tomatoes. Their liquid adds sweetness and acidity to the stew.

1. In a small bowl, stir together 2 tablespoons of the oil, 2½ teaspoons salt, ½ teaspoon black pepper, the cinnamon, cumin, paprika, coriander and cayenne. In a medium bowl, toss the chicken with half the spice paste, rubbing the meat to coat evenly; set aside.

2. In a large Dutch oven over medium-high, combine the onion, garlic, the remaining 2 tablespoons of oil and ¼ teaspoon salt. Cook until the onion is browned and softened, 7 to 9 minutes. Add the ginger and remaining spice paste and cook, stirring constantly, for 1 minute. Add the broth, tomatoes and apricots and bring to a boil, scraping up any browned bits. Add the chicken, return to a boil, then reduce heat to medium-low and simmer for 10 minutes.

3. Add the squash and olives, return to a simmer and cook, partially covered, until the liquid has thickened and the squash is tender, 20 to 25 minutes, stirring occasionally and adjusting the heat to maintain a medium simmer.

4. Meanwhile, in a medium bowl, stir together ½ cup of the cilantro, the pistachios and lemon zest. Stir the spinach into the stew and cook until wilted, 1 to 2 minutes. Stir in the remaining ½ cup of cilantro and the lemon juice, then taste and season with salt and pepper. Serve topped with the cilantro-pistachio mixture.

Carne Adovada

Start to finish: **5 hours (50 minutes active)**
Servings: **8**

---

3 ounces New Mexico chilies, stemmed, seeded and torn into pieces

3 ounces guajillo chilies, stemmed, seeded and torn into pieces

4 cups boiling water

5 pounds boneless pork butt roast, trimmed of excess fat and cut into 1½-inch cubes

Kosher salt and ground black pepper

2 tablespoons lard or grapeseed oil

2 medium white onions, chopped

6 medium garlic cloves, minced

4 teaspoons cumin seed

4 teaspoons ground coriander

1 teaspoon dried oregano, preferably Mexican

¾ teaspoon cayenne pepper

1 tablespoon molasses

Lime wedges, to serve

Sour cream, to serve

Fresh cilantro leaves, to serve

We found that 3 ounces of New Mexico chilies—the widely available medium-hot chilies grown in the state—and 3 ounces of fruity, mildly smoky Mexican guajillos gave us just the right flavor. If guajillos are hard to find, another 3 ounces of New Mexico chilies can be substituted. Pork butt, which is cut from the shoulder, is a fatty cut. Trimming as much fat as possible from the meat—not just from the surface but also from between the muscles—helps prevent a greasy stew. After trimming, you should have 4 to 4½ pounds of pork. If the stew nonetheless ends up with fat on the surface, simply use a wide, shallow spoon to skim it off. This adovado is rich and robust; it pairs perfectly with Mexican rice, stewed pinto beans and/or warmed flour tortillas.

Don't use a picnic shoulder roast for this recipe. The picnic cut, taken from the lower portion of the shoulder, has more cartilage and connective tissue, which will make trimming more difficult. Also, don't use blackstrap molasses, which has a potent bittersweet flavor.

1. Place all of the chilies in a large bowl, add the boiling water and stir. Let stand, stirring occasionally, until the chilies have softened, about 30 minutes. Transfer half of the mixture to a blender and blend until smooth, about 1 minute. Add the remaining mixture and blend until smooth, scraping down the blender as needed. Measure ½ cup of the chili puree into a small bowl, cover and refrigerate until needed. Pour the remaining puree into a medium bowl and set aside; do not scrape out the blender jar. Pour ½ cup cool water into the blender, cover tightly and shake to release all of the puree.

2. Place the pork in a large bowl. Add 2 teaspoons salt and the chili-water mixture in the blender. Stir to coat, then cover and refrigerate for 1 hour.

3. Heat the oven to 325°F with a rack in the lower-middle position. In a large Dutch oven over medium, heat the lard until shimmering. Add the onions and cook, stirring occasionally, until softened, 8 to 10 minutes. Stir in the garlic, cumin, coriander, oregano and cayenne, then cook until fragrant, about 30 seconds. Stir in ½ cup water and the chili puree from the medium bowl. Add the pork. Stir to combine, then cover the pot, place in the oven and cook for 2 hours.

4. Remove the pot from the oven. Uncover, stir and return, uncovered, to the oven. Continue to cook until the pork is tender, another 1¼ to 1½ hours. Remove from the oven and set on the stove over medium heat and simmer, stirring occasionally, until the sauce has thickened slightly, 8 to 10 minutes.

5. Stir in the reserved ½ cup chili puree and the molasses. Taste and season with salt and pepper. Serve with lime wedges, sour cream and cilantro leaves.

Chicken **en Cocotte**

Start to finish: 1 hour 35 minutes (15 minutes active)
Servings: 4

___

4- to 4½-pound whole chicken, wings tucked and legs tied

Kosher salt and ground black pepper

5 tablespoons salted butter, divided

1 large yellow onion, peeled and cut into 8 wedges

8 medium garlic cloves, peeled and halved

1½ cups dry white wine

10 thyme sprigs

3 tablespoons lemon juice

2 tablespoons Dijon mustard

½ cup finely chopped fresh tarragon

CHICKEN EN COCOTTE WITH APRICOTS AND SHALLOTS

Substitute 8 large shallots (peeled and halved) for the onion, omit the mustard and decrease the tarragon to ¼ cup. When the shallots and garlic are lightly browned, after about 5 minutes, add 3 ounces dried apricots (thinly sliced), ½ teaspoon red pepper flakes, and ¼ teaspoon saffron threads (optional) and cook until fragrant, about 30 seconds. Add the wine and proceed with the recipe.

There is little prep involved in this chicken en cocotte—or chicken in a pot—and most of the cooking is hands-off. A cocotte is simply a covered oven-safe dish or casserole similar to a Dutch oven. We found that cooking the chicken breast side down in the pot allows the delicate white meat to gently poach in the wine while the legs cook up above, a technique that helps equalize the cooking of the white meat (done at 160°F) and dark meat (done between 175°F to 180°F). Allowing the chicken to rest breast side up after prevents the white meat from overcooking.

Don't use a Dutch oven smaller than 7 quarts or a chicken larger than 4½ pounds. *If the bird fits too snugly, there won't be enough space for heat to circulate, hindering even cooking.*

1. Heat the oven to 400°F with a rack in the lower-middle position. Using paper towels, pat the chicken dry then season with salt and pepper.

2. In a large Dutch oven over medium, melt 1 tablespoon of butter. Add the onion and garlic and cook until lightly browned, about 5 minutes. Add the wine and bring to a simmer. Lay the thyme sprigs on the onion mixture. Set the chicken, breast down, on the thyme and onions.

3. Cover and bake until a skewer inserted into the thickest part of the breast meets no resistance or the thickest part of the breast reaches 160°F and the thighs reach 175°F to 180°F, 55 to 65 minutes. Using tongs inserted into the cavity of the chicken, carefully transfer it to a large baking dish, turning it breast up. Let rest for at least 15 minutes.

4. Meanwhile, remove and discard the thyme sprigs. Tilt the pot to pool the liquid to one side and use a wide spoon to skim off and discard the fat. Bring to a simmer over medium and cook until thickened and reduced to about 1 cup (with solids), about 5 minutes. Off heat, whisk in the remaining 4 tablespoons butter, the lemon juice and mustard. Taste and season with salt and pepper.

5. Remove the legs from the chicken by cutting through the hip joints. Remove and discard the skin from the legs, then separate the thighs from the drumsticks. Remove the breast meat from the bone, remove and discard the skin, then cut each breast crosswise into thin slices. Arrange the chicken on a platter. Transfer the sauce to a bowl, stir in the tarragon and serve with the chicken.

Sumac-Spiced Chicken (*Musakhan*)

Start to finish: **1 hour 15 minutes**
Servings: **4**

2 pounds boneless, skinless chicken thighs, trimmed

Kosher salt and ground black pepper

6 tablespoons extra-virgin olive oil, divided

½ cup pine nuts, toasted, divided

1 large yellow onion, halved lengthwise and thinly sliced

4 medium garlic cloves, thinly sliced

4 tablespoons ground sumac, divided

2 teaspoons sweet paprika

Four 8-inch pita bread rounds

½ cup lightly packed flat-leaf parsley, chopped

Tahini, to serve

Deep-red ground sumac is the star of this Palestinian dish. Its tart, citrusy flavor is nicely balanced by the sweetness of the sautéed onion and the rich pine nuts. Look for sumac in well-stocked grocery stores, spice shops and Middle Eastern markets; it can also be ordered online.

Don't skip the tahini for drizzling at the table. Its nutty flavor and richness perfectly complement the chicken. And don't forget to stir the tahini well before serving.

1. Pat the chicken dry, then season with salt and pepper. In a large Dutch oven over medium-high, heat 1 tablespoon of oil until barely smoking. Add half the chicken in a single layer and cook until well browned, 5 to 7 minutes. Transfer to a bowl. Repeat with 1 tablespoon of the remaining oil and the remaining chicken. Set aside.

2. Chop ¼ cup of the pine nuts and set aside. In the Dutch oven over medium, heat 2 tablespoons of the remaining oil. Add the onion and cook, stirring, until softened slightly, about 5 minutes. Add the garlic, chopped pine nuts, 3 tablespoons of sumac and the paprika. Cook, stirring, until fragrant, 30 to 60 seconds. Add 3 cups water, stir and bring to a simmer. Return the chicken to the pot. Cover, reduce to medium-low and simmer until a skewer inserted into the chicken meets no resistance, 25 to 30 minutes.

3. Meanwhile, heat the oven to 450°F with a rack in the middle position. Use a slotted spoon to transfer the chicken to a bowl, then use 2 forks to shred the meat. Bring the liquid in the pot to a simmer over medium-high. Cook, stirring, until most of the moisture has evaporated, 10 to 15 minutes. Return the chicken to the pot and stir in the remaining ¼ cup whole pine nuts. Taste and season with salt and pepper. Cover and set aside.

4. Brush the pita on both sides with the remaining 2 tablespoons oil and arrange the rounds on a rimmed baking sheet. Bake until warm and soft, 5 to 7 minutes. Sprinkle the pita with the remaining 1 tablespoon sumac, cut each in half and transfer to a platter. Stir the parsley into the chicken. Drizzle with tahini and serve with the pita.

Southern Thai-Style Fried Chicken

Start to finish: 40 minutes, plus marinating
Servings: 4

3 tablespoons ground cumin

3 tablespoons ground coriander

3 tablespoons ground
white pepper, divided

1 large egg white

¼ cup fish sauce

1 bunch fresh cilantro, finely chopped

2 serrano chilies, stemmed
and finely chopped

2 pounds boneless, skinless
chicken thighs, trimmed, each cut
crosswise into 3 strips

2 cups cornstarch

Kosher salt

2 quarts peanut oil, plus more
if needed

Lime wedges, to serve

Sweet chili sauce, to serve
(see note; optional)

Gai tod hat yai, fried chicken from the southern region of Thailand, inspired this recipe, but for ease, we use boneless, skinless thighs cut into strips instead of the typical bone-in, skin-on parts. Toasted spices are added to the marinade so they infuse the chicken with flavor; they're also dusted onto the pieces after frying for additional seasoning. The chicken is customarily sprinkled with crisp fried shallots after cooking, but we opted out of this garnish, as the spices themselves provide plenty of bold flavor. If you like, you can purchase fried shallots in most Asian grocery stores; scatter them over the chicken just before serving. If you're not up for making our extra-easy version of Thai sweet chili sauce, serve with store-bought sweet chili sauce, or simply offer lime wedges for squeezing.

Don't marinate the chicken for longer than an hour or it will be too salty. Don't crowd the pot when frying. Cook only a third of the chicken at a time so the temperature of the oil won't drop drastically, which results in greasy chicken.

1. In a 10-inch skillet over medium, toast the cumin and coriander until fragrant and just beginning to color, 2 to 3 minutes. Transfer to a small bowl and stir in 1 tablespoon of white pepper; set aside.

2. In a large bowl, whisk together the egg white, fish sauce and ¼ cup water. Stir in the cilantro, chilies and 3 tablespoons of the spice mixture. Add the chicken and stir to thoroughly coat, then cover and refrigerate for 30 to 60 minutes.

3. Set a wire rack in a rimmed baking sheet. In a large bowl, whisk together the cornstarch, the remaining 2 tablespoons white pepper and 2 teaspoons salt.

4. Drain the chicken in a colander. Scraping off excess marinade, add ⅓ of the chicken to the cornstarch mixture and toss to coat completely, then firmly press the pieces into the cornstarch.

Transfer the pieces to the prepared rack in a single layer, shaking to remove excess coating. Repeat with the remaining chicken and cornstarch mixture, working in two more batches.

5. Set another wire rack in a rimmed baking sheet. In a large Dutch oven over medium-high, heat the oil to 350°F (the oil should be at least 2 inches deep; add more if needed). Add ⅓ of the chicken pieces and cook, stirring occasionally to prevent sticking, until golden brown, about 5 minutes. Using a slotted spoon or wire skimmer, transfer the chicken to the second rack and season on all sides with about ⅓ of the reserved spice mixture. Allow the oil to return to 350°F, then repeat with the remaining chicken and spice mixture, working in two more batches. Serve with lime wedges and sweet chili sauce (if using).

CHANGE THE WAY YOU COOK:
PUT SEASONINGS ON REPEAT

Finishing a dish with a repeat hit of seasoning used during cooking creates layers of interest and helps reinforce flavor.

TANGY-SWEET CHILI SAUCE

Start to finish: **10 minutes**
Makes about **¾ cup**

This side dish makes good use of the fond left in the porchetta's roasting pan.

1 cup white vinegar

½ cup white sugar

Kosher salt

3 tablespoons chili-garlic sauce

In a small saucepan over medium-high, bring the vinegar, sugar and ¼ teaspoon salt to a boil, stirring to dissolve the sugar. Cook until the mixture thickens and is reduced to about ¾ cup, 10 to 12 minutes. Off heat, stir in the chili-garlic sauce. Cool to room temperature.

Breads

Easy Flatbread Dough / 375

Toppings for Easy Flatbread Dough / 376

Italian Flatbread (*Piadine*) / 379

Piadine Toppings / 380

Multigrain Soda Bread / 382

Potato-and-Herb Focaccia / 384

Pita Bread / 386

Taiwanese Flaky Scallion Pancakes / 388

Pumpkin Seed Rolls / 391

Portuguese Cornbread (*Broa*) / 392

Whipped Cream Biscuits / 394

Macerated Strawberries with
Lime and Tangy Whipped Cream / 395

French Spice Bread (*Pain d'Épices*) / 396

Brown Butter–Cardamom
Banana Bread / 399

9

SHAPING FLATBREAD (PIZZA) DOUGH

1. Place one ball of dough on a lightly-floured counter.

2. Using your hands, begin patting and stretching the dough into an oval.

3. A ruler helps ensure that the dough reaches the correct dimensions.

4. Continue stretching the dough, making sure it is of even thickness.

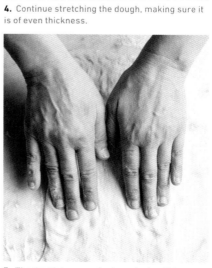

5. The dough is properly shaped when it forms a 6-by 12-inch oval.

Easy Flatbread Dough

Start to finish: 1½ hours (30 minutes active)
Makes two 12-inch pizzas or flatbreads

241 grams (1¾ cups) bread flour, plus more for dusting

1½ teaspoons instant yeast

1¾ teaspoons kosher salt

¾ cup plain whole-milk Greek-style yogurt

1 tablespoon honey

This versatile dough is a breeze to make in a food processor and can be used for pizzas with various toppings or Middle Eastern–style flatbreads. The addition of Greek yogurt helps create a supple dough that's easy to work with and bakes up with a chewy-soft crumb and subtle richness. For convenience, the dough can be made a day in advance. After dividing the dough in half and forming the pieces into rounds, place each portion in a quart-size zip-close bag that's been misted with cooking spray, seal well and refrigerate overnight. Allow the dough to come to room temperature before shaping.

Don't undermix the dough in the food processor; it needs a full minute of processing to build the gluten that provides structure and strength. When done, the dough may be warm to the touch; this is normal.

1. In a food processor, combine the flour, yeast and salt, then process until combined, about 5 seconds. Add the yogurt, honey and ¼ cup water. Process until the mixture forms a ball, about 30 seconds; the dough should be tacky to the touch and should stick slightly to the sides of the bowl. If it feels too dry, add more water, 1 tablespoon at a time, and process until incorporated. Continue to process until the dough is shiny and elastic, about 1 minute.

2. Transfer the dough to a lightly floured counter. Flour your hands and knead the dough a few times, until it forms a smooth ball. Divide the dough in half and form each half into a taut ball by rolling it against the counter in a circular motion under a cupped hand. Space the

balls about 6 inches apart on a lightly floured counter, then cover with plastic wrap. Let rise until doubled in volume, 1 to 1½ hours.

3. About 1 hour before baking, heat the oven to 500°F with a baking steel or stone on the upper-middle rack. Working one at a time, gently stretch each ball on a lightly floured counter to an oval approximately 6 inches wide and 12 inches long. The dough is now ready to top and bake.

CHANGE THE WAY YOU COOK:
ADD YOGURT TO MAKE DOUGH FLAVORFUL AND FLEXIBLE

Adding tangy yogurt to dough is an easy way to boost flavor. It also makes the dough more tender and easier to work with.

Toppings for Easy Flatbread Dough

ZA'ATAR FLATBREADS

Start to finish: 25 minutes
Makes two 12-inch oval flatbreads

6 tablespoons extra-virgin olive oil

2 tablespoons sesame seeds, toasted

2 tablespoons za'atar

Semolina, for dusting

Easy flatbread dough (p. 375)

About 1 hour before baking, heat the oven to 500°F with a baking steel or stone on the upper-middle rack. In a small bowl, stir together the oil, sesame seeds and za'atar. Lightly dust a baking peel, inverted baking sheet or rimless cookie sheet with semolina.

Transfer one portion of the shaped dough to the peel and, if needed, reshape into a 6-by-12-inch oval. Spoon half of the oil mixture evenly over the entire surface of the dough. Slide the dough onto the baking steel and bake until the edges are golden brown, 7 to 9 minutes.

Using the peel, transfer the baked flatbread to a wire rack. Let cool for about 10 minutes. Meanwhile, top and bake the second portion of dough in the same way. Serve warm.

SPICED BEEF FLATBREADS WITH YOGURT AND TOMATOES

Start to finish: 45 minutes
Makes two 12-inch oval flatbreads

1 medium shallot, roughly chopped

1 cup lightly packed fresh flat-leaf parsley, roughly chopped, plus more to serve

¼ cup chopped drained roasted red peppers, patted dry

2 tablespoons tomato paste

1¼ teaspoons ground cumin

¾ teaspoon sweet smoked paprika

⅛ to ¼ teaspoon cayenne pepper

Kosher salt and ground black pepper

8 ounces 85 percent lean ground beef or ground lamb

Semolina, for dusting

Easy flatbread dough (p. 375)

1 large egg white, beaten

Plain whole-milk yogurt, to serve

Chopped tomato, to serve

Chopped red onion, to serve

About 1 hour before baking, heat the oven to 500°F with a baking steel or stone on the upper-middle rack. In a food processor, combine the shallot, parsley, roasted peppers, tomato paste, cumin, paprika, cayenne, 1¼ teaspoons salt and ½ teaspoon black pepper. Process until finely chopped, about 30 seconds, scraping the bowl as needed. Add the beef and pulse just until incorporated, 3 or 4 pulses.

Lightly dust a baking peel, inverted baking sheet or rimless cookie sheet with semolina. Transfer one portion of the shaped dough to the peel and, if needed, reshape into a 6-by-12-inch oval. Brush the surface of the dough with a thin but even layer of egg white, then spread half of the beef mixture over the surface. Slide the dough onto the baking steel or stone and bake until the edges are golden brown, 9 to 11 minutes.

Using the peel, transfer the flatbread to a wire rack. Top and bake the second portion of dough in the same way. Serve warm with yogurt, chopped tomatoes, chopped onion and additional chopped parsley.

Italian Flatbread (*Piadine*)

Start to finish: 30 minutes
Makes four 10-inch flatbreads

½ cup water, divided

¼ cup plain whole-milk yogurt

274 grams (2 cups) bread flour

2 teaspoons kosher salt

1½ teaspoons baking powder

63 grams (⅓ cup) lard, room temperature

Flatbread is among the quickest of quick breads. Leavened or not, folded, topped or used as a scoop, it appeals with promises of warm, fresh dough. Fast. One of our favorite variations originated in Romagna, in northern Italy. There they throw together flour, salt, water or milk, and lard or olive oil to make a quick dough. After a short rest, the flatbread—a piadina—is cooked on a griddle or skillet. The cooked piadine then are stuffed with sweet or savory fillings and folded in half to make a sandwich. We started by finding the right fat for our dough. Butter was wrong. Olive oil gave us a pleasant texture and flavor, but something still was missing. So we gave lard a shot. And what a difference. The piadine were tender with just the right chew. But we wanted yet more suppleness and found our answer in naan, a tender flatbread from India that adds a scoop of yogurt to the dough. It seemed heretical in an Italian bread, but fat hinders gluten development, keeping bread soft. It worked well in our piadine and gave the dough more complex flavor. Though it was not as flavorful, vegetable shortening worked as a substitute for lard. If the dough doesn't ball up in the processor, gather it together and briefly knead it by hand. For a simple topping, brush the cooked piadine with our spicy garlic oil (p. 524), or try one of the fillings on the following pages.

1. In a liquid measuring cup, whisk together ¼ cup of the water and the yogurt. In a food processor, combine the flour, salt and baking powder. Process for 5 seconds. Add the lard and process until combined, about 10 seconds. With the processor running, add the yogurt mixture. With the processor still running, add the remaining water 1 tablespoon at a time until the dough forms a smooth, moist ball, about 1 minute.

2. Divide the dough into 4 pieces. Roll each into a ball, then cover with plastic wrap. Let rest for 15 minutes. Meanwhile, prepare toppings.

3. Roll each dough ball into a 10-inch round. Poke the surfaces all over with a fork. Heat a 12-inch cast-iron skillet over medium until a drop of water sizzles immediately, 4 to 6 minutes. One at a time, place a dough round in the skillet and cook until the bottom is charred in spots, 1 to 2 minutes. Using tongs, flip and cook for 30 seconds. Transfer to a plate and cover loosely with foil.

Piadine **Toppings**

LAHMAJOUN

Start to finish: **30 minutes**
Makes **4 piadine**

Made with ground meat, tomatoes and spices, lahmajoun is a common topping for flatbread in Armenia. If you prefer, swap in ground lamb.

8 ounces 80 percent lean ground beef

½ large yellow onion, finely chopped (about ¾ cup)

1 large red bell pepper, cored and finely chopped

2 teaspoons red pepper flakes

1 teaspoon smoked paprika

1 teaspoon ground cumin

Kosher salt and ground black pepper

14½-ounce can fire-roasted crushed tomatoes

½ cup plain whole-milk Greek-style yogurt

4 tablespoons lemon juice, divided

2 cups lightly packed fresh flat-leaf parsley leaves

2 cups lightly packed fresh mint leaves, torn

In a 12-inch nonstick skillet over medium, cook the beef, stirring and breaking up the meat, until beginning to brown, 2 to 3 minutes. Add the onion, bell pepper, pepper flakes, paprika, cumin, 2 teaspoons salt and 1 teaspoon pepper. Cook, stirring occasionally, for 5 minutes. Add the tomatoes and cook until most of the liquid has evaporated, about 8 minutes.

In a small bowl, whisk together the yogurt and 2 tablespoons of the lemon juice. In a medium bowl, combine the parsley, mint and the remaining 2 tablespoons of lemon juice. Season with salt and pepper. Spread the beef mixture evenly over half of each piadina. Drizzle with the yogurt mixture, top with the herbs and fold in half.

PROSCIUTTO, ARUGULA AND RICOTTA

Start to finish: **10 minutes**
Makes **4 piadine**

In Romagna, piadine often are served with cured meats, greens and fresh cheeses that soften with the warmth of the freshly cooked bread. If possible, purchase fresh-cut prosciutto, sliced as thinly as possible, and allow it to come to room temperature. The flavor and texture of ricotta cheese varies widely by brand; we like Calabro.

¾ cup whole-milk ricotta cheese

½ teaspoon grated lemon zest,
plus 2 tablespoons lemon juice

Kosher salt and ground black pepper

8 slices prosciutto, room temperature

4 ounces baby arugula (about 4 cups)

3 tablespoons extra-virgin olive oil

In a medium bowl, stir together the ricotta and lemon zest. Taste and season with salt and pepper. Spread the ricotta mixture evenly over half of each piadina, then top with 2 slices of the prosciutto. In a medium bowl, toss the arugula with the lemon juice and a pinch of salt. Mound on top of the prosciutto. Drizzle with the oil and fold.

Multigrain Soda Bread

Start to finish: 1 hour 20 minutes (10 minutes active), plus cooling
Makes 2 small loaves

---

2 cups plain whole-milk yogurt

161 grams (1 cup) 10-grain
hot cereal mix

315 grams (2¼ cups)
whole-wheat flour

163 grams (1¼ cups) all-purpose flour

42 grams (3 tablespoons packed)
brown sugar

1½ teaspoons kosher salt

1 teaspoon baking powder

1 teaspoon baking soda

½ cup pepitas, toasted (optional)

10 tablespoons (1¼ sticks) salted
butter, melted

Soda bread by definition already is a quick bread, but a few shortcuts helped us make it even faster. Our goal was a flavorful mixed grain soda bread—minus the chore of a long, expensive and hard to find ingredient list. Our solution was premixed multigrain porridge, which gave us 10 grains in one package. We saved even more time by soaking the cereal in yogurt—a convenient replacement for the more classic buttermilk—before mixing it into the dough. This softened the grains and meant we didn't have to cook the porridge on its own. For a little more texture and toasted flavor, we added pepitas. Some recipes call for working cold butter into the dough. We stayed in the fast lane on that step, too, borrowing a technique from scone making and stirring melted butter into our dry ingredients. It was fast, easy and less messy. If you can't find 10-grain cereal mix (Bob's Red Mill makes one), use a five- or seven-grain hot cereal or porridge mix instead.

Don't use Greek-style yogurt for this recipe; it won't mix with and hydrate the grains. We liked whole-milk yogurt, but low-fat will work, too.

1. Heat the oven to 350°F with a rack in the middle position. Line a baking sheet with kitchen parchment. In a medium bowl, stir together the yogurt and cereal; let sit for 15 minutes. Meanwhile, in a large bowl, whisk together both flours, the sugar, salt, baking powder, baking soda and pepitas, if using.

2. Whisk 8 tablespoons of the butter into the yogurt mixture. Add the mixture to the dry ingredients and fold until no dry flour remains; the dough will be thick and look wet and slightly sandy. Pile the dough into 2 even mounds on the prepared pan. Dampen your hands, then shape into 6-inch rounds.

3. Use a sharp serrated knife to cut a ½-inch-deep X into the top of each loaf. Bake until lightly browned and hollow-sounding when tapped, 50 to 60 minutes. Immediately brush the loaves all over with the remaining 2 tablespoons of butter. Transfer to a wire rack and let cool completely.

Potato-and-Herb **Focaccia**

Start to finish: 3½ hours (30 minutes active)
Makes one 13-by-9-inch loaf

___

8 ounces Yukon Gold potatoes
(about 2 small or 1 large), cut into
¾-inch pieces

6 sprigs fresh rosemary or
thyme, plus 2 tablespoons chopped
fresh herbs

3 garlic cloves, smashed and peeled

3½ teaspoons kosher salt, divided

457 grams (3⅓ cups) bread flour

4 tablespoons extra-virgin
olive oil, divided

2 teaspoons instant yeast

2 teaspoons white sugar

½ cup Kalamata olives, pitted
and slivered (optional)

1½ ounces Parmesan cheese,
grated (about ¾ cup) (optional)

Ground black pepper

Common to the Puglia region of Italy, potato focaccia is a particularly moist version of the classic Italian bread. We embedded ours with deep herbal flavors by seasoning the cooking water for the potatoes with rosemary or thyme, as well as garlic. Then we made the starchy, herb-infused cooking liquid do double duty, using it in the dough, too. Yukon Gold potatoes gave the focaccia color and texture, and didn't require peeling (the soft skins disappeared into the dough). For our herbs, we liked a combination of rosemary and thyme, but oregano and bay leaves worked, too. After the dough comes together, you may need to add more cooking liquid (up to ¼ cup) to achieve the proper texture; the dough should be soft and sticky, and just barely clear the sides of the bowl. The focaccia is delicious with a sprinkling of herbs and black pepper, but Kalamata olives and Parmesan cheese were welcome additions. Flaky sea salt, such as Maldon, was a nice touch, as well.

Don't use a glass baking dish. The bread won't brown and crisp properly. If you don't have a metal baking pan, stretch the focaccia into a rough 13-by-9-inch rectangle and bake on a rimmed baking sheet.

1. In a medium saucepan over high, combine 3 cups water, potatoes, herb sprigs, garlic and 2 teaspoons salt. Cover and bring to a boil. Uncover, reduce heat to medium and simmer until the potatoes are tender, 12 to 14 minutes. Drain, reserving the cooking liquid. Discard the herb sprigs, then return the potatoes, garlic and any loose herb leaves to the pan. Use a potato masher or fork to mash until smooth and creamy. Transfer to the bowl of a stand mixer fitted with a dough hook attachment; let the cooking liquid cool until just barely warm, 20 to 30 minutes (it should be no more than 115°F). Meanwhile, oil a large bowl.

2. To the stand mixer bowl, add the flour, 2 tablespoons of the oil, the yeast, the sugar and remaining 1½ teaspoons of salt. Add 1¼ cups of the reserved cooking water, then mix on low speed until the dough comes together, about 1 minute. Increase to medium-high and mix until the dough clears the sides of the bowl but sticks to the bottom, 3 to 5 minutes, adding more cooking liquid 1 tablespoon at a time as needed (dough should be very soft and sticky and just clear the sides of the bowl). Use an oiled silicone spatula to transfer the dough to the prepared bowl. Cover with plastic wrap and let sit in a warm, draft-free area until puffed but not quite doubled, 30 to 60 minutes.

3. Spread the remaining 2 tablespoons of oil over the bottom and sides of a 13-by-9-inch metal baking pan. Transfer the dough to the pan and use oiled fingers to spread in an even layer, pressing into the corners. Cover and let sit in a warm, draft-free area until puffed, 30 to 60 minutes.

4. Heat the oven to 400°F with a rack in the middle position. Use a chopstick to poke the dough all over, then sprinkle with the chopped herbs, olives and Parmesan, if using, and a few grinds of pepper. Bake until the edges are browned and crisp and the top is golden, 35 to 40 minutes. Cool in the pan on a wire rack for 10 minutes, then remove from the pan and cool on the rack. Serve warm or at room temperature.

Pita **Bread**

Start to finish: **4 hours (40 minutes active)**
Servings: **Ten 5½-inch pita rounds**

4 tablespoons grapeseed
or other neutral oil, divided

171 grams (1¼ cups) bread flour,
plus more for dusting

175 grams (1¼ cups)
whole-wheat flour

2¼ teaspoons instant yeast

2 teaspoons white sugar

¾ cup warm water (100°F to 110°F),
plus more if needed

¼ cup plain whole-milk yogurt

2½ teaspoons kosher salt

This pita bread, made with whole-wheat flour and whole-milk yogurt, is full-flavored and has a pleasant chew. To ensure the breads puff nicely and form pockets, they're baked two at a time on a heated baking steel or stone. We preferred a stand mixer for making the dough, but a food processor worked, too. To make the dough in a processor, combine both flours, the yeast and sugar in the work bowl and pulse until combined. Add the water, yogurt and 2 tablespoons of oil and process until a smooth, slightly sticky ball forms, about 1 minute. Add additional water, 1½ teaspoons at a time (up to 2 tablespoons total), if the dough feels too dry. Let the dough rest in the processor for 5 minutes, then add the salt and process until smooth and pliable, about 1 minute. Knead by hand on a lightly floured counter for 1 minute, then transfer to an oiled medium bowl and turn to coat. Cover with plastic wrap and let rise in a warm, draft-free spot until not quite doubled in bulk. Continue with the recipe from the third step to shape and bake. It's not unusual if one or two of the rounds don't puff during baking—the bread will still taste great. The ones that do puff will not deflate as they cool. Store leftover rounds in a zip-close bag for up to a day. To warm, wrap the pitas in foil and heat for 4 minutes at 300°F.

Don't forget to heat the baking steel or stone for a full hour before baking. And do cover the pita breads with a towel when they come out of the oven to keep them soft.

1. Coat a medium bowl with 1 teaspoon of oil; set aside. In the bowl of a stand mixer fitted with the dough hook, add both flours, the yeast and sugar. Mix on low until combined, about 5 seconds. Add the water, yogurt and 2 tablespoons of oil. Mix on low until a smooth ball forms, about 3 minutes. Feel the dough; it should be slightly sticky. If not, add water 1½ teaspoons at a time (no more than 2 tablespoons total), mixing after each addition, until slightly sticky. Let rest in the mixer bowl for 5 minutes.

2. Add the salt and knead on low until smooth and pliable, 10 minutes. Transfer to the prepared bowl, forming it into a ball and turning to coat with oil. Cover with plastic wrap and let rise in a warm, draft-free area until well risen but not quite doubled in volume, 1 to 1½ hours.

3. Dust a rimmed baking sheet evenly with bread flour. Transfer the dough to the counter. Using a dough scraper or bench knife, divide the dough into 10 pieces (about 2 ounces each). Form each into a tight ball and place on the prepared baking sheet. Brush each ball with ½ teaspoon of the remaining oil, then cover with a damp kitchen towel. Let rise in a warm, draft-free area until well risen but not quite doubled, 30 to 60 minutes. Meanwhile, heat the oven to 500°F with a baking steel or stone on the upper-middle rack.

4. Lightly dust two rimmed baking sheets with bread flour and lightly dust the counter. Place a dough ball on the counter; use a lightly floured rolling pin to roll the ball into a round ⅛ inch thick and 5½ inches in diameter. Set on one of the prepared baking sheets. Repeat with the remaining dough balls, placing them in a single layer on the baking sheets. Cover with a damp kitchen towel and let rest for 10 minutes.

5. Lightly dust a peel with bread flour, then place 2 dough rounds on the peel without flipping them. Working quickly, open the oven and slide the rounds onto the baking steel. Immediately close the door. Bake until the breads have puffed and are very lightly browned, about 3 minutes. Using the peel, remove the breads from the oven. Transfer to a wire rack and cover with a dry kitchen towel. Repeat with the remaining dough rounds. Serve warm or at room temperature.

Taiwanese Flaky Scallion Pancakes

Start to finish: 2 hours plus 24-hour rest
Makes 8 pancakes

1 large egg

582 grams (4¼ cups) bread flour, plus more for dusting

Kosher salt

2 sticks (16 tablespoons) salted butter, 1 melted and 1 at room temperature

½ cup peanut or canola oil, plus more for counter

1 cup finely chopped scallions

These flaky scallion pancakes are similar to Malaysian or Indonesian roti and are rich in flavor yet light because of the many delicate layers. You'll need a large, smooth table or countertop for working. The pancakes are best when the dough is made and refrigerated a day ahead, but they can be shaped and frozen, then thawed and cooked just before serving. To do so, once the pancakes have been pressed into 8-inch ovals, freeze them in a single layer on baking sheets lined with lightly oiled kitchen parchment. Freeze until rigid, then stack between sheets of lightly oiled parchment and place in a large zip-close bag. Seal and freeze for up to a month. When ready to cook, thaw on the parchment liners just until pliable, then cook as directed.

Don't use all-purpose flour. Bread flour is essential to make a dough that can be stretched paper-thin. Don't worry if the dough forms a few tears or holes as you stretch it; they won't matter in the finished pancakes. Don't skimp on the oil used on the countertop; a thin but thorough coating is required.

1. In a 2-cup liquid measuring cup or small bowl, whisk together 1¼ cups water and the egg. In a stand mixer fitted with the dough hook, combine the flour and 2 teaspoons salt; mix on medium until well combined, about 1 minute. Add the melted butter to the water-egg mixture then, with the mixer running on medium, slowly add to the flour and mix until incorporated, about 1 minute. Reduce to medium-low and knead until a smooth, elastic dough forms, about 7 minutes.

2. Transfer the dough to a very lightly floured counter and divide into 8 portions (about 4 ounces each). Shape each into a taut ball. On an unfloured area of the counter, roll each portion against the counter under a cupped hand until the surface of the ball is completely smooth. Pour the oil into a 13-by-9-inch baking dish. Place the balls in the dish and rotate to coat with oil on all sides. Cover with plastic wrap and refrigerate overnight.

3. Remove the dough from the refrigerator and let stand at room temperature

for at least 1 hour or up to 2 hours. Using your hands, spread 2 to 3 tablespoons of oil in an even layer on a large area of counter (about 2 feet square). Working with 1 dough ball at a time, use your fingertips to push the dough gently out from the center until it forms an 8-inch round. Flip the round, adding more oil as needed to the counter to keep the surface slicked, and continue to push and stretch the dough until it forms a paper-thin round about 18 inches in diameter; you should be able to see through the dough. Shape the dough into an 18-inch square. If at any point the dough isn't moving easily, add more oil to the counter.

4. Grease your hands with 1 tablespoon of the room-temperature butter, then gently rub the entire surface of the dough with butter. Sprinkle with ½ teaspoon salt. Using your fingertips, lift the far edge of the dough square and fold the top third of the dough down toward you, then fold the bottom third up as if folding a letter; align edges as much as possible. The dough will spring back slightly as you fold, leaving you with a long strip about 4 inches wide. Scatter 2 tablespoons of the scallions over the strip and gently press them in. Fold over 4 inches of one end of the strip, then continue folding the 4-inch area until you reach the other end of the strip. Transfer to an oiled plate and cover with plastic wrap. Repeat with the remaining dough; you'll need 2 plates, each holding 4 packets.

5. Heat the oven to 350°F with a rack in the middle position. Heat a 10-inch cast-iron or nonstick skillet over medium-low until flecks of water instantly sizzle when they hit the pan, 3 to 5 minutes. Place 1 dough packed on an oiled counter and gently spread it into an 8-inch oval of even thickness; it's fine if the oval is not perfectly shaped. Transfer the oval to the skillet, reduce heat to low and cook, occasionally rotating the pancake in the pan, until the bottom is golden brown and crisp, 5 to 7 minutes. Flip the pancake and cook until the second side is golden brown and crisp, another 5 to 7 minutes. While the pancake cooks, shape another dough packed into an 8-inch oval.

6. Using a spatula, transfer the pancake to a cutting board and cover with a dry kitchen towel. Using your hands, scrunch the pancake, pushing the edges together to help the layers separate. Flatten the pancake, then rotate 90 degrees, re-cover with the towel and repeat the scrunching process. Flatten the pancake and place it on a wire rack set in a rimmed baking sheet. Repeat the entire process until all the dough squares have been cooked. Transfer the pancakes to the oven and bake until heated through, about 3 minutes.

Pumpkin Seed Rolls

Start to finish: 3½ hours (1 hour active)
Makes 15 rolls

For the sponge:

70 grams (½ cup) rye flour

½ cup warm (100°F) water

1 tablespoon honey

2 teaspoons instant yeast

For the dough:

1 cup shelled pumpkin seeds (pepitas)

½ cup sesame seeds

4 tablespoons (½ stick) salted butter, cut into 4 pieces and chilled

343 grams (2½ cups) bread flour, plus more for dusting

1 cup room-temperature (70°F) water

2½ teaspoons kosher salt

1 large egg, lightly beaten

Flaky salt, such as Maldon sea salt

Rye flour brings texture to these pumpkin seed rolls that are based on a classic Bavarian bread, Kürbiskern Brötchen. We added toasted pumpkin seeds, as is traditional, and threw in some sesame seeds, as well. Then we processed the seeds with chilled butter in a food processor to create a nut butter, which we added to the sponge before kneading for a tender, moist and flavorful crumb. These rolls are best served the day they are baked. For ease, they can be made in the morning, then reheated in a 350°F oven for 10 minutes just before serving. The seed-butter mixture can be prepared up to three days ahead and refrigerated. Just be sure to pull it out an hour before using to bring it to room temperature.

Don't be tempted to add extra flour when mixing the dough; it will look and feel quite sticky, but will firm up as it rises. Otherwise, the rolls won't have enough chew.

1. To make the sponge, in the bowl of a stand mixer, whisk together the rye flour, warm water, honey and yeast. Cover and let sit until doubled and bubbly, about 1 hour.

2. Meanwhile, in a 12-inch skillet over medium, combine the pumpkin and sesame seeds and toast, stirring, until the sesame seeds are golden (some pumpkin seeds will pop), 5 to 8 minutes. Measure out ½ cup of the mixture and set aside. Transfer the rest to a food processor and process until finely ground, about 1 minute. Add the butter and process until just melted and combined, about another 20 seconds.

3. When the sponge is ready, add the bread flour, water and seed-butter mixture. Mix with the dough hook on low until just combined, about 1 minute. Let sit for 5 minutes. Add the kosher salt, then mix on low until the dough forms a mass around the hook but still adheres to the sides, about 5 minutes. The dough should look and feel sticky but not wet. Cover the bowl and let rise until tripled in size, about 1 hour.

4. Heat the oven to 450°F with a rack in the middle position. Line a baking sheet with kitchen parchment. Turn the dough out onto a well-floured surface, being careful not to deflate it. Lightly flour the top of the dough and gently press it into a 10-by-6-inch rectangle. To create 15 equal portions of dough (about 2 ounces each), cut the rectangle into thirds lengthwise, then into fifths crosswise.

5. Gently round each portion into a ball, creating a smooth, taut surface and pinching together any seams on the bottom. Arrange the rolls evenly on the prepared baking sheet. Brush the tops generously with the egg and sprinkle the reserved seed mixture over them, pressing very gently to adhere. Top each with a small sprinkle of flaky salt. Cover and let rise until nearly doubled in size, 30 to 35 minutes.

6. Bake until deep golden brown, 20 to 25 minutes, rotating the pan once halfway through. Using tongs, immediately transfer the rolls to a wire rack. Let cool for at least 30 minutes before serving.

Portuguese Cornbread (*Broa*)

Start to finish: 4½ hours (15 minutes active)
Makes 1 loaf

204 grams (1⅔ cups) corn flour

2 tablespoons honey

1 cup boiling water, plus ¼ cup
room-temperature (70°F) water

137 grams (1 cup) bread flour,
plus more for dusting

70 grams (½ cup) rye flour

2 teaspoons instant yeast

2 teaspoons kosher salt

Known as broa, Portuguese cornbread shares little but its name with
the cakey, honeyed version familiar to Americans. Beneath a crackling,
creviced crust, the heart of broa is dense, moist and deeply flavored.
Traditionally, the bread is made with corn flour, which is dried corn that is
ground finer than cornmeal. If you can't find corn flour, you can use finely
ground cornmeal, but the bread will have some granularity in the crumb.
This hearty loaf is delicious sliced and spread with salted butter. Stored in
an airtight container or zip-close bag, leftover broa will keep for up to three
days at room temperature; the flavor and texture are best if the bread is
toasted before serving.

*Don't let the loaf rise for longer than indicated, as the bread may bake up with
an unpleasantly boozy, slightly sour flavor. Unlike most bread doughs that double
in bulk during rising, this one increases only by about 50 percent.*

1. Line a rimmed baking sheet with
kitchen parchment. In a stand mixer
fitted with the paddle attachment, mix
the corn flour, honey and boiling water
on low until evenly moistened and a
thick mash forms, 30 to 60 seconds.
Turn off the mixer and let stand
until just warm to the touch, about
30 minutes.

2. Add the room-temperature water,
bread and rye flours, yeast and salt.
Using the dough hook attachment, mix
on low, scraping down the bowl as
needed, until a cohesive dough forms,
about 5 minutes; the dough should
clear the sides of the bowl and feel
tacky but not excessively sticky.

3. Turn the dough out onto the counter
and use your hands to shape the dough
into a ball about 5 inches in diameter.
Set on the prepared baking sheet, dust
the top with flour and cover with a
kitchen towel. Let rise in a warm, draft-
free spot until the volume increases by
about half, 1 to 1½ hours. Meanwhile,
heat the oven to 500°F with a rack in
the middle position.

4. Bake the bread for 15 minutes.
Reduce the oven to 300°F and continue
to bake until deep golden brown, another
30 to 35 minutes. Transfer the bread
from the baking sheet to a wire rack
and let cool completely, about 2 hours.

Whipped Cream **Biscuits**

Start to finish: 30 minutes, plus cooling
Makes 8 biscuits

260 grams (2 cups) all-purpose flour

1½ tablespoons white sugar, divided

2½ teaspoons baking powder

½ teaspoon kosher salt

¼ teaspoon baking soda

⅔ cup heavy cream, plus more
as needed

½ cup sour cream

4 tablespoons (½ stick) salted
butter, chilled and cut into ¼-inch
cubes, plus 1 tablespoon, melted

We first heard of whipped cream biscuits from a central Pennsylvanian cook, then later found recipes for them in a handful of Southern cookbooks. We think they fall in the same category as whipped cream cake, which gets some of its lift from the cream. Instead of relying exclusively on baking powder or baking soda for leavening, these biscuits benefit from the air trapped in stiffly beaten cream. The result is a particularly fluffy texture that doesn't have the heavy-handed richness of an all-butter biscuit. This recipe is designed to work as a dessert, not a breakfast biscuit, and that makes it an ideal candidate for strawberry shortcake. We wanted a bolder filling than one finds in the average shortcake. To avoid waste—as well as the need to reroll scraps—we cut our biscuits into squares. For a savory variation, decrease the sugar to 2 teaspoons and skip the final sprinkle.

Don't forget to decrease the temperature when you put the biscuits in the oven. Starting the biscuits in a very hot oven helped them rise and brown better, but keeping them at that temperature will overcook them.

1. Heat the oven to 475°F with a rack in the middle position. Line a baking sheet with kitchen parchment. In a large bowl, whisk together the flour, 1 tablespoon of the sugar, the baking powder, salt and baking soda. In a second large bowl, use a whisk or electric mixer to beat the cream and sour cream to soft peaks; set aside. Scatter the butter cubes over the flour. With your fingertips, rub together until the butter is thoroughly and evenly dispersed in the flour.

2. Add the whipped cream mixture to the flour mixture. Use a large rubber spatula to fold and press until large clumps form and no dry flour remains. Use your hand to knead the dough in the bowl until it forms a shaggy mass, adding additional cream 1 tablespoon at a time, if needed.

3. Turn the dough out onto a lightly floured counter and divide in half. Form each piece into a rough 5-inch square about ¾ inch thick. With a bench scraper or chef's knife, cut each square into 4 pieces. Evenly space the biscuits on the prepared baking sheet. Brush the tops with the melted butter and sprinkle with the remaining ½ tablespoon sugar.

4. Place the baking sheet in the oven and immediately reduce the temperature to 425°F. Bake until golden brown on top and bottom, 15 to 18 minutes, rotating the pan halfway through. Let cool on the baking sheet for 10 minutes.

MACERATED STRAWBERRIES WITH LIME

We favored small to medium strawberries for this recipe. If your berries are quite large, cut them into 1-inch pieces instead of quartering them.

Don't hull your strawberries before washing them; they may get water-logged and lose flavor.

Start to finish: **20 minutes**
Makes **about 4 cups**

2 pounds strawberries, washed, dried, hulled and quartered

¼ cup white sugar

4 teaspoons grated lime zest

½ teaspoon kosher salt

In a large bowl, use a potato masher or fork to mash 2 cups of the strawberries until few chunks remain. Stir in the sugar, lime zest and salt. Fold in the remaining strawberries. Cover and let sit until syrupy, at least 15 minutes or up to 2 hours.

TANGY WHIPPED CREAM

Adding a dollop of sour cream to heavy cream can balance the sweetness of a cake and help define the flavor of mediocre fruit. We also add brown sugar and vanilla, lending a depth and complexity to a treat that typically is one note flat.

Start to finish: **5 minutes**
Makes **about 2 cups**

1 cup heavy cream

¼ cup sour cream

2 tablespoons packed brown sugar

½ teaspoon vanilla extract

Pinch of kosher salt

In the bowl of a stand mixer, combine all ingredients. Using the whisk attachment, mix on low until uniform and frothy, about 30 seconds. Increase speed to medium-high and whip until soft peaks form, 1 to 2 minutes.

French Spice Bread (*Pain d'Épices*)

Start to finish: 1 hour 25 minutes (10 minutes active), plus cooling
Makes one 9-inch loaf

228 grams (1¾ cups) all-purpose flour

100 grams (1 cup) almond flour

1½ teaspoons ground cinnamon

1 teaspoon baking soda

1 teaspoon ground ginger

½ teaspoon ground mace

Kosher salt and ground black pepper

8 tablespoons (1 stick) salted butter, melted, plus more for the pan

334 grams (1 cup) honey

½ cup whole milk

2 large eggs

2 tablespoons minced crystallized ginger

1 tablespoon finely grated fresh ginger

2 teaspoons grated orange zest

Honey-based spice breads and cakes have been produced in one form or another throughout Europe since the Middle Ages. For good reason: The hygroscopic honey retains moisture, ensuring the breads remain moist during storage. Its antibacterial properties also act as a preservative. Meanwhile, the spices—and therefore the flavor—only improve with time. We wanted a lighter, less sweet alternative to the more common gingerbread, something that tasted as good straight up as it did toasted and topped with butter and marmalade for a quick breakfast or afternoon-coffee accompaniment. This French version is just that. For a fruitier version, add 1 cup golden raisins, chopped dates, figs or dried apricots. Melting the butter in a liquid measuring cup in the microwave, then using the same cup for the honey, made it easy to measure out and add the honey; it slid right out. For maximum spice flavor, we used pepper and three kinds of ginger. If you can't find crystallized (candied) ginger, just skip it; the cake still will be delicious. And if you can't find ground mace, substitute ¼ teaspoon each of ground nutmeg and allspice.

Don't use baking spray in place of butter. While spray is fine in many situations, butter helps create the dark crust that sets pain d'épices apart from other quick breads. Use melted butter and a pastry brush to liberally coat the inside of the pan.

1. Heat the oven to 325°F with a rack in the upper-middle position. Coat the bottom and sides of a 9-by-5-inch loaf pan with butter. In a medium bowl, whisk together both flours, the cinnamon, baking soda, ground ginger, mace and ½ teaspoon each of salt and pepper. In a large bowl, whisk together the butter and honey until smooth. Add the milk, eggs, crystallized ginger, fresh ginger and orange zest; whisk until thoroughly combined.

2. Add the flour mixture to the wet ingredients and fold only until no dry flour remains. Transfer the batter to the prepared pan. Bake until firm to the touch and a toothpick inserted at the center comes out with a few moist crumbs, 65 to 70 minutes. Let cool in the pan on a wire rack for 10 minutes. Remove from the pan and let cool completely, about 2 hours.

Brown Butter–Cardamom
Banana Bread

Start to finish: **1 hour 15 minutes (25 minutes active)**
Makes **one 9-inch loaf**

260 grams (2 cups) all-purpose flour

1 teaspoon baking powder

1 teaspoon baking soda

1 teaspoon kosher salt

8 tablespoons (1 stick) salted butter,
plus more for the pan

1¼ teaspoons ground cardamom

2 cups mashed bananas
(about 4 very ripe bananas)

149 grams (¾ cup packed)
dark brown sugar

2 large eggs

2 teaspoons vanilla extract

1 tablespoon white sugar

Banana bread is one of the most common baked goods made at home. Unfortunately, most taste just that–common. We wanted a revved-up recipe that would produce flavorful results without additional effort. So we paired one of banana's most complementary spices—cardamom—with nutty browned butter. Toasting the cardamom briefly in the hot butter intensified the flavor. For just the right texture, we found we needed two leaveners. Baking powder gave the bread lift; baking soda resulted in a well-browned top and a dense crumb. Measuring the bananas in a 1-cup dry measuring cup was important; the difference in moisture between four small and four large bananas could throw off the balance of the ingredients. While we preferred the deeper flavor of dark brown sugar here, light brown works just as well. Sprinkling granulated sugar over the top of the loaf just before baking created a crisp, brown crust that we loved.

1. Heat the oven to 350°F with a rack in the upper-middle position. Lightly coat a 9-by-5-inch loaf pan with butter. In a large bowl, whisk together the flour, baking powder, baking soda and salt.

2. In a medium saucepan over medium, melt the butter. Once melted, continue to cook, swirling the pan often, until the butter is fragrant and deep brown, 2 to 5 minutes. Remove pan from the heat and immediately whisk in the cardamom. Carefully add the bananas (the butter will sizzle and bubble up) and whisk until combined. Add the brown sugar, eggs and vanilla, then whisk until smooth. Add the banana mixture to the flour mixture and, using a silicone spatula, fold until just combined and no dry flour remains.

3. Transfer the batter to the prepared pan and sprinkle evenly with the white sugar. Bake until the loaf is well browned, the top is cracked and a toothpick inserted at the center comes out clean, 50 to 55 minutes, rotating the pan halfway through. Cool the bread in the pan on a wire rack for 10 minutes, then turn out the loaf and cool completely before serving. Cooled bread can be wrapped tightly and stored at room temperature for up to 4 days or refrigerated for a week.

Small Sweets

Chocolate Meringue Cookies / 403

Lamingtons / 404

Chocolate-Almond Spice Cookies / 407

Triple Ginger Scones
with Chocolate Chunks / 409

Tahini Swirl Brownies / 411

Rosemary–Pine Nut Cornmeal
Cookies / 412

Semolina Polvorones / 414

Swedish Gingersnaps (*Pepparkakor*) / 417

Date-Stuffed Semolina Cookies
(*Ma'amoul*) / 418

Australian Oat-Coconut Cookies
(*Anzac Biscuits*) / 421

Rye Chocolate Chip Cookies / 422

10

Chocolate Meringue Cookies

Start to finish: 1 hour 10 minutes (40 minutes active)
Makes 24 cookies

8 ounces bittersweet chocolate, finely chopped, divided

4 tablespoons (½ stick) salted butter, cut into 4 pieces

20 grams (¼ cup) cocoa powder

½ teaspoon instant espresso powder

3 large egg whites

145 grams (⅔ cup) packed light brown sugar

1 teaspoon vanilla extract

½ teaspoon kosher salt

These rich, yet airy flourless chocolate cookies have crisp edges and chewy interiors. They rely on whipped egg whites for their structure. To ensure your whites attain the proper volume with beating, make sure the mixer bowl, whisk and whisk attachment are perfectly clean and without any trace of grease or fat. Either Dutch-processed or natural cocoa works well in this recipe. Leftover cookies can be stored in an airtight container for up to three days; the edges will lose their crispness but the cookies will still taste good.

Don't omit the step of heating the egg whites and sugar over the saucepan of simmering water. This ensures the sugar fully dissolves so the cookies bake up with shiny, crisp exteriors. But also make sure you don't overheat the mixture (100°F is the ideal temperature), which can cause the whites to cook. Also, the melted chocolate mixture should still be warm when you fold in the whipped egg whites. If it has cooled and thickened, it will be impossible to fold in the whites without deflating them. If needed, before folding in the whites, return the bowl of chocolate to the saucepan and re-melt the mixture.

1. Heat the oven to 350°F with racks in the upper- and lower-middle positions. Line 2 baking sheets with kitchen parchment. Measure out 2½ ounces (½ cup) of the chopped chocolate and set aside.

2. In a medium saucepan over high, bring 1 inch of water to a boil, then reduce heat to maintain a simmer. In a medium bowl, combine the remaining 5½ ounces chopped chocolate, the butter, cocoa and espresso powder. Set the bowl on the saucepan over the simmering water (the bottom of the bowl should not touch the water) and let the mixture melt until completely smooth, stirring often with a silicone spatula. Set aside to cool slightly; keep the saucepan and water over the heat.

3. In the bowl of a stand mixer, whisk together the egg whites, sugar, vanilla and salt. Set the bowl on the saucepan over the simmering water and, while whisking constantly, heat the mixture to 100°F. Attach the bowl to the mixer fitted with the whisk attachment and whip on medium-high until the mixture holds soft peaks when the whisk is lifted, 3 to 4 minutes.

4. Using a silicone spatula, fold ⅓ of the egg white mixture into the chocolate mixture until almost completely combined. Add the remaining egg whites and fold until a few streaks of white remain. Add the reserved chopped chocolate and fold gently until no white streaks remain.

5. Drop the batter in 2-tablespoon mounds spaced 1½ inches apart on the prepared sheets. Bake until the tops have cracked but the interiors still look moist, 12 to 14 minutes, switching and rotating the sheets halfway through. Cool on the baking sheets for 10 minutes, then transfer the cookies to a wire rack to cool completely, about 30 minutes.

Lamingtons

Start to finish: 4½ hours (50 minutes active)
Makes 16 individual cakes

For the cake:

150 grams (1¼ cups) cake flour, plus more for pan

3 large egg whites, room temperature

½ cup whole milk, room temperature

½ teaspoon vanilla extract

214 grams (1 cup) white sugar

1 teaspoon baking powder

½ teaspoon kosher salt

6 tablespoons (¾ stick) salted butter, cut into 6 pieces, room temperature

For the glaze:

¾ cup whole milk, room temperature

4 ounces unsweetened chocolate, chopped

¼ cup refined coconut oil

124 grams (1 cup) powdered sugar

⅛ teaspoon kosher salt

225 grams (2½ cups) unsweetened shredded coconut

The inspiration for these Lamingtons—small chocolate-coated, coconut-covered cakes from Australia—came from Le Petit Grain boulangerie in Paris. We skipped the customary jam filling, but these treats are so delicious we don't think you'll notice. We bake a simple butter cake in a square pan, then cut the cooled cake into two-bite cubes. Freezing the cubes before coating them with the chocolate glaze allows for easy handling, and helps the coating firm up quickly. The cake can be cut and frozen up to two days in advance, but if you freeze it for more than just an hour or so, be sure to wrap it well to protect it from drying out. Finished Lamingtons will keep in an airtight container in the refrigerator for one day or in the freezer for several days (if frozen, let stand at room temperature for about 30 minutes before serving).

Don't cut the cake while it's warm. Allow it to cool completely, about 2 hours, so it cuts cleanly and neatly. And make sure to use a serrated knife; a regular knife will crush the cake's delicate crumb.

1. To make the cake, heat the oven to 325°F with a rack in the middle position. Mist the interior of an 8-inch square baking pan with cooking spray, dust with flour, then tap out the excess. Line the bottom with kitchen parchment. In a 2-cup liquid measuring cup or small bowl, whisk together the egg whites, milk and vanilla; set aside.

2. In a stand mixer fitted with the paddle attachment, combine the flour, sugar, baking powder and salt, then mix on low until combined, about 10 seconds. With the mixer running, add the butter one piece at a time. Once all the butter has been added, continue mixing until sandy and no large butter pieces remain, 2 to 3 minutes. With the mixer still running, pour in all but ¼ cup of the egg-milk mixture and mix until combined. Increase to medium-high and beat until the mixture is light and fluffy, about 1 minute. Reduce to medium, then slowly add the remaining egg mixture, scraping the bowl once or twice.

3. Transfer the batter to the prepared pan and spread evenly. Bake until light golden brown and a toothpick inserted at the center comes out clean, 30 to 35 minutes. Cool in the pan on a wire rack for 10 minutes, then run a paring knife around the edges to loosen. Invert the cake onto a large plate, lift off the pan and remove and discard the parchment. Re-invert the cake onto the rack to be right side up and cool completely, about 2 hours.

4. Line a rimmed baking sheet with kitchen parchment. Using a serrated knife, trim off the edges of the cake, then cut the cake into 16 even squares. Place the squares on the prepared baking sheet, cover with plastic wrap and freeze until firm, at least 1 hour or up to 2 days.

5. To make the glaze, in a medium saucepan over high, bring 1 inch of water to a boil, then reduce to medium-low. In a medium heat-proof bowl that fits on top of the saucepan, combine the milk, chocolate and coconut oil. Set the bowl on the saucepan, over the simmering water, and warm the mixture, whisking gently and occasionally, until melted and smooth. Remove the bowl from the pan, then whisk in the powdered sugar and salt; reserve the saucepan and warm water. Place the coconut in a small bowl.

6. Remove the cake squares from the freezer. Using your fingers, dip 1 cake square into the chocolate and turn to coat each side, then scrape off any excess against the edge of the bowl. Toss in the coconut to coat on all sides, then return to the baking sheet. Repeat with the remaining cake squares, chocolate glaze and coconut. If the glaze cools and becomes too thick, return the bowl to the saucepan and gently rewarm the glaze. Let the coated cakes stand until the glaze sets slightly, about 30 minutes.

Chocolate-Almond Spice Cookies

Start to finish: 1¼ hours (30 minutes active), plus cooling
Makes about 24 cookies

¾ teaspoon ground cinnamon

½ teaspoon ground cardamom

½ teaspoon ground ginger

339 grams (1⅓ cups plus ¼ cup white sugar

250 grams (2½ cups) blanched almond flour

26 grams (¼ cup) cocoa powder

1 teaspoon kosher salt

4 egg large whites, lightly beaten

1½ teaspoons vanilla extract

5 ounces bittersweet chocolate, finely chopped

This recipe is a loose interpretation of the Swiss chocolate-almond holiday cookie known as Basler brunsli. Traditionally, the dough is rolled and cut into shapes before baking, but we opted for an easier drop cookie studded with bits of chocolate. Even without butter, these cookies are intensely rich—and they happen to be gluten-free, too. Both Dutch-processed cocoa and natural cocoa work. If you have a 2-tablespoon spring-loaded scoop, use it for portioning the dough; otherwise, two soup spoons get the job done. The dough can be made ahead and refrigerated in an airtight container for up to 24 hours; bring to room temperature before shaping and baking. The baked and cooled cookies keep well in a well-sealed container at room temperature for up to two days.

Don't skip toasting the almond flour; it gives the cookies a fuller, deeper flavor. But don't forget to allow the almond flour to cool after toasting; if the flour is too hot when the egg whites are added, the whites will cook. Take care not to overbake the cookies or they will become tough.

1. **Heat the oven to 375°F** with racks in the upper- and lower-middle positions. Line 2 baking sheets with kitchen parchment. In a small bowl, stir together the cinnamon, cardamom and ginger. Measure ¼ teaspoon of the spice mixture into another small bowl, stir in the 54 grams (¼ cup) sugar and set aside.

2. **In a 12-inch skillet** over medium, combine the almond flour and remaining spice mixture. Cook, stirring frequently and breaking up any lumps, until fragrant and lightly browned, 5 to 7 minutes. Transfer to a large bowl and let cool until barely warm to the touch, 15 to 20 minutes.

3. **Into the almond flour mixture,** whisk in the remaining 285 grams (1⅓ cups) sugar, the cocoa and salt. Use a spatula to stir in the egg whites and vanilla until evenly moistened. Stir in the chocolate. The dough will be sticky.

4. **Using two soup spoons,** drop a few 2-tablespoon portions of dough into the spiced sugar, then gently roll to coat evenly. Arrange the sugar-coated balls on the prepared baking sheets about 2 inches apart. Repeat with the remaining dough.

5. **Bake until the cookies** have cracks in their surfaces and a toothpick inserted into a cookie at the center of the baking sheets comes out with few crumbs attached, 12 to 15 minutes, switching and rotating the sheets halfway through. Let the cookies cool on the baking sheets for 5 minutes, then transfer to a rack to cool completely.

Triple Ginger Scones
with Chocolate Chunks

Start to finish: 1¼ hours (40 minutes active) / Makes 12 scones

455 grams (3½ cups) all-purpose flour, plus more for dusting

67 grams (5 tablespoons) white sugar

4 teaspoons baking powder

½ teaspoon baking soda

2 tablespoons ground ginger

1½ teaspoons grated nutmeg

2½ teaspoons kosher salt

1½ teaspoons ground black pepper

1¼ cups cold buttermilk

2 tablespoons finely grated fresh ginger

1 tablespoon grated orange zest

18 tablespoons (2 sticks plus 2 tablespoons) salted butter, cut into ½-inch pieces and chilled

150 grams (1 cup) roughly chopped bittersweet chocolate

154 grams (1 cup) finely chopped crystallized ginger

1 large egg, beaten

These rich, flavor-packed oversized scones are the creation of Briana Holt of Tandem Coffee + Bakery in Portland, Maine. Ginger in three different forms—ground, fresh and crystallized—give these breakfast pastries plenty of kick, as does ground black pepper. Keep both the butter and buttermilk in the refrigerator until you're ready to use them so they stay as cold as possible, which makes the dough easier to handle. Holt recommends serving the scones after they've cooled to room temperature, but we also loved them warm, while the chocolate is soft and melty.

Don't worry if the flour-butter mixture doesn't form a cohesive dough immediately after all the buttermilk has been added. In fact, it will be very crumbly, but a brief kneading and the act of shaping and pressing the mixture into disks will bring it together. When kneading, though, take care not to overwork the dough, which will result in tough, not tender, scones.

1. Heat the oven to 375°F with racks in the upper- and lower-middle positions. Line 2 rimmed baking sheets with kitchen parchment. In a large bowl, whisk together the flour, sugar, baking powder, baking soda, ground ginger, nutmeg, salt and pepper. In a 2-cup liquid measuring cup or a small bowl, stir together the buttermilk, grated ginger and orange zest.

2. To a food processor, add about ½ of the flour mixture and scatter the butter over the top. Pulse until the butter is in large pea-sized pieces, 10 to 12 pulses. Transfer to the bowl with the remaining flour mixture. Add the chocolate and crystallized ginger, then toss with your hands until evenly combined. Pour in about ⅓ of the buttermilk mixture and toss just a few times with your hands, making sure to scrape along the bottom of the bowl, until the liquid is absorbed. Add the remaining buttermilk in 2 more additions, tossing after each. After the final addition of buttermilk, toss until no dry, floury bits remain. The mixture will be quite crumbly and will not form a cohesive dough.

3. Lightly dust the counter with flour, turn the mixture out onto it, then give it a final toss. Divide it into 2 even piles, gathering each into a mound, then very briefly knead each mound; it's fine if the mixture is still somewhat crumbly. Gather each mound into a ball, then press firmly into a cohesive 5-inch disk about 1½ inches thick. Brush the tops of each disk lightly with beaten egg. Using a chef's knife, cut each disk in half, then cut each half into 3 wedges. Place 6 wedges on each prepared baking sheet, spaced evenly apart.

4. Bake until the scones are deep golden brown, 27 to 30 minutes, switching and rotating the baking sheets halfway through. Cool on the baking sheets on wire racks for 5 minutes, then transfer directly to a rack and cool for at least another 5 minutes. Serve warm or at room temperature.

Tahini Swirl **Brownies**

Start to finish: 40 minutes
Makes **16** brownies

---

4 tablespoons (½ stick) salted butter plus more for pan

4 ounces bittersweet chocolate, finely chopped

16 grams (3 tablespoons) cocoa powder

3 large eggs

240 grams (1 cup plus 2 tablespoons) white sugar

1 tablespoon vanilla extract

1 teaspoon kosher salt

180 grams (¾ cup) tahini

43 grams (⅓ cup) all-purpose flour

Tired of one-note brownies, we looked to the Middle East for a grown-up version of this American standard. We loved the halvah brownie from Tatte Bakery & Cafe in Cambridge, Massachusetts. Halvah is fudge-like candy from the Middle East made from tahini, a rich sesame seed paste. At Milk Street, we fiddled with how much tahini to use—its fat content was the major problem. To start, we reduced the tahini and the amount of butter, substituted cocoa powder for some of the chocolate and added an egg to cut through the rich brownie base. Then, we reversed our thinking and instead of trying to add tahini to a classic brownie batter, we added chocolate to a tahini base. For a final touch, we swirled reserved tahini batter into the chocolate to create a visual and textural contrast and let the tahini flavor shine. The best way to marble the brownies was to run the tip of a paring knife through the dollops of batter. Be sure to fully bake these brownies—they are extremely tender, even wet, if not baked through. The tahini's flavor and color will intensify over time, so make a day ahead for a more pronounced sesame taste.

Don't skip stirring the tahini before measuring; the solids often sink to the bottom.

1. Heat the oven to 350°F with a rack in the middle position. Line an 8-inch square baking pan with 2 pieces of foil with excess hanging over the edges on all sides. Lightly coat with butter.

2. In a medium saucepan over medium, melt the butter. Off heat add the chocolate and cocoa, whisking until smooth.

3. In a large bowl, whisk the eggs, sugar, vanilla and salt until slightly thickened, about 1 minute. Whisk in the tahini. Fold in the flour until just incorporated. Transfer ½ cup of the mixture to a small bowl. Add the chocolate mixture to the remaining tahini mixture and fold until fully combined.

4. Pour the batter into the prepared pan, spreading evenly. Dollop the reserved tahini mixture over the top, then swirl the batters together. Bake until the edges are set but the center remains moist, 28 to 32 minutes. Cool in the pan on a wire rack for 30 minutes. Use the foil to lift the brownies out of the pan and cool on the rack for at least another 30 minutes; the longer they cool, the better they cut. Cut into 2-inch squares.

Rosemary–Pine Nut Cornmeal Cookies

Start to finish: 1½ hours (30 minutes active), plus cooling
Makes 24 cookies

195 grams (1½ cups)
all-purpose flour

72 grams (½ cup) fine cornmeal

107 grams (½ cup) white sugar

1 tablespoon minced fresh rosemary

2 teaspoons grated orange zest

16 tablespoons (2 sticks)
salted butter, softened, divided

1 cup pine nuts

63 grams (2 tablespoons) honey

This cookie is sweet enough to track as a treat, but pairs as well with Parmesan as it does a glass of milk. Our inspiration was a hazelnut-rosemary biscotti by Claudia Fleming, the former pastry chef of New York's Gramercy Tavern who famously blended savory flavorings into classically sweet dishes. We chose to reimagine Fleming's biscotti as crisp, pat-in-the-pan shortbread. Same crunchy texture without the hassle of rolling, slicing and twice-baking. The dough got sticky in a warm kitchen, but 10 minutes in the refrigerator fixed that. Letting the cookies cool completely before cutting produced uneven shards; 15 minutes was the sweet spot for a sturdy but sliceable texture.

Don't use dried rosemary. Fresh has a better flavor and softer texture.

1. Heat the oven to 325°F with a rack in the lower-middle position. Line a 13-by-9-inch baking pan with foil, letting the edges hang over the long sides of the pan. In a bowl, combine the flour and cornmeal; set aside.

2. In the bowl of a stand mixer fitted with the paddle attachment, combine the sugar, rosemary and orange zest. Mix on low until the sugar is moistened and begins to clump, 1 to 2 minutes. Add 14 tablespoons of the butter, increase to medium-high and beat until light and fluffy, 3 to 5 minutes, scraping down the bowl twice. Reduce to low and gradually add the flour mixture (this should take about 30 seconds). Scrape down the bowl and mix on low until the dough forms around the paddle, about 1 minute.

3. Crumble the dough evenly over the bottom of the prepared pan. Coat the bottom of a dry measuring cup with oil, then use it to press the dough into an even layer. Sprinkle the pine nuts over the dough in a single layer and press down firmly.

4. In a small bowl, microwave the remaining 2 tablespoons of butter until melted. Add the honey and stir until combined. Brush the mixture over the bars, then bake until the top is deep golden brown, 40 to 45 minutes.

5. Let the bars cool in the pan for 15 minutes. Using the foil, lift the bars and transfer to a cutting board. Cut into 24 pieces. Let the bars cool completely on a wire rack before serving. The cooled cookies can be stored in an airtight container at room temperature for up to 1 week.

Semolina **Polvorones**

Start to finish: 3 hours (45 minutes active), plus cooling time
Makes 24 cookies

54 grams (¼ cup) white sugar

1½ teaspoons grated orange zest

57 grams (½ cup) coarsely chopped walnuts

128 grams (¾ cup) semolina flour

½ teaspoon cinnamon

2 large egg yolks

½ teaspoon vanilla extract

⅛ teaspoon kosher salt

87 grams (⅔ cup) all-purpose flour

10 tablespoons (1¼ sticks) salted butter, cut into ½-inch pieces and chilled

Powdered sugar, to coat

Polvorones are Spanish cookies popular across Latin America, Spain and the Phillipines. They're basically a simple shortbread—and sadly can be simply bland. Our inspiration was a lesser-known Basque variation made with semolina and spiced with orange zest and cinnamon. We also borrowed a Filipino technique of toasting the flour first. In fact, we toasted both our walnuts and semolina to give the cookies deep, complex flavor. Adding the ground cinnamon to the hot semolina bloomed it, bringing out its aroma. Flattening the cookies too much made them delicate; ½-inch-thick discs held up best when tossed in powdered sugar. Likewise, the cookies are fragile when hot out of the oven, so let them cool several minutes before transferring to a wire rack. You can bake both sheets of cookies at once on the upper and lower-middle racks, but we got more even browning baking one sheet at a time.

Don't be alarmed if the semolina smokes slightly during toasting. And don't coat the cookies with powdered sugar until you're ready to serve them; they look best immediately after they're sugared.

1. In a food processor, pulse together the white sugar and orange zest. In a 10-inch skillet over medium, toast the walnuts, stirring, until lightly browned and fragrant, 3 to 5 minutes. Transfer to the food processor. Wipe the skillet clean, then add the semolina and toast, stirring, until beginning to brown, 2 to 3 minutes. Reduce heat to medium-low and toast, stirring constantly, until speckled, golden brown and fragrant, another 2 to 3 minutes. Off the heat, stir in the cinnamon, then transfer to a plate and cool to room temperature.

2. In a small bowl, use a fork to beat the yolks and vanilla. Add the salt to the walnuts and sugar, then process until coarsely ground, about 10 seconds. Add the flour and semolina mixture, then process until combined, about 5 seconds. Add the butter and pulse until the mixture resembles damp sand,

10 to 12 pulses. Drizzle in the yolk mixture and pulse until large clumps gather around the blade. Transfer the dough to the counter and knead briefly, then wrap in plastic wrap and refrigerate for at least 1 hour and up to 2 days.

3. Heat the oven to 325°F with a rack in the middle position. Line 2 baking sheets with kitchen parchment. Roll the dough into 24 balls (1 tablespoon each) and arrange evenly on the baking sheets. Press the balls gently into discs about ½ inch thick.

4. One at a time, bake each sheet until well browned, 23 to 28 minutes, rotating halfway through. Let the cookies cool on the sheet for 10 minutes, then transfer to a wire rack and cool completely. Just before serving, gently drop each cookie into powdered sugar to coat.

Swedish Gingersnaps (*Pepparkakor*)

Start to finish: 3½ hours (30 minutes active), plus cooling
Makes about 24 cookies

217 grams (1⅔ cups)
all-purpose flour

¼ teaspoon baking soda

8 tablespoons (1 stick) salted butter

100 grams (½ cup packed)
dark brown sugar

78 grams (6 tablespoons) white sugar

¼ cup dark corn syrup

2½ tablespoons ground ginger

1 tablespoon finely grated
fresh ginger

1 teaspoon cinnamon

¾ teaspoon finely grated orange zest

¾ teaspoon kosher salt

½ teaspoon ground cloves

¼ teaspoon ground black pepper

⅛ teaspoon cayenne pepper

1 large egg

Turbinado sugar, for sprinkling

In search of a cookie that would deliver grown-up gingerbread flavor, we came across Swedish gingersnaps, a cookie that goes as well with wine as coffee. For these cookies, we needed to balance dark brown and white sugars to get a workable dough that crisped properly. Baking soda helped with browning and gave the cookies lift, making them crunchy but not hard. The pepparkakor's distinctive spice came from ground and fresh ginger, black pepper and cayenne, and we pumped up all of them. The dough can be made up to two days in advance. The cookies keep for up to a week in an airtight container.

Don't portion the dough right after mixing; it will be too soft and sticky. Because it is made with melted butter (to avoid using a stand mixer), the dough must chill first.

1. In a large bowl, whisk together the flour and baking soda; set aside. In a medium saucepan over medium, combine the butter, both sugars, the corn syrup, both gingers, the cinnamon, orange zest, salt, cloves, black pepper and cayenne. As the butter melts, whisk until the sugar dissolves and the mixture begins to simmer. Remove from the heat. Cool until just warm to the touch, about 30 minutes.

2. Whisk the egg into the cooled mixture until smooth. Add to the dry ingredients and fold until no dry flour remains. Refrigerate for at least 2 hours or up to 2 days.

3. Heat the oven to 350°F with racks in the upper- and lower-middle positions. Line 2 baking sheets with kitchen parchment. Working with a tablespoon of dough at a time, use dampened hands to roll into balls. Arrange 12 dough balls on each baking sheet, spacing evenly.

4. Lay a sheet of plastic wrap over the balls on each sheet and use the bottom of a dry measuring cup to flatten each to about ¼ inch thick. Remove the plastic and sprinkle each cookie with a generous pinch of turbinado sugar. Bake until richly browned, 14 to 16 minutes, switching and rotating the baking sheets halfway through. Cool on the sheet for 10 minutes, then transfer to a wire rack and cool completely.

Date-Stuffed Semolina Cookies (*Ma'amoul*)

Start to finish: **1 hour (30 minutes active)**, plus cooling
Makes **36 cookies**

For the dough:

170 grams (1 cup) semolina flour

130 grams (1 cup) all-purpose flour

71 grams (⅓ cup) white sugar

½ teaspoon kosher salt

10 tablespoons (1¼ sticks) salted butter, cut into 10 pieces and chilled

2 tablespoons plain whole-milk yogurt

2 teaspoons rose water

1 teaspoon vanilla extract

Powdered sugar, for dusting (optional)

For the filling:

5 ounces (1 cup) medjool dates, pitted

4 ounces (1 cup) walnut pieces, lightly toasted and cooled

1 tablespoon honey

2 teaspoons grated orange zest

½ teaspoon ground cardamom

¼ teaspoon kosher salt

These semolina-based cookies stuffed with dates, nuts or other fillings are a popular Middle Eastern treat often served on holidays. Though they are often made using a complex molding technique, we simplified and came up with a rolling method anyone could do. A combination of semolina and all-purpose flours gave our cookies a rich, crumbly texture and complex flavor. Chilled butter prevented the dough from getting overly sticky, but if your kitchen is particularly warm and the dough is soft and shiny after mixing, refrigerate it for 30 minutes before proceeding. Covering the dough with plastic wrap while making the filling and rolling it out between sheets of kitchen parchment further prevented the dough from drying out. If the dough begins to crack while shaping the cookies, gently pinch the cracks back together. You can substitute pistachios for the walnuts, but the filling will take an extra minute or so to form into a paste. While rose water is traditional, a good substitute is 2 teaspoons each of orange juice and orange zest, plus ¼ teaspoon almond extract. These cookies keep for up to three days in an airtight container at room temperature.

Don't use deglet dates. Soft, plump medjool dates were essential to producing the proper consistency of the paste, and they made for a moister, more flavorful filling.

1. Heat the oven to 325°F with racks in the upper- and lower-middle positions. Line 2 baking sheets with kitchen parchment.

2. For the dough, in a food processor combine both flours, the white sugar and salt. Process until combined, about 5 seconds. Add the butter and process until the butter is completely incorporated, 15 to 20 seconds. Add the yogurt, rose water and vanilla, then process until the dough comes together, about 1 minute. Transfer to the counter and knead until the dough is smooth, then cover with plastic wrap and set aside.

3. For the filling, in the processor, combine all filling ingredients and process until a smooth paste forms, 45 to 60 seconds.

4. To assemble the cookies, set the dough between 2 sheets of kitchen parchment and roll into a 12-by-9-inch rectangle, cutting and patching the dough together as needed. Cut the dough into thirds lengthwise to form three 12-by-3-inch strips. Divide the filling into thirds and roll each portion into a 12-inch rope. Place one rope down the middle of each strip of dough, then wrap the dough completely around the filling. Pinch the seam to seal. Place each roll seam side down and cut each crosswise into 12 rounds, gently reshaping if necessary. Evenly space the cookies seam side down on the prepared baking sheets.

5. Bake until the bottoms are golden but the tops are still pale, 25 to 30 minutes, switching and rotating the sheets halfway through. Cool the cookies on the sheets for 5 minutes, then transfer to a wire rack and cool completely, about 30 minutes. Dust with powdered sugar, if desired.

Australian Oat-Coconut Cookies
(*Anzac Biscuits*)

Start to finish: **30 minutes** / Makes **24 cookies**

---

125 grams (1¼ cups)
old-fashioned rolled oats

112 grams (1¼ cups) unsweetened
shredded coconut

158 grams (1 cup plus 2 tablespoons)
whole-wheat flour

10 tablespoons (1¼ sticks)
salted butter

100 grams (½ cup packed)
dark brown sugar

¼ cup brewed coffee

63 grams (3 tablespoons) honey

2 teaspoons vanilla extract

1 teaspoon grated orange zest

1 teaspoon baking soda

In Australia and New Zealand, Anzac Day (April 25) honors servicemen and women past and present. The date marks the day the Australian and New Zealand Army Corps (ANZAC) landed at Gallipoli in Turkey during World War I. There are a number of traditions associated with the day, including the Dawn Service marking the pre-dawn landing on Gallipoli. And there are more lighthearted rituals, such as the drinking of "gunfire coffee"—black coffee with a splash of rum—and the eating of Anzac biscuits, an oat and coconut cookie that is both simple and delicious. We wanted a bolder more modern rendition. Though golden syrup is traditional, we found honey and dark brown sugar were good stand-ins. And toasting the coconut and the oats deepened the flavor of the biscuits. Be sure to have all ingredients measured beforehand; it's important to combine everything as soon as possible after the baking soda has been incorporated into the wet ingredients. Underbaking the cookies gave them chewy centers. An oiled 1 tablespoon measuring spoon helped portion out the cookies.

Don't roll these cookies into balls. It will compress them and result in dense cookies.

1. Heat the oven to 350°F with racks in the upper- and lower-middle positions. Line 2 baking sheets with kitchen parchment. In a large skillet over medium-high, toast the oats, stirring often, until fragrant and beginning to brown, about 5 minutes. Reduce the heat to medium-low and add the coconut. Toast until golden, stirring constantly, 1 to 2 minutes. Transfer to a large bowl. Stir in the flour. Wipe out the skillet.

2. Return the skillet to medium-low and add the butter, sugar, coffee, honey, vanilla and orange zest. Cook, whisking, until the butter melts and the mixture boils. Off heat, add the baking soda and

stir until completely mixed, pale and foamy. Add to the oatmeal mixture and stir until just combined.

3. Scoop or drop heaping tablespoons of dough, spaced about 2 inches apart, onto the prepared baking sheets. Bake until the cookies have risen and are deep golden brown but still soft at the center, 8 to 10 minutes, switching and rotating the pans halfway through. Cool on the pans for 5 minutes, then transfer to a wire rack to cool completely.

Rye Chocolate Chip Cookies

Start to finish: 1 hour (20 minutes active), plus cooling
Makes 24 cookies

---

130 grams (1 cup) all-purpose flour

¾ teaspoon kosher salt

½ teaspoon baking soda

140 grams (1 cup) finely ground
rye flour (see note)

12 tablespoons (1½ sticks) salted
butter, cut into pieces and chilled

268 grams (1¼ cups) white sugar

2 large eggs

1 tablespoon molasses,
preferably blackstrap

1 tablespoon vanilla extract

1¼ cups good-quality dark chocolate
chips or 7½ ounces bittersweet
chocolate, roughly chopped

113 grams (1 cup) pecans, toasted
and chopped (optional)

We've eaten plenty of Toll House chocolate chip cookies. And while they're good, we wanted something different—a more complex cookie with a robust flavor that could balance the sugar and chocolate. We found inspiration on a visit to Claire Ptak's Violet bakery in London, where she's a fan of switching things up. Think rye flour for an apricot upside-down cake. Rye is a little bitter, a little savory, and it makes the perfect counterpoint for the sugary high notes of a chocolate chip cookie. First, though, we had to make a few adjustments. Rye has less gluten than all-purpose flour so it bakes differently and requires more liquid. We decided to go almost equal parts rye and all-purpose flours and recommend that you weigh for best results. Toasting the rye flour added complex, nutty flavor that balanced the sweetness of the cookies. Rye flour texture and flavor varies from brand to brand; we preferred the cookies' spread and chew when made with Arrowhead Mills Organic Rye, with Bob's Red Mill Dark Rye as a close second. A touch of molasses deepened the flavor and added slight bitterness. These cookies continue to firm up after they come out of the oven; it is best to check them early and err on the side of under-baking.

Don't use coarsely ground rye flour, as it absorbs moisture differently than finely ground, causing these cookies to spread too much during baking. Unfortunately, labels usually do not specify, but if the flour is visible in its packaging, coarsely ground has a granularity similar to cornmeal; finely ground rye has a powderiness much like all-purpose flour. We found Hodgson Mills rye flour, which is widely available, to be too coarse.

1. Heat the oven to 350°F with a rack in the upper-middle and lower-middle positions. Line 2 baking sheets with kitchen parchment. In a medium bowl, whisk together the all-purpose flour, salt and baking soda. In a 12-inch skillet over medium-high, toast the rye flour, stirring constantly, until fragrant and darkened by several shades, 3 to 5 minutes. Remove the skillet from the heat, add the butter and stir until melted, then transfer to a small bowl. Let cool for 10 minutes, stirring once or twice. The mixture will still be warm.

2. In a large bowl, whisk together the sugar, eggs, molasses and vanilla until smooth, about 30 seconds. Gradually stir in the rye mixture. Add the flour mixture and stir until combined. Stir in the chocolate chips and nuts, if using. Let rest until a finger pressed into the dough comes away cleanly, about 5 minutes.

3. Drop 2-tablespoon mounds of dough about 2 inches apart on the prepared baking sheets. Bake until the edges feel set when gently pressed but the centers are still soft, 13 to 15 minutes, switching and rotating the baking sheets halfway through. Let cool on the sheets for 5 minutes, then transfer to a wire rack and cool for 10 minutes.

Desserts

Caramel Oranges / 426

Chocolate, Prune and Rum Cake / 429

Austrian Plum Cake
(*Zwetschgenkuchen*) / 431

Foolproof Single-Crust Pie Dough / 432

Brown Sugar Tart / 434

Chocolate Tart / 437

Pumpkin Tart with Honey-Orange
Whipped Cream / 439

Lemon Tart / 441

Sherry-Soaked French Toast (*Torrijas*) / 443

Rye-on-Rye Sticky Toffee Pudding / 445

Browned Butter and
Coconut Loaf Cake / 446

Caprese Chocolate and Almond Torte / 449

Lemon-Buttermilk Pound Cake / 450

Chocolate-Hazelnut (*Gianduja*)
Crostata / 453

Senegalese Mango and
Coconut Rice Pudding / 455

French Apple Cake / 457

Maple-Whiskey Pudding Cakes / 458

French Walnut Tart / 460

Salted Butter Caramel
Chocolate Mousse / 463

Pistachio-Cardamom Cake / 464

Salted Peanut and Caramel Tart / 466

Toasted Bread Pudding
with Cream and Pistachios / 469

Tangerine-Almond Cake
with Bay-Infused Syrup / 470

Chocolate-Orange Tart / 472

Lemon-Almond Pound Cake / 474

Ricotta-Semolina Cheesecake / 479

Coconut Cashew Cake (*Sanwin Makin*) / 481

Macanese Sweet Potato Cake
(*Batatada*) / 483

Stovetop Chocolate Cake / 484

Spanish Almond Cake
(*Tarta de Santiago*) / 487

Maple–Browned Butter Pie / 488

11

Caramel Oranges

Start to finish: 40 minutes, plus chilling
Servings: 6

8 medium navel or Cara Cara oranges
(about 4½ pounds) or a combination

214 grams (1 cup) white sugar

2 cinnamon sticks or star anise pods

2 tablespoons salted butter

Oranges with caramel sauce were the hit of dessert carts across London in the 1960s. The dish never caught on in America and eventually faded overseas. But with its bright flavors and fresh-yet-familiar combination of fruit and caramel, we felt it was a classic worth reviving. Our inspiration was a recipe in Nigella Lawson's cookbook, "Forever Summer." She bathes peeled and sliced oranges in caramel spiked with cardamom, and suggests serving them with yogurt. Cardamom was good, but we preferred cinnamon sticks, as well as star anise. Cara Cara oranges are good if you can find them, but navel work fine. Be sure to remove all the bitter white pith. Substituting fresh orange juice for the water in a traditional caramel amplified the flavor of the dish tremendously.

1. Juice 2 of the oranges to yield ¾ cup juice. If 2 oranges don't yield enough juice, add water to measure ¾ cup total.

2. Slice off the top and bottom ½ inch from each of the remaining 6 oranges. Stand each orange on one of its flat ends and use a sharp knife to cut down and around the fruit, following the contours of the flesh, slicing away the skin and white pith. Turn each orange on its side and thinly slice crosswise into rounds. In a 13-by-9-inch baking dish, shingle the rounds in a single layer.

3. In a medium saucepan, combine the sugar, ¼ cup of the orange juice and the cinnamon or star anise; bring to a boil over medium-high, this should take 2 to 3 minutes. Cook, swirling the pan occasionally, until the sugar begins to color at the edges, another 3 to 5 minutes. The bubbles should go from thin and frothy to thick and shiny.

4. Reduce heat to medium-low and cook, swirling the pan often, until the sugar is coppery-brown, 1 to 3 minutes. Remove the pan from the heat, add the butter, then whisk until melted.

5. Add a splash of the remaining orange juice and whisk until smooth (the mixture will steam and bubble vigorously), then add the remaining orange juice and whisk until fully incorporated. If the caramel separates and sticks to the pan, return it to the heat and simmer until the hardened caramel dissolves.

6. Pour the caramel evenly over the oranges, cover with plastic wrap, then refrigerate for at least 3 hours and up to 6 hours.

7. Allowing the caramel to drip off into the baking dish, use a slotted spoon to transfer the oranges to a serving platter or plates. Remove and discard the cinnamon or star anise from the caramel, then whisk to recombine and mix in any juices. Pour the caramel over the oranges.

ORANGE CARAMEL SAUCE

Don't think about the caramel's color for the first few minutes. The sugar mixture will melt, frothing furiously as the heat increases and moisture evaporates, then finally subside into larger, shinier bubbles before it changes color. If the sugar browns too quickly, slide the pan off the heat and whisk steadily to incorporate air, which cools it.

Chocolate, Prune and **Rum Cake**

Start to finish: **1 hour 20 minutes (30 minutes active), plus cooling**
Servings: **12**

9 tablespoons (1 stick plus
1 tablespoon) salted butter
(1 tablespoon softened)

8 ounces pitted prunes
(about 1½ cups), finely chopped

⅓ cup dark rum

1 tablespoon molasses

12 ounces bittersweet chocolate,
finely chopped

6 large eggs, separated

125 grams (⅓ cup plus ¼ cup)
white sugar, divided

½ teaspoon kosher salt

Claire Ptak has a fairly revolutionary approach to baking—soft-whipped egg whites! undermixed batter!—that sets her apart from most bakers. We were smitten with her chocolate, prune and whiskey cake when we tasted it at her Violet bakery in East London. When we got the recipe back to Milk Street, we knew we needed to adjust it to be more approachable for the American home cook. Ptak uses almond flour in her batter, but we preferred the lighter, more mousse-like texture we got by leaving it out. We followed her lead in under whipping the egg whites and just barely mixing them into the batter. We found dark rum was delicious warm or cool and better complemented the molasses than whiskey. We preferred bar chocolates with 60 to 70 percent cacao. Chocolate chips contain stabilizers that can change the cake's texture; it's best to avoid them. We liked this served with whipped cream.

1. Heat the oven to 325°F with a rack in the middle position. Coat the bottom and sides of a 9-inch springform pan evenly with the 1 tablespoon of softened butter.

2. In a 2-cup microwave-safe liquid measuring cup, combine the prunes, rum and molasses. Microwave until the rum is bubbling, 45 to 60 seconds. Let sit for 15 minutes, stirring occasionally.

3. In a medium saucepan over medium, melt the remaining 8 tablespoons of butter. Remove the pan from the heat and immediately whisk in the chocolate until melted and completely smooth. In a large bowl, whisk together the egg yolks and 71 grams (⅓ cup) of the sugar until pale and glossy, about 30 seconds. Slowly add the melted chocolate mixture and whisk until smooth. Stir in the prune mixture.

4. Using a stand mixer with a whisk attachment, whip the egg whites and salt on medium-high until light and foamy, about 1 minute. With the mixer running, slowly sprinkle in the remaining 54 grams (¼ cup) of sugar and continue to whip until the whites are thick and glossy and hold soft peaks, about 1 minute.

5. Whisk a third of the whipped egg whites into the chocolate mixture to lighten it. Gently fold in the remaining whites with a rubber spatula until the batter is marbled but not fully blended.

6. Pour the batter into the prepared pan. If needed, smooth the top with a spatula. Bake until the edges of the cake are firm and cracked, 35 to 40 minutes. The center will be just set, but will jiggle. Cool the cake in the pan on a wire rack for at least 1 hour before serving. The cake will settle and sink as it cools.

Austrian Plum Cake
(*Zwetschgenkuchen*)

Start to finish: 1½ hours (10 minutes active) / Servings: 8

130 grams (1 cup) all-purpose flour, plus more for pan

107 grams (½ cup) white sugar, plus 2 tablespoons for sprinkling

¾ teaspoon baking powder

½ teaspoon kosher salt

8 tablespoons (1 stick) salted butter, cut into 8 pieces, room temperature

1 large egg, plus 1 large egg yolk

1½ teaspoons vanilla extract

1¼ pounds ripe but firm medium plums, quartered and pitted

Powdered sugar, to serve

This simple cake showcases tangy-sweet summertime plums. Both red and black varieties work beautifully. Just make sure to choose medium plums that are ripe but still have a little firmness; soft, ultra-juicy fruits will make the center of the cake wet and soggy. Italian prune plums are great, too; use the same weight. But since they are small, cut them into halves instead of quarters. Ripe but firm pluots, a plum-apricot hybrid, are another excellent alternative. The flavor and texture of this cake are best the day of baking, but leftovers can be stored overnight in an airtight container at room temperature.

Don't forget to allow time for the butter to soften. Cold, firm butter won't blend well into the dry ingredients. And don't underbake this cake; the plums let off a lot of juice that slows down the baking, especially at the center. When testing for doneness, make sure there are no moist crumbs clinging to the toothpick.

1. Heat the oven to 325°F with a rack in the middle position. Mist the bottom and sides of a 9-inch springform pan with cooking spray, then dust evenly with flour; tap out the excess.

2. In a stand mixer with the paddle attachment, mix the flour, 107 grams (½ cup) of the sugar, the baking powder and salt on low until combined, about 5 seconds. With the mixer running, add the butter 1 piece at a time and continue mixing just until the mixture resembles moist sand, 2 to 3 minutes. Add the egg, egg yolk and vanilla. Increase to medium-high and beat until pale and fluffy, about 1 minute, scraping down the bowl as needed.

3. Transfer the batter to the prepared pan and spread in an even layer. Arrange the plum quarters on top of the batter in 2 concentric circles, placing the pieces on their cut sides. Sprinkle with the remaining 2 tablespoons sugar. Bake until golden brown and a skewer inserted at the center comes out clean, 1 to 1¼ hours. Let cool in the pan on a wire rack for 30 minutes, then remove the pan sides. Serve warm or at room temperature, dusted with powdered sugar.

Foolproof Single-Crust Pie Dough

Start to finish: 2½ hours (30 minutes active), plus cooling
Makes one 9-inch pie shell

___

3 tablespoons water

2 teaspoons cornstarch

146 grams (1 cup plus 2 tablespoons) all-purpose flour

2 teaspoons white sugar

¼ teaspoon kosher salt

10 tablespoons (1 stick plus 2 tablespoons) salted butter, cut into ½-inch pieces and chilled

2 tablespoons sour cream

Finding that sweet spot in pie dough can be a challenge. Drier doughs are less likely to shrink during blind baking, but they can be stiff and difficult to roll out. Moist doughs are easier to work with, but tend to slump in the oven. We stabilize our basic but excellent pastry dough by borrowing a technique known as tangzhong that is used to make Japanese milk bread, the soft, pillowy staple of Asian bakeries. Moisture makes dough easier to work with, but it also activates gluten, which makes pie dough tough. We wanted to add moisture without activating gluten. The tangzhong technique does this by mixing a small portion of the flour with boiling water to make a paste that then gets mixed into the dough. The paste adds moisture, but also traps it, preventing it from triggering the gluten. Inspired by this, we used cornstarch blended with water for the paste, heating it briefly to create a gel. The gel trapped the water, preventing it from reacting with the proteins in the flour. We also added sour cream to the dough, which contains a small peptide called glutathione. This peptide can be a baker's secret weapon because it reduces the ability of the proteins in wheat to react and form gluten. Result: a softer, more forgiving dough that rolls out easily and resists slumping in the pan during prebaking.

Don't skimp on the pie weights. Use enough to come three-quarters of the way up the sides. We like ceramic pie weights, but 1 pound dry beans or rice works, too. Avoid glass pie weights; they are too heavy and retain heat too long. And don't remove the foil and weights until the dough is set and dry. A moist or partially set crust can slump or shrink after the weights are removed. To check, lift up some of the foil and feel the edge of the pie or tart with your finger.

1. In a small bowl, whisk together the water and cornstarch. Microwave until set, 30 to 40 seconds, stirring halfway through. Chill in the freezer for 10 minutes.

2. Once the cornstarch mixture has chilled, in a food processor, combine the flour, sugar and salt, then process until mixed, about 5 seconds. Add the chilled cornstarch mixture and pulse until uniformly ground, about 5 pulses. Add the butter and sour cream, then process until the dough comes together and begins to collect around the blade, 20 to 30 seconds. Pat the dough into a 4-inch disk, wrap in plastic wrap and refrigerate for at least 1 hour and up to 48 hours.

3. When ready to bake, heat the oven to 375°F with a rack in the middle position. On a well-floured counter, roll the dough into a 12-inch circle. Hang the dough over the rolling pin and transfer to a 9-inch pie pan. Gently ease the dough into the pan by lifting the edges while pressing down into the corners of the pan. Trim the edges, leaving a ½-inch overhang, then tuck the overhang under itself so the dough is flush with the rim of the pan. Crimp the dough with your fingers or the tines of a fork, then chill in the freezer for at least 15 minutes.

4. To blind bake, line the chilled crust with heavy-duty foil and fill with enough pie weights to come three-quarters up. Bake until the edges are light golden brown, about 25 minutes, rotating the pan halfway through. Remove the foil and weights and bake until the bottom of the crust just begins to color, another 5 to 7 minutes. Let cool on a wire rack for 1 hour before filling. Once baked and cooled, the crust can be wrapped in plastic wrap and kept at room temperature for up to 2 days.

Brown Sugar Tart

Start to finish: 1¾ hours (30 minutes active), plus cooling
Servings: 8

1 recipe single-crust pie dough
(p. 432)

100 grams (8 tablespoons packed)
dark brown sugar, divided

1 tablespoon all-purpose flour

⅛ teaspoon kosher salt

4 large egg yolks

1¼ cups heavy cream

2 teaspoons vanilla extract

The inspiration for this simple yet rich tart was a French-Canadian sugar tart that originated in Waterloo, the Belgian town that was the site of Napoleon Bonaparte's 1815 defeat. Our brown sugar tart has two distinct layers: a rich, lightly sweet egg-yolk custard on top, and a thick bed of brown sugar on the bottom. Using just egg yolks in the custard resulted in a silkier, creamier texture than whole eggs, and adding flour prevented the tart from forming a skin on top. We wanted the brown sugar layer to be distinct from the custard layer, but found that adding a few tablespoons of the sugar to the custard mixture rounded out the flavor. While light brown sugar worked fine, we preferred the deep, more robust flavor of dark brown.

Don't use old, hard brown sugar. If your sugar is clumpy and dry, it will never fully incorporate into the custard mixture.

1. Heat the oven to 375°F with racks in the middle and lowest positions. On a well-floured counter, roll the dough into a 12-inch circle. Wrap the dough loosely around the rolling pin and transfer to a 9-inch tart pan with a removable bottom. Gently ease the dough into the corners of the pan, then trim the edges flush with the pan rim. Freeze for 15 minutes.

2. Line the chilled tart shell with heavy-duty foil and fill with enough pie weights to come three-quarters up, then place it on a rimmed baking sheet. Bake on the oven's lowest rack until the edges are light golden brown, 25 to 30 minutes, rotating the pan halfway through. Remove the foil and weights, then bake until the bottom of the crust just begins to color, another 5 to 7 minutes. Remove the pan from the oven and reduce the oven temperature to 325°F.

3. In a medium bowl, combine 25 grams (2 tablespoons) of the sugar with the flour and salt. Add the yolks and whisk until combined. Add the cream and vanilla and whisk until smooth. Sprinkle the remaining 75 grams (6 tablespoons) of sugar over the warm crust and gently press into an even layer.

4. Slowly pour the custard over the sugar. Bake on the oven's middle rack until the edges are set but the center jiggles slightly, about 25 minutes. Cool in the pan on a wire rack for at least 1 hour. Remove the outer metal ring and serve at room temperature.

Chocolate Tart

Start to finish: 1 hour 20 minutes (25 minutes active), plus cooling
Servings: 8

1 recipe single-crust pie dough
(p. 432)

6 tablespoons salted butter

6 ounces bittersweet chocolate,
finely chopped

2 large eggs, plus 1 large egg yolk

40 grams (5 tablespoons)
all-purpose flour

54 grams (¼ cup) white sugar

2 teaspoons vanilla extract

⅛ teaspoon kosher salt

When it comes to French-style chocolate tarts, there's a fine line between elegant and unpleasant. There's much to be said for the flavor of fine bitter chocolate, but it can be overwhelming. We aimed for a balance with more richness than is common. Flour and eggs provided structure, preventing the filling from being too gooey or pudding-like, while butter and an extra egg yolk added richness.

Don't be alarmed by how soft the center is when you remove the tart from the oven. The edges will be set, but the center still will be quite soft.

1. Heat the oven to 375°F with racks in the middle and lowest positions. On a well-floured counter, roll the dough into a 12-inch circle. Wrap the dough loosely around the rolling pin and transfer to a 9-inch tart pan with a removable bottom. Ease the dough into the pan, then trim the edges flush with the rim. Freeze for 15 minutes.

2. Line the chilled tart shell with heavy-duty foil and fill with enough pie weights to come three-quarters up, then place it on a rimmed baking sheet. Bake on the oven's lowest rack until the edges are light golden brown, 25 to 30 minutes, rotating the pan halfway through. Remove the foil and weights, then bake until the bottom of the crust just begins to color, another 5 to 7 minutes. Set aside. Leave the oven on.

3. In a medium saucepan over medium, melt the butter. Remove from the heat and add the chocolate, whisking until smooth. Whisk in the remaining ingredients until fully incorporated; the filling should appear shiny. If the mixture separates during whisking, don't worry. Just keep whisking; it will smooth out again. Pour into the warm crust and smooth the top. Bake on the baking sheet on the middle rack until the edges are just set, 8 to 10 minutes. Cool in the pan on a wire rack for at least 15 minutes. Remove the outer ring from the pan. Serve warm or at room temperature.

Pumpkin Tart

Start to finish: 1 hour 40 minutes (40 minutes active), plus cooling
Servings: 8

1 recipe single-crust pie dough
(p. 432)

15-ounce can pumpkin puree

149 grams (¾ cup packed)
dark brown sugar

¼ cup bourbon

8-ounce container (1 cup)
crème fraîche

3 large eggs

¼ teaspoon kosher salt

We love pumpkin pie, but we don't love how dense and cloying it can be. We wanted a lighter, fresher take with a pronounced pumpkin flavor. Canned pumpkin puree was a great place to start, but we intensified the flavor by giving it a quick sauté with dark brown sugar. This simmers off excess moisture and adds caramel flavors. Deglazing the pan with bourbon added a complexity we loved, but an equal amount of orange juice worked well, too. Crème fraîche gave the filling tang and richness that other dairy products couldn't match.

Don't use canned pumpkin pie filling for this recipe. Look for unsweetened canned pumpkin puree; the only ingredient listed should be pumpkin.

1. Heat the oven to 375°F with racks in the middle and lowest positions. On a well-floured counter, roll the dough into a 12-inch circle. Wrap the dough loosely around the rolling pin and transfer to a 9-inch tart pan with a removable bottom. Ease the dough into the pan, then trim the edges flush with the rim. Freeze for 15 minutes.

2. Line the chilled tart shell with heavy-duty foil and fill with enough pie weights to come three-quarters up, then place it on a rimmed baking sheet. Bake on the oven's lowest rack until the edges are light golden brown, 25 to 30 minutes, rotating the pan halfway through. Remove the foil and weights, then bake until the bottom of the crust just begins to color, another 5 to 7 minutes. Remove the pan from the oven and reduce the oven temperature to 325°F.

3. While the crust bakes, in a 12-inch nonstick skillet over medium-high, combine the pumpkin and sugar. Cook, stirring frequently, until the mixture is thickened, dark and leaves a film on the pan, about 10 minutes. Transfer to a 2-cup liquid measuring cup (the yield should be 1½ cups).

4. Add the bourbon to the skillet, return to medium-high heat and stir, scraping up any browned bits; add to the pumpkin mixture.

5. In a food processor, combine the pumpkin mixture and crème fraîche; process until smooth. Scrape down the bowl, add the eggs and salt, then process until smooth, about 1 minute. Pour the filling into the warm crust, smoothing the top. Bake on the baking sheet on the middle rack until the edges start to puff and crack and the center sets, 30 to 35 minutes.

6. Cool in the pan on a wire rack for at least 30 minutes. Remove the outer metal ring and serve warm or at room temperature.

HONEY-ORANGE WHIPPED CREAM

Start to finish: 5 minutes
Makes about 3 cups

Don't use creamed, thick or crystallized honey for this recipe. For the cream and honey to properly mix, a thin, pourable honey is needed.

1½ cups heavy cream

3 tablespoons honey

½ teaspoon grated orange zest

In the bowl of a stand mixer, combine all ingredients. Using the whisk attachment, mix on low until frothy, about 30 seconds. Scrape the bowl with a spatula to make sure the honey is incorporated. Mix on medium-high and whip until soft peaks form, 2 to 3 minutes.

Lemon Tart

Start to finish: 1 hour 40 minutes (25 minutes active), plus cooling
Servings: 8

1 recipe single-crust pie dough (p. 432)

107 grams (½ cup) white sugar

1 tablespoon grated lemon zest

1 teaspoon grated orange zest

⅛ teaspoon kosher salt

2 large eggs, plus 2 large egg yolks

6 tablespoons heavy cream

5 tablespoons lemon juice (1 to 2 lemons)

3 tablespoons orange juice

We love the fresh, bright flavor of lemon tarts, but the classic tarte au citron is acidic enough to strip the enamel off your teeth. We wanted to tame the tartness of lemon without relying on heaps of sugar. Pairing lemon with sweeter, mellower orange worked great. Using both the juice and the zest of both citruses provided complex, well-rounded flavor. Rubbing the zest into the sugar helped release the aromatic, flavorful oils. Using a combination of whole eggs and yolks gave us the best texture. The richness of the yolks and the cream also helped balance the lemon.

Don't eat this tart warm. The flavor and texture are best when chilled, or at least at room temperature.

1. Heat the oven to 375°F with racks in the middle and lowest positions. On a well-floured counter, roll the dough into a 12-inch circle. Wrap the dough loosely around the rolling pin and transfer to a 9-inch tart pan with a removable bottom. Ease the dough into the pan, then trim the edges flush with the rim. Freeze for 15 minutes.

2. Line the chilled tart shell with heavy-duty foil and fill with enough pie weights to come three-quarters up, then place it on a rimmed baking sheet. Bake on the oven's lowest rack until the edges are light golden brown, 25 to 30 minutes, rotating the pan halfway through. Remove the foil and weights, then bake until the bottom of the crust just begins to color, another 5 to 7 minutes. Remove the pan from the oven and reduce the oven temperature to 325°F.

3. In a bowl, combine the sugar, both zests and the salt. Rub together with your fingers until fragrant and the mixture begins to clump. Add the eggs and yolks and whisk until pale and slightly thickened, about 1 minute. Whisk in the cream and both juices. Skim the foam off the top.

4. Pour the filling into the warm tart shell and bake on the baking sheet on the middle rack until set, 20 to 25 minutes. Cool in the pan on a wire rack until room temperature, at least 1 hour. Remove the outer metal ring and serve, or chill completely before serving.

Sherry-Soaked **French Toast** (*Torrijas*)

Start to finish: **25 minutes** / Servings: 4

Four 1-inch-thick slices challah bread, halved on diagonal

1 cup dry sherry

124 grams (1 cup) powdered sugar

2 teaspoons grated orange zest, divided, plus ¼ cup orange juice

54 grams (¼ cup) white sugar

¼ teaspoon cinnamon

⅛ teaspoon ground cloves

4 large eggs

65 grams (½ cup) all-purpose flour

½ cup grapeseed or other neutral oil

This is our take on torrijas, Spain's version of French toast. Cinnamon and citrus are traditional flavorings, and dry sherry infuses the bread with its subtle nuttiness and caramel undertones. Challah isn't typical for torrijas, but we liked its eggy richness and tender crumb. Torrijas are especially good warm from the oven, when the outsides are delicately crisp and the insides are soft and custardy, but they're also great at room temperature. Unlike regular French toast, the bread for torrijas is sweetened throughout, so skip syrup for serving—berries or a fresh fruit compote are the best accompaniments. You'll need a thermometer to gauge the temperature of the oil for frying.

Don't use stale challah. Stale bread will soak up too much of the sherry mixture.

1. Heat the oven to 350°F with a rack in the middle position. In a large baking dish, arrange the challah in a single layer. In a medium bowl, whisk the sherry, powdered sugar, 1 teaspoon of zest and the orange juice. Pour the mixture over the bread; do not wash the bowl. Let stand for 5 minutes, then flip each piece of bread. Let stand until the bread absorbs most of the liquid, another 5 minutes.

2. Meanwhile, in a small, shallow bowl, stir together the remaining 1 teaspoon zest, the white sugar, cinnamon and cloves. In the same bowl used for the sherry mixture, whisk together the eggs, flour and 1 tablespoon of the sugar-spice mixture. When the bread has finished soaking, one at a time, remove the slices from the baking dish and dunk in the egg mixture, coating on both sides, then return to the baking dish.

3. In a 12-inch skillet over medium, heat the oil to 350°F. Set a wire rack in a rimmed baking sheet. When the oil is ready, place half of the slices in the pan and cook until golden brown, about 1 minute. Using a thin metal spatula, flip each piece and cook until the second sides are golden brown, about 1 minute. Transfer to the prepared baking sheet. Repeat with the remaining slices of bread. Place the baking sheet in the oven and bake until the centers of the bread slices are firm and set, about 5 minutes.

4. Using tongs, dip each slice into the remaining sugar-spice mixture, turning to coat, then transfer to a serving plate. Serve warm.

Rye-on-Rye Sticky Toffee Pudding

Start to finish: 1½ hours (30 minutes active), plus cooling
Servings: 10

For the cake:

8 ounces pitted dates (about 1½ cups)

1 cup brewed coffee

130 grams (1 cup) all-purpose flour, plus more for pan

105 grams (¾ cup) rye flour

1 teaspoon baking powder

1 teaspoon kosher salt

½ teaspoon baking soda

199 grams (1 cup packed) dark brown sugar

4 large eggs

2 teaspoons vanilla extract

1 teaspoon ground allspice

12 tablespoons (1½ sticks) salted butter, melted and cooled slightly, plus more for pan

For the toffee sauce:

199 grams (1 cup packed) dark brown sugar

218 grams (⅔ cup) light corn syrup

2 teaspoons finely grated orange zest

⅛ teaspoon kosher salt

6 tablespoons rye whiskey

8 tablespoons (1 stick) salted butter, cut into 8 pieces and chilled

To update Britain's sticky toffee pudding—a steamed, too-often bland dessert hidden under a gluey, cloying syrup—we worked backward, starting with the sauce. Instead of the traditional cream, we gave the toffee glaze a transatlantic twist by spiking it with rye whiskey. The whiskey's spice and heat cut through the sweetness of the dark brown sugar and corn syrup; orange zest added brightness. For the cake itself, we wanted to mirror the flavor of the rye, so we used a blend of rye and all-purpose flours. Dates that are steeped in coffee, then pureed, gave body and an earthiness that boosted the rye flavor. Together, the nutty rye and bitter coffee balanced the cake's sweetness. To up the dessert's elegance, we made it in a Bundt pan. Covering the pan with foil kept the cake rich and moist. This mimicked the gentle heat of steaming in a water bath (bain marie), but was far less fussy.

Don't chop the dates. Their texture was unpleasant in the finished dish. The food processor is the best bet. And be sure to check your dates for pits.

FOR THE CAKE:

1. Heat the oven to 325°F with a rack in the middle position. Lightly coat a 12-cup nonstick Bundt pan with butter and flour. In a medium saucepan over medium-high, bring the dates and coffee to a boil. Remove from the heat and let sit for 15 minutes. In a large bowl, whisk together both flours, the baking powder, salt and baking soda.

2. Transfer the coffee-date mixture to a food processor, add the sugar and process until smooth, about 1 minute. Add the eggs, vanilla and allspice. Then, with the processor running, add the butter. Pour the date mixture over the flour mixture and whisk gently until combined. Transfer to the prepared pan, cover tightly with foil and bake until firm and a toothpick inserted at the center comes out clean, 55 to 65 minutes. Remove the foil and cool in the pan on a rack for 15 minutes.

FOR THE SAUCE:

3. While the cake cools, in a medium saucepan over medium-high, combine the sugar, corn syrup, orange zest and salt. Bring to a boil, then cook until the mixture hits 240°F, 2 to 3 minutes. Reduce heat to low and add the whiskey, 2 tablespoons at a time, allowing the bubbling to subside before adding more. Whisk in the butter 2 tablespoons at a time until melted and smooth.

4. Invert the cake onto a serving platter. Brush the top and sides generously with the warm toffee sauce. Slice and serve drizzled with additional sauce. The sauced, cooled cake can be wrapped tightly in plastic wrap and kept at room temperature for up to 3 days. Cooled sauce can be refrigerated for up to 1 week. To reheat, wrap the cake in foil and place in a 300°F oven until warmed. Microwave the sauce until bubbling.

Browned Butter and Coconut Loaf Cake

Start to finish: **5 hours (45 minutes active)**
Makes **one 9-inch loaf**

For the cake:

10 tablespoons (1¼ sticks) salted butter

36 grams (½ cup plus 1 tablespoon) unsweetened shredded coconut

98 grams (¾ cup) all-purpose flour

135 grams (1 cup) spelt flour

1¼ teaspoons baking powder

¼ teaspoon kosher salt

1 cup plus 2 tablespoons buttermilk, room temperature

1¼ teaspoons vanilla extract

214 grams (1 cup) white sugar, divided

4 large eggs, room temperature

For the syrup:

2 tablespoons coconut milk

31 grams (2 tablespoons) white sugar

For the glaze:

62 grams (½ cup) powdered sugar

1 tablespoon plus 1 teaspoon coconut milk

¼ teaspoon kosher salt

This moist, dense, buttery loaf cake comes from Briana Holt of Tandem Coffee + Bakery in Portland, Maine. It's baked until the exterior is deeply browned, developing rich, toasty flavors and an amazing aroma. A coconut syrup is brushed on while the cake is still warm and, after cooling, a coconut glaze coats the surface. Holt uses spelt flour, a whole-grain flour with a subtle nuttiness. If you prefer, you can use all-purpose flour instead; if so, the total amount of all-purpose would be 228 grams (1¾ cups). Don't use whole-wheat flour in place of the spelt flour, as it changes the texture of the cake. Stored in an airtight container, the cake will keep at room temperature for up to three days.

Don't attempt to warm the buttermilk to room temperature by heating it in the microwave or in a saucepan. Buttermilk curdles if overheated, so it's best to let it stand on the counter until it reaches room temperature. If you're in a rush, warm it very gently in a warm water bath. Don't be afraid to brown the butter until the milk solids (the bits that separate out to the bottom) are deeply browned—almost black in color. They won't taste scorched in the finished cake. Rather, they will infuse it with a rich, nutty flavor and aroma.

1. To make the cake, in a medium saucepan over medium, heat the butter, occasionally swirling the pan and scraping the bottom with a wooden spoon, until dark amber and the milk solids at the bottom are almost black, 8 to 10 minutes. Transfer to the bowl of a stand mixer, making sure to scrape in all of the milk solids. Cool until the butter is opaque, spreadable and cool to the touch, about 1 hour.

2. While the butter cools, heat the oven to 350°F with a rack in the middle position. Spread the shredded coconut in a 9-by-5-inch loaf pan and toast in the oven until golden brown, 5 to 7 minutes, stirring once about halfway through. Measure 1 tablespoon of the toasted coconut into a small bowl, then transfer the remainder to a medium bowl; set both aside. Let the pan cool.

3. Mist the loaf pan with cooking spray. Line it with an 8-by-12-inch piece of kitchen parchment, fitting the parchment into the bottom and up the pan's long sides; mist the parchment with cooking spray. To the medium bowl with the coconut, whisk in both flours, the baking powder and salt. In a liquid measuring cup or small bowl, stir together the buttermilk and vanilla.

4. Add the white sugar to the cooled browned butter. In the stand mixer with the paddle attachment, mix the butter and sugar on medium until well combined, about 2 minutes, scraping the bowl about halfway through. With the mixer running on medium, add the eggs one at a time, scraping the bowl after the first 2 additions. Beat on medium until the mixture is shiny and lightened in color, about 1 minute. With the mixer running on low, add half of the flour, then the buttermilk mixture, followed by the remaining flour mixture. Mix on low for about 10 seconds, then stop the mixer. Using a silicone spatula, fold the batter just until the flour is incorporated, scraping the bottom of the bowl to ensure no pockets of butter or flour remain.

5. Transfer the batter to the prepared pan and smooth the surface. Bake until the top is deeply browned and a tooth-pick inserted into the center comes out with a few small crumbs attached, 75 to 80 minutes.

6. While the cake bakes, make the syrup. In a small microwave-safe bowl, stir together the coconut milk, white sugar and 2 tablespoons water. Micro-wave on high for 30 seconds, stirring once about halfway through to ensure the sugar is dissolved. Set aside to cool.

7. When the cake is done, cool in the pan on a wire rack for 15 minutes. Using the parchment overhang as handles, remove the cake from the pan and set on the rack. With a toothpick, poke holes in the top of the cake at 1-inch intervals. Brush all of the syrup onto the cake, allowing it to soak in. Cool to room temperature, about 2 hours. Remove and discard the parchment.

8. To make the glaze, in a medium bowl, whisk the powdered sugar, coconut milk and salt until smooth. Spoon over the cooled cake, spreading it to cover the surface and allowing it to drip down the sides slightly. Sprinkle with the reserved 1 tablespoon toasted coconut. Allow the glaze to dry for at least 5 minutes before serving.

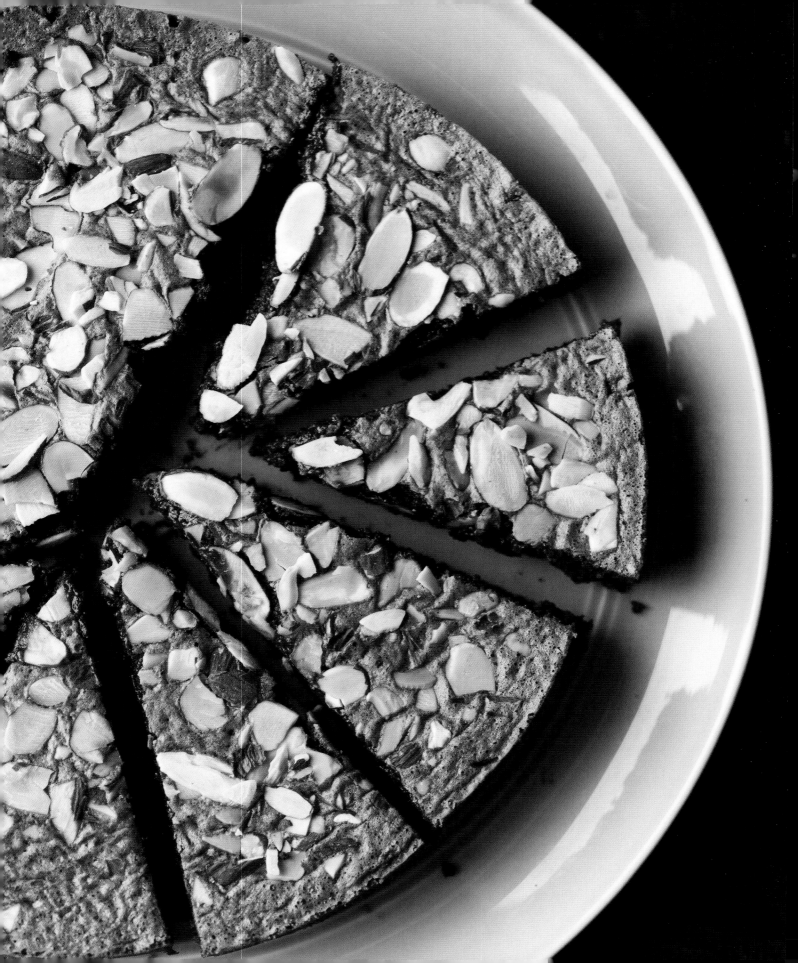

Caprese Chocolate and Almond Torte

Start to finish: 1 hour 10 minutes (20 minutes active)
Servings: 10

233 grams (2⅓ cups) sliced almonds

5 large eggs

2 teaspoons vanilla extract

8 ounces bittersweet chocolate (see note), roughly chopped

199 grams (1 cup) packed dark brown sugar

1 teaspoon kosher salt

This flourless chocolate cake from Capri, Italy (where it is called torta caprese), gets its rich, almost brownie-like texture from ground almonds and a generous amount of egg. Before grinding the nuts, we toast them to intensify their flavor and accentuate the deep, roasted notes of the chocolate. We preferred the cake made with bittersweet chocolate containing 70 to 80 percent cocoa solids. You can, of course, use a lighter, sweeter bittersweet chocolate, but the cake will have less chocolate intensity. Serve slices warm or at room temperature dolloped with unsweetened whipped cream.

Don't forget to reduce the oven to 300°F after toasting the almonds. Also, don't overbake the cake or its texture will be dry and tough. Whereas most cakes are done when a toothpick inserted at the center comes out clean, a toothpick inserted into this one should come out with sticky, fudgy crumbs, similar to brownies.

1. Heat the oven to 350°F with a rack in the middle position. Spread the almonds in an even layer on a rimmed baking sheet and toast in the oven until golden brown, 8 to 10 minutes, stirring once about halfway through. Cool to room temperature.

2. While the almonds cool, reduce the oven to 300°F. Mist the bottom and sides of 9-inch round cake pan with cooking spray, line the bottom with a round of kitchen parchment, then mist the parchment. Crack the eggs into a liquid measuring cup and add the vanilla; set aside.

3. In a food processor, process 185 grams (2 cups) of the almonds until finely ground, 20 to 30 seconds. Add the chocolate and pulse until the chocolate is finely ground, 10 to 15 pulses. Add the sugar and salt, then process until well combined, about 30 seconds, scraping

the bowl as needed. With the machine running, gradually pour in the egg mixture. Continue processing until the batter is smooth and homogenous, about another 15 to 20 seconds. Remove the blade and scrape the bowl.

4. Pour the batter into the prepared pan, then sprinkle evenly with the remaining 48 grams (⅓ cup) almonds. Bake until the center feels firm when gently pressed and a toothpick inserted at the center comes out with moist, fudgey crumbs attached, 30 to 35 minutes.

5. Let cool in the pan on a wire rack for 30 minutes. Run a knife around the sides of the cake, then invert onto a rack. Peel off the parchment and reinvert the cake onto a platter. Serve warm or at room temperature.

Lemon-Buttermilk **Pound Cake**

Start to finish: 1½ hours (30 minutes active)
Servings: 8

---

13 tablespoons (1½ sticks plus
1 tablespoon) salted butter, room
temperature, divided

467 grams (2 cups plus 3 tablespoons)
white sugar, plus extra, divided

330 grams (2¾ cups) cake flour

½ teaspoon baking soda

½ teaspoon kosher salt

¾ cup buttermilk

2 tablespoons grated lemon zest,
plus 3 tablespoons lemon juice

5 large eggs, separated

Pound cake historically has had a propensity to density. So thick was the batter of equal parts butter, sugar, flour and eggs that 18th-century cookbook author Hannah Glasse recommended beating it for an hour. But despite all that flogging, and even with modern techniques, the cakes remained resolutely heavy. We figured there was a better way. For our pound cake, we separated the eggs, a trick we learned from pastry chef Kathryn King of Atlanta's Aria restaurant. She makes a lemon-buttermilk pound cake she got from her grandmother that is lofty and light. Gently whipping the egg whites, a trick lifted from sponge cakes, built lightness into the cake. King also adds baking soda, unusual in a pound cake, as well as buttermilk and lemon juice, which contribute a slightly tart flavor and add acid. We made minor tweaks, whisking the dry ingredients instead of sifting them and using a stand mixer to whip the whites, combine lemon zest and sugar, and beat the batter. King, like Violet bakery's Claire Ptak, emphasizes under-whipping the whites. Likewise, we took a gentler hand when creaming the butter and sugar. At Aria, the cake is sliced, buttered, toasted and served with fresh fruit and whipped cream. It's also delicious plain with just a spoonful of tangy whipped cream.

Don't overbeat the whites. They should appear smooth and glossy, with gentle peaks that curl back on themselves. And don't wait until the end of the baking time to check the cake for doneness; pans cook at different rates due to color and composition.

1. Heat the oven to 325°F with a rack in the middle position. Rub 1 tablespoon of the butter evenly over a Bundt pan, then use a pastry brush to ensure it gets into all corners. Sprinkle in a bit of sugar, then turn the pan to evenly coat all surfaces.

2. In a bowl, whisk together the flour, baking soda and salt. In a liquid measuring cup, combine the buttermilk and lemon juice; set aside.

3. In a stand mixer with a whisk attachment, whip the egg whites on medium-high until light and foamy, about 1 minute. With the mixer running, slowly sprinkle in 39 grams (3 tablespoons) of the sugar and continue to whip until the whites are thick and glossy and hold soft peaks, about 1 minute. Transfer the whites to a bowl and set aside, then add the remaining 2 cups of sugar and the lemon zest to the stand mixer's bowl.

4. Using the paddle attachment, mix 428 grams (2 cups) of the sugar and zest on low until the sugar appears moistened and begins to clump, about 1 minute. Add the remaining 12 tablespoons of butter and mix on medium-low until the mixture is cohesive, then increase the mixer to medium-high and beat until pale and fluffy, about 3 minutes. Reduce the mixer to low and add the yolks, one at a time, mixing until incorporated.

5. Add a third of the flour mixture, then mix on low. Add half of the buttermilk mixture, then mix again. Repeat the process of adding and mixing, ending with the final third of flour. Fold ⅓ of the whipped egg whites into the batter until combined, then gently fold in the remaining whites until barely combined. Transfer the batter to the prepared pan and smooth the top.

6. Bake until the cake is golden brown and bounces back when gently pressed, 50 to 60 minutes, rotating the pan halfway through baking. Cool the cake in the pan on a wire rack for 10 minutes, then remove from the pan and cool completely.

Chocolate-Hazelnut (*Gianduja*) Crostata

Start to finish: 1 hour 15 minutes (45 minutes active)
Servings: 10

163 grams (1¼ cups) hazelnuts

65 grams (½ cup) all-purpose flour

35 grams (¼ cup) whole-wheat flour

214 grams (1 cup) white sugar, divided

¼ teaspoon baking powder

Kosher salt

6 tablespoons (¾ stick) salted butter, cut into ½-inch cubes and chilled

1 large egg yolk, plus
3 large egg whites

2½ teaspoons vanilla extract, divided

4 ounces bittersweet chocolate, chopped

1 teaspoon instant espresso powder

The chewy, rich filling for this dessert was inspired by gianduja, a chocolate-hazelnut paste first created in Turin, Italy. The crust, made with whole-wheat flour, is simply pressed into the bottom of a springform pan; its nuttiness pairs perfectly with the intense filling. If you like, dust the baked crostata with powdered sugar before serving, or top wedges with unsweetened whipped cream or crème fraîche. The crostata is best served the same day, but leftovers can be covered in plastic wrap and refrigerated overnight; bring to room temperature before serving.

Don't underprocess the hazelnut and sugar mixture. Grinding it until fine and paste-like is key to the filling's thick, decadent texture.

1. Heat the oven to 375°F with a rack in the lowest position. Evenly mist a 9-inch springform pan with cooking spray. Spread the hazelnuts on a rimmed baking sheet and toast until deep golden brown, about 10 minutes. Wrap the nuts in a kitchen towel and rub vigorously to remove the skins. Set aside.

2. In a food processor, combine both flours, 53 grams (¼ cup) of sugar, the baking powder and ¼ teaspoon salt. Process until combined, about 5 seconds. Scatter the butter over the mixture and pulse until it resembles coarse sand, 10 to 12 pulses. Add the egg yolk and ½ teaspoon of vanilla extract, then process until evenly moistened and clumping together, 20 to 30 seconds.

3. Transfer the dough to the prepared pan; do not wash the food processor. Press into an even layer covering the bottom of the pan and prick with a fork about every ½ inch. Bake until the crust is golden at the center and slightly darker at the edges, 15 to 20 minutes.

4. Meanwhile, make the filling. In a small microwave-safe bowl, microwave the chocolate on 50 percent power, stopping to stir every 30 seconds, until smooth and melted, about 3 minutes. Set aside.

5. In the food processor, pulse the hazelnuts until roughly chopped, about 8 pulses; measure out ¼ cup and set aside. Add the remaining 161 grams (¾ cup) sugar and process until the mixture resembles wet sand and sticks to the corners of the bowl, about 2 minutes. Scrape the bowl. Add the egg whites, the remaining 2 teaspoons vanilla extract, espresso powder and ½ teaspoon salt. Process until smooth, about 10 seconds. Add the chocolate and process until incorporated, another 10 seconds, scraping the sides as needed.

6. Spread the chocolate-hazelnut mixture in an even layer on the crust, then sprinkle the reserved chopped nuts around the perimeter. Bake until slightly puffed and the edges begin to crack, 20 to 25 minutes.

7. Let cool on a wire rack until the edges pull away from the sides of the pan, about 15 minutes. Remove the pan sides. Serve the crostata warm or at room temperature.

Senegalese Mango and
Coconut Rice Pudding

Start to finish: 1 hour (plus cooling)
Servings: 4

2 tablespoons honey

14- to 16-ounce ripe mango, peeled, pitted and cut into ½-inch chunks

Kosher salt

1 tablespoon lime juice

45 grams (½ cup) unsweetened shredded coconut

14-ounce can coconut milk

2 tablespoons white sugar

2 teaspoons vanilla extract

2 cups cooked and cooled long-grain white rice (see note)

Senegalese coconut rice pudding—called sombi—usually has a porridge-like consistency and is eaten as a snack or for breakfast. We preferred it a little thicker and enjoyed it as dessert, so after learning the recipe from Pierre Thiam in Dakar, we adapted the version in his book "Yolele!" and paired it with diced mango that is gently cooked in caramelized honey. This recipe calls for 2 cups of cooked long-grain rice. Rinse and drain ¾ cup long-grain white rice, then combine it with 1 cup water in a small saucepan. Bring to a boil over medium-high, then cover, reduce to low and cook until the water has been absorbed, about 15 minutes. Transfer the rice to a kitchen parchment–lined baking sheet or large plate and cool to room temperature.

Don't stir the mango too often as it cooks; each time the lid is removed, steam escapes. This can dry out the mango too quickly and cause it to scorch.

1. In a 10-inch nonstick skillet over medium-high, cook the honey without stirring for 2 minutes; it will bubble vigorously and smell lightly caramelized. Stir in the mango, ¾ cup water and ¼ teaspoon salt, then bring to a simmer. Cover, reduce to medium-low and cook, stirring only occasionally, until very tender and the moisture has completely evaporated, 25 to 30 minutes. (If most of the liquid has evaporated after about only 15 minutes but the mango is still firm, reduce to low to prevent scorching.) Off heat, stir in the lime juice.

2. Meanwhile, in a medium saucepan over medium-high, toast the coconut, stirring occasionally, until golden brown, 1½ to 2 minutes. Stir in the coconut milk, sugar, vanilla and ½ teaspoon salt, then bring to a simmer. Reduce to medium-low and cook, stirring occasionally, until slightly thickened, about 5 minutes.

3. Remove ¼ cup of the coconut mixture and set aside. Add the rice and 1 cup water to the saucepan and stir to combine. Cook over medium, stirring frequently, until the liquid is absorbed and the rice is creamy, 15 to 20 minutes. Remove from the heat and let cool for 15 minutes.

4. Spoon the rice pudding into serving bowls, top with the mango and drizzle with the reserved coconut mixture. Serve warm.

French Apple Cake

Start to finish: 1 hour (25 minutes active), plus cooling
Servings: 8

8 tablespoons (1 stick) salted butter, plus more for pan

¼ teaspoon ground allspice

1½ pounds Granny Smith apples, peeled, cored, cut into ¼-inch slices

1 pound Braeburn or Golden Delicious apples, peeled, cored cut into ¼-inch slices

156 grams (12 tablespoons) white sugar, divided

½ teaspoon kosher salt

2 tablespoons brandy or Calvados

86 grams (⅔ cup) all-purpose flour, plus more for pan

1 teaspoon baking powder

2 large eggs

2 teaspoons vanilla extract

This simple dessert is less cake than sautéed apples set in a thick, custardy crumb under a golden, sugary crust. We liked using two varieties of apples, one tart and one sweet—the variation in the apples' sweetness gave the cake a full, complex flavor. The cake is delicious served plain, but we also loved it with crème fraîche or ice cream.

Don't use a spatula to scrape the browned butter out of the skillet—simply pour it into the bowl. A skim coat of butter in the pan is needed to cook the apples. And don't slice the cake until it has fully cooled; if it is at all warm, the texture at the center will be too soft.

1. Heat the oven to 375°F with a rack in the middle position. Coat a 9-inch springform pan with butter, dust with flour, then tap out the excess.

2. In a 12-inch skillet over medium-high, melt the butter. Cook, swirling the pan frequently, until the milk solids are golden brown and the butter has a nutty aroma, 1 to 3 minutes. Pour into a small heat-safe bowl; don't scrape the skillet. Stir the allspice into the butter. Set aside.

3. Add all the apples, 26 grams (2 tablespoons) of sugar and the salt to the still-hot skillet and set over medium-high. Cook, stirring occasionally, until the moisture released by the apples has evaporated and the slices are beginning to brown, 12 to 15 minutes. Add the brandy and cook until evaporated, 30 to 60 seconds. Transfer to a large plate, spread in an even layer and refrigerate uncovered until cool to the touch, 15 to 20 minutes.

4. In a small bowl, whisk together the flour and baking powder. In a large bowl, whisk together the eggs, vanilla and 117 grams (9 tablespoons) of the sugar; gradually whisk in the butter. Add the flour mixture and stir until smooth; the batter will be very thick. Add the cooled apples and fold until evenly coated. Transfer to the prepared pan, spread in an even layer and sprinkle with the remaining 1 tablespoon sugar.

5. Bake until the cake is deeply browned, 35 to 40 minutes. Let cool completely in the pan on a wire rack, about 2 hours. Run a knife around the inside of the pan and remove the sides before slicing.

Maple-Whiskey Pudding Cakes

Start to finish: 45 minutes (20 minutes active)
Servings: 4

6 tablespoons maple syrup

1 teaspoon cider vinegar

6 tablespoons whiskey, divided

8 tablespoons (1 stick) salted butter, divided

¾ teaspoon kosher salt, divided

107 grams (½ cup) white sugar

¼ cup whole milk

1 large egg

1 teaspoon vanilla extract

90 grams (¾ cup) pecans, toasted

65 grams (½ cup) all-purpose flour

1 teaspoon baking powder

These individual desserts bake up with a gooey sauce beneath a layer of rich, tender cake. We tried a few different types of whiskey. Our favorites were Jameson for its clean, bright flavor and Rittenhouse rye for its spicy depth. This recipe can easily be doubled to serve eight. Serve the pudding cakes warm, with vanilla ice cream or lightly sweetened whipped cream.

Don't stir the maple-whiskey syrup into the batter after dividing it among the batter-filled ramekins. With baking, the syrup will form a sauce at the bottom.

1. In a small saucepan over medium, combine ½ cup water, the maple syrup, vinegar, 4 tablespoons of whiskey, 2 tablespoons of butter and ¼ teaspoon of salt. Bring to a boil, stirring occasionally. Reduce to low and simmer for 5 minutes. Remove from the heat and set aside.

2. In another small saucepan over medium, melt the remaining 6 tablespoons butter. Cook, swirling the pan, until the milk solids at the bottom are deep golden brown and the butter has the aroma of toasted nuts, about 5 minutes. Transfer to a medium bowl and cool to room temperature.

3. Meanwhile, heat the oven to 325°F with a rack in the middle position. Mist four 6-ounce ramekins with cooking spray and place on a rimmed baking sheet. When the butter is cool, whisk in the sugar, milk, egg, vanilla and remaining 2 tablespoons whiskey. Set aside.

4. In a food processor, process the pecans until finely ground and beginning to clump, 30 to 40 seconds. Add the flour, baking powder and the remaining ½ teaspoon salt, then pulse until combined, about 5 pulses. Add the butter mixture and pulse until a smooth, thick batter forms, about 5 pulses, scraping down the bowl once.

5. Divide the batter evenly among the prepared ramekins. Gently pour the maple mixture over the batter in each ramekin. Do not stir. Bake until the cakes are puffed and the centers jiggle only slightly, 25 to 30 minutes. Let cool on the baking sheet for 10 minutes before serving; the cakes will fall slightly as they cool.

French Walnut Tart

Start to finish: 2¼ hours (20 minutes active)
Servings: 10

For the tart shell:

87 grams (⅔ cup) all-purpose flour

46 grams (⅓ cup) whole-wheat flour

40 grams (3 tablespoons) white sugar

½ teaspoon kosher salt

6 tablespoons (¾ stick) salted butter,
cut into ½-inch cubes and chilled

1 large egg yolk

1 teaspoon vanilla extract

For the filling:

107 grams (½ cup) white sugar

¼ cup honey

⅓ cup crème fraîche

4 tablespoons (½ stick) salted butter

1 tablespoon cider vinegar

¼ teaspoon kosher salt

2 large egg yolks

230 grams (2½ cups) walnuts,
roughly chopped and lightly toasted
(see note)

This simple tart comes from the Perigord region of France, an area known for its walnuts. A cookie-like pastry shell is filled with the rich, subtly bitter nuts and buttery caramel. Our version tones down what often is cloying sweetness with a small measure of crème fraîche and a dose of cider vinegar (you won't detect it in the finished dessert). Whole-wheat flour in the crust plays up the earthiness of the walnuts. To toast the walnuts, spread them in an even layer on a rimmed baking sheet and bake at 325°F until fragrant and just starting to brown, about 8 minutes, stirring just once or twice; do not overtoast them or they will taste acrid. The dough-lined tart pan can be prepared in advance; after the dough is firm, wrap tightly in plastic and freeze for up to two weeks. The tart is superb lightly sprinkled with flaky sea salt and accompanied by crème fraîche or unsweetened whipped cream.

Don't overcook the caramel. Aim for an amber hue; if it gets much darker than that, the finished tart will taste bitter.

1. Heat the oven to 325°F with a rack in the lower-middle position. Mist a 9-inch tart pan with removable bottom with cooking spray. Line a rimmed baking sheet with kitchen parchment.

2. To make the tart shell, in a food processor, combine both flours, the sugar and salt, then process until combined, about 5 seconds. Scatter the butter over the mixture and pulse until it resembles coarse sand, 10 to 12 pulses. Add the egg yolk and vanilla, then process until the mixture is evenly moistened and cohesive, 20 to 30 seconds; the mixture may not form a single mass.

3. Crumble the dough into the prepared tart pan, evenly covering the surface. Using the bottom of a dry measuring cup, press into an even layer over the bottom and up the sides; the edge of the dough should be flush with the rim. Use a fork to prick all over the bottom, then freeze until the dough is firm, 15 to 30 minutes.

4. While the dough chills, to make the filling, pour ¼ cup water into a medium saucepan. Add the sugar and honey into the center, avoiding contact with the sides. Cook over medium, swirling the pan frequently, until the mixture is amber in color, about 8 minutes. Off heat, add the crème fraîche, butter, vinegar and salt, then whisk until the butter is melted and the mixture is well combined. Let cool until just warm, about 30 minutes.

5. While the caramel cools, set the dough-lined tart pan on the prepared baking sheet. Bake until lightly browned, about 30 minutes. Cool on the baking sheet on a wire rack for about 5 minutes.

6. Whisk the yolks into the warm honey filling, then add the nuts and stir until evenly coated. Pour the filling into warm tart shell, then gently spread in an even layer. Bake until the edges of the filling begin to puff and the center jiggles only slightly when gently shaken, 25 to 35 minutes.

7. Let the tart cool on the baking sheet on a wire rack for about 1 hour. Remove the pan sides. Serve warm or at room temperature.

Salted Butter Caramel
Chocolate Mousse

Start to finish: 30 minutes, plus cooling and chilling / Servings: 6

---

104 grams (½ cup) white sugar

3 tablespoons salted butter, cut into ½-inch cubes

¾ cup heavy cream

6 ounces bittersweet or semisweet chocolate, chopped

4 large eggs, separated

Generous ¼ teaspoon fleur de sel (see note)

With butter-and-cream richness, bittersweet notes from the chocolate and caramel, and sea salt to cut through the sugar, this simple six-ingredient dessert from "My Paris Kitchen" by David Lebovitz is far greater than the sum of its parts. You can whip the egg whites by hand using a whisk, or use a handheld or stand mixer. Whatever method, make sure the bowl and whisk are perfectly clean and free of any residual oil, which will prevent the egg whites from achieving maximum loft. (Note that the eggs here are not cooked.) Fleur de sel is a hand-harvested, somewhat coarse-grained sea salt from France. Just about any variety of finishing sea salt can be substituted, but don't use very coarse salt (the type meant for grinding). The salt particles in the mousse don't fully dissolve; the little bursts of salinity are what makes this dessert so unique and delicious.

Don't overwhip the egg whites; stop whisking when they hold stiff peaks. Over-beaten egg whites appear dry and won't incorporate well with other ingredients.

1. Spread the sugar evenly over the bottom of a medium sauté pan or wide medium saucepan, then set the pan over medium. As the sugar begins to melt at the edges, use a silicone spatula to push the liquefied sugar toward the center. Continue to cook, stirring gently, until all the sugar is melted, caramelizes to a deep amber color and begins to smoke, 3 to 5 minutes. Remove the pan from the heat, quickly add the butter and stir until melted. Gradually whisk in the cream and continue to whisk to dissolve any hardened bits of caramel.

2. Once the cream mixture is smooth, add the chocolate and stir gently until melted and smooth. Transfer the mixture to a large bowl and cool to room temperature, stirring occasionally. Whisk in the egg yolks.

3. In another large bowl, whip the egg whites until they hold stiff peaks. Using a silicone spatula, fold about ⅓ of the whites into the chocolate mixture, sprinkling in the fleur de sel. Fold in the remaining whites just until no streaks of white remain.

4. Divide the mousse into serving glasses or bowls, or transfer it to a large serving bowl. Cover and refrigerate for at least 8 hours or up to 24 hours.

Pistachio-Cardamom Cake

Start to finish: 1 hour 10 minutes (15 minutes active), plus cooling
Makes one 9-inch loaf

___

214 grams (1 cup) white sugar

2 teaspoons grated orange zest, plus ¼ cup orange juice (about 1 orange)

185 grams (1⅓ cups) shelled, unsalted pistachios, toasted and cooled

130 grams (1 cup) all-purpose flour, plus more for pan

2 teaspoons baking powder

1½ teaspoons ground cardamom

1 teaspoon kosher salt

4 large eggs

½ cup plus 2 tablespoons plain whole-milk Greek-style yogurt

¼ cup olive oil, plus more for pan

2 teaspoons vanilla extract

93 grams (¾ cup) powdered sugar

Baking a cake can be daunting. Enter the loaf cake, as easy as a quick bread but with more polish. Rose Bakery in Paris, created by Briton Rose Carrarini and her French husband, Jean-Charles, has elevated the style to an art form, producing tempting loaf cakes in all manner of flavors. We were particularly taken by a green-tinged, nut-topped pistachio cake. For our version, we paired toasted pistachios with cardamom and ground orange zest, giving it a distinctly Middle Eastern flavor. Combining ground nuts with rich Greek-style yogurt, olive oil and plenty of eggs ensured a moist, appealingly coarse crumb. We got the best results from grinding the nuts until they were nearly as fine as flour, but still had some texture. If you can't find unsalted pistachios, reduce the salt in the recipe by half. Cooling the cake was essential to maintain the thick consistency of the glaze.

Don't skip toasting the pistachios. The differences in flavor and texture were significant between raw and toasted. Toast the nuts at 300°F until they're quite fragrant and begin to darken, 10 to 15 minutes.

1. Heat the oven to 325°F with a rack in the middle position. Lightly coat a 9-by-5-inch loaf pan with olive oil and flour. In a food processor, combine the white sugar and orange zest; process until the sugar is damp and fragrant, 5 to 10 seconds. Transfer to a large bowl.

2. Add the pistachios to the processor and pulse until coarse, 8 to 10 pulses. Set aside 2 tablespoons of the nuts for topping. Add the flour, baking powder, cardamom and salt to the processor with the nuts. Process until the nuts are finely ground, about 45 seconds.

3. To the sugar mixture, whisk in the eggs, ½ cup of the yogurt, the oil, orange juice and vanilla. Add the nut-flour mixture and fold until mixed. Transfer the batter to the prepared pan, and smooth the top. Bake until golden brown, firm to the touch and a toothpick inserted at the center comes out with moist crumbs, 50 to 55 minutes. Cool in the pan on a wire rack for 15 minutes. Remove from the pan and let cool completely, about 2 hours.

4. In a small bowl, whisk the remaining 2 tablespoons of yogurt with the powdered sugar until thick and smooth. Spread over the top of the cake. Sprinkle with the reserved nuts. Let set for 10 minutes before serving.

Salted Peanut and Caramel Tart

Start to finish: 2½ hours (1 hour active)
Makes one 9-inch tart

___

For the tart shell:

130 grams (1 cup) all-purpose flour

50 grams (½ cup) almond flour

66 grams (⅓ cup) white sugar

½ teaspoon kosher salt

6 tablespoons (¾ stick) salted butter, cut into ½-inch cubes and softened

1 large egg yolk

1 teaspoon vanilla extract

For the peanut butter–meringue filling:

188 grams (¾ cup) creamy (smooth) peanut butter (see note)

2 large egg whites

1 teaspoon vanilla extract

⅛ teaspoon kosher salt

164 grams (½ cup) corn syrup

107 grams (½ cup) white sugar

For the peanut-caramel topping:

54 grams (¼ cup) white sugar

3 tablespoons heavy cream

2 tablespoons salted butter, cut into 2 pieces

68 grams (½ cup) dry-roasted, salted peanuts, roughly chopped

Flaky sea salt, such as Maldon (optional)

The peanut butter and marshmallow sandwich—also known as the Fluffernutter—is inarguably all-American. And Le Petit Grain, a Parisian boulangerie headed by Edward Delling-Williams, created a delicious riff on that childhood favorite with their elegant individual tartlets called tartes cacahuètes (literally, peanut tarts). A buttery, cookie-like pastry is filled with an airy peanut butter meringue that is topped with caramel-coated roasted peanuts. For ease, our version makes a single 9-inch tart. Pay attention to the timing in the recipe, which can be tricky. To make the meringue filling, the whipped egg whites and sugar syrup need to be ready at the same time. If your egg whites reach soft peaks before the syrup is ready, reduce the mixer speed to low while you wait for the syrup to finish; this prevents the whites from turning dry and stiff. You'll need a candy or digital thermometer for gauging the doneness of the sugar syrup. The finished tart will keep at room temperature for up to 12 hours. If you're storing it longer than an hour or so before serving, wait to add the flaky salt garnish until just before serving and cover the tart with plastic wrap or foil.

Don't use natural peanut butter (the variety that requires stirring to mix in the oil on the surface); even the creamy variety of natural peanut butter has a slight grittiness that's detectable in the tart filling. Make sure the mixer bowl and whisk attachment for whipping the meringue are perfectly clean; a trace of fat will prevent the egg whites from attaining the proper volume.

1. To make the tart shell, mist a 9-inch tart pan with removable bottom with cooking spray and set on a rimmed baking sheet. In a stand mixer fitted with the paddle attachment, combine both flours, the sugar and salt, then mix on low until combined, about 5 seconds. With the mixer on low, add the butter one piece at a time. When all the butter has been added, continue mixing on low until the mixture resembles coarse sand, about 2 minutes. Add the yolk and vanilla, then mix on low until the dough is evenly moistened and cohesive, 2 to 3 minutes; the dough may not form a single mass.

2. Crumble the dough into the prepared tart pan, covering the bottom as evenly as possible. Using the bottom of a dry measuring cup, press the dough into an even layer over the bottom and up the sides of the pan. Prick the bottom and sides about every ½ inch with a fork. Set in the freezer on the baking sheet to chill until firm, at least 15 minutes or up to 1 hour.

3. Meanwhile, heat the oven to 300°F with a rack in the middle position. When the tart shell is firm, bake it on the baking sheet until deep golden brown, 1 to 1¼ hours. Let cool on the baking sheet set on a wire rack for at least 15 minutes.

4. To make the peanut butter–meringue filling, put the peanut butter in a small microwave-safe bowl; set aside. In a clean, dry mixer bowl,

combine the egg whites, vanilla and salt, then attach to the mixer along with the whisk attachment. In a small saucepan, combine the corn syrup, sugar and ¼ cup water. Bring to a boil over medium-high and cook until the syrup reaches 238°F, 3 to 4 minutes; swirl the pan once or twice before the syrup reaches a boil. When the syrup has boiled for 2 minutes, begin whipping the whites on medium and whip until they hold very soft peaks when the whisk is lifted, about 1 minute. When the syrup reaches 238°F, remove the pan from the heat and let stand just until the bubbling slows, no more than 15 seconds. Then with the mixer running on medium-high, slowly pour the hot syrup into the egg whites, aiming for the area between the whisk and the sides of the bowl. After all the syrup has been added, continue whipping on medium-high until the bowl is just warm to the touch, about 3 minutes; do not overbeat.

5. Meanwhile, microwave the peanut butter on high until pourable, 30 to 60 seconds, stirring once about halfway through. When the egg whites are ready, reduce the mixer to low and pour in the peanut butter. Once all the peanut butter is added, stop the mixer, then fold with a silicone spatula until homogenous, taking care not to deflate the whites. Gently pour the filling into the tart shell and spread in an even layer; set aside.

6. For the peanut-caramel topping: Place 2 tablespoons water in a small saucepan. Carefully pour the sugar into the center of the pan, and stir gently with a clean spoon just until the sugar is evenly moistened. Bring to a boil over medium and cook, gently swirling the pan (do not stir) until the syrup is deep amber-colored and lightly smoking, 5 to 6 minutes. Carefully pour in the cream (the mixture will bubble and steam vigorously), then stir to combine. Add the butter, remove from the heat and continue stirring until the butter is melted and incorporated. Stir the peanuts into the caramel.

7. Working quickly, pour the caramel mixture evenly over the filling, then use a small spatula to gently spread it to the edges; be careful not to push the peanuts into the filling. Let cool for at least 15 minutes. Remove the outer ring from the tart pan, then sprinkle lightly with flaky salt (if using). Serve at room temperature.

Toasted Bread Pudding
with Cream and Pistachios

Start to finish: **30 minutes, plus chilling** / Servings: **10**

5 ounces melba toast

268 grams (1¼ cups) white sugar

1 teaspoon lemon juice

2 tablespoons salted butter,
cut into 2 pieces

1 tablespoon plus 1 teaspoon
orange blossom water, divided

8-ounce container mascarpone
cheese

½ cup heavy cream

135 grams (1 cup) raw unsalted
shelled pistachios, chopped

Pomegranate seeds, raspberries or
strawberries, to serve (optional)

In her book "The Palestinian Table," Reem Kassis explains that the name of this dessert, aish el saraya, translates as "bread of the royal palaces." Made from syrup-soaked toasted bread (we call for melba toast) topped with creamy whipped mascarpone and finished with pistachios and pomegranate seeds, it is simple to make, but offers elegant and rich flavors and textures. If you are not a fan of orange blossom water, which has an intensely floral aroma, instead use three or four strips of orange zest in the syrup (remove the zest before pouring the syrup over the bread) and 1 teaspoon vanilla extract in the mascarpone mixture.

Don't overwhip the mascarpone mixture or it will turn too stiff and have a curdled appearance.

1. Mist a 9-inch round springform pan with cooking spray and set aside. In a food processor, process the melba toast until the largest pieces are pea-sized, 30 to 45 seconds. Transfer to a large bowl and set aside.

2. In a small saucepan over medium-high, combine 1¼ cups water, the sugar and lemon juice. Bring to a boil, stirring to dissolve the sugar. Reduce to medium and cook until the syrup is slightly thickened, 3 to 4 minutes. Remove from heat, add the butter and 1 tablespoon orange blossom water, then stir until the butter is melted.

3. Pour the hot syrup over the melba toast and set aside until all of the liquid has been absorbed, about 10 minutes, stirring occasionally. Transfer to the prepared springform pan and press into an even layer. Cool to room temperature.

4. In a stand mixer with the whisk attachment, whip the mascarpone, cream and remaining 1 teaspoon orange blossom water on medium-high until smooth and the mixture holds stiff peaks when the whisk is lifted, about 1 minute; do not overbeat.

5. Spread the mascarpone mixture over the bread, smoothing it with the back of a spoon or a small spatula. Sprinkle the pistachios over the top. Cover and refrigerate for at least 2 hours or up to 24 hours. To serve, remove the sides of the pan. Top with pomegranate seeds or berries (if using), then cut into wedges.

Tangerine-Almond Cake
with Bay-Infused Syrup

Start to finish: 1 hour 10 minutes (20 minutes active), plus cooling
Servings: 8

For the cake:

225 grams (2¼ cups) blanched almond flour

87 grams (⅔ cup) all-purpose flour

½ teaspoon baking powder

214 grams (1 cup) white sugar

1½ tablespoons finely grated tangerine zest (4 to 5 tangerines)

2 teaspoons finely grated lemon zest (1 to 2 lemons)

¾ teaspoon kosher salt

12 tablespoons (1½ sticks) salted butter, room temperature, plus more for pan

4 large eggs, room temperature

3 tablespoons sliced almonds

For the syrup:

71 grams (⅓ cup) white sugar

3 tablespoons tangerine juice

2 tablespoons lemon juice

3 small bay leaves

Syrup-soaked cakes are largely foreign to U.S. bakers, though they're common throughout eastern Mediterranean countries. Easy to make, the cakes also keep well because of the hygroscopic (water retaining) nature of the syrup. Our tangerine-almond cake has a moist, pleasantly dense texture thanks in part to almond meal. (Use blanched almond flour; unblanched almond meal makes for a drier and less appealing cake.) We infuse our citrus syrup with bay leaves, adding an herbal note. We loved the unique flavor of tangerines in this cake, but if you can't find them, substitute orange zest and juice. If you don't have an 8-inch round cake pan, use a 9-inch pan and reduce the baking time to about 45 minutes.

Don't invert the cake without the buttered parchment. The cake's exterior is tacky and will easily stick to other surfaces, peeling off the crust and the almonds.

1. Heat the oven to 325°F with a rack in the middle position. Butter the bottom and sides of an 8-inch round cake pan. Line the bottom with a round of kitchen parchment, then butter the parchment. In a medium bowl, whisk together the almond flour, all-purpose flour and baking powder.

2. In the bowl of a stand mixer with a paddle attachment, mix the sugar, both zests and the salt on low until the sugar appears moistened and clumps, about 1 minute. Add the butter and mix on medium-low until the mixture is cohesive. Increase the mixer to medium-high and beat until pale and fluffy, about 3 minutes. Reduce the mixer to low and add the eggs, one at a time, scraping down the bowl after each addition.

3. Add the dry ingredients and mix on low just until combined, 10 to 15 seconds. Use a silicone spatula to fold the batter until no streaks of flour remain. The batter will be very thick. Scrape the batter into the prepared pan. Spread into an even layer, then sprinkle the almonds

on top. Bake until the cake is golden brown and the center feels firm when lightly pressed, about 55 minutes, rotating the pan halfway through.

4. Meanwhile, make the syrup. In a small saucepan over medium, combine all ingredients. Bring to a simmer, stirring until the sugar dissolves. Remove from heat and let the syrup steep until needed.

5. When the cake is done, return the syrup to a simmer over medium. Use a toothpick or skewer to poke holes all over the cake's surface. Brush all of the hot syrup evenly onto the hot cake. Cool the cake in the pan until barely warm to the touch, about 30 minutes.

6. Lightly butter a sheet of kitchen parchment, then place it on the cake, buttered side down. Invert a large plate on top of the parchment, then invert the plate and cake pan together. Lift off the pan and remove the parchment round. Re-invert the cake onto a serving platter and let cool completely.

Chocolate-Orange Tart

Start to finish: 2 hours (45 minutes active), plus cooling
Servings: 8

___

For the tart shell:

130 grams (1 cup) all-purpose flour

50 grams (½ cup) almond flour

71 grams (⅓ cup) white sugar

½ teaspoon kosher salt

6 tablespoons salted butter, cut into ½-inch cubes and chilled

1 large egg yolk

1 teaspoon vanilla extract

For the filling:

78 grams (6 tablespoons) white sugar

2 teaspoons grated orange zest plus 2 tablespoons orange juice

½ teaspoon kosher salt

¼ teaspoon cinnamon

1½ cups (12 ounces) whole-milk ricotta cheese

1 large egg plus 1 large egg yolk

1 teaspoon vanilla extract

1½ ounces semisweet chocolate, chopped

The filling of this tart was inspired by the chocolate, orange and ricotta tart served at Rose Bakery in Paris, but we found the crust in the pastry case of Vancouver's Beaucoup Bakery—a crisp, slightly crunchy almond meal affair that had us at first bite. Rose Carrarini's decadent cheesecake-style filling is made with ricotta, cream, orange zest and dark chocolate, all bound together with a little flour. We added cinnamon and lightened our take, leaving out cream and flour and reducing the amount of chocolate so the ricotta and orange came through more clearly. For the crust, we used all-purpose and almond flours and pressed the dough right into the tart pan (no rolling). The result had great flavor and texture, and it didn't shrink or slump when blind baked. For do-ahead ease, the tart shell can be prepped, pressed into the pan, pricked all over, then frozen for up to two weeks; do not thaw before baking.

Don't use skim-milk ricotta; whole-milk is needed for a rich, creamy consistency. Some ricottas with more lactose will brown more deeply than others. We liked Calabro, which is low in lactose.

1. Heat the oven to 300°F with a rack in the middle position. Mist a 9-inch tart pan with a removable bottom with cooking spray. Set on a baking sheet and set aside.

2. To make the tart shell, in a food processor, combine both flours, the sugar and salt; process until combined, about 5 seconds. Scatter the butter over the dry ingredients and pulse until the mixture resembles coarse sand, 10 to 12 pulses. Add the yolk and vanilla, then process until the mixture is evenly moistened and cohesive, 20 to 30 seconds; the mixture may not form a single mass.

3. Crumble the dough into the tart pan, evenly covering the surface; do not wash the food processor. Using the bottom of a dry measuring cup, press the dough into an even layer over the bottom and up the sides of the pan. Use a fork to prick the dough all over the bottom and sides, then freeze until firm, at least 15 minutes or up to 1 hour.

4. Bake on the baking sheet until the tart shell is deep golden brown, 1 to 1¼ hours. Let cool on the sheet on a wire rack for 15 minutes. Increase the oven to 350°F.

5. Meanwhile, prepare the filling. In the food processor, combine the sugar, orange zest, salt and cinnamon; process until the sugar is moistened and fragrant, about 15 seconds. Add the ricotta and process until smooth, about 30 seconds, scraping the bowl as needed. Add the egg, egg yolk, orange juice and vanilla, then process until combined, another 10 to 15 seconds.

6. Pour the filling into the still-warm crust, then sprinkle evenly with the chocolate. Carefully slide the baking sheet into the oven and bake until the filling is slightly puffed at the edges but the center still jiggles slightly, 25 to 35 minutes. Let cool completely on the wire rack, about 2 hours.

7. If serving the tart at room temperature, remove the outer ring from the tart pan. If serving the tart chilled, keep the outer ring in place and refrigerate uncovered for 1 hour, or until the chocolate is set, then loosely cover with plastic wrap. Refrigerate for up to 2 days; remove the outer ring from the pan before serving.

Lemon-Almond Pound Cake

Start to finish: 1½ hours (20 minutes active), plus cooling
Makes one 9-inch loaf

___

195 grams (1½ cups) all-purpose flour, plus more for the pan

4 large eggs, room temperature

2 teaspoons vanilla extract

241 grams (1 cup plus 2 tablespoons) plus 54 grams (¼ cup) white sugar

2 tablespoons grated lemon zest, plus 3 tablespoons lemon juice, divided

100 grams (1 cup) almond flour

1½ teaspoons baking powder

1 teaspoon kosher salt

14 tablespoons (1¾ sticks) salted butter, cut into 14 pieces, room temperature

3 tablespoons sliced almonds

CHANGE THE WAY YOU COOK:
MAKING THE BEST OF ZEST

Grating citrus zest directly into other ingredients helps prevent loss of flavorful oils on the cutting board. But when grating zest, make sure to use only the outer colored portion of the peel; the white pith underneath is bitter and astringent.

For this plush, velvety pound cake, we took a cue from Rose Carrarini of Rose's Bakery in Paris and replaced some of the wheat flour with almond flour. Almond flour makes the cake's crumb extra tender and moist and gives it a more interesting texture than wheat flour alone. Grating the lemon zest directly into the mixer bowl allows you to capture the maximum amount of flavorful essential oils; rather than fish out the zest to then measure it, we usually just eyeball it. We finish the cake with a tangy-sweet lemon glaze, brushing it on while the loaf is still hot so the syrup is readily absorbed. Thanks to generous amounts of eggs and butter, this cake keeps well. Store it in an airtight container at room temperature for up to three days.

Don't use cold butter or cold eggs. The butter must be softened to room temperature so it integrates into the sugar-flour mixture. And the eggs must be at room temperature, too, not chilled, so they don't cause the butter to stiffen up when added to the mixer. Lastly, don't rotate the cake as it bakes. Jostling the pan increases the chance the batter will deflate, resulting in a dense, underrisen cake.

1. Heat the oven to 325°F with a rack in the middle position. Coat a 9-by-5-inch loaf pan with cooking spray, dust evenly with flour, then tap out the excess. In a 2-cup liquid measuring cup or small bowl, beat the eggs and vanilla until combined; set aside.

2. In a stand mixer fitted with the paddle attachment, mix the 241 grams sugar and the lemon zest on low until fragrant, about 1 minute. Add both flours, the baking powder and salt and mix until combined, about 10 seconds. With the mixer on low, add the butter a piece at a time. Once all the butter has been added, continue mixing on low until the mixture is crumbly and no powdery bits remain, 1 to 2 minutes.

3. With the mixer still running, add the egg mixture in a slow, steady stream and mix for about 10 seconds. Increase to medium-high and beat until the batter

is light and fluffy, 1 to 1½ minutes, scraping the bowl once or twice. The batter will be thick.

4. Transfer the batter to the prepared pan and smooth the surface, then sprinkle evenly with the sliced almonds. Bake for 45 minutes, then reduce the oven to 300°F. Continue to bake until the top is deep golden brown and a toothpick inserted at the center of the cake comes out clean, another 30 to 35 minutes.

5. While the cake bakes, in a small saucepan over medium-low, heat the remaining 54 grams sugar and 2 tablespoons of lemon juice, stirring often, until the sugar dissolves and the mixture reaches a simmer. Immediately remove from the heat and stir in the remaining 1 tablespoon lemon juice. Set aside to cool.

6. When the cake is done, cool in the pan on a wire rack for 10 minutes. Invert the cake onto the rack, then turn it upright. Using a toothpick, poke small holes in the surface at 1-inch intervals. Brush all of the lemon-sugar syrup onto the cake, allowing it to soak in. Cool completely before slicing, about 2 hours.

MAKING LEMON-ALMOND POUND CAKE

1. In a stand mixer with the paddle attachment, mix the 241 grams (1 cup plus 2 tablespoons) sugar and lemon zest on low until fragrant, about 1 minute.

2. After adding both flours, the baking powder and salt, keep the mixer on low and add the 14 tablespoons room-temperature butter one piece at a time.

3. After all the butter has been added to the bowl, continue mixing on low until the mixture is crumbly and no powdery bits remain, 1 to 2 minutes.

4. With the mixer still running on low, pour in the egg and vanilla mixture in a slow, steady stream, then continue to mix for about 10 seconds.

5. Increase the speed to medium-high and beat until light and fluffy, 1 to 1½ minutes, scraping down the bowl once or twice. The batter will be thick.

6. Transfer to a loaf pan; smooth the surface. Sprinkle with almonds, then bake at 325°F for 45 minutes. Reduce to 300°F and bake for another 30 to 35 minutes.

7. Cool the cake in the pan for 10 minutes. After inverting the cake onto the rack, use a toothpick to poke small holes in the surface at 1-inch intervals.

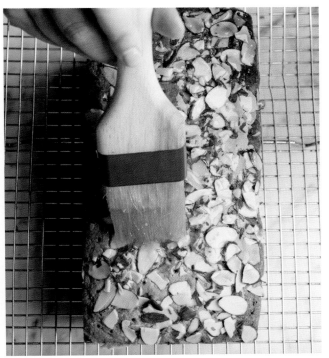

8. Brush the lemon syrup onto the surface of the cake, allowing it to soak in. Cool the cake completely before slicing, about 2 hours.

Ricotta-Semolina **Cheesecake**

Start to finish: **1 hour (20 minutes active), plus cooling and chilling**
Servings: **10**

161 grams (¾ cup) white sugar, divided

2 teaspoons grated lemon zest, plus 1 tablespoon lemon juice

16-ounce container (2 cups) whole-milk ricotta

8-ounce container (1 cup) mascarpone

43 grams (¼ cup) semolina flour, plus more for the pan

4 large eggs, separated

2 tablespoons dry Marsala wine

¾ teaspoon kosher salt

This is a delicate dessert that mimics the texture of a New York–style cheesecake without the heft. It takes inspiration from a style of cake prepared in Germany and Italy. Instead of cream cheese, whole-milk ricotta kept it light; our favorite supermarket brand is Calabro. Mascarpone added plenty of flavor and a rich, creamy texture. Whipped egg whites also helped keep things light, and semolina flour gave structure to the cheese mixture and created a "crust" on the exterior. Lemon zest and juice brightened the flavors, and Marsala added an Italian touch while also cutting through the richness. If you don't have Marsala, dry sherry is a good substitute. A citrus curd or fruit compote made a great topping for this barely sweet cheesecake. Or try our flavorful fruit compotes (p. 543).

Don't be surprised if the cake cracks as it cools. The whipped egg whites give it a light, fluffy texture, but also make it delicate enough that cracks are inevitable.

1. Heat the oven to 350°F with a rack in the middle position. Coat the bottom and sides of a 9-inch springform pan with cooking spray, then dust evenly with semolina, tapping out the excess.

2. In a food processor, combine ½ cup of the sugar and the lemon zest. Process until moist and fragrant, about 15 seconds. Add the ricotta and mascarpone and process until smooth, about 30 seconds, scraping the sides as needed. Add the semolina, egg yolks, Marsala, lemon juice and salt, then process until combined, about 10 seconds. Transfer to a large bowl.

3. In a stand mixer with a whisk attachment, whip the egg whites on medium-high until light and foamy about 1 minute. With the mixer running, slowly add the remaining ¼ cup of sugar and continue to whip until the whites hold soft peaks, 1 to 2 minutes. Add a third of the egg whites to the cheese mixture and fold until combined. Add the remaining whites and fold until just incorporated. Transfer to the prepared pan, spreading in an even layer and tapping on the counter to release air bubbles.

4. Bake until the top is lightly browned and the cake is just set but still jiggles when shaken, 40 to 45 minutes. Let cool completely in the pan on a wire rack, about 2 hours. Cover and refrigerate for at least 2 hours. Run a knife around the inside of the pan and remove the pan sides before slicing.

Coconut Cashew Cake (*Sanwin Makin*)

Start to finish: 1 hour
Makes one 9-inch cake

170 grams (1 cup) semolina flour

30 grams (⅓ cup) plus 2 tablespoons unsweetened shredded coconut, divided

14-ounce can coconut milk

218 grams (1 cup packed) light brown sugar

4 tablespoons (½ stick) salted butter, melted and slightly cooled

3 large eggs

1½ teaspoons baking powder

½ teaspoon ground cardamom

½ teaspoon kosher salt

32 grams (¼ cup) unsalted roasted cashews, chopped

Rich with the flavor of coconut, traditional Burmese semolina cake is made by cooking the semolina into a thick, dense porridge before baking. We lightened the cake's texture by using a straightforward cake-mixing method and added ground cardamom for fragrance and flavor. Toasting the semolina and shredded coconut first brings out their nuttiness, and soaking them in coconut milk softens their texture so the cake bakes up with a soft, plush crumb. Roasted cashews added texture and visual appeal to the golden-brown cake. Though this dessert is usually served chilled, we liked it better at room temperature and even slightly warm, with lightly sweetened whipped cream on the side.

Don't use light coconut milk, which lacks the richness of full-fat coconut milk. And don't forget to stir the coconut milk before using. Avoid cream of coconut and sweetened coconut flakes, both of which contain added sugar. They will make the cake too sweet.

1. Heat the oven to 350°F with a rack in the middle position. Mist the bottom and sides of a 9-inch round cake pan with cooking spray. Line the bottom with a round of kitchen parchment, then mist the parchment.

2. On a rimmed baking sheet, combine the semolina and the 30 grams (⅓ cup) of shredded coconut in an even layer. Toast until fragrant and golden at the edges, 10 to 12 minutes, stirring halfway through. Transfer to a large bowl, immediately add the coconut milk and whisk to combine. Set aside until the liquid is absorbed, 15 minutes.

3. Increase the oven to 375°F. To the semolina mixture, add the brown sugar, butter, eggs, baking powder, cardamom and salt. Whisk until well combined; the batter will be very thin. Pour the batter into the prepared pan and sprinkle with the cashews and remaining 2 tablespoons shredded coconut.

4. Bake until a toothpick inserted at the center comes out clean, 28 to 33 minutes. Let cool on a wire rack for 20 minutes. Run a knife around the edges, then invert the cake onto the rack and remove the pan and parchment. Re-invert onto a serving plate. Serve warm or at room temperature.

Macanese Sweet Potato Cake
(*Batatada*)

Start to finish: **3 hours (20 minutes active)**
Servings: **12**

100 grams (½ cup) coconut oil, melted and slightly cooled, plus more for pan

12 ounces orange-fleshed sweet potatoes, peeled and cut into 1-inch chunks

195 grams (1½ cups) all-purpose flour

60 grams (⅔ cup) unsweetened shredded coconut

2 teaspoons ground ginger

2 teaspoons baking powder

½ teaspoon baking soda

1 teaspoon kosher salt

199 grams (1 cup) packed dark brown sugar

1 tablespoon grated lime zest, plus 2 tablespoons juice

3 large eggs

¾ cup whole milk

1 tablespoon vanilla extract

93 grams (¾ cup) powdered sugar

Sweet potatoes give this simple cake rich flavor but a light crumb. Yellow sweet potatoes are the traditional choice, but we preferred the color of orange-fleshed sweet potatoes. Both unrefined and refined coconut oil worked; the former has a fuller, more intense flavor and aroma that accentuate the shredded coconut in the cake. You'll need a food processor with at least an 11-cup capacity to accommodate the sweet potato puree.

Don't use sweetened shredded coconut. It will make the cake much too sweet.

1. Heat the oven to 350°F with a rack in the middle position. Coat a 13-by-9-inch metal baking pan with coconut oil. Place the sweet potatoes in a microwave-safe medium bowl, cover and microwave on high for about 5 minutes, stirring once halfway though, until the potatoes are completely tender. Carefully uncover and set aside to cool slightly.

2. In a food processor, combine the flour, coconut, ginger, baking powder, baking soda and salt. Process until the coconut is finely ground, 1 to 2 minutes. Transfer to a large bowl. In the processor, combine the brown sugar and lime zest, then process until fragrant, about 30 seconds. Add the sweet potatoes and process until completely smooth, 60 to 90 seconds, scraping the bowl as needed.

3. Add the eggs, milk and vanilla, then process until combined, about 10 seconds. With the machine running, add the melted coconut oil through the feed tube, then process until fully incorporated. Pour the sweet potato mixture into the dry ingredients and gently whisk to combine. Transfer the batter to the prepared pan and spread evenly.

4. Bake until the cake is golden brown and a toothpick inserted at the center comes out clean, 30 to 35 minutes. Let cool in the pan on a wire rack for 15 minutes.

5. Meanwhile, in a small bowl, whisk the powdered sugar and the lime juice until smooth. Brush the glaze evenly onto the warm cake. Let the cake cool completely in the pan, about 2 hours.

Stovetop Chocolate Cake

Start to finish: 35 minutes (10 minutes active), plus cooling
Servings: 8

___

130 grams (1 cup) all-purpose flour

29 grams (⅓ cup) cocoa powder

1 teaspoon baking soda

½ teaspoon kosher salt

218 grams (1 cup packed)
light brown sugar

2 large eggs

1 teaspoon instant espresso powder

½ cup sour cream

6 tablespoons (¾ stick) salted butter,
melted and slightly cooled

1½ teaspoons vanilla extract

Steaming a standard chocolate cake batter produced a light, moist cake, and let us avoid having to turn on the oven. To elevate the cake above the water that steams it, we fashioned a ring from foil. Brown sugar and espresso powder gave the cake complexity, while sour cream added richness and a welcome tang. We liked serving this cake dusted with powdered sugar or topped with whipped cream. If your Dutch oven has a self-basting lid—bumps or spikes on the underside—lay a sheet of parchment or foil over the top of the pot before putting the lid in place to prevent water from dripping onto the surface.

Don't open the Dutch oven too often while steaming, but do check that the water is at a very gentle simmer. You should see steam emerging from the pot. If the heat is too high, the water will boil away before the cake is cooked.

1. Cut an 18-inch length of foil and gently scrunch together to form a snake about 1 inch thick. Shape into a circle and set on the bottom of a large Dutch oven. Add enough water to reach three-quarters up the coil. Mist the bottom and sides of a 9-inch round cake pan with cooking spray. Line the bottom with a round of kitchen parchment, then mist the parchment. Place the prepared pan in the pot on top of the foil coil.

2. Sift the flour, cocoa powder and baking soda into a medium bowl, then whisk in the salt. In a large bowl, whisk the sugar and eggs until slightly lightened, about 30 seconds. Whisk in ½ cup water, the espresso powder, sour cream, butter and vanilla. Add the flour mixture and whisk gently until just combined.

3. Pour the batter into the prepared pan. Cover and heat on high until the water boils. Reduce to low and steam, covered, until the center of the cake is just firm to the touch, about 23 minutes.

4. Turn off the heat and remove the lid. Let stand until the cake pan is cool enough to handle. Transfer the pan to a wire rack, then run a paring knife around the edges. Let cool completely, then invert the cake onto a plate and remove the pan and parchment. Re-invert onto a serving plate.

Spanish Almond Cake
(*Tarta de Santiago*)

Start to finish: **1 hour 10 minutes, plus cooling (10 minutes active)** / Servings: 8

240 grams (1 cup plus 2 tablespoons) white sugar

3 large eggs, plus 3 large egg whites

½ teaspoon kosher salt

¼ teaspoon almond extract

¼ teaspoon vanilla extract

250 grams (2½ cups) blanched almond flour

35 grams (3 tablespoons) turbinado or demerara sugar

37 grams (⅓ cup) sliced almonds, roughly chopped

This flourless cake from Galicia, Spain, traditionally is made with separated eggs and flavored with citrus and/or cinnamon. We liked it made more simply, with whole eggs and just a small measure of vanilla and almond extracts. A sprinkling of chopped almonds and coarse raw sugar on top gives the surface a chewy-crisp crust that contrasts wonderfully with the dense, plush crumb of the cake's interior. Crème fraîche and fresh berries are perfect accompaniments. Allow the cake to cool to room temperature before serving.

Don't underbake the cake. Rather than use a skewer or toothpick to test the center for doneness, check the browning and crust development. The cake is ready when the surface is deeply browned and the crust feels firm when gently pressed with a finger.

1. Heat the oven to 350°F with a rack in the middle position. Mist the bottom and sides of a 9-inch round cake pan with cooking spray, line the bottom with a round of kitchen parchment, then mist the parchment.

2. In a large bowl, combine the white sugar, whole eggs and egg whites, salt and both extracts. Whisk vigorously until well combined, 30 to 45 seconds; the mixture will be slightly frothy but the sugar won't be fully dissolved. Add the almond flour and whisk until incorporated. Pour the batter into the prepared pan, then sprinkle evenly with the turbinado sugar and chopped almonds. Bake until deeply browned and the crust feels firm when gently pressed with a finger, 45 to 55 minutes. Let cool in the pan on a wire rack for 10 minutes.

3. Run a knife around the edges of the cake, then invert onto a plate. Remove the pan and parchment then re-invert the cake onto a serving plate. Let cool completely before serving.

Maple–Browned Butter Pie

Start to finish: 3 hours (45 minutes active), plus cooling
Makes one 9-inch pie

For the crust:

98 grams (¾ cup) all-purpose flour, plus more for dusting

70 grams (½ cup) whole-wheat flour

13 grams (1 tablespoon) white sugar

½ teaspoon kosher salt

7 tablespoons salted butter, cut into ½-inch pieces and chilled

6 to 8 tablespoons ice water

For the filling:

8 tablespoons (1 stick) salted butter, cut into 4 pieces

107 grams (½ cup) white sugar

111 grams (⅓ cup) honey

18 grams (2 tablespoons) fine cornmeal

1 teaspoon kosher salt

3 large eggs, plus 1 large egg yolk, well beaten

½ cup maple syrup (see note)

½ cup heavy cream

2 teaspoons vanilla extract

2 teaspoons cider vinegar

Maldon sea salt flakes, to serve (optional)

This dessert is the creation of Briana Holt of Tandem Coffee + Bakery in Portland, Maine. The nutty flavor and flaky yet sturdy texture of the whole-wheat pastry perfectly complement the browned butteriness and silkiness of the custard filling. We recommend using the darkest maple syrup you can find so the smoky maple notes hold their own with the butter, eggs and cream. A sprinkle of flaky sea salt just before serving balances the filling's sweetness and adds a pleasing crunchy contrast, but this flourish is optional. The pie can be covered with plastic wrap and refrigerated for up to two days; bring to room temperature before serving.

Don't skip or skimp on the pie weights when prebaking the crust; they're essential for preventing the dough from shrinking, slipping and bubbling. We highly recommend using metal or ceramic pie weights. These materials conduct heat well, unlike dried beans and rice—common pantry-staple pie weights—so they aid with browning, and their hefty weight holds the dough in place as it bakes. Also, don't forget to lower the oven temperature to 325°F after placing the prebaked crust on a wire rack.

1. To make the crust, in a food processor, combine both flours, the sugar and salt; process until combined, about 5 seconds. Scatter the butter over the flour mixture, then pulse until the pieces are the size of small peas, 10 to 14 pulses. Transfer the mixture to a medium bowl. Sprinkle with 1 tablespoon ice water, then toss with a silicone spatula, making sure to scrape along the bottom of the bowl until the water has been absorbed. Repeat with the remaining ice water, adding it 1 tablespoon at a time, until the mixture forms pebbly clumps; you may not need all the water. Using your hands, press the clumps together firmly into a rough ball, then form the ball into a 4-inch disk. Wrap tightly in plastic wrap and refrigerate for 1 hour.

2. Heat the oven to 375°F with a rack in the middle position. On a well-floured counter and using a rolling pin, roll the dough into a 12-inch circle. Drape the dough over the rolling pin and transfer to a 9-inch pie plate. Gently ease the dough into the plate by lifting the edges while pressing down into the corners. Trim the edges, leaving a ½-inch overhang, then tuck the overhang under itself so the dough is flush with the rim of the pan. Using your fingers, crimp and flute the edge of the dough. Refrigerate uncovered until firm, about 30 minutes, or cover with plastic wrap and refrigerate for up to 8 hours.

3. Line the chilled dough with a large piece of heavy-duty foil, pressing the foil into the corners and up the sides of the pie plate, then fill evenly with 2 cups pie weights; loosely fold the foil to cover the fluted edge. Bake until the edges of the crust are light golden brown, about 35 minutes. Transfer to a wire rack and remove the foil and weights. Reduce the oven to 325°F.

4. While the crust is baking, make the filling. In a 10-inch skillet over medium-high, melt the butter. Cook, swirling the pan frequently, until the milk solids at the bottom are golden brown and the butter has a nutty aroma, 1 to 3 minutes. Scrape the butter into a medium heat-proof bowl and let cool until warm, about 15 minutes.

5. To the browned butter, whisk in the sugar, honey, cornmeal and kosher salt. Add the eggs and yolk, then whisk slowly and gently until well combined. Add the maple syrup, cream, vanilla and vinegar, then whisk gently until homogenous. Pour the filling into the crust (it's fine if the crust is still warm).

6. Bake until the edges of the filling are puffed and the center jiggles when the pie plate is gently shaken, 40 to 45 minutes. Transfer to the wire rack and let stand until the filling is fully cooled and set, 3 to 4 hours. Sprinkle with Maldon salt (if using).

Staples, Sauces and Seasonings

Ancho Chili Salsa Roja / 492

Tomatillo-Avocado Salsa / 493

Greek Dips / 494

Harissa with Three Variations / 496

Honey-Chili Sauce / 501

Colombian Avocado Salsa
(*Ají de Aguacate*) / 503

Tamarind Dipping Sauce / 504

Japanese-Style Salt-Pickled Radish and
Red Onion (*Yasai no Sokuseki-zuke*) / 507

Slow-Roasted Tomatoes / 509

Homemade Chipotles in Adobo Sauce / 511

Cilantro-Jalapeño Adobo Sauce / 512

Pickled Vegetables (*Escabeche*) / 514

Central Mexican Guacamole / 519

Jalapeño-Mint Sauce / 520

Pickled Chilies (*Nam Prik*) / 523

Spicy Garlic-and-Herb Oil / 524

Spiced Yogurt Dressing / 526

Sweet-and-Sour Mint Dressing
(*Sekanjabin*) / 528

Fig-Olive Tapenade / 533

Whipped Feta / 535

Miso-Ginger Dressing / 536

Green Goddess Tofu Dressing / 538

Fruit Chutney / 540

Fruit Compotes / 542

12

Ancho Chili Salsa Roja

Start to finish: **15 minutes** / Makes **about 1½ cups**

3 medium ancho chilies, stemmed, seeded and torn into pieces

Boiling water

1 large garlic clove, smashed and peeled

1 medium shallot, roughly chopped

1 medium vine-ripened tomato, cored and roughly chopped

2 teaspoons white sugar

Kosher salt

In this salsa, fresh tomato, garlic and shallot complement the earthy, smoky notes of ancho chilies. Use it as a dip for tortilla chips, spooned onto tacos or in a marinade for beef, pork or chicken.

1. In a 12-inch skillet over medium, toast the chilies, pressing with a wide metal spatula and flipping once or twice, until fragrant and a shade darker in color, 2 to 4 minutes. Transfer to a medium bowl and pour in enough boiling water to cover. Let stand until softened, about 10 minutes.

2. Drain the chilies and discard the soaking liquid. Transfer to a food processor or blender. Add the garlic, shallot, tomato, sugar, 1 teaspoon salt and ½ cup water. Process until finely chopped and well combined, about 20 seconds, scraping the sides as needed.

Tomatillo-Avocado **Salsa**

Start to finish: **15 minutes** / Makes 1½ cups

3 medium tomatillos (about 6 ounces), husked, cored and halved

¼ cup lightly packed fresh cilantro

3 scallions, roughly chopped

2 serrano chilies, stemmed, seeded and roughly chopped

1 medium garlic clove, smashed and peeled

1 tablespoon grapeseed or other neutral oil

Kosher salt

1 ripe avocado, halved, pitted, peeled and roughly chopped

2 teaspoons lime juice

This smooth, herbal salsa is a nice alternative to tomato-based versions. The tartness of the tomatillos balances the creamy richness of the avocado. We greatly preferred serrano chilies over jalapeños here, as they provided more fruitiness and flavor. Serve with tortilla chips, tacos, quesadillas, enchiladas and fried or scrambled eggs.

Don't forget to seed the serrano chilies. This salsa is meant to be creamy and cooling, not sharp and spicy. Also, be sure to roughly chop the chilies before adding them to the processor so they break down easily.

In a food processor, combine the tomatillos, cilantro, scallions, chilies, garlic, oil and 1¼ teaspoons salt. Process until finely chopped, about 1 minute. Add the avocado and lime juice, then process until smooth and creamy, about 1 minute, scraping the bowl as needed. Taste and season with salt.

Greek Dips

TZATZIKI

Start to finish: **15 minutes**
Makes **about 3½ cups**

The cucumber-yogurt dip known as tzatziki is often seasoned with lemon juice in the U.S. But in Greece cooks prefer red wine vinegar because it adds sharp acidity without the citrus notes to compete with the other ingredients. Thick and cooling, tzatziki can be served as a dip, but it's also an ideal condiment or accompaniment for grilled meats and seafood and fried foods.

Don't use nonfat Greek yogurt. Without any fat, the flavor of the tzatziki is weak and thin. Also, when shredding the cucumbers, don't shred the cores, as the seeds are watery and have a slight bitterness and unappealing texture.

2 English cucumbers, halved crosswise

Kosher salt

1¾ cups plain whole-milk or low-fat Greek yogurt

½ cup extra-virgin olive oil

3 medium garlic cloves, finely grated

3 tablespoons chopped fresh mint, plus more to serve

3 tablespoons chopped fresh dill, plus more to serve

4 teaspoons red wine vinegar

1. Set a colander in a medium bowl, then set a box grater in the colander. Grate the cucumber halves on the grater's large holes, rotating and grating only down to the seedy core. Discard the cores. Sprinkle the shredded cucumber with 2 teaspoons salt and toss. Set aside to drain for 10 minutes.

2. Meanwhile, in a medium bowl, whisk the yogurt, oil, garlic, mint, dill and vinegar.

3. A handful at a time, squeeze the shredded cucumber to remove as much liquid as possible, then set on a cutting board; reserve 2 teaspoons of the cucumber liquid. Finely chop the squeezed cucumber, then stir into the yogurt mixture. Stir in the reserved cucumber liquid and ½ teaspoon salt. Transfer to a serving bowl and sprinkle with additional mint and dill.

SPICY FETA DIP (*TIROKAFTERI*)

Start to finish: **10 minutes**
Makes **about 3½ cups**

Tirokafteri is a Greek cheese-based dip or spread that
can be flavored numerous ways. In our version, we build
complexity by combining two cheeses with different
characteristics: creamy, tangy chèvre (fresh goat cheese)
and firm, briny feta. Roasted red peppers give the dip
sweetness and color; the Anaheim chili and hot smoked
paprika lend some heat. If you don't have hot smoked
paprika, you can substitute with ½ teaspoon sweet
smoked paprika plus ¼ teaspoon cayenne pepper.

*Don't add more Anaheim chili if you're looking to increase
the spiciness. Instead, up the hot paprika or toss a Fresno
chili into the food processor before pureeing.*

8 ounces chèvre (fresh goat cheese)

½ cup drained roasted red peppers, patted dry

1 Anaheim chili, stemmed, seeded and chopped

3 tablespoons extra-virgin olive oil,
plus more to serve

¾ teaspoon hot smoked paprika

½ teaspoon honey

Kosher salt and ground black pepper

6 ounces feta cheese, crumbled (1½ cups)

½ cup fresh dill, chopped, plus more to serve

1. In a food processor, combine the goat cheese, roasted
peppers, Anaheim chili, oil, paprika, honey, ½ teaspoon
salt and ¼ teaspoon black pepper. Process until smooth,
about 1 minute, scraping the bowl as needed.

2. Transfer to a medium bowl. Fold in the feta and dill,
then taste and season with salt and pepper. Transfer
to a serving bowl and top with additional oil, dill and
black pepper.

Harissa

Start to finish: **15 minutes**
Makes **about 1½ cups**

4 dried New Mexico chilies, stemmed, seeded and torn into rough pieces

½ cup grapeseed or other neutral oil

6 medium garlic cloves, peeled

1 teaspoon caraway seeds

1 teaspoon cumin seeds

1 cup drained roasted red peppers, patted dry

½ cup drained oil-packed sun-dried tomatoes

1 tablespoon white balsamic vinegar

Kosher salt

Cayenne pepper

Our version of harissa, the spicy condiment that originated in North Africa, adds delicious punch to dips, soups, sauces and vinaigrettes. New Mexico chilies did the best job of matching harder-to-find North African chilies, bringing balanced heat. For more fire, a bit of cayenne can be added. Plenty of recipes call for either sun-dried tomatoes or roasted red peppers; we found a combination gave our harissa the sweet, ketchup-like profile Americans love and helped make it more of an all-purpose sauce, rather than simply a hot sauce. Frying the chilies, whole spices and garlic in oil was easier and works better than the traditional method of toasting in a dry skillet. And while most recipes call for rehydrating the dried chilies, we found the hot oil softened them adequately, giving the harissa a pleasant, slightly coarse texture. Adding garlic to the mix mellowed its bite, and leaving the cloves whole ensured they wouldn't burn (and meant less prep work). We favored white balsamic vinegar for its mild acidity and slight sweetness. Lemon juice or white wine vinegar sweetened with a pinch of sugar is a good substitute.

In a small saucepan over medium, combine the chilies, oil, garlic, caraway and cumin. Cook, stirring often, until the garlic is light golden brown and the chilies are fragrant, about 5 minutes. Carefully transfer the mixture to a food processor and add the red peppers, tomatoes, vinegar and ¾ teaspoon of salt. Process until smooth, about 3 minutes, scraping the bowl once or twice. Season with salt and cayenne. Serve immediately or refrigerate in an airtight container for up to 3 weeks.

HARISSA HISTORY

Harissa (pronounced ha-REE-sah) may well be one of the original hot sauces, and it has enjoyed a bit of piggyback popularity as Sriracha and other spicy condiments have attracted near cultish followings. Chilies didn't land in Africa until the mid-16th century via conquerors, colonialists and traders returning from Central America. The easy-to-grow ingredient found a warm reception in arid African climates, adding an affordable kick to previously bland grain-based diets. Tunisia is credited with the birth of harissa, but it is popular across the region. Tunisians have a stronger predilection for spice than their neighbors, so their harissa emphasizes heat over nuance. In Morocco, where the cuisine is more complex, tomato paste, rose water and preserved lemon might play into the condiment's flavor. Our recipe is honest to its origins but suited to the foods and flavors of the American palate. We use our harissa sauce in all kinds of ways, including adding some kick to roasted potatoes (p. 121).

GREEK YOGURT-HARISSA DIP

Start to finish: **5 minutes**
Makes **about 2 cups**

This works well as an appetizer with crudités and crackers or as a sandwich spread with cold cuts, leftover chicken or grilled lamb.

2 cups plain whole-milk Greek-style yogurt

3 tablespoons harissa

2 tablespoons chopped fresh parsley, mint or a combination

1 teaspoon white sugar

Kosher salt and ground black pepper

In a bowl, stir together the yogurt, harissa, herbs and sugar. Season with salt and pepper.

HARISSA-CILANTRO VINAIGRETTE

Start to finish: **5 minutes**
Makes **about ½ cup**

This dressing pairs well with assertive greens or can be drizzled over roasted beets, cauliflower or broccoli. It's also a terrific sauce for salmon.

2 tablespoons lemon juice

1 tablespoon harissa

1 tablespoon water

2 teaspoons honey

Kosher salt

5 tablespoons extra-virgin olive oil

Ground black pepper

2 tablespoons chopped fresh cilantro

In a bowl, whisk together the lemon juice, harissa, water, honey and ¼ teaspoon of salt. Add the oil and whisk until emulsified. Season with additional salt and pepper, then stir in the cilantro.

SPICY HARISSA DIPPING SAUCE

Start to finish: **5 minutes**
Makes **1 cup**

Use this sauce anytime you'd reach for ketchup.

¾ cup mayonnaise

2 tablespoons harissa

2 tablespoons ketchup

Hot sauce

In a bowl, stir together the mayonnaise, harissa and ketchup. Season with hot sauce, to taste.

Honey-Chili Sauce

Start to finish: **5 minutes**
Makes **about ¾ cup**

167 grams (½ cup) honey

3 tablespoons unseasoned rice vinegar

1 tablespoon chili-garlic sauce

You can pay big money for spicy honey these days, or you can make your own. Our version skews Asian by spiking mild honey with chili-garlic sauce, and it takes honey to some unexpected places. Any mild honey, such as clover, will work. It's great drizzled over sweet potatoes, grilled or roasted vegetables, corn on the cob, or chicken or pork. And don't stop there. Consider a drizzle over pepperoni pizza, or on a soppresatta and mozzarella sandwich. Or use it to jazz up a grilled cheese.

In a small bowl, stir together all ingredients.

Colombian Avocado Salsa
(*Ají de Aguacate*)

Start to finish: **15 minutes** / Makes 3½ cups

4 scallions, cut into 1-inch lengths

2 Anaheim chilies, stemmed, seeded and cut into rough 1-inch pieces

1 habanero chili, stemmed and seeded

1¼ cups lightly packed fresh cilantro

2 tablespoons white vinegar

Kosher salt

3 ripe avocados (see note), halved and pitted

3 hard-cooked large eggs, peeled and chopped

2 tablespoons lime juice

1 plum tomato, cored, seeded and finely chopped

Colombian food does not tend to be spicy, so we seeded the chilies for this salsa. The Anaheims gave the sauce deep pepper flavor, while the habanero added fruitiness and heat.

Don't use fully ripe avocados, which made thin salsa. They should give only slightly when pressed.

1. In a food processor, process the scallions and all 3 chilies until finely chopped, about 20 seconds. Add the cilantro, vinegar and 1½ teaspoons salt. Process until the cilantro is finely chopped, about 10 seconds, scraping the sides as needed.

2. In a medium bowl, mash the flesh from 2 avocado halves and ⅓ of the chopped eggs with a fork until mostly smooth but with some lumps. Roughly chop the remaining 4 avocado halves and transfer to the bowl. Add the lime juice and fold with a silicone spatula to combine.

3. Reserve 2 tablespoons of the chopped tomato and 2 tablespoons of the remaining chopped eggs for garnish. Mix the remaining tomato and eggs into the avocado mixture, then gently fold in the chili-cilantro mixture. Taste and season with salt.

4. Transfer the salsa to a serving bowl and top with the reserved tomato and chopped eggs.

Tamarind Dipping Sauce

Start to finish: 20 minutes
Makes about 2 cups

---

2 lemon grass stalks, trimmed to the lower 6 inches, dry outer layers discarded, chopped

1 large shallot, chopped

3 tablespoons grapeseed or other neutral oil

1 serrano chili, stemmed and chopped

1 tablespoon tomato paste

1 tablespoon finely grated fresh ginger

2 ounces tamarind pulp, seeds removed

5 tablespoons packed light brown sugar

¼ cup fish sauce

1 tablespoon soy sauce

3 tablespoons lime juice (1 to 2 limes)

Ground black pepper

We developed this sauce to go alongside our Chiang Mai chicken, but it's also great with sticky Asian spareribs, stirred into Asian soups, drizzled over steamed or sticky rice, as a base for steaming mussels, or tossed with sliced cucumber and torn mint leaves for a quick salad. And it's good with grilled meats, poultry and fish, especially salmon. Tamarind is a brown pod containing seeds and a sticky, sour pulp. Tamarind pulp is most commonly available as blocks and will keep for several weeks in the refrigerator. A blender gave the sauce its smooth consistency. For a milder flavor, remove the seeds and ribs from the chili. If you can find palm sugar, it would be an authentic substitute for the brown sugar.

1. **In a medium saucepan** over medium, combine the lemon grass, shallot, oil and chili. Cook, stirring, until just beginning to brown, 3 to 5 minutes. Add the tomato paste and ginger and cook, stirring constantly, until fragrant, about 30 seconds. Add 2½ cups water, the tamarind and sugar. Bring to a boil, then reduce heat to medium-low and simmer until the tamarind has softened, about 15 minutes. Off heat, stir in the fish sauce and soy sauce.

2. **Let the mixture cool slightly,** then transfer to a blender. Blend until smooth, about 1 minute. Strain through a fine mesh strainer, pressing on the solids; discard the solids. Stir in the lime juice, then taste and season with pepper. Use immediately or refrigerate for up to 2 weeks.

Japanese-Style Salt-Pickled Radish and Red Onion (*Yasai no Sokuseki-zuke*)

Start to finish: **45 minutes (10 minutes active)** / Makes **about 2 cups**

10 ounces small red radishes, thinly sliced, or 10 ounces daikon, peeled, halved lengthwise and thinly sliced

Kosher salt

½ small red onion, thinly sliced

1 tablespoon grated lemon zest

2-inch square kombu seaweed, cut or broken into 5 pieces

These simple pickles are made with salt to draw out the vegetables' water, and the salty liquid that results serves as a brine for curing. Lemon zest pairs well with the peppery radishes and onion, and a small piece of kombu seaweed adds savoriness. After draining and rinsing, the pickles can be refrigerated for up to two days. Serve them as a crunchy condiment to round out a meal.

Don't be afraid to firmly massage the radishes with the salt. But after adding the onion, massage gently and briefly, just until the onion wilts.

1. In a 1-quart zip-close bag, combine the radishes and 1 teaspoon salt. Seal the bag, removing as much air as possible, then massage the salt into the radishes. When liquid begins to collect and the radishes are wilted, after about 1 minute, add the onion. Reseal the bag, again removing as much air as possible, and gently massage until the onion is just wilted, another 30 seconds.

2. Add the zest and kombu, reseal the bag, removing as much air as possible, then massage to evenly distribute and soften the kombu. Lay the bag flat in a baking dish or rimmed baking sheet. Top with a second baking dish or baking sheet and weigh down with about 4 pounds of cans or filled bottles. Let stand at room temperature for 30 minutes, or refrigerate for up to 1 day.

3. Drain in a colander and discard the kombu. Rinse under cold water. Drain well, squeezing gently to remove as much moisture as possible.

Slow-Roasted Tomatoes

Start to finish: 3½ hours (15 minutes active)
Makes about 32 halves

¼ cup white balsamic vinegar

¼ cup tomato paste

2 teaspoons kosher salt

1 teaspoon ground black pepper

4 pounds plum tomatoes
(about 16 medium), halved
lengthwise

¼ cup extra-virgin olive oil

We love what a burst of bright tomato flavor can do for a recipe. But supermarket tomatoes are a disappointment, especially during winter. So we looked for a way to improve year-round tomatoes and found it by way of a slow roast to concentrate flavor. We began by coating halved plum tomatoes with a mix of tomato paste and vinegar, then roasting them on kitchen parchment–lined baking sheets along with garlic. We tried several variations of vinegar, including white and regular balsamic; we found white balsamic worked best. Mixing olive oil into the coating mixture made the vinegar and tomatoes burn and stick to the parchment. Drizzling the olive oil over the tomatoes separately worked better. Medium plum tomatoes, roughly 4 ounces each, were ideal. If your tomatoes are smaller, start checking them after three hours in the oven.

1. Heat the oven to 325°F with a rack in the middle position. Line a rimmed baking sheet with kitchen parchment. In a large bowl, whisk together the vinegar, tomato paste, salt and pepper. Add the tomatoes and toss to coat. Arrange the tomatoes cut side up on the prepared baking sheet. Drizzle evenly with the oil.

2. Roast until the tomatoes are shriveled, caramelized and lightly charred at the edges, about 3½ hours, rotating the pan halfway through. Serve immediately, or let cool, transfer to a lidded container and refrigerate for up to 1 week.

SLOW ROAST FOR FAST FLAVOR

A jar of slow-roasted tomatoes can launch a host of meals and accent a variety of dishes. Use them as a relish for sandwiches, add them to soups or stews, toss them with pasta, serve them over grilled polenta, or spoon them over grilled or fried fish. Chop a few and toss with herbs like basil, parsley and thyme for a quick relish. For a quick version of fagioli all'uccelletto (beans braised in tomato sauce), toss a handful of chopped slow-roasted tomatoes with a drained can of white beans, chopped sage, a pinch of red pepper flakes and a few tablespoons of olive oil. Heat until bubbling and creamy; serve with crusty bread.

Homemade Chipotles in Adobo Sauce

Start to finish: **45 minutes (5 minutes active)**
Makes **16 chipotles with sauce**

20 dried morita chipotle chilies
(about 1¼ ounces), stems removed

1 medium yellow onion,
roughly chopped

6 garlic cloves

⅓ cup cider vinegar

¼ cup ketchup

¼ cup packed light brown sugar

1 teaspoon ground cumin

1 teaspoon ground coriander

1 teaspoon kosher salt

½ teaspoon dried thyme

Canned chipotles in adobo are a great pantry staple. The chilies (or even just a spoonful of the sauce) are an easy way to add moderate heat and deep, smoky flavor to sauces, soups, meats and sandwiches. They are made by drying and smoking jalapeño peppers, then packing them in a rich sauce made from tomatoes and even more chilies. We love homemade even more; the texture of the chilies is firmer and the sauce is thicker and more robustly flavored. Be sure to use dried morita chipotles, which are shiny and dark. They are smaller, sweeter and smokier than tan-colored meco chipotles, which tend to be leathery and nutty.

In a medium saucepan, combine the chipotles and 3 cups water. Bring to a boil, then simmer for 20 minutes. Remove all but 4 of the chilies from the pan and set aside. In a blender, combine the cooking water and the remaining 4 chipotles. Add the remaining ingredients. Blend until mostly smooth, then return to the pan. Add the reserved chilies, then simmer, stirring occasionally, until thickened, about 20 minutes. Cool, then refrigerate. The chipotles keep for up to 1 month.

TURN UP THE HEAT

Chipotle peppers—actually smoked and dried jalapeños—can contribute deep, smoky-sweet flavor and body to a host of different dishes. We like them chopped and stirred into a pot of braised pinto or black beans, or pureed into a can or two of black beans for quick refried beans. They are terrific mixed into mayonnaise for an instant sauce. Or add to a basic tomato sauce with a handful of cilantro and a pinch each of cumin and cinnamon for a simple enchilada sauce. This sauce can also be used to smother a burrito, known as burrito ahogado or "drowned burrito." Smear some of the sauce into a grilled cheese or add a spoonful to mac and cheese (and garnish with toasted pepitas). A chopped chili or two can add welcome spiciness to a basic meat stew.

Cilantro-Jalapeño Adobo Sauce

Start to finish: 20 minutes
Makes about 1 cup

4 large jalapeño chilies

6 large garlic cloves, unpeeled

5 cups (about 4 ounces) lightly packed fresh cilantro leaves and tender stems

6 tablespoons extra-virgin olive oil

1 tablespoon lime juice, plus more as needed

¾ teaspoon kosher salt

½ teaspoon sugar

Spanish for marinade, adobo can be many things, but it began as a blend of olive oil, vinegar and spices that was slathered over meat and other foods to keep them from spoiling. We wanted a sauce that could go with just about anything and were inspired by a Mexican-style adobo from Rick Bayless, who blends together garlic, serrano chilies, cilantro, parsley and oil. We wanted to cut back on the oil and heat, so we chose jalapeño peppers over serrano chilies; the latter can vary widely in heat level from dud to scud. We dropped the parsley and went all in on cilantro; its fresh, clean flavor was even bolder when it didn't need to compete with another herb. Our sauce packs moderate heat; if you prefer a milder version, replace two of the jalapeños with one large Anaheim or poblano chili. Since it's blended with oil, the herb sauce can be refrigerated for up to three weeks.

Don't forget to wash and dry your herbs. Cilantro can be quite sandy. A salad spinner is the easiest way to wash and dry it.

1. Heat the broiler with an oven rack 6 inches from the element. Arrange the jalapeños and garlic on a rimmed baking sheet and broil, turning as necessary, until the chilies are evenly blistered and the garlic skins are spotted brown, 8 to 10 minutes. If the garlic blackens too quickly, remove it first. Cover with foil and let sit until cool enough to handle, about 10 minutes. Peel, stem and seed the chilies and peel the garlic, trimming away any scorched bits.

2. In a food processor, combine the chilies, garlic and all remaining ingredients. Process until smooth, 1 to 2 minutes, scraping the bowl as needed. Taste and adjust salt and lime juice as desired.

A SAUCE FOR ALL SEASONS

Cilantro-jalapeño adobo sauce adds an easy punch of spicy, fresh flavor to numerous dishes, including:

Quesadillas: Smear a thin layer of adobo on tortillas before filling and toasting.

Rice: Fold adobo into a pot of cooked rice (about 1 tablespoon per cup of rice), then season with plenty of lime juice. Serve with grilled meats or alongside stewed beans.

Beans: Stir into cooked pinto or black beans, either whole or refried. Or puree with canned beans to make a spread for tortas or quesadillas.

Meats: Use the adobo as a dipping sauce for roasted or grilled beef or a rich pork shoulder.

Fish: Thin with additional olive oil, then spoon over seared scallops or roasted salmon or halibut; garnish with lime wedges.

Sweet potatoes: Thin the sauce with Greek-style yogurt and drizzle over roasted sweet potato wedges or use as a dipping sauce.

Sandwiches: Stir together equal parts adobo and mayonnaise, then use as a sandwich spread, particularly with turkey, chicken or on a BLT.

Vinaigrettes: Add a spoonful to any neutral-flavored vinaigrette (use citrus juice, rice vinegar or white balsamic vinegar for the acid).

Eggs: Fold into barely set scrambled eggs, drizzle over fried eggs or add to egg salad.

Hummus: Swirl a spoonful into the top hummus. This works equally well with baba ghanoush.

Polenta: Spoon a tablespoon or two over polenta topped with toasted pumpkin seeds, crumbled queso fresco and avocado.

Pickled Vegetables (*Escabeche*)

Start to finish: **45 minutes** (30 minutes active), plus cooling
Makes **about 4 cups**

1 large red onion (¾ pound), halved and thinly sliced lengthwise

½ pound carrots, peeled, halved lengthwise and thinly sliced on diagonal

2 jalapeño chilies, thinly sliced crosswise

5 teaspoons kosher salt

1 cup distilled white vinegar

107 grams (½ cup) white sugar

½ teaspoon black peppercorns

½ teaspoon coriander seeds

¼ teaspoon red pepper flakes (optional)

6 allspice berries

1 bay leaf

Escabeche translates as marinade, or pickle, and refers to a variety of pickled dishes popular in Spanish and Latin American cooking. Here, we pickle vegetables for a piquant side dish. Salting the vegetables before pickling them enhanced their crispness and intensified their final flavor. That's because salting removes water, allowing them to better absorb the brine. Once cooled, the pickled vegetables can be eaten immediately, but their flavor improves with time. We left the whole spices in the brine to infuse even more during storage.

Don't slice the onions crosswise. We preferred the texture and appearance of onions sliced from pole to pole. And the thinner the slices the better; aim for about ⅛-inch thickness.

1. In a bowl, toss together the onions, carrots, jalapeños and salt. Let sit for 30 to 60 minutes. Transfer the vegetables to a colander and rinse well, then set aside to drain.

2. Meanwhile, in a medium saucepan over high, combine the vinegar, 1 cup water, sugar, peppercorns, coriander, pepper flakes, if using, allspice and bay leaf. Bring to a boil, then reduce to medium and simmer for 5 minutes.

3. Transfer the vegetables to a canning jar or heatproof, lidded container. Pour the hot brine over them, ensuring they are fully submerged. Cool to room temperature, about 2 hours, then cover and refrigerate for up to 1 month.

HOW TO SERVE ESCABECHE

○ On burgers, sandwiches, wraps, tacos and nachos

○ With pulled pork, chili, brisket and grilled fish, poultry or steaks

○ Chopped into slaws and potato, tuna, egg or chicken salads

○ In a grilled cheese sandwich, and on green or grain salads

○ As a condiment for charcuterie platters, smoked fish and baked potatoes

○ As a garnish for crostini or bruschetta

GET INTO A PICKLE

The pickling brine for our escabeche can be used:

- To poach fish or boneless chicken breasts (use equal parts water and brine)

- In place of citrus juice in salsa or ceviche

- In vinaigrettes, store-bought barbecue sauces and bloody mary cocktails

- To deglaze a pan

- To braise chicken or pork (use pickling brine for 20 percent of the liquid)

- To brighten the flavor of cooked beans (stir in brine immediately after cooking)

- To glaze vegetables (combine brine, butter and a sweetener, such as maple syrup, honey or sugar)

Other uses for pickling brine:

MUSTARD VINAIGRETTE

Start to finish: 5 minutes
Makes about 1 cup

To vary this recipe, add minced garlic, shallot or fresh thyme and/ or a squeeze of honey.

1 tablespoon Dijon mustard

3 tablespoons pickling brine

¾ cup extra-virgin olive oil

Kosher salt and ground black pepper

In a bowl, whisk together the mustard and brine until smooth. Continue to whisk and add the oil slowly until the dressing is emulsified, about 15 seconds. Season with salt and pepper.

SPICY PEANUT SAUCE

Start to finish: 10 minutes
Makes about 1 cup

This recipe works equally well with creamy or chunky peanut butter.

½ cup natural peanut butter

¼ cup pickling brine

1 tablespoon soy sauce

1 tablespoon white sugar

1 garlic clove, minced

½ teaspoon red pepper flakes

2 tablespoons water, plus more as needed

In a blender, combine all ingredients. Blend until smooth, adding water 1 tablespoon at a time to achieve desired consistency.

VINEGAR-BASED BARBECUE SAUCE

Start to finish: 10 minutes
Makes about 1⅓ cups

1 cup pickling brine

¼ cup ketchup

2 tablespoons packed brown sugar

1 tablespoon red pepper flakes

1 teaspoon ground black pepper

Kosher salt

In a medium bowl, whisk together all ingredients except the salt. Season to taste.

Central Mexican **Guacamole**

Start to finish: **10 minutes** / Servings: 4

4 tablespoons finely chopped
fresh cilantro, divided

1 to 2 serrano chilies, stemmed
and finely chopped

2 tablespoons finely chopped
white onion

Kosher salt

3 ripe avocados, halved and pitted

1 pint (10 ounces) grape tomatoes,
finely chopped

Many guacamole recipes are a muddle of flavors. We prefer the simplicity of Central Mexican guacamole, which is seasoned with just three things—serrano chilies, white onion and cilantro. No garlic. No lime juice. Whether you use a mortar and pestle or a mixing bowl and the back of a fork, the onions, chilies and cilantro get mashed to a paste that permeates the avocados. Though acid is needed to balance the fat of the avocados and slow down oxidation (that ugly browning), lime juice can overpower guacamole. In Central Mexico, tomato provides the acid. Chopped fresh tomatoes offer a gentler acidity and flavor that—unlike limes—complement rather than compete with the other ingredients. Guacamole hinges on the ripeness of the avocados; they should be soft but slightly firm.

Don't discard the seeds from the chilies. This recipe relies on them for a pleasant heat.

In a bowl, combine 2 tablespoons of the cilantro, the chilies, onion and ½ teaspoon salt. Mash with the bottom of a dry measuring cup until a rough paste forms, about 1 minute. Scoop the avocado flesh into the bowl and coarsely mash with a potato masher or fork. Stir in half of the tomatoes until combined. Taste and season with salt. Transfer to a serving bowl and sprinkle with the remaining cilantro and tomatoes.

Jalapeño-Mint Sauce

Start to finish: **5 minutes**
Makes about **1¼ cups**

---

1 cup lightly packed fresh mint leaves

⅔ cup extra-virgin olive oil

3 medium jalapeño chilies, stemmed, seeded and roughly chopped

2 tablespoons lime juice

1 tablespoon honey

2 teaspoons finely grated fresh ginger

1 garlic clove, smashed

¾ teaspoon kosher salt, plus more as needed

This light, bright sauce takes moments to prepare and pairs particularly well with grilled or roasted fish, especially meaty swordfish, halibut and salmon. We also like it as a sauce alongside grilled vegetables and roasted cauliflower. Or use it as a sauce for tacos or lettuce wraps, or as a dressing for room-temperature pasta salads. Three-inch jalapeños—ribs and seeds removed—worked best for balanced heat. If you prefer a spicier sauce, incorporate a few seeds.

Don't let this sauce sit for more than an hour or two; it's best served soon after it is made. If it begins to separate, stir to recombine.

In a food processor, combine all ingredients. Process until smooth, about 1 minute, scraping the bowl as necessary. Taste and season with salt. Serve immediately.

Pickled Chilies (*Nam Prik*)

Start to finish: **35 minutes (5 minutes active)**
Makes **1 cup**

---

4 jalapeño chilies, stemmed, seeded (if desired) and thinly sliced crosswise

¼ cup fish sauce

¼ cup lime juice (1 to 2 limes)

1 teaspoon white sugar

These jalapeño chilies pickled in fish sauce, lime juice and a little sugar are a milder variation of the often fiery Thai dressing called nam prik. The chilies, and their sauce, add a balanced hit of heat, sweet and acid. We find them a delicious way to add bright flavor to our Thai fried rice (p. 142), or any Thai or Vietnamese dish. Whisk in a little peanut oil for a quick salad, vegetable or slaw dressing. Add a spoonful to stews, or even scrambled eggs or roasted or sautéed vegetables.

In a bowl, stir together all ingredients. Refrigerate for at least 30 minutes or up to 1 week.

Spicy Garlic-and-Herb Oil

Start to finish: **10 minutes**
Makes **about 1 cup**

2 cups lightly packed fresh
flat-leaf parsley leaves

½ cup plus 2 tablespoons
extra-virgin olive oil

½ cup coarsely chopped
fresh chives

¼ cup coarsely chopped fresh dill

1 tablespoon red pepper flakes

1 large garlic clove, smashed
and peeled

1 teaspoon kosher salt

½ teaspoon ground black pepper

This herb-rich oil is great brushed on to warm piadine (p. 379). It also can be served as a dip for bread. If you like, substitute fresh oregano, marjoram or mint for the dill. Other uses: Drizzle over pasta, polenta and fried eggs, or use as a base for vinaigrettes with lemon juice or white balsamic vinegar.

In a food processor, combine all ingredients and process until smooth, about 20 seconds, scraping the bowl as needed.

Spiced Yogurt Dressing

Start to finish: **5 minutes**
Makes **about 1½ cups**

1 cup plain whole-milk
Greek-style yogurt

2 teaspoons ground coriander

¾ teaspoon ground cumin

½ teaspoon ground turmeric

½ teaspoon kosher salt

¼ teaspoon ground black pepper

⅛ to ¼ teaspoon cayenne pepper

⅛ teaspoon finely grated garlic

3 tablespoons extra-virgin olive oil

3½ teaspoons red wine vinegar

1 teaspoon honey

Water, as needed

Our spiced yogurt dressing was inspired by Madhur Jaffrey, the Delhi-born actress, cookbook author and television chef who has spent decades exploring the food of her homeland and beyond. We loved the yogurt dressing in her book, "Vegetarian India." The warm spices in this thick dressing work with everything from simple salads of romaine or spinach to poached salmon, herbed chickpeas and roasted vegetables, such as beets, cauliflower and broccoli. Use it to dress farro or barley salads, as a dipping sauce for whole artichokes, over warm or room-temperature potatoes or with grilled or roasted lamb. For a thinner consistency, add water, a tablespoon at a time, whisking until smooth after each addition. Because it is made without herbs or much garlic, it refrigerates well for up to five days.

Don't overdo the garlic. More than ⅛ teaspoon of finely grated raw garlic—use a wand-style grater—easily overpowered the dressing.

In a medium bowl, whisk together the yogurt, coriander, cumin, turmeric, salt, pepper, cayenne and garlic. Add the oil, vinegar and honey, then whisk until smooth. Add water, 1 tablespoon at a time, to reach desired consistency.

Sweet-and-Sour Mint Dressing (*Sekanjabin*)

Start to finish: **10 minutes active, plus 1 hour cooling** / Makes **about ½ cup**

½ cup plus 2 tablespoons cider vinegar, divided

167 grams (½ cup) clover honey

½ teaspoon kosher salt

1½ cups lightly packed fresh mint

French vinaigrette may be the dressing we know best, but step out of Europe and the choices multiply. In many cultures, sauces—not just vinegar and oil—dress vegetables, grains or greens. The range of acids and fats expands, as does the potential for sweeteners and wild cards such as tamarind paste, miso or a bold splash of fish, soy or oyster sauce. We were introduced to one of the simplest, most appealing dressings by Yasmin Khan, author of "The Saffron Tales." The Iranian dressing sekanjabin is an ancient blend of cider vinegar, honey or sugar, and mint concentrated into a syrup to use straight as a dressing or diluted in a drink. We preferred unfiltered cider vinegars. And we loved the dressing on cold roasted vegetables.

Don't use a distinctively flavored honey, such as orange blossom or buckwheat. The flavor will overpower the delicate mint.

In a small saucepan over medium, combine ½ cup of the vinegar, the honey and salt. Simmer until large bubbles appear and the mixture reduces to about ½ cup, about 7 minutes. Off the heat, add the mint, pushing it into the syrup. Let cool to room temperature. Strain into a bowl, pressing the solids. Stir in the remaining 2 tablespoons of vinegar. Cool. Refrigerate for up to 1 month.

Three ways to use sekanjabin:

BROILED EGGPLANT WITH CHILIES AND CILANTRO

Start to finish: 20 minutes
(10 minutes active)
Servings: 4

2 pounds eggplant, cut crosswise into 1-inch slices

½ cup olive oil

Kosher salt and ground black pepper

½ cup chopped fresh cilantro

2 tablespoons chili-garlic sauce

2 tablespoons sweet-and-sour mint dressing

Heat the broiler and set an oven rack 6 inches from it. Line a rimmed baking sheet with foil. Arrange the eggplant on the foil and brush both sides with the olive oil. Season with salt and pepper. Broil until well browned, about 10 minutes. Flip each slice and broil again until well browned, another 5 to 10 minutes. Let cool. In a large bowl, combine the cilantro, chili-garlic sauce and dressing. Cut each eggplant slice into 6 pieces and toss with the dressing.

ROASTED BROCCOLI RAAB WITH FENNEL AND CHILI FLAKES

Start to finish: 30 minutes
(10 minutes active)
Servings: 4

1 pound broccoli raab, ends trimmed, well dried

½ cup olive oil

1 tablespoon ground fennel

1 teaspoon kosher salt

1 teaspoon ground black pepper

1 teaspoon red pepper flakes

2 tablespoons sweet-and-sour mint dressing

Heat the oven to 500°F with an oven rack in the middle position. Line a rimmed baking sheet with foil. In a large bowl, toss the broccoli raab with the oil, fennel, salt, black pepper and red pepper flakes. Transfer to the baking sheet, reserving the bowl. Roast, stirring halfway through, until just beginning to brown, 12 to 15 minutes. Let cool. Return to the bowl and toss with the dressing.

ROASTED CAULIFLOWER WITH CURRY AND MINT

Start to finish: 45 minutes
(10 minutes active)
Servings: 4

½ cup olive oil

1 teaspoon curry powder

1 teaspoon ground cumin

1 teaspoon kosher salt

½ teaspoon ground black pepper

2 medium heads cauliflower (about 4 pounds total), cored and cut into 2-inch pieces

3 tablespoons minced fresh mint

2 tablespoons sweet-and-sour mint dressing

Heat the oven to 475°F with an oven rack in the middle position. Line a rimmed baking sheet with foil. In a large bowl, combine the oil, curry powder, cumin, salt and pepper. Add the cauliflower and toss. Transfer to the prepared baking sheet, reserving the bowl. Arrange the pieces cut side down. Roast until well browned, about 30 minutes. Let cool. In the reserved bowl, combine the mint with the dressing. Add the cauliflower and toss to coat.

Fig-Olive **Tapenade**

Start to finish: **20 minutes**
Makes **about 2 cups**

5 ounces (1 cup) dried black mission figs, stemmed

1 cup Kalamata olives, pitted, rinsed and patted dry

½ cup oil-cured olives, pitted

¼ cup capers, rinsed and squeezed dry

2 oil-packed anchovy fillets, patted dry

1 teaspoon minced fresh rosemary

½ teaspoon grated orange zest

½ teaspoon red pepper flakes

¼ cup extra-virgin olive oil

A paste made of figs and olives may sound like an oddball pairing, but the two work well together. The sweetness of the figs mitigates the brine and bitterness of the olives. A combination of Kalamata and more pungent oil-cured olives provided the best balance of flavor and creamy texture. To easily pit the olives, whack them with the side of a chef's knife to flatten, then simply use your fingers to pull out the pits. Soaking the figs made up for any difference in moisture content and ensured they ground easily to a smooth paste. We love this tapenade smeared on crostini, either alone or with fresh cheese or caramelized onions, as a dip for crudités, tossed with steamed vegetables or potatoes, as a topping for beef, chicken or fish, combined with olive oil and vinegar for a quick vinaigrette, or stirred into pasta.

Don't forget to check your olives for pits, even if they're labeled "pitted." We prefer to buy olives with pits and prep them ourselves, but pitted olives will work.

1. In a small saucepan, bring 1 cup water to a boil. Add the figs, remove from the heat, then cover and let sit for 15 minutes. Drain the figs, reserving the soaking liquid. In a food processor, combine the figs, both olives, capers, anchovies, rosemary, zest, pepper flakes and 2 tablespoons of the fig soaking liquid. Process until a smooth paste forms, 1 to 2 minutes, scraping the bowl halfway through.

2. With the processor running, add the oil in a steady stream and process until incorporated, about 30 seconds. Transfer to a bowl or lidded container and let sit for 1 hour before serving. Tapenade can be refrigerated for up to 3 weeks.

Whipped **Feta**

Start to finish: **15 minutes**
Makes **about 1½ cups**

8 ounces feta cheese

2 tablespoons lemon juice

1 garlic clove, peeled and smashed

3 ounces cream cheese, room temperature

⅓ cup extra-virgin olive oil

½ teaspoon smoked paprika

½ teaspoon red pepper flakes

¼ teaspoon ground black pepper

2 tablespoons chopped fresh mint leaves, plus more to garnish

2 tablespoons chopped mild Peppadew peppers

This easy, whipped feta cheese spread is based on the traditional Greek dip, htipiti (pronounced h'tee-pee-tee). There are many variations, some as simple as feta, red pepper flakes and extra-virgin olive oil, others with herbs and roasted red peppers. We shifted to Peppadew peppers, which added a sweet-tart kick to balance the creaminess of the cheese. A brief soak in water removed some of the salt from the cheese and made it easier to control the dish's seasoning. Raw garlic tasted harsh and bitter; infusing lemon juice with a smashed clove provided gentler flavor. Processing the feta and cream cheese before adding the remaining ingredients was the key to a light, whipped texture. To increase the heat, use cayenne pepper or hot Peppadews, or add more red pepper flakes. The whipped feta can be refrigerated for up to a week. This makes the perfect dip for crudités or pita points, or use as garnish on pasta or grilled meats and vegetables. It's terrific as a sandwich spread, too, especially when topped with sautéed greens—spinach, kale or chard—and a fried egg. Try serving it alongside lamb chops or even slices of seared steak.

Don't use pre-crumbled feta. It can be dry and chalky. Look for block feta packed in brine, ideally made with sheep's or goat's milk.

1. In a medium bowl, cover the feta with fresh tap water and let sit for 10 minutes. In a small bowl, combine the lemon juice and garlic and let sit for 10 minutes. Discard the garlic clove. Drain the feta and pat dry, then crumble.

2. In a food processor, combine the feta and cream cheese. Process until smooth, about 30 seconds. Add the oil, lemon juice, paprika, pepper flakes and black pepper. Process until well mixed, about 30 seconds. Scrape the bowl, add the mint and Peppadews, then pulse until combined.

3. Taste and season with pepper flakes and black pepper. Refrigerate for at least 30 minutes before serving. Garnish with mint.

Miso-Ginger Dressing

Start to finish: **10 minutes**
Makes **about 1 cup**

⅓ cup walnuts

⅓ cup white miso

1 teaspoon grated lemon zest, plus ¼ cup lemon juice (1 to 2 lemons)

¼ cup water

1-ounce piece fresh ginger, peeled and thinly sliced

1 teaspoon Dijon mustard

1 teaspoon honey

½ teaspoon ground white pepper

½ cup grapeseed or other neutral oil

Miso and ginger are mainstays of the Japanese kitchen. This recipe combines them with items common to the Western pantry—Dijon mustard and honey—to create a zesty dressing. The creamy texture and mild, sweet-salty flavor of white miso, also called shiro miso, worked best. Walnuts gave the dressing richness and body. If the dressing becomes too thick after being refrigerated, gradually whisk in water to thin it. Because of its creamy, thick texture, this dressing goes well with heartier salad greens, as well as vegetables, grains, beans, chicken and fish.

Don't toast the walnuts. They provide texture, but their flavor should be subtle. Toasting them makes them too assertive.

In a blender, combine all ingredients except the oil. Blend until the walnuts are finely ground and the dressing is smooth, about 1 minute. Add the oil and blend until emulsified, about 30 seconds.

USE THIS DRESSING:

- On a chopped salad of romaine, cucumbers, cherry tomatoes, radishes, red onion and mint

- On a radicchio, endive and arugula salad with roasted beets and toasted chopped walnuts

- Tossed with or drizzled over blanched vegetables, especially green beans, asparagus, broccoli, cauliflower and carrots

- As a sauce for poached whitefish or salmon

- As a dressing for cabbage slaws—thinly sliced red, white or napa cabbage with grated carrots, sliced scallions, diced jalapeño and herbs, such as fresh parsley, cilantro, basil or mint

- As dressing for a shredded chicken salad with blanched sugar snap peas, thinly sliced red pepper and celery and fresh herbs

- As dressing for a rice salad with diced celery, cucumber, toasted chopped almonds, raisins, sliced scallions and chopped parsley or mint

- Drizzled on grilled vegetables, especially eggplant, zucchini, yellow squash, asparagus and onions

Green Goddess Tofu Dressing

Start to finish: **5 minutes, plus chilling**
Makes **about 1½ cups**

2 tablespoons white balsamic vinegar

1 small garlic clove, smashed

8 ounces drained silken tofu (1 cup)

¾ cup lightly packed fresh flat-leaf parsley leaves

⅓ cup coarsely chopped fresh chives

¼ cup grapeseed or other neutral oil

2 tablespoons chopped fresh tarragon

1½ teaspoons grated lemon zest

1 oil-packed anchovy fillet

½ teaspoon kosher salt

¼ teaspoon ground black pepper

Green goddess salad dressing is one of those enchantingly retro recipes most of us have heard of even if we haven't actually tried it. The original recipe went heavy on the mayonnaise and later versions included sour cream and even avocado. We took the dressing to a lighter place with silken tofu, which provided a creamy base. From there we piled on the herbs. We liked parsley's clean, herbaceous flavor combined with the mellow onion note of chives and tarragon's distinctive licorice flavor. Lemon zest added a hit of citrus, but the juice was too sharp. Instead, we opted for sweet-tart white balsamic vinegar. We preferred the more neutral flavor of shelf-stable tofu—found in the Asian foods aisle—over its refrigerated counterpart. While the dressing can be served right away, we preferred to let the flavors meld for at least an hour. It keeps for up to four days refrigerated.

Don't use dried tarragon. If fresh tarragon isn't available, substitute 3 tablespoons of chopped fresh dill or basil.

In a blender, combine all ingredients. Blend until smooth and uniformly pale green, 1 to 2 minutes. Transfer to a jar and refrigerate for at least 1 hour.

USE THIS DRESSING:

- Rice salad with chopped toasted almonds, diced celery and peas

- Chopped chicken salad with bacon, avocado and tomatoes

- Shredded chicken salad with spinach, sliced cucumbers, grated carrots and sliced red cabbage

- Fusilli pasta salad with grilled zucchini, summer squash, olives and cherry tomatoes

- Broiled or grilled fish

- Shrimp or seafood salad with diced celery, red pepper and lemon zest on frisee

- Romaine and watercress salad with chopped hard-cooked eggs and avocado

Fruit **Chutney**

Start to finish: 25 minutes, plus cooling
Makes about 2½ cups

1 large red onion, diced
(about 1½ cups)

2 tablespoons salted butter

1 tablespoon grapeseed
or other neutral oil

Kosher salt

2 teaspoons coriander seeds,
crushed

1 teaspoon yellow mustard
seeds, crushed

2 Granny Smith apples,
peeled, cored and diced

¼ cup white sugar

⅓ cup dried apricots, diced

⅓ cup dried cherries,
coarsely chopped

⅓ cup dried currants

⅓ cup cider vinegar

⅓ cup water

In India, chutney, or chatni, refers to a variety of sauces made from numerous ingredients. Elsewhere in the world, it is translated mostly as a sweet-savory jam-like condiment. In our version—which was inspired by a chutney by London baker Claire Ptak—red onion lent a slight, pleasant bite. A combination of salted butter and neutral oil worked best for sauteing. Sulfured and unsulfured dried apricots fared equally well in this recipe. The cooled chutney can be refrigerated for up to two weeks. Our favorite way to use this chutney was in a gooey grilled cheese (see sidebar), but it also is great as a topping for grilled pork chops, in a turkey sandwich or simply as a component on a cheese board.

Don't grind the mustard and coriander seeds. Crush them with a mortar and pestle, or use the side of a wide chef's knife to crush them against the cutting board.

In a medium saucepan over medium, combine the onion, butter, oil and ⅛ teaspoon salt. Cook, stirring occasionally, until the onion is softened, 9 to 11 minutes. Add the coriander and mustard seeds and cook for 1 minute. Stir in the apples, sugar and ¼ teaspoon salt. Cook until the sugar is dissolved, about 1 minute. Add the apricots, cherries, currants, vinegar and water, then stir to combine. Bring to a simmer and cook until the chutney is thickened but the apples still hold their shape, 10 to 12 minutes. Remove from the heat and cool.

GRILLED CHEESE
WITH FRUIT CHUTNEY

Start to finish: **10 minutes**
Makes **1 sandwich**

Homemade chutney is the highlight of this sandwich, but if you use store-bought, look for Stonewall Kitchen Apple Cranberry Chutney or another high-quality variety with a thick texture. This recipe is easily doubled using a 12-inch skillet.

3 to 4 tablespoons chutney

Two ½-inch-thick slices sourdough or seeded rye bread

2 to 3 ounces Gruyere, Comte, Gouda or raclette cheese, thinly sliced

1 tablespoon salted butter, softened

Kosher salt

1. Evenly spread the chutney over 1 slice of bread, then top with the cheese in an even layer, followed by the second slice of bread. Spread half the butter over the top of the sandwich, then sprinkle with a pinch of salt.

2. Heat a 10-inch stainless steel or cast-iron skillet over medium-high for 2 minutes. Reduce heat to low and add the sandwich, buttered side down. Spread the remaining butter over the top of the sandwich, then cover the pan and cook until the bottom is golden brown, 3 to 5 minutes.

3. Flip the sandwich and cook, covered, until the second side is golden brown and the cheese is melted, 2 to 3 minutes. If the bread toasts faster than the cheese melts, remove from the heat and let sit, covered, for 1 to 2 minutes, or until the cheese is fully melted.

Fruit Compotes

Compote is French for "mixture" and generally refers to fruit that's been slowly stewed in syrup long enough to soften, but not lose its shape. Unlike preserves and conserves, it's usually made fresh for consumption with a particular meal. Just what that meal should be is up to you. Our fruit compotes play well with yogurt, oatmeal and granola in the morning, but also can help elevate a bowl of ice cream or slice of pound cake later in the afternoon. These compotes are perfect served over cakes—we particularly like the blueberry-lavender with our lemon-buttermilk pound cake (p. 450) and ricotta cheesecake (p. 479).

SPICED APRICOT COMPOTE

Start to finish: 15 minutes,
plus cooling
Makes about 2 cups

We liked the texture and tartness
pomegranate seeds gave this
compote, but they can be omitted.
Both sulfured and unsulfured
apricots worked.

12 ounces dried apricots
(about 2 cups), roughly chopped

1¼ cups water

2 tablespoons packed light
brown sugar

Two 3½-inch cinnamon sticks

2 star anise pods

Two 3-inch strips lemon zest,
plus ½ teaspoon lemon juice

Pinch of kosher salt

⅓ cup pomegranate seeds

In a medium saucepan over
medium-high, combine the apricots,
water, sugar, cinnamon, star anise,
lemon zest and salt, then bring to
a boil. Reduce to medium-low and
simmer, stirring occasionally, until
the apricots are plump and softened, and the liquid is thick and
syrupy, 10 to 12 minutes. Off heat,
stir in the lemon juice and pomegranate seeds. Discard the cinnamon sticks, star anise and zest.
Cool to room temperature.

BLUEBERRY-LAVENDER COMPOTE

Start to finish: 10 minutes,
plus cooling
Makes about 2 cups

Frozen blueberries can be substituted for fresh, but be sure to thaw
and drain them first.

15 ounces blueberries
(about 3 cups)

54 grams (¼ cup) white sugar

Two 2-inch strips lemon zest,
plus ¼ teaspoon lemon juice

¼ teaspoon dried lavender

Pinch of kosher salt

In a medium saucepan, use a
potato masher or fork to mash half
of the berries. Stir in the sugar,
lemon zest, lavender and salt.
Bring to a boil over medium-high,
stirring frequently. Add the remaining blueberries and return to a boil.
Reduce heat to medium-low and
simmer, stirring occasionally, until
the juices thicken and most of the
berries have popped, 6 to 8 minutes.
Off heat, stir in the lemon juice.
Discard the zest. Cool to room
temperature.

APPLE-PEAR COMPOTE

Start to finish: 25 minutes,
plus cooling
Makes about 2 cups

Gala, Golden Delicious, Cortland
or Jonagold apples all worked well;
Bartlett and Anjou pears were our
favorite. Calvados or apple brandy
also was delicious in place of the
bourbon. To make it easier to fish
out the cloves at the end, stick them
through the lemon zest before
adding them to the pan.

2 apples (12 to 16 ounces), peeled,
cored and cut into ½-inch chunks

2 firm, ripe pears (12 to 16 ounces),
peeled, cored and cut into ½-inch
chunks

½ cup bourbon

109 grams (½ cup) packed light
brown sugar

Two 3-inch strips lemon zest,
plus 1 teaspoon lemon juice

5 whole cloves

Pinch of kosher salt

In a medium saucepan over
medium-high, combine all ingredients but the lemon juice, then bring
to a boil. Reduce to medium-low,
cover and cook, stirring occasionally, until the fruit is soft but still
intact, about 15 minutes. Uncover,
increase heat to medium-high and
cook until the liquid is thick and
syrupy, 5 to 7 minutes. Off heat,
stir in the lemon juice. Discard the
zest and cloves. Cool to room
temperature.

Index

A

acids, 4–5, 349, 450

Acurio, Gastón, 178

adobado (seasoning), 356

adobo sauce, 513
    chipotles in, 510–11
    cilantro-jalapeño, 512–13
    Filipino chicken, 352–53

afelia (Cypriot cracked potatoes), 117

agave, 14

ají de aguacate (Columbian avocado salsa), 502–3

alcohol. *See* beer; sherry; spirits; wine

Aleppo pepper, 7, 37, 43, 280

allspice, 7

almond flour
    cakes with, 470, 474
    chocolate spice cookies with, 407

almonds
    cake with tangerine and, 470–71
    Caprese torte with, 448–49
    kale salad with smoked, 84–85
    Middle Eastern rice with, 148–49
    pound cake with lemon and, 474–77
    quinoa pilaf with, 140–41
    Spanish cake with, 486–87
    spice cookies with, 406–7
    Trapanese pesto with, 184–85

anchovies, 10
    Brussels sprouts with, 106–7
    spaghetti with, 188–89, 192–93

Andoh, Elizabeth, 50, 146, 211

Andrés, José, 67

anise, Thai braised pork and eggs with, 226–27

Anzac biscuits, 420–21

apples
    compote with, 543
    French cake of, 456–57
    salad of celery root, fennel, and, 80–81

apricots
    chicken en cocotte with, 367
    chicken tagine with, 362–63
    spiced compote with, 543

arugula
    gemelli pasta with, 172–73
    piadine topping with, 381
    salmon salad with, 212–13
    skirt steak salad with, 218–19

asparagus, soba noodles with, 180–81

avocado
    guacamole of, 518–19
    how to fan, 77
    salads with, 76–77, 104–5, 212–13
    salsas with, 493, 502–3

B

baking powder, 27

baking sheets, roasting on, 293–94

baking soda, 382–83, 450

baleadas, Honduran, 263

banana bread, brown butter–cardamom, 398–99

barbecue sauce, vinegar-based, 516

basil
    campanelle pasta with, 162–63
    pesto with, 184–85, 186
    stir-fried chicken with, 254–55

Bastianich, Lidia, 193

batatada (Macanese sweet potato cake), 482–83

bay leaves, 7
    sweet potato gratin with, 120–21
    syrup infused with, 470–71

Bayless, Rick, 512

beans
    adobo sauce for, 513
    braised in tomato sauce, 509
    Greek soup of white, 56–57
    pasta with, 170–71
    puree of black, 214, 215, 216
    refried, 262–63, 274–75, 511
    rinsing canned, 170
    soaking, 256, 262
    soup of black, 262, 263
    sweet-and-spicy ginger green, 126–27
    Turkish, 256–57
    See also chickpeas; lentils

beef
    Austrian stew of, 334–35
    Colombian braised, 298–99
    flatbreads with spiced, 377
    herb-rubbed roast of, 318–19
    kibbeh, 204–5
    lahmajoun with, 380
    lomo saltado (stir-fry) with, 234–35
    pasta with ragu of, 351
    salads with, 218–19, 328–29

sandwiches of broccoli rabe and, 351
    spiced topping of, 277
    spicy salad of, 224–25
    stew with chickpeas and, 306–7
    stew with orange, olive, and, 342–43
    stir-fried cumin, 258–59
    Taiwanese soup with, 52–53
    Turkish beans with, 256–57
    Turkish meatballs of, 270–71
    Tuscan stew of, 350–51
    Vietnamese shaking, 248–49

beer, turkey roasted with, 300–301

biscuits
    Anzac, 420–21
    whipped-cream, 394–95

blueberry-lavender compote, 543

boeuf à la gardiane (beef, orange and olive stew), 342–43

bok choy
    beef noodle soup with, 52–53
    yakiudon with, 164–65

bò lúc lac (Vietnamese shaking beef), 248–49

Bras, Michel, 341

bread
    brown butter–cardamom banana, 398–99
    flatbread, 204–5, 374–81
    French spice, 396–97
    French toast with challah, 442–43
    for grilled cheese with fruit chutney, 541
    for molletes, 216–17
    multigrain soda, 382–83
    pizza dough, 242–45
    Portuguese corn-, 392–93
    potato-and-herb focaccia, 384–85
    pudding of toasted, 468–69
    pumpkin seed rolls, 390–91
    for Turkish meatballs, 270–71
    whipped-cream biscuits, 394–95
    See also pancakes; pita bread; tortillas

bread cubes or crumbs
    chickpea and harissa soup with, 45
    herbed dressing with, 302–3
    kale salad with, 84–85
    spaghetti with, 189
    Spanish garlic soup with, 66–67
    Spanish-style eggs with, 30–31

brine, pickling, 514–17

broa (Portuguese cornbread), 392–93

broccoli, stir-fried, 134–35

broccoli rabe

    with fennel and chili flakes, 530

    sandwiches of beef and, 351

broth

    chicken, 55

    chicken adobo with coconut, 352–53

    chicken poached in, 296–97

    for herbed dressing, 302–3

    rice cooked in, 297

    vegetable, 156, 157

    See also soups

brownies, tahini swirl, 410–11

brown sugar, 14

    braised beef with, 298

    storage of, 434

    tamarind dipping sauce with, 504

    tart of, 434–35

Brussels sprouts, skillet-charred, 106–7

bulgur, 17, 205

    beef kibbeh with, 204–5

    salad with tomatoes and, 100–101

    soaking, 79

    tabbouleh with, 78–79

burrito abogado, 511

butter, 2, 3

    banana bread with browned, 398–99

    cooking spray vs., 396

    eggs cooked in, 22, 23

    gnocchi sauce with, 183

    loaf cake with browned, 446–47

    mashed potatoes with caraway-mustard, 128–29

    mousse with salted, 462–63

    multigrain soda bread with, 382

    pasta toasted in, 149

    pie with maple and browned, 488–89

    pine nuts toasted in, 203

    soba noodles with miso, 180–81

    softening for cakes, 474

    See also peanut butter

buttermilk

    coconut loaf cake with, 446–47

    ginger scones with, 409

    pound cake with, 450–51

cabbage

    cod steamed with, 236–37

    miso-shiitake soup with, 40–41

    pork stir-fried with fermented, 264–65

    Thai-style coleslaw of, 82–83

cacio e pepe (cheese and pepper), 194–95

cai dao (Chinese cleaver), 114–15

cakes

    Austrian plum, 430–31

    butter and coconut loaf, 446–47

    Caprese chocolate and almond, 448–49

    chocolate, prune, and rum, 428–29

    coconut cashew, 480–81

    French apple, 456–57

    fruit compotes for, 542

    Lamington, 404–5

    lemon-almond pound, 474–77

    lemon-buttermilk pound, 450–51

    Macanese sweet potato, 482–83

    maple-whiskey pudding, 458–59

    pistachio-cardamom, 464–65

    ricotta-semolina cheesecake, 478–79

    rye-on-rye sticky toffee, 444–45

    scallion pancakes, 34–35, 388–89

    Spanish almond, 486–87

    steaming, 445, 484

    stovetop chocolate, 484–85

    strawberry shortcake, 394–95

    tangerine-almond, 470–71

camarones enchipotlados (shrimp in chipotle sauce), 288–89

canh (Vietnamese meatball and watercress soup), 62–63

capers

    spaghetti with, 192–93

    Turkish scrambled eggs with, 36–37

caramel

    fish in sauce of, 286–87

    mousse with, 462–63

    oranges in sauce of, 426–27

    tart with, 466–67

caraway seeds

    Austrian beef stew with, 334–35

    mashed potatoes with, 128–29

carcamusa (pork and chorizo with peppers), 252–53

cardamom, 7

    banana bread with, 398–99

caramel oranges with, 426

pistachio cake with, 464–65

carne adovada (pork and chili stew), 364–65

carnitas, 260–61

Carrarini, Jean-Charles, 464

Carrarini, Rose, 464, 472, 474

carrots

    beef stew with, 342–43

    French salad of, 92–93

    gingery pickled, 313

    grating, 92

    quinoa pilaf in juice of, 140–41

cashews

    cake with coconut and, 480–81

    cauliflower with, 130–31

    dukkah with, 131

cauliflower

    with curry and mint, 530

    roasted and miso-glazed, 108–9

    with tahini, 130–31

celery root (celeriac)

    grating, 125

    puree of, 124–25

    salad of apples, fennel, and, 80–81

cereal, multigrain, 382

Chang, David, 180

cheese

    bread pudding with mascarpone, 468–69

    cheesecake with ricotta, 478–79

    chocolate-orange tart with ricotta, 472–73

    dip with feta and chèvre, 494

    gemelli pasta with chèvre, 172–73

    grating, 196

    green enchiladas with mozzarella, 272–73

    grilled, with fruit chutney, 541

    lentil salad with Gorgonzola, 266–67

    melting, 173

    molletes with mozzarella, 216

    pasta all'amatriciana with pecorino Romano, 174–75

    pasta with pepper and pecorino Romano, 194–95

    Peruvian pesto with Parmesan, 178–79

    pesto alla Genovese with Parmesan, 186

    piadine topping with ricotta, 381

pizza sauce with fontina and Parmesan, 242, 243

risotto with Parmesan, 156–57

salad of greens and Parmesan, 90–91

shrimp with feta, 232–33

spaghetti and pancetta with pecorino Romano, 196–97

spaghetti carbonara with pecorino Romano, 198–99

Spanish ratatouille with manchego, 230–31

tlayudas with mozzarella, 214

Trapanese pesto with pecorino Romano, 184–85

vegetable broth with Parmesan, 157

whipped feta, 534–35

zucchini and herb salad with Parmesan, 98–99

cheesecake, ricotta-semolina, 478–79

Chermoula sauce, salmon packets with, 346–47

chicken

boiling or poaching, 268

Burmese, 284–85

Cape Malay curry of, 332–33

chiang mai, 358–59

Chinese white-cooked, 296–97

en cocotte, 366–67

couscous with, 338–39

crispy Sichuan-chili, 336–37

crispy under a brick, 314–17

Filipino adobo, 352–53

Georgian soup with, 54–55

green enchiladas with, 272–73

Japanese fried, 304–5

lemon-saffron, 344–45

marinating, 349, 358, 370

Mexican soup with, 60–61

noodle soup with, 48–49

Oaxacan green mole with, 250–51

orange–guajillo chili pulled, 246–47

piri piri, 320–21

red chili spatchcocked roast, 356–57

Senegalese braised, 348–49

shredding, 269

Sichuan salad of, 268–69

Singapore satay of, 238–39

with snap peas and basil, 254–55

Somali soup of, 70–71

spatchcocking, 314, 316–17, 356

sumac-spiced, 368–69

tagine of, 362–63

teriyaki rice bowls, 210–11

Thai-style fried, 370–71

three-cup, 222–23

traybaked with poblano and salsa, 292–95

za'atar cutlets of, 280–81

za'atar-roasted, 326–27

chickpeas

Israeli hummus of, 276–77

lamb or beef stew with, 306–7

Punjabi, 206–7

salad with pita and, 202–3

soup with harissa and, 44–45

chikhirtma (Georgian chicken soup), 54–55

chili(es), 497

broccoli rabe with, 530

Brussels sprouts with, 106–7

campanelle pasta with habanero, 163

chicken traybake with, 292–95

chicken with orange and guajillo, 246–47

Chinese noodles with, 168–69

dried, 9

eggplant with, 530

Filipino chicken adobo with, 352

guacamole with, 518–19

harissa with, 496

hot sauce with tomatillo and, 214, 215, 272

Indian tomato rice with, 154–55

margarita with, 325

Mexican chicken soup with, 60–61

piri piri chicken with, 320

pork stews with, 72–73, 364–65

refried black beans with, 262

salsas with, 492, 493, 502–3

sauce of serrano, 71

Sichuan chicken with, 336–37

spatchcocked chicken with, 356–57

spicy beef salad with, 225

stir-fried cumin beef with, 258

Swiss chard with, 112–13

tacos with, 330–31

tlayudas with, 214

Turkish scrambled eggs with, 36–37

See also chipotles; jalapeños

chili-garlic sauce, 10

chili-lime sauce with, 359

eggplant with, 530

honey-chili sauce with, 500–501

tangy-sweet sauce with, 371

chili paste, Korean, 46, 312–13

chili powder

ancho, 331

Korean, 35, 312–13

piri piri chicken with, 320

chili sauce, tangy-sweet, 371

chimichurri, stuffed pork loin with, 308–11

chipotles, 9, 511

in adobo sauce, 510–11

refried beans with, 275

shrimp in sauce of, 288–89

chives, gnocchi sauce with, 183

chocolate

cake with prune and rum, 428–29

Caprese torte with, 448–49

cookies with chips of, 422–23

crostata with, 452–53

ginger scones with, 408–9

Lamington cakes with, 404–5

meringue cookies with, 402–3

mousse with, 462–63

spice cookies with, 406–7

stovetop cake of, 484–85

tahini swirl brownies with, 410–11

tarts with, 436–37, 472–73

chole (Punjabi chickpeas with potato), 206–7

chorizo

browning, 31

Mexican vs. Spanish, 214

mussels with, 282–83

pork and peppers with, 252–53

Spanish-style eggs with, 30–31

tlayudas with, 214

chutney, fruit, 540–41

cilantro, 7

adobo sauce with, 512–13

cumin-coriander potatoes with, 110–11

eggplant broiled with, 530

harissa vinaigrette with, 498

napa coleslaw with, 82–83

spicy beef salad with, 224–25

cinnamon, Thai braised pork and eggs with, 226–27

citrus zest and juice, 4, 343, 345, 474

See also lemon; lime; orange

Clark, Sam and Sam, 117

cleavers, Chinese, 114–15

cocoa. *See* chocolate

coconut

cookies with, 420–21

cream of, 82

Lamington cakes with, 404–5

loaf cake with, 446–47

rice pudding with, 454–55

rice with, 144–45

semolina cake with, 480–81

sweet potato cake with, 482–83

coconut milk

chicken adobo with, 352–53

fish braised in, 278–79

lentil stew with, 58–59

"light," 82, 481

napa coleslaw with, 82–83

rice with ginger and, 150–51

coconut oil, 3, 59, 65

coconut water, 287

cocotte (covered pot), 367

coffee, "gunfire," 421

compotes, fruit, 542–43

cookies

Australian oat-coconut, 420–21

chocolate-almond spice, 406–7

chocolate meringue, 402–3

date-stuffed semolina, 418–19

rosemary–pine nut cornmeal, 412–13

rye chocolate chip, 422–23

semolina polvorones, 414–15

Swedish gingersnaps, 416–17

cooking spray, 3, 396

coriander, 7

cracked potatoes with, 116–17

fruit chutney with, 540

potatoes with, 110–11

corn

campanelle pasta with, 162–63

sauces with grated, 163

cornmeal, 139

cookies with, 412–13

cornbread with, 392–93

polenta of, 138–39, 513

cornstarch

cheese sauces with, 195

Japanese fried chicken with, 304

pie dough with, 432

couscous

chicken with, 338–39

herb-and-pistachio, 152–53

Israeli, 153

cream

biscuits with, 394–95

bread pudding with, 468–69

of coconut, 82

gochujang sour, 313

honey-orange whipped, 439

pie dough with sour, 432

pizza sauce with, 243

tangy whipped, 395

crostata, chocolate-hazelnut, 452–53

crostini, fig-olive tapenade on, 532–33

croutons. *See* bread cubes or crumbs

cucumbers

salad of smashed, 88–89

tzatziki with, 494

cumin, 7

chickpea and harissa soup with, 44–45

potatoes with, 110–11

stir-fried beef with, 258–59

curry

Cape Malay chicken, 332–33

cauliflower with, 530

chickpea with potato, 206–7

eggs braised with, 28–29

fish braised with, 278–79

D

dashi, 41

dates, 418, 445

quinoa pilaf with, 140–41

semolina cookies with, 418–19

toffee pudding with, 444–45

Delling-Williams, Edward, 466

dill, oven-poached salmon with, 340–41

dipping sauces

chili-lime, 359

Japanese fried chicken with, 304–5

spicy harissa, 498

tamarind, 504–5

vinegar-peanut, 238–39

dips, Greek, 494–95

spicy feta, 494

tzatziki, 494

whipped feta, 534–35

yogurt–harissa, 498

dressings

ginger-soy, chicken with, 296–97

green goddess tofu, 538–39

herbed (savory), 302–3

miso-ginger, 536–37

spiced yogurt, 526–27

sweet-and-sour mint, 528–31

tips for clingy, 87, 92

See also vinaigrettes

Duguid, Naomi, 285

dukkah (Egyptian nut-and-seed seasoning), 130, 131

Dunlop, Fuchsia, 112, 169

Dutch oven, 126, 304, 367, 484

E

eetch (bulgur-tomato salad), 100–101

eggplant

roasted with chilies and cilantro, 530

Spanish ratatouille with, 230–31

spicy Egyptian, 122–23

eggs

adobo sauce on, 513

caramel chocolate mousse with, 462–63

chickpea and harissa soup with, 44–45

Chinese noodles with, 168–69

Chinese stir-fried, 32–33

chocolate, prune, and rum cake with, 429

chocolate and almond torte with, 448–49

Colombian salsa with, 502–3

curry braised, 28–29

fluffy olive oil scrambled, 22–23

French toast with, 442–43

Georgian chicken soup with, 54–55

Japanese potato salad with, 94–95

Korean scallion pancakes with, 34–35

Persian herb omelet of, 26–27

pork and rice with, 220–21

pork loin stuffed with, 308–11

soba noodles with, 180–81

spaghetti carbonara with, 198–99

Spanish garlic soup with, 66–67

Spanish-style, 30–31

sunny-side up, 23

tart custard with, 434

temperature for cakes, 474

Thai braised pork and, 226–27

Turkish scrambled, 36–37

whipping whites of, 403, 429, 450, 463, 466, 479

enchiladas

chipotles for, 511

verdes (green), 272–73

escabeche (pickled vegetables), 514–17

F

fasolada (Greek white bean soup), 56–57

fats, 2–3

skimming off, 312

See also butter; lard; oil; tahini

fatteh (pita and chickpea salad), 202–3

fattoush (pita bread salad), 96–97

fennel, 9

broccoli rabe with, 530

cracked potatoes with, 116–17

pasta con fagioli with, 170–71

porchetta with, 360–61

roasted, 361

salad with, 80–81

shrimp and feta cheese with, 233

figs, tapenade with, 532–33

fish

adobo sauce for, 513

curry-coconut braised, 278–79

ginger-scallion cod, 236–37

Vietnamese caramel, 286–87

See also salmon

fish sauce, 10

beef salad with, 328

fried rice with, 142

napa coleslaw with, 82–83

turkey basted with, 300

five-spice powder, 226

flatbread

beef kibbeh on, 204–5

dough for, 374–75

Italian, 378–81

spiced beef, 377

toppings for, 376–77, 380–81

za'atar, 376

Fleming, Claudia, 412

flour, 14, 17

all-purpose, 14

bread, 14, 388

corn, 392

graham, 14, 382

potato, 35

spelt, 446

toasting, 414, 422, 470

See also almond flour; rye flour; semolina flour

focaccia, potato-and-herb, 384–85

foil packet

pork roasted in, 322, 324–25

salmon steamed in, 347

French toast, sherry-soaked, 442–43

fruit chutney, 540–41

fruit compotes, 542–43

G

garam masala (seasoning), 28, 206

garides saganaki (shrimp with feta cheese), 232–33

garlic

Brussels sprouts with, 106–7

chicken en cocotte with, 366–67

chili sauce with, 10, 359, 371, 501, 530

cooking, 111

grating, 526

lentil salad with, 266–67

oil with herbs and, 524–25

spaghetti with, 189

Spanish soup with, 66–67

Spanish-style eggs with, 30–31

gianduja (chocolate-hazelnut paste), 453

ginger

carrots pickled with, 313

chicken with dressing of soy and, 296–97

cod steamed with, 236–37

dressing of miso and, 536–37

French spice bread with, 396

grating, 112, 520

green beans with, 126–27

rice with coconut and, 150–51

scones with, 408–9

Swedish gingersnaps with, 416–17

Swiss chard with, 112–13

yakiudon with pickled, 164–65

glass baking dishes, 384

Glasse, Hannah, 450

gluten and glutathione, 375, 432

gnocchi, potato, 182–83

gochugaru (Korean chili powder), 35

pulled pork with, 312–13

sour cream with, 313

gochujang (Korean chili paste), 46, 312–13

Goldstein, Darra, 55

grains, 17

flavorful liquids for, 140

hydrating, 79, 153

for multigrain soda bread, 382

pilaf of quinoa, 140–41

See also bulgur; couscous; rice

grapes, fattoush with, 96–97

grapeseed oil, 3

gravy, brown ale turkey with, 300

green goddess tofu dressing, 538–39

greens

herbs as, 203

salad of walnuts, Parmesan, pancetta, and, 90–91

sizzling in oil, 112–13

tenderizing, 85

See also kale

guacamole, central Mexico, 518–19

Gutenbrunner, Kurt, 335

Guzmán, Gonzalo, 73

H

halvah, 411

ham

Japanese potato salad with, 94–95

piadine topping with prosciutto, 381

harissa, 496–97

chicken couscous with, 338–39

chickpea soup with, 44–45

eggplant with, 122–23

potatoes roasted with, 132–33

ways to use, 498

Hazan, Marcella, 173

hazelnuts

crostata with, 452–53

salad with, 80–81

herbs, 4, 7

bread dressing with, 302–3

brown ale turkey with, 300

bulgur-tomato salad with, 100–101

couscous with, 152–53

eggplant with fresh, 122–23

focaccia with potatoes and, 384–85

Greek dips with, 494, 498

Middle Eastern rice with, 148–49

oil with garlic and, 524–25

omelet with, 26–27

risotto with, 156–57

roast beef rubbed with, 318–19

as salad greens, 203

salad with zucchini with, 98–99

tabbouleh with, 78–79

washing and drying, 512

See also specific herb

Holt, Briana, 446, 488

hominy

Mexican chicken soup with, 60–61

pozole rojo (stew) with, 72–73

honey, 14

Brussels sprouts with, 106

carrot salad with, 92

chili sauce with, 500–501

French walnut tart with, 460

maple–browned butter pie with, 488

pork tenderloin with, 208–9

spice bread with, 396

sweet-and-sour dressing with, 528–29

whipped cream with, 439

horseradish

apple, celery root, and fennel salad with, 80–81

grating, 81

mashed potatoes with, 128–29

sauce of fresh, 318, 319

hot pot, Japanese, 41

htipiti (Greek dip), 535

hummus

adobo sauce for, 513

beef topping for, 277

Israeli, 276–77

J

Jaffrey, Madhur, 155, 526

jalapeños

adobo sauce with, 512–13

lomo saltado with, 234–35

mint sauce with, 520–21

pickled, 522–23

pico de gallo with, 217, 299

smoked, 9, 511

juice

carrot, 140–41

citrus, 4, 345

margarita with pineapple, 325

K

kai yang (chiang mai chicken), 358–59

kale

salad with, 84–85

Spanish-style eggs with, 30–31

tenderizing, 85

karaage (Japanese fried chicken), 304–5

Kassis, Reem, 469

kawarma (spiced beef topping), 277

kecap manis (sweet soy sauce), 13

Khan, Yasmin, 528

khao kua (toasted rice powder), 225

khao tom (Thai rice soup), 68–69

kimchi, 13

pancakes with, 35

pork stir-fried with, 264–65

kimchi jjigae (pork and kimchi stew), 46–47

King, Kathryn, 450

knives, cleaver-like, 114–15

kofta, Turkish, 271

kuku sabzi (Persian herb omelet), 26–27

kuru fasulye (Turkish bean stew), 256

L

lablabi (chickpea and harissa soup), 44–45

lahmajoun, 380

laksa (shrimp and chicken noodle soup), 48–49

lamb

stew with chickpeas and, 306–7

Turkish beans with, 256–57

Lamingtons (chocolate-coconut cakes), 404–5

larb neua (spicy beef salad), 224–25

lard, 2, 3, 262

Italian flatbread with, 379

pork slow-cooked in, 260

refried beans with, 262

lavender, blueberry compote with, 543

Lawson, Nigella, 213, 426

Lebovitz, David, 463

Lee, Edward, 279

lemon, 4

chicken with saffron and, 344–45

pasta con fagioli with, 170

pasta with pistachios, tomatoes, mint, and, 177

pound cakes with, 450–51, 474–77

salad with parsley and, 280–81

spaghetti with, 166–67, 192–93

tangerine-almond cake with, 470–71

tart of, 440–41

lemon grass

Burmese chicken with, 285

chiang mai chicken with, 358

lentils

Lebanese rice and, 158–59

salad with Gorgonzola and, 266–67

stew with red, 58–59

substituting types of, 59, 159, 266

Turkish soup with, 42–43

Lett, Travis, 106

lime, 4

chicken braised with, 348–49

dipping sauce with chilies and, 359

guacamole with, 519

sauce of yogurt and, 270–71

strawberries macerated with, 395

Vietnamese shaking beef with, 249

lomo saltado (beef stir-fry), 234–35

lu rou fan (Taiwanese pork and rice), 220–21

M

ma'amoul (date-stuffed semolina cookies), 418–19

mace, French spice bread with, 396

Madison, Deborah, 140

Mallmann, Francis, 354

mango

rice pudding with, 454–55

salad with, 104–5

maple syrup

pie with browned butter and, 488–89

pudding cakes with, 458–59

margarita, chili-pineapple, 325

marjoram, vinaigrette with, 76–77

masabacha (Israeli hummus), 276–77

masalas (seasoning), 28, 206

meat
adobo sauce for, 513
grain of, 328
moisture for cooking, 343
sauce for, 225
searing, 306
See also beef; lamb; pork
meatballs
Turkish, 270–71
Vietnamese soup with, 62–63
menemen (Turkish scrambled eggs), 36–37
migas (crumbs), Spanish-style eggs with, 30–31
milk, goat, 173
See also buttermilk; coconut milk; cream
mint, 7
cauliflower with, 530
napa coleslaw with, 82–83
pasta with pistachios, tomatoes, and, 176–77
pita and chickpea salad with, 202–3
sauce with jalapeño and, 520–21
spicy beef salad with, 224–25
sweet-and-sour dressing with, 528–31
mirin, 17, 211
miso, 13
cauliflower glazed with, 108–9
dressing of ginger and, 536–37
pulled pork with, 312–13
soba noodles with, 180–81
soups with, 40–41, 50–51
mojo sauce, pork shoulder with, 322–25
mole verde (green), chicken with, 250–51
moo palo (Thai braised pork and eggs), 226–27
mousse, salted butter caramel chocolate, 462–63
mujaddara (Lebanese lentils and rice), 158–59
musakhan (sumac-spiced chicken), 368–69
mushrooms, pizza with portobello, 242–45
See also shiitake mushrooms
mussels with chorizo and tomatoes, 282–83
mustard, vinaigrette with Dijon, 516
mustard seeds, 9
avocado salad with pickled, 76–77

fruit chutney with, 540
mashed potatoes with, 128–29

N

nabemono (hot pot), 41
nam prik (pickled chilies), 522–23
Napoleon Bonaparte, 434
ndambe (black-eyed pea and sweet potato stew), 64–65
noodles
Asian, 17
with asparagus, miso butter, and egg, 180–81
buckwheat, 180
Chinese chili-and-scallion, 168–69
with pickled ginger, 164–65
soups with, 48–49, 52–53
See also pasta
nutmeg, 9

O

oats, cookies with rolled, 420–21
oil, 2–3
coconut, 3, 59, 65
garlic-and-herb, 524–25
greens sizzled in, 112–13
mixing cheese with, 173
olive, 3, 22–23, 57
sesame, 3, 169, 265
sesame seeds browned in, 169
Sichuan chili, 336, 337
olive oil, 3
adding to soup, 57
extra-virgin, 22
fluffy scrambled eggs with, 22–23
olives
beef stew with, 342–43
shrimp and feta cheese with, 233
tapenade with, 532–33
omelet, Persian herb, 26–27
onions
chicken braised with, 348–49
chicken traybake with, 292–95
crisping, 159
Lebanese lentils and rice with, 158–59
lomo saltado with, 234–35
pickled red, 214, 260, 261, 506–7
slicing, 514
See also scallions; shallots

orange, 4
beef stew with, 342–43
caramel oranges, 426–27
chicken with guajillo chilies and, 246–47
pork caramelized with, 354–55
tarts with, 441, 472–73
whipped cream with, 439
orange blossom water, 460
oregano, 7
Orr, Peter, 182
Ottolenghi, Yotam, 79, 153
oven temperature, 28, 318, 394
Oxaal, Stephen, 77

P

pain épices (spice bread), 396–97
pajeon (Korean scallion pancakes), 34–35
palm sugar, 14, 504
panade technique, 271
pancakes
Korean scallion, 34–35
Taiwanese scallion, 388–89
pancetta
pasta all'amatriciana with, 174–75
porchetta with, 360
salad with vinaigrette of, 90–91
spaghetti with, 196–97, 198–99
Thai fried rice with, 142
paprika, 9
Austrian beef stew with, 334–35
hot smoked, 111, 494
parchment paper
inverting cake on, 470
roasting pork in, 322, 324–25
roasting tomatoes on, 509
parsley, salad with lemon and, 280–81
pasta, 17
all'amatriciana, 174–75
beef ragu with, 351
campanelle, 162–63
caramelizing, 149
with cheese and pepper, 194–95
with chèvre, arugula, and walnuts, 172–73
con fagioli, 170–71
cooking tips for, 167, 175, 180, 189, 193
Middle Eastern rice with toasted, 148–49

nuts added to, 177

Peruvian pesto with, 178–79

pesto alla Genovese with, 186–87

with pistachios, tomatoes, and mint, 176–77

Trapanese pesto with, 184–85

whole-wheat, with yogurt and tahini, 190–91

See also noodles; spaghetti

patates mekhalel (cumin-coriander potatoes), 110–11

peanut butter, 466

sauces with, 238–39, 516

tart with, 466–67

peanut oil, 3

pears, compote with, 543

peas

stew with black-eyed, 64–65

stir-fried chicken with snap, 254–55

See also chickpeas

pepitas. *See* pumpkin seeds

peposo alla fornacina (Tuscan beef and black pepper stew), 350–51

Peppadew peppers, 13

shrimp and feta cheese with, 233

skirt steak salad with, 218–19

whipped feta with, 534–35

pepparkakor (gingersnaps), 416–17

pepper (seasoning), 7

Aleppo, 7, 37, 43, 280

black, 7, 194–95

red, flaked, 9, 106, 169, 530

Tuscan beef stew with black, 350–51

white, 10, 226

peppercorns

chicken salad with, 268

crispy chicken with, 336, 337

roast beef with, 318–19

Sichuan, 10, 134–35

peppers

feta dip with red, 494

pork and chorizo with piquillo, 252–53

Spanish ratatouille with bell, 230–31

See also chili(es); chipotles; jalapeños; Peppadew peppers

pernil asado (Cuban-style pork shoulder), 322

pesto

alla Genovese, 186–87

Peruvian, 178–79

tips for, 186, 187

Trapanese, 184–85

Phan, Charles, 126

piadine (Italian flatbread), 378–81

pickling

carrots, 313

chilies, 522–23

ginger, 164, 165

mustard seeds, 76–77

radishes, 506–7

red onions, 214, 260, 261, 506–7

tomatoes, 256–57

vegetables, 86–87, 514–17

pico de gallo, 299

braised beef with, 298

molletes with, 216–17

pies

dough for single-crust, 432–33

maple-browned butter, 488–89

See also tarts

pie weights, 432, 488

pilaf, quinoa, 140–41

pinchos morunos (spice-crusted pork tenderloin), 208–9

pineapple, tacos with, 330–31

pineapple juice, margarita with, 325

pine nuts

beef kibbeh with, 204–5

cornmeal cookies with, 412–13

pesto alla Genovese with, 186

pita and chickpea salad with, 202–3

spaghetti with, 188–89

sumac-spiced chicken with, 369

Pisco Sour, 179

pistachios

bread pudding with, 468–69

cake with, 464–65

couscous with, 152–53

pasta with tomatoes, mint, and, 176–77

roasted cauliflower with, 108–9

pisto manchego (Spanish ratatouille), 230–31

pita bread, 386–87

salads with, 96–97, 202–3

sumac-spiced chicken on, 368–69

Turkish meatballs with, 270–71

pizza, roasted mushroom, 242–45

plates, warming, 23

plums, cake topped with, 430–31

poaching

salmon in oven, 340–41

whole-bird, 268, 296–97

polenta

adobo sauce for, 513

soft, 138–39

polvorones, semolina, 414–15

pomegranate molasses, 4

bulgur-tomato salad with, 100–101

fattoush with, 96–97

Turkish beans with, 256–57

pork

Argentinian stuffed loin of, 308–11

caramelized tenderloin of, 354–55

carne adovada with, 364–65

carnitas with, 260–61

chorizo and peppers with, 252–53

Cuban-style, with mojo sauce, 322–25

fennel-rosemary porchetta of, 360–61

Korean stew with kimchi and, 46–47

miso-gochujang pulled, 312–13

pozole rojo (stew) with, 72–73

sesame stir-fried, 264–65

soup with vegetables, miso, and, 50–51

spice-crusted tenderloin of, 208–9

tacos with, 330–31

Taiwanese five-spice, 220–21

Thai braised eggs and, 226–27

Thai rice soup with, 68–69

Vietnamese soup with, 62–63

See also chorizo; ham; pancetta

posta negra (Colombian braised beef), 298–99

potatoes

Austrian salad of, 102–3

celery root puree with, 124–25

cracked, 116–17

cumin-coriander, 110–11

focaccia with herbs and, 384–85

gnocchi of, 182–83

harissa roasted, 132–33

Japanese salad of, 94–95

mashed, with caraway-mustard butter, 128–29

Punjabi chickpeas with, 206–7

sweet, gratin of, 120–21

Yukon Gold, 95, 103, 182, 384

See also sweet potatoes

potato starch, 14, 35

pound cake, lemon-buttermilk, 450–51

pozole rojo (pork, chili, and hominy stew), 72–73

prosciutto, piadine topping with, 381

prunes

braised beef with, 298

cake with, 428–29

roast beef with, 318–19

Ptak, Claire, 422, 429, 450, 540

pudding

mango and coconut rice, 454–55

maple-whiskey pudding cakes, 458–59

rye-on-rye sticky toffee, 444–45

toasted bread, 468–69

pumpkin seeds

rolls with, 390–91

salmon salad with, 212–13

pumpkin tart, 438–39

Q

quesadillas, adobo sauce for, 513

quinoa pilaf, 140–41

R

radishes, salt-pickled, 506–7

raisins, spaghetti with, 188–89

Ramirez, Erik, 140

ratatouille, Spanish, 230–31

red pepper flakes, 9

rice, 17

adobo sauce for, 513

basmati, 17, 142, 155

Burmese chicken over, 284–85

chicken curry with, 332–33

chicken teriyaki with, 210–11

coconut, 144–45

coconut-ginger, 150–51

Indian tomato, 154–55

Japanese-style, 146–47

jasmine, 17, 142, 144

Lebanese lentils and, 158–59

liquids for cooking, 140, 297

mango and coconut pudding of, 454–55

Middle Eastern, 148–49

pre-cooking, 68, 143

rinsing or soaking, 149, 155

risotto of, 156–57

Somali soup with, 70–71

spicy beef salad with, 224–25

Taiwanese pork with, 220–21

Thai fried, 142–43

Thai soup with, 68–69

toasted powdered, 225

Turkish lentil soup with, 42–43

Ricker, Andy, 142

Rindsgulasch (Austrian beef stew), 334–35

risotto, 156–57

rof (Senegalese condiment), avocado and mango salad with, 104–5

rosemary

cornmeal cookies with, 412–13

pasta con fagioli with, 170

porchetta with, 360–61

rose water, 418

rum, 18

cake with, 428–29

coffee with, 421

rye flour, 14

chocolate chip cookies with, 422–23

toffee pudding with, 444–45

rye whiskey, 17

Singapore Sling with, 240–41

toffee pudding with, 444–45

S

saffron

chicken with lemon and, 344–45

risotto with, 156

sage

gnocchi sauce with, 183

pork caramelized with, 354–55

sake to kinoko takikomi gohan (rice with salmon and mushrooms), 146–47

salads

apple, celery root, and fennel, 80–81

Austrian potato, 102–3

avocado with pickled mustard seeds, 76–77

bulgur-tomato, 100–101

Eventide green, 86–87

fattoush, 96–97

French carrot, 92–93

greens with walnuts, Parmesan, and pancetta, 90–91

herbs in, 203

hot-smoked salmon, 212–13

Japanese potato, 94–95

kale, with almonds and picada crumbs, 84–85

lemon-parsley, 280–81

lentil, with Gorgonzola, 266–67

napa coleslaw, 82–83

pita and chickpea, 202–3

Senegalese avocado and tomato, 104–5

Sichuan chicken, 268–69

skirt steak, 218–19

smashed cucumber, 88–89

spicy beef, 224–25

Thai beef, 328–29

Thai-style coleslaw, 82–83

zucchini and herb, 98–99

See also dressings; vinaigrettes

salmon

chraimeh, 228–29

Japanese rice with, 146–47

marinating, 341

oven-poached, 340–41

packets, with Chermoula, 346–47

salad with hot-smoked, 212–13

salsa

ancho chili, 492

chicken traybake with tomato, 292–95

Colombian avocado, 502–3

pico de gallo, 216–17, 298, 299

tomatillo-avocado, 493

salt, 9

beans soaked with, 256

chicken broiled over, 238

French sea, 463

greens tenderized with, 85

pasta cooked with, 180, 193

radish and onion pickled in, 506–7

vegetables dried with, 89

sandwiches

adobo sauce for, 513

beef and broccoli rabe, 351

grilled cheese with fruit chutney, 541

pulled pork, 312–13

sanwin makin (coconut cashew cake), 480–81

sauces

adobo, 352–53, 510–13

barbecue, vinegar-based, 516

berbere, 71

butter, sage, and chive, 183

caramel, 286–87, 426–27

carbonara, 199

Chermoula, salmon packets with, 346–47

chili, 10

chili-garlic, 10, 359, 371, 500–501, 530

chipotle, shrimp in, 288–89

cornstarch in, 195

creamy, 163, 173, 175

fontina-Parmesan cheese, 242, 243

green chili, 71

green chili and tomatillo, 214, 215, 272

harissa, 132–33, 496–98

honey-chili, 500–501

horseradish, 318, 319

jalapeño-mint, 520–21

lime-yogurt, meatballs with, 270–71

meat, 225

mojo, pork shoulder with, 322–25

piri piri, 320

spicy peanut, 516

tangy-sweet chili, 371

toffee, sticky pudding with, 444–45

tomato, beans braised in, 509

yogurt-tahini, 205

See also dipping sauces; fish sauce; pesto; soy sauce

scallions

Chinese noodles with, 168–69

cod steamed with, 236–37

mushroom pizza with, 242–45

pancakes with, 34–35, 388–89

pork stir-fried with, 264–65

Swiss chard with, 112–13

scones, triple ginger, 408–9

seasonings, 10–15

adobado, 356

dry mixed, 306

dukkah, 130, 131

finishing dish with, 370

masalas, 28, 206

shichimi togarashi, 9–10, 164, 304

Sichuan, 336, 337

toban djan, 52

See also pepper; spices; za'atar

seaweed

pickled radish and onion with, 507

soups with, 40–41, 50–51

vinaigrette of nori, 86–87

sekanjabin (sweet-and-sour mint

dressing), 528–31

semolina flour, 17

cheesecake with, 478–79

coconut cashew cake with, 480–81

date-stuffed cookies with, 418–19

polvorones with, 414–15

sesame oil, 3, 265

sesame seeds

Chinese noodles with, 169

pork stir-fried with, 264–65

rolls with, 390–91

shallots

chicken en cocotte with, 367

fried, 69

kale salad with, 85

tabbouleh with, 78–79

Thai rice soup with, 68–69

Thai-style fried chicken with, 370

sherry, 17, 296

French toast with, 442–43

pork and rice with, 221

vinegar made from, 4, 85

See also wine

shichimi togarashi (seasoning), 9–10, 164, 304

shiitake mushrooms, 10, 12

Japanese rice with, 146–47

pork and kimchi stew with, 46–47

pork stir-fried with, 264–65

soups with, 40–41, 50–51

yakiudon with, 164–65

shoyu, 13

shrimp

in chipotle sauce, 288–89

with feta cheese, 232–33

noodle soup with, 48–49

pancakes with, 35

saving shells of, 49

Silverton, Nancy, 243

Singapore Sling, 240–41

skillets

Brussels sprouts charred in, 106–7

lids for, 117, 126

nonstick, 24, 142, 206

seasoning, 24–25

steel vs. cast-iron, 24, 106

sombi (Senegalese coconut rice pudding), 455

Sortun, Ana, 97, 280

soups

black bean, 262, 263

chickpea and harissa, 44–45

Georgian chicken, 54–55

Greek white bean, 56–57

Mexican chicken, 60–61

miso-shiitake, 40–41

pork and vegetable miso, 50–51

shrimp and chicken noodle, 48–49

Somali chicken, 70–71

Spanish garlic, 66–67

Taiwanese beef noodle, 52–53

Thai rice, 68–69

Turkish lentil, 42–43

Vietnamese meatball and watercress, 62–63

See also broth; stews

soy sauce, 13

chicken adobo with, 352

chicken teriyaki with, 211

chicken with dressing of ginger and, 296–97

lomo saltado with, 234–35

pork and rice with, 221

spaghetti

all'amatriciana, 174–75

with anchovies, pine nuts, and raisins, 188–89

with lemon, anchovies, and capers, 192–93

al limone, 166–67

with pancetta (alla Gricia), 196–97

Roman carbonara of, 198–99

See also pasta

spatchcocking chicken, 314, 316–17, 356

spices, 7–11

French bread with, 396–97

freshness of, 306

pork tenderloin crusted with, 208–9

Taiwanese pork with, 220–21

See also seasonings; specific spice

spinach

chicken tagine with, 362–63

lentil stew with, 58–59

Peruvian pesto with, 178–79

Thai stir-fried, 118–19

spirits, 17–18

cakes with, 428–29, 458–59

chili-pineapple margarita, 325

coffee with, 421
    Pisco Sour, 179
    Singapore Sling, 240–41
    Tequila at High Noon, 357
    toffee pudding with, 444–45
    See also sherry; vermouth
squash, chicken tagine with butternut, 362–63
    See also zucchini
starches, 14, 17
    cornstarch, 195, 304, 432
    potato, 14, 35
stews
    Austrian beef, 334–35
    beef, orange, and olive, 342–43
    black-eyed pea and sweet potato, 64–65
    carne adovada, 364–65
    chicken couscous, 338–39
    chicken tagine, 362–63
    lamb or beef and chickpea, 306–7
    pork and kimchi, 46–47
    pozole rojo, 72–73
    red lentil, 58–59
    Turkish bean, 256–57
    Tuscan beef and black pepper, 350–51
    See also soups
stir-frying
    broccoli, 134–35
    chicken with snap peas and basil, 254–55
    cumin beef, 258–59
    eggs with tomatoes, 32–33
    green beans, 126–27
    lomo saltado, 234–35
    sesame pork, 264–65
    spinach, 118–19
    yakiudon with pickled ginger, 164–65
stock. *See* broth
strawberries, macerated, with lime, 395
stuffing, herbed, 302–3
sugar, 14
    browning, 427
    palm, 14, 504
    panela, 298
    See also brown sugar
sumac, 10
    chicken spiced with, 368–69
    fattoush with, 97
    tabbouleh with, 78–79

sweeteners, 14
    See also honey; maple syrup; sugar
sweet potatoes
    adobo sauce for, 513
    gratin of, 120–21
    Macanese cake with, 482–83
    stew with black-eyed peas and, 64–65
Swiss chard, hot oil–flashed, 112–13
syrup, cake with bay-infused, 470–71

T

tabbouleh, Lebanese-style, 78–79
tacos al pastor, 330–31
    See also tortillas
tagine, chicken, 362–63
tagliata (Italian sliced steak), 218–19
tahini, 3
    brownies with, 410–11
    cauliflower with, 130–31
    hummus with, 276–77
    pasta with, 190–91
    sauce with yogurt and, 205
    stirring, 276, 369, 411
    sumac-spiced chicken with, 369
tallarines verde (Peruvian pesto), 178–79
tamari, 13, 304
tamarind, 13, 15
    dipping sauce with, 504–5
tangerine, almond cake with, 470–71
tangia (lemon-saffron chicken), 344–45
tangzhong technique for pastry, 432
tapenade, fig-olive, 532–33
tarragon, green goddess tofu dressing with, 538–39
tarta de Santiago (Spanish almond cake), 486–87
tarts
    brown sugar, 434–35
    chocolate, 436–37
    chocolate-orange, 472–73
    dough for, 432–33
    French walnut, 460–61
    lemon, 440–41
    peanut and caramel, 466–67
    pumpkin, 438–39
teriyaki donburi (chicken teriyaki rice bowls), 210–11
Thiam, Pierre, ix, 104, 349, 455
thyme, oven-poached salmon with, 340–41

tirokafteri (spicy feta dip), 494
tlayudas, 214–15
toban djan (chili-bean paste), 52
toffee sauce, rye-on-rye sticky pudding with, 444–45
tofu
    green goddess dressing with, 538–39
    miso-shiitake soup with, 40–41
    pork and kimchi stew with, 46–47
    pork and vegetable miso soup with, 50–51
    shrimp and chicken noodle soup with, 48–49
tomatillos
    hot sauce with chiles and, 214, 215, 272
    Mexican chicken soup with, 60–61
    salsa with, 493
tomatoes
    avocado and mango salad with, 104–5
    beans with pickled, 256–57
    beef flatbreads with, 377
    campanelle pasta with, 162–63
    chicken traybake with salsa of, 292–95
    Chinese stir-fried eggs with, 32–33
    guacamole with, 518–19
    Indian rice with, 154–55
    lomo saltado with, 234–35
    mussels with slow-roasted, 282–83
    pasta all'amatriciana with, 174–75
    pasta and beef ragu with, 351
    pasta con fagioli with, 170–71
    pasta with pistachios, mint, and, 176–77
    pico de gallo with, 217, 299
    pork and chorizo with, 252–53
    salad with bulgur and, 100–101
    salmon chraimeh with, 228–29
    salsa roja with, 492
    shrimp and feta cheese with, 233
    slow-roasted, 508–9
    Spanish ratatouille with, 230–31
    Trapanese pesto with, 184–85
    Turkish scrambled eggs with, 36–37
ton-jiru (pork and vegetable miso soup), 50–51
toppings
    flatbread, 376–77, 380–81
    spiced beef, 277
torrijas (sherry-soaked French toast), 442–43

torte, Caprese chocolate and almond, 448–49
tortillas
    carne adovada on, 364–65
    carnitas on, 260–61
    green enchiladas with, 272–73
    green mole and chicken with, 250–51
    pulled chicken on, 246–47
    refried beans on, 263
    shrimp in chipotle sauce on, 288–89
    spatchcocked roast chicken on, 356–57
    tacos with, 330–31
    tlayudas with, 214
tsitsila tabaka (crispy chicken under a brick), 314–17
turkey, brown ale, 300–301
tzatziki (cucumber-yogurt dip), 494

V

vanilla bean, sweet potato gratin with, 120–21
vegetables
    broth of, 156, 157
    Chinese cleavers for, 114–15
    drying with salt, 89
    grating, 92
    pickling, 86–87, 313, 506–7, 514–17, 522–23
    roasting, 293–94
    sizzling in oil, 112
verjus, 4
vermouth, 18
    cracked potatoes with, 116–17
    oven-poached salmon with, 340–41
vinaigrettes
    adobo sauce for, 513
    harissa-cilantro, 498
    marjoram, 76–77
    mustard, 516
    nori, 86–87
    pancetta, 90–91
    shallot-sherry, 85
    See also dressings
vinegar, 4–5
    balsamic, 4, 92
    pickling brine with, 514–17
    sauces with, 238–39, 516
    sherry, 4, 85
Vongerichten, Jean-Georges, 347

W

walnuts
    French tart with, 460–61
    gemelli pasta with, 172–73
    miso-ginger dressing with, 536–37
    salad of greens and, 90–91
    toasting, 90
water
    coconut, 287
    flavorful substitutions for, 140
    orange blossom, 460
    pasta, 167, 180, 193
    rose, 418
    soaking beans in, 256, 262
watercress
    soup with meatballs and, 62–63
    Vietnamese shaking beef with, 248–49
Watson, Quealy, 82
wheat, cracked, 17
wine, 18
    beef stews with, 343, 350–51
    cheesecake with Marsala, 479
    mirin, 17, 211
    See also sherry

Y

yam neua (Thai beef salad), 328–29
yasai no sokuseki-zuke (Japanese pickled radish and onion), 506–7
yassa ginaar (Senegalese braised chicken), 348–49
yogurt
    flatbread with, 375, 377
    Greek vs. traditional, 191, 271, 382
    harissa dip with, 498
    multigrain soda bread with, 382
    pita and chickpea salad with, 202–3
    sauces with, 205, 270–71
    spiced dressing with, 526–27
    tzatziki with, 494
    whole-wheat pasta with, 190–91
    yosenabe (hot pot), 41

Z

za'atar (seasoning), 13–14
    chicken with, 280–81, 326–27
    flatbreads with, 376
    pita and chickpea salad with, 203
zucchini

    salad of shaved, 98–99
    Spanish ratatouille with, 230–31
Zwetschgenkuchen (Austrian plum cake), 430–31

ACKNOWLEDGMENTS

Milk Street is a real place with, oddly enough, real people. It's a small crew, but I want to thank everyone who has made this book a reality. In particular, I want to acknowledge J.M. Hirsch, our tireless editorial director, Matthew Card, food editor, Michelle Locke, books editor, and Dawn Yanagihara, recipe editor, for leading the charge on conceiving, developing and editing all of this. Jennifer Baldino Cox, our art director, and the entire design team who deftly captured the look and feel of Milk Street, including Brianna Coleman, Connie Miller, Christine Tobin, Gary Tooth, Catherine Smart, Brian Samuels, Channing Johnson, Ben Schaefer, Catrine Kelty, Kristin Teig, Joyelle West, Michael Piazza, Heidi Murphy, Monica Mariano, Molly Shuster, and Sally Staub. Our team of production cooks and recipe developers kept the bar high, throwing out recipes that did not make the cut and improving those that did. Our team includes Diane Unger, Erin Register, Courtney Hill, Julia Rackow, Phoebe Maglathlin, Rose Hattabaugh, and Angie Marvin. Also, Elizabeth Germain, Bianca Borges, Erika Bruce, Laura Russell and Jeanne Maguire. Deborah Broide, Milk Street director of media relations, has done a spectacular job of introducing Milk Street to the world.

We also have a couple of folks to thank who work outside of 177 Milk Street. Michael Szczerban, editor, and everyone at Little, Brown and Company have been superb and inspired partners in this project. Yes, top-notch book editors still exist! And my long-standing book agent, David Black, has been instrumental in bringing this project to life both with his knowledge of publishing and bourbon. Thank you, David!

Finally, a sincere thank you to my business partner and wife, Melissa, who manages our media department, from television to radio. Melissa has nurtured the Milk Street brand from the beginning so that we ended up where we thought we were going in the first place! Thanks.

And, last but not least, to all of you who have supported the Milk Street project. Everyone has a seat at the Milk Street table, so pull up a chair and dig in!

Christopher Kimball